The Parables of Jesus

STUDIES IN THE SYNOPTIC GOSPELS

by Herman Hendrickx, CICM

The Infancy Narratives
The Passion Narratives of the Synoptic Gospels
The Resurrection Narratives of the Synoptic Gospels
The Sermon on the Mount
The Parables of Jesus

The Parables of Jesus

Herman Hendrickx

Geoffrey Chapman
London

Harper & Row, Publishers
San Francisco

A Geoffrey Chapman book published by
Cassell Ltd
1 Vincent Square, London SW1P 2PN

Harper & Row, Publishers, Inc.
1700 Montgomery Street
San Francisco, California 94111

This edition first published 1986

ISBN 0 225 66486 0 (Geoffrey Chapman)
        0-06-254815-8 (Harper & Row)

Scripture quotations, unless otherwise indicated, are from the Revised Standard Version Bible (RSV), Catholic Edition, copyrighted © 1965 and 1966 by the Division of Christian Education of the National Council of Churches of Christ in the USA, and used by permission. The abbreviations JB, NAB and NEB denote, respectively, the Jerusalem Bible, the New American Bible and the New English Bible.
Quotations from the *Gospel of Thomas* are taken from *The Nag Hammadi Library* (general editor James M. Robinson; New York: Harper and Row, 1972), and used with permission.

British Library Cataloguing in Publication Data
Hendrickx, Herman
    The parables of Jesus.—Rev. ed.—
    (Studies in the Synoptic Gospels)
    1. Jesus Christ—Parables
    I. Title   II. The parables of Jesus then
    and now   III. Series
    226'.806   BT375.2

Cover illustration: The Pharisee and the tax collector. Sixth-century mosaic in S. Apollinare Nuovo, Ravenna. Reproduced by courtesy of the Mansell Collection.

Typeset by Scribe Design, Gillingham, Kent
Printed and bound in Great Britain by Biddles Limited, Guildford

Contents

Foreword to the First Edition

It is a great honour to introduce the author of this book. He is a profound biblical scholar, a prolific writer of extraordinary gifts, and above all a confrere. A professor at the CICM Maryhill School of Theology (MST) and staff member of the East Asian Pastoral Institute, he has lectured in almost all parts of the country and of Asia. He has written many books, among which are: **The Story Behind the Gospels** (now translated in Pilipino), **The Infancy Narratives, The Passion Narratives, The Resurrection Narratives, The Bible on Justice** and **The Sermon on the Mount.** He is Fr Herman Hendrickx, CICM, a missionary from Belgium.

Fr Hendrickx is not an activist type, but his awareness of contemporary problems and his deep insights on the Holy Scriptures make him one of the few outstanding exegetes we have in the country today. Priests, Sisters, seminarians and pastoral workers, who are immersed in the work with the poor, the oppressed and the marginalized and who are searching for a deeper and greater understanding of the Word of God in the light of the present world situation, especially in the Philippines today, look up to him.

The publication of this book comes out at an opportune time when we CICMs in the Philippines mark our Diamond Jubilee this year: 75 challenging years of missionary presence and service in the Philippine Church. I take pride in my confrere's unique contribution to the People of God in the Philippines through his innumerable and scholarly books and commentaries on God's Word so much in demand in our times.

Rev. Ernesto M. Amigleo, CICM
Provincial Superior
2 November 1982

Preface

This book had its beginning in a series of lectures and sessions on the parables given to several groups of theology students, religious and catechists over a period of about ten years. The positive response of several of these groups as well as the kind appreciation expressed in reviews on my previous books, encouraged me to thoroughly revise my notes in the light of recent scholarship.

It will be readily understood that the purpose and the format of this book does not allow for a heavily technical apparatus. The origin of the book, also, made it difficult to account in detail for every idea or formulation for which I am indebted to New Testament scholarship. That is why, except for a few quotations and explanatory notes, practically all notes were omitted. We trust that the extensive bibliography will enable any interested reader to discover the extent to which I am indebted to many excellent biblical scholars for whom I wish to express here my deep admiration. It is because I want to make the fruits of their labours available to a larger public that this book was written.

The bibliography of more than six hundred titles on the parables in general and on about fifteen parables is, with a few exceptions, limited to the literature of the past twenty years. It is intended for those who would like to pursue further studies on the interesting subject of the parables.

I should like to thank all those who had a share in the publication of this book. I am especially indebted to Rev. John Linskens, CICM, for his lectures and the many notes on the parables he shared with me during the past fifteen years; to the many religious, catechists, and lay leaders who by their response and questions challenged me to express my thoughts more accurately, and last but not least to Rev. Andres R. Arboleda, Jr, SSP, book editor of the Society of Saint Paul in Manila, who accepted the manuscript, and whose kind concern was so obvious throughout the successive stages of publication of the first edition.

Note on the revised edition

The first edition of this book was published in 1983 and could take into account the literature on the Parables only up to 1981. The author and the publisher, Geoffrey Chapman, therefore decided to complete and update the bibliography and make a few minor revisions of the text. The 'Reflections' at the end of each chapter have been expanded. In them I try to give some suggestions for a communitarian application of the parables, either through personal reflections or pertinent quotations. Thus we hope to contribute somewhat to breaking through the predominantly individual interpretation of the parables. We trust that these changes will make the book more readable and useful for the reading public we have in mind.

I would like to express here my special gratitude to Miss Anne Boyd, Chief Editor, without whose interest this second edition would not have been possible, and Miss Fiona McKenzie, Senior House Editor, for her highly expert editing.

1 And he spoke to them in parables

Jesus the narrator

Anybody who consults the Synoptic Gospels to see how Jesus conveyed his message is confronted by the remarkable fact that he seldom expressed himself directly on a particular matter. Statements like 'whoever divorces his wife and marries another, commits adultery against her' (Mk 10:11) occur rarely, compared with the abundance of parabolic language and stories. In fact, about a third of Jesus' teachings recorded in the gospels are 'in parables'. How should this be explained?

The first reason why we possess so many stories and figurative statements of Jesus is clearly related to the fact that he was a speaker, not a writer. Jesus did not write down his teachings after due reflection. He spoke left and right on various occasions and to a more or less accidental public. His parables are 'situational'.

A second reason is that Jesus' teaching did not come down to us directly but through the channel of the early Christian tradition. Much of what Jesus said was not passed on by this oral tradition, in which lapidary sayings and stories had a much better chance of surviving than discussions and other more abstract forms of speech.

But even if we take into account these qualifications, it remains true that Jesus seems to have expressed himself mainly in parable stories. Again, however, some further considerations are in order. Jesus spoke in a whole range of forms, from short metaphors via more extended comparisons to the full-length stories of the prodigal son and the good Samaritan.

The word parable is derived from the Greek word *parabolē*, often used by the Synoptics, which suggests the placings of things side by side for the sake of comparison. The statement 'there is nothing outside a man which by going into him can defile him; but the things which come out of a man are what defile him' (Mk 7:15) is called a parable by the disciples (Mk 7:17). Similarly, the saying about the fig tree (Mk 13:28) and the proverb 'Physician, heal yourself' (Lk 4:23). *Parabolē* is the Greek equivalent for the Hebrew *mashal* and, like the latter, can be used for a proverb (Lk 4:23); maxims (Lk 14:7–11); a riddle (Mk 7:15–17); an example story (Lk 12:16–21); figurative speech (Mk 4:33); a simile (Mt 13:33); a metaphor (Mt 5:14); and finally parables, and parables with simple allegorical features (Mk 12:1–9). Thus a 'parable' can be anything from a single-line metaphor or simile to a long narrative.

The parables can be classified according to whether they relate an existing reality or are invented. The 'parable' of the leaven is not invented. To the invented stories belong the parables proper, and the example story or paradigm. The example story differs from the parable in that it does not lead listeners to a point where their own existence is drawn into the story, since the occurrence is narrated as an example which should be generalized as a whole. But it has recently been pointed out that the distinction between parable and example story is problematic in as far as it presupposes Jülicher's distinction between the word-picture (*Bild*) and its object (*Sache*). Anyway, any attempt to classify the parables has its problems, and many long-accepted concepts, definitions, and distinctions have been challenged in the past decade, e.g., what is now more and more considered as 'the faulty contrast between parable and allegory'.[1]

Some people shrug their shoulders at the fact that the gospels contain so many parable 'stories'. They overlook, however, how powerful a story can be (cf. II Sam 12:1–7, Nathan's parable of the ewe lamb). Stories fulfil a very important function in communication among people; they lead to insights and are often more effective than abstract considerations.

The reason why Jesus spoke so often in parables can be gleaned from the situation in which he operated. He had an urgent message: 'The time is fulfilled, and the Kingdom of God is at hand'. This called for immediate action: 'repent, and believe in the gospel' (Mk 1:15). There was no time to lose, not so much because Jesus' ministry would be short, but rather because of the nearness of the kingdom of God. Jesus' eschatology is not a doctrine of the last things, but it is 'realistic eschatology'. The combination of promise and realism necessarily leads to conflict. Modern parable research, therefore, often stresses the crisis element in Jesus' parables. Jesus as parable narrator can be known only by studying *how* he spoke in parables. Then it can also be understood *what* he intended to say in his parables.

Jesus was often confronted by a suspicious, even a hostile audience. His purpose in speaking in parables was neither to convey general religious truths to them nor to enter into a debate, but rather to win them over to his views. The parables, then, were means of dialogue. At the same time, they were means of avoiding dealing with questions in a purely theoretical way. They owed their effectiveness to a constant appeal to experience, either that of the audience or Jesus' own unique experience.

The parables are taken from ordinary life[2]

The answers given to the question whence the data used in the parables are derived are rather diverse, and so a closer look at the materials of the parables is called for.

The materials of the parables

In the relatively simple parables like those of the 'pieces of unshrunk cloth on an old garment' and 'new wine into old wineskins' (Mk 2:21–22), some exegetes have recognized a stereotyped and quite artificial imagery. Others have insisted that a great number of images used in the parables are derived from biblical tradition which gave them a religious dimension easily understod by Jewish listeners. The parables were endowed with metaphorical features which promoted allegorical interpretation. But others have reacted against what they considered an exaggeration and emphasize the parables' realism,[3] human character, and secularity.

A few nuances are in order. There is no need for radical opposition between immediate experience and reference to cultural inheritance which has become a part of life. To the Jewish listeners references to Old Testament figures and events did not lie outside their horizon. One cannot *a priori* exclude the presence in Jesus' parables of traditional images or references to well-known biblical texts. But most of the time these biblical references seem to be later additions or clarifications, and, therefore, it is unlikely that they belong to the original parable (cf., e.g., the allusion to Isa 5:1–2 and the quotation from Ps 118[117]:22–23 in Mk 12:1–12). And while the parables use a number of conventional characters like the king, the shepherd, the judge, many of the actions ascribed to these figures in the parables are not so conventional.

Interrogative form

Twenty-two parables begin with a question: 'What do you think?', 'Who among you...?', or just 'How...?' The whole parable then becomes a question which calls for an answer from the listeners. The parable narrator does not impose anything; he asks for the listeners' opinion.

Sometimes the question is found at the end of the parable. The data which the listeners have received in the story they have just heard enable them to get a better idea of exactly what the question is concerned with. The parable of the wicked tenants ends with the question, 'What will the owner of the vineyard do?' (Mk 12:9 and parallels); the parable of the two sons: 'Which of the two did the will of his father?' (Mt 21:31); and the parable of the good Samaritan: 'Which of these three, do you think, proved neighbour to the man who fell among the robbers?' (Lk 10:36).

Sometimes the question is not directly addressed to the listeners but is integrated into the parable. In these cases the character to whom the question is addressed in the parable story never gives the answer. In reality the question is addressed to the listeners, who are expected to give the answer. Thus the question of the owner of the vineyard, 'Do you begrudge my generosity?' (literally, 'Is your eye bad, because I am good?'), apparently addressed to the protesting labourers, is in fact intended for the listeners. The same is true for God's question addressed to the rich fool, 'This night your soul is required of you; and the things you have prepared, whose will they be?' (Lk 12:20).

But questions are not the only way to make the listener think. This is clear in the parable of the thief who comes during the night: '*But know this*, that if the householder had known at what hour the thief was coming, he would have been awake and would not have left his house to be broken into' (Lk 12:39; Mt 24:43). This appeals to the listener for approval. At times this appeal is implicit and simply flows from the solemn final statement: '*For I tell you*, none of those men who were invited shall taste my banquet' (Lk 14:24); 'It was fitting to make merry (literally, '*there must be* merry-making') and be glad, for this your brother was dead, and is alive; he was lost, and is found' (Lk 15:32).

On the level of the redaction or literary composition of the gospels there was certainly a tendency to change the interrogative form, which goes better with oral style, into the affirmative, which is more literary and goes better with the tone of catechesis. The gospel tradition contains a good number of examples of this shift from the interrogative to the affirmative form. One may wonder, therefore, whether the affirmative conclusions of a number of parables were substituted for an original interrogative conclusion. Anyway, the interrogative form occurs so often that there cannot be any doubt that it belonged to Jesus' way of telling parables.

The use of the interrogative form obviously presupposes that the listeners are capable of giving the answer the narrator expects. Apparently the correct answer would not be based on logical reasoning or on the authority of the Scriptures, but would be inspired by the experiences and the wisdom of the milieu in which the listeners lived. This shows that use of the parables today will face some questions of inculturation and contextualization.

Relevance of the parable method

It seems superfluous to underline the relevance of Jesus' parable approach, in so far as it is an active method which confronts the listeners with a question and expects their answer, or at least draws them into an event in which they cannot remain passive onlookers, but are called to play a part, to take a stand, and to express agreement. By its very nature the parable genre is the opposite of the sacred eloquence of a homily intended for an audience which is not permitted any intervention and to which only rhetorical questions are addressed. The tone of the parable is that of a conversation in which the partner is invited to make known a reaction and to express an opinion. Today we are aware that religious instruction cannot achieve its goal without the active participation of those for whom it is intended.

It may be more important to draw attention to the presuppositions of this active contribution by the listeners. The world of the parables with its customs and habits is as a rule foreign to present-day listeners, while it was exactly their rootedness in that milieu which made Jesus' parables click with what occupied the minds and hearts of his listeners, so that they could be drawn into the action and the intended goal could be reached.

In the course of time the distance between the original audience of the parables and contemporary Christians has constantly grown. There are only two ways to bridge this distance. The first consists in giving people all the necessary information to enable them to set aside temporarily the familiar image of their own way of life and to immerse themselves in the world of Galilean farmers and fishermen. However, this procedure is very complicated and presupposes a rather culturally sophisticated public. Is the understanding of the parables, then, reserved for an elite? This would be a very un-Christian thought. The gospel is intended in the first place for the poor who do not have access to higher education. There must, therefore, be another way which corresponds better to the spirit which prompted Jesus to have recourse to the more direct parabolic language: a method which starts from the actual circumstances of the life of contemporary people.

'To start from life' is the slogan which has led to a number of worthwhile efforts and experiments which at the same time make one realize the difficulties (even the dangers) of the method. Starting from an actual life-experience, one raises a number of questions which stimulate the group to reflection and dialogue. Then comes the Bible text, again followed by questions intended to lead to common reflection. The initial life-experience is selected in such a way that it prepares for the interpretation of the scripture text. Its choice presupposes some exegetical homework on the part of the moderator, allowing him or her to bring out the point of the text to which the reflection on a real life-situation should lead.

Undoubtedly this approach is demanding for the moderator. Other approaches are possible. It is important not to forget that, in order to be faithful to Jesus' practice, one must place the gospel in the midst of life, in the midst of one's own life, and that one must help others to read it in their life, in close relation to their experience. For that purpose it is not sufficient to explain what the parables meant for the listeners of Jesus' time who lived in circumstances very different from ours.

Directed towards life

In his parables Jesus speaks to people about (actual) life as they know it from experience to ensure their involvement in the reaction to the story told or the situation described. The active role thus allotted to the listeners is not intended to help them gather more knowledge and better understanding or remember one or another doctrine. By eliciting a reaction, the parables intend to set into motion a process leading to a change of life. They intend not so much to convey information as to impel people to action: their outlook on life has a direct impact on attitude and behaviour. They do not put any pressure upon the listeners to make a decision in any one direction, and yet these are confronted by the necessity of making a decision which will determine their further life.

This procedure was not new in Israel. It was in line with a tradition whose best-known example is Nathan's parable of the rich man who took a poor man's only lamb (II Sam 12:1–7). After telling the story, the prophet did not have to formulate any questions. David reacted immediately: this man deserves death. And Nathan needed to add only one more word to make the king realize that this judgment was his own. Agreeing with this and admitting his guilt, the king became another man: a criminal became a penitent. Most of the time Jesus' parables work in the same way.

Two opposite views

Often a parable opposes two opinions concerning the same matter: one corresponds to the opinion of the listeners, the other to that of

Jesus. The clearest example is found in the parables in which a character appears who gives the point of view of the listeners after which Jesus presents his own point of view by the mouth of the principal figure of the story. The parable of the workers in the vineyard (Mt 20:1–15) is told in such a way that the listeners spontaneously identify themselves with the workers who started work early in the morning, and share their view that it is unjust to give the same salary for one hour as for twelve hours of work. They are made to listen to the explanation of the owner of the vineyard and especially the concluding question addressed to the listeners which expresses Jesus' own view: 'Do you begrudge my generosity?' (Mt 20:15). The same procedure is found in the parable of the prodigal son (Lk 15:11–32): the indignation of the elder son expresses the criticism of a particular group of people, to whom Jesus replies with the words of the father inviting the displeased son to acknowledge the prodigal son as his brother.

Other parables too can be approached in similar fashion: the parable of the two sons (Mt 21:28–31), addressed to people who say yes but do not do what is expected from them; the parable of the great supper (Lk 14:16–24), intended for people who do not heed the call and then find out to their surprise who those are who do respond; the parable of the weeds among the wheat (Mt 13:24–30), in which the servants who want to remove the weeds represent the view of those to whom the parable is addressed.

But it is not necessary for the parable to contain an explicit conversation. Here belong especially the parables derived from nature in which two opposite situations are often found, one expressing the view of the listeners, the other the view of Jesus. The parable of the sower (Mk 4:3–8 and parallels) begins with a series of failures which undoubtedly reflect the impression Jesus' activity made on his listeners, but ends with the image of a marvellous success which expresses Jesus' own certainty. The same contrast is found in the parable of the mustard seed (Mk 4:30–32 and parallels): to the smallness and insignificance of the beginning is opposed the great effect that follows.

These examples support the conclusion that Jesus' parables often contain an invitation to follow a certain direction; starting from one way of looking at things one discovers that there is another, better way. This view is, of course, the view of the narrator, as opposed to the view of the listeners. They are led from their initial position which was considered solid to a point where they can see that the opposite view is more solid. They will have to reconsider their point of view. It remains to be seen whether they are ready to do so.

Towards a change in behaviour

Jesus' parables do not dwell on descriptions or definitions of people or things. Instead of saying what people or things *are*, they express what people *do* and how things *happen*. A number of parables deal with the kingdom of God, but one should not expect to find in them a definition of the kingdom. Jesus wants to make us see that the kingdom of God is coming, how it comes, and what we should do to enter it. The parables do not reveal unchanging truths intended to be known.

A good number of parables or parabolic statements directly aim at a line of conduct to which Jesus wants to impel his listeners or against which he wants to warn them. This is especially the case in four example stories: the good Samaritan (Lk 10:30–37), the rich fool (Lk 12:16–20), the rich man and Lazarus (Lk 16:19–31), and the Pharisee and the tax collector (Lk 18:9–14). The same is true of the parables of the unforgiving debtor (Mt 18:23–34), the dishonest steward (Lk 16:1–8), the wicked tenants (Mk 12:1–9), the talents (Mt 25:14–30), and the twin parables of the old garment and the old wineskins (Mk 2:21–22), the treasure and the pearl (Mt 13:44–46), the tower and the war (Lk 14:28–32). These and other parables are concerned with practical behaviour.

Many parables deal with God's behaviour. But God's behaviour is never described for its own sake. Jesus speaks of it because of the consequences his listeners should draw from it for their own conduct. The most typical example is found in the statement in which Jesus describes God as one who 'makes his sun rise on the evil and on the good, and sends rain on the just and on the unjust' (Mt 5:45). The fact that God makes no distinction here was a very difficult theological problem for the rabbis: how could this be reconciled with God's justice? Jesus is not concerned with this theological problem. He thinks only of the example which his disciples should follow. Similarly, Jesus describes the love with which God cares for birds and flowers (Mt 6:26, 30; Lk 12:24, 28), a warning against anxiety. Likewise, the conduct of a father towards his son (Mt 7:9–11), of a friend towards his friend (Lk 11:5–8), of a master towards his servants (Lk 17:7–10), of a judge towards a widow (Lk 18:2–5) are described to help us understand God's attitude towards people, but always with the intention that we draw from it the consequences for people's behaviour towards God and each other.

The same occurs in the parables in which Jesus speaks of God's behaviour in relation to what shocked people in his own behaviour. His friendly association with sinners offended people who, in their attitude towards these outcasts, could not understand what they meant in the eyes of God who loved them. Only when they change their attitude towards those who are their brothers (Lk 15:32) and friends (Mt 20:15), will they be able to see in Jesus' conduct a revelation of God's love. His failures and the insignificance of his appearance in comparison with the great events evoked by the kingdom of God could give rise to doubts about the fact that with Jesus' mission the final stage of saving history was inaugurated. By their contrasting images several parables show that the way God is acting now corresponds to the way things happen in ordinary life (Mk 4:3–8, 26–29, 30–32; Mt 13:24–30, 31–33, 47–48). So there is no reason to doubt that Jesus is backed up by God and that he is the eschatological bringer of salvation. This series of parables is apparently intended to confirm the doubtful.

The parables of Jesus are almost always concerned with the behaviour of the listeners: either they deal directly with their behaviour or, where this does not seem to be the case and the parable's purport seems rather theological, they are ultimately still concerned with behaviour. Even if the listeners must change their point of view, the ultimate intent is a change of behaviour in consequence of a new outlook on reality. In so far as the parables teach something, it is always a teaching which should become part of life. It should result in conversion, reconciliation, etc.

In this connection, it should be noted that the biblical concept of reconciliation is often fatefully mistaken for the ideological harmonization of society. Jesus' proclamation is indeed a word of reconciliation, but reconciliation is act, decision, and creative action, not a theory of the harmony of estates, of solidarity of the classes and the whole of society. The Christian faith is not intended to confirm society, but to change it.

Contemporary life

Jesus stood in the reality of nature and the human community. He observed events, he spoke to people of what they themselves could see or establish. He observed things together with them, knowing how they thought. He gave evidence of clear insight which inspired confidence. He talked about a world they were familiar with, and knew what he was talking about and the people he was talking to.

The way people look or can look at things is only a starting point to enable the listeners to discover that another view on things is possible, and that the latter is more correct. The narrator, therefore, does not confirm current opinion. He criticizes it and opposes to it his own point of view, but in such a way as to remain on the level of ordinary life. On that very level he invites the listeners to agree with him. Therefore, he does not lead them immediately to the religious level, where he would enter into conflict with convictions which are firmly rooted in current ways of thinking. He first meets his listeners on a seemingly neutral ground on which he intends to make them receptive to another image of the world, the image on which his own religious conviction rests.

The 'method' Jesus used in the parables remains important today. It is clear that religious instruction will not get far with rational, logical arguments. Religious conviction is not imposed by means of an appeal to one's own or others' authority, or under pressure of rational argumentation. A method which appeals to experience and the observation of reality stands a much better chance of succeeding, even though it remains indirect and its conclusions rest on analogy. The best way to bring people to that new outlook of life to which the gospel message invites them is to make them see the familiar reality with new eyes.

The parables do not only make one see and judge things in a new way; they invite to *behaviour* corresponding to that new outlook. It is not sufficient to contemplate things in such a way that one can adopt Jesus' judgment: one must also assume the consequences. The parables debouch into life. They do so by inspiring attitudes and behaviour, not by prescribing rules or offering recipes which only have to be applied. Jesus indicates the direction in which he invites people to go; but this does not relieve them from the responsibility of choosing the right means to move ahead. The behaviour to which one is invited is not programmed. The recommendations or warnings are discreet, the opposite of casuistry, without altering the demanding character of the message.

A Christian proclamation based on Jesus' parable method cannot but elicit the question how the message will become part of our life, an invitation to a new behaviour. One can talk about *receiving* the gospel only when, together with a new outlook on the world and a new understanding of life, it brings about a renewed way of behaviour towards God and people. In this connection it may be noted that rather than a single point or significant idea, a parable has a 'cluster' of (theological) motifs which together press the listener/reader to make a single response. But then it has been suggested again 'that it is more accurate and helpful to speak of the meaning of the *whole* parable and the meaning of its *parts* than to speak of "one point" and "many points"'.[4]

How does a parable function?[5]

A good parable should create distance, provoke, and appeal.

The person who begins to tell a parable creates the immediate impression of talking about something which seems to have little connection with the circumstances of the moment. At first the listeners must wonder what the purpose of this story is. In this sense it can be said that a parable *creates distance* or alienates. Simon the Pharisee must have been surprised when all of a sudden Jesus began to tell a story about a creditor and two debtors (Lk 7:40–43).

Just because a parable is somewhat irritating it has *provoking* power. It impels people to think and sharpens their attention. It is not by accident that so many parables begin with a question. It is clear that over the heads of the characters of the parable the question is addressed to the listeners. They are made to think and are expected to react and to answer. Evidently the listeners want to see and understand, the more so because the parables often reverse the situation. Indeed, Jesus often tells rather unusual and paradoxical things, which shock or even irritate the listeners. That the labourers who worked only one hour receive as much as those who worked the whole day is shocking. This 'shock-effect' is intended to force people to question their own conventional way of life and regard it from another point of view, i.e., from the new possibilities of life disclosed by the parables. In other words, by the intentional insertion of irritating, surprising or paradoxical features, the parables challenge one's spontaneous, current way of acting. The father of the prodigal son not only forgives his son, he does some 'crazy' things as well; he is standing outside waiting for his son; he runs to meet him; he embraces him and insists that his home-coming should be lavishly celebrated. By stressing this surprising mercy of the father, the parable discloses a new world, a new way of life. The author of the parable does this in the hope that his listeners will understand, and even more, that henceforth they will act likewise.

A parable, therefore, does not only intend to bring people to new insight; it also contains an *appeal*, a call to live differently; it does not so much give information as impel to action. A parable confronts the listeners with the choice between two points of view or possibilities of life: the short-sighted attitude of refusal of forgiveness or the new broadminded and wholehearted mercy proposed by Jesus on behalf of God. Those who listen to a parable must choose between their own point of view and that of Jesus; they are unavoidably confronted by a decision. They are no longer the same people as before; they cannot remain neutral; they must react, positively or negatively. They must straighten out things here and now; they must open themselves for a new world, the world of God, which Jesus discloses in his parables, or stubbornly close themselves to it.

By continually telling new parables, with ever new 'shock-effects', Jesus tries to get his listeners, and each of us, out of their and our everyday conformist conduct and to win them and us over to this new world of God, whom he calls his Father, so that they and we too may be good and merciful as the heavenly Father is. In the parables Jesus always starts from life towards life. He tells people about real life as they know it from experience, but in such a way that they start to question this life and open themselves to a new life, a life as God wants it and as it was presented and exemplarily lived by Jesus himself, on God's behalf.

Those, then, who tell a parable, old or new, should see to it that they achieve this effect; they should change the life of their listeners. They must succeed in making people who hear the parable see the trusted reality with new eyes and live it in a new way. A parable saying should never return empty. A parable should not only 'teach', but also and especially 'convert'.

The three levels of tradition[6]

In a complete explanation of the gospel parables three levels or phases must be distinguished: firstly, the meaning of the parable as it was pronounced by Jesus; secondly, the form in which it was passed on by the early Christian communities after Easter; and thirdly, the form of the parable as it is now found in the gospel. On this third level — but the first to be encountered when one sets out to study the gospels — the reader is often confronted with differing versions of the same parable. A certain amount of observation and interpretation of the differences which occur between the parallel versions of the same parable is a must if one wants to reach an understanding of the parables in their earliest meaning. To discover the meaning intended by the evangelist or final redactor one should pay special attention to the literary context. The intention of the early Christian tradition is usually discovered in certain details, unevenness and seams in the texts, and sometimes also in concluding formulas which did not originate with Jesus but were added at a later time. To understand what the parable meant as spoken by Jesus, one must first try to scan the (reconstructed) text of the parable in all its nuances and listen with fresh attention to the original parable, paying special attention to the basic idea or the point of the story or comparison. One should also try to place the parable back into Jesus's life and ask in what situation Jesus would have pronounced this parable, who were the people to whom he originally addressed himself, and how this parable fits into the totality of his message.

The parables are, for the most part, authentic words of Jesus. After thirty years of life in a Middle Eastern, oral-tradition peasant community, and fully aware of the active role of the early Christian

Palestinian community, Kenneth Bailey could state that he did not find any 'convincing reason to question the basic authenticity of the parables as parables of Jesus of Nazareth'.[7]

On all three levels it is the community rather than individual Christians who are addressed in the first place.

> It is not to man as individual man, initially, that the parables apply, but to man in his religious context as part of a community, yet they do so in nonreligious terms, at once identifying his religious life with life itself and the community of the religious with the human community. For the basic modern question in human relationships, interpersonal or international, is whether other people or peoples are to be treated as human beings. The importance of the modern critical study of the parables is not to limit their interpretation to what may be recovered of their impact in Jesus' time, nor even their meaning in the *Sitz im Leben*, the life situation of the church in the evangelists' times. The importance of the analytical survey of the original import is that they be not treated as offering generalized universal 'truths' but as proclamations concerning the situation of man under *this* God in a situation which, since Jesus and because of Christ, has been and always will be critical. Quite obviously this has its application to the individual, but if God's purpose be not needlessly and invalidly confined to the church, it applies mutatis mutandis to the succeeding generations of men and to the social structures which, since the decline of Christendom, carry the burden of fulfilling God's work in the world — or fail to do so.[8]

A note on contemporary parable interpretation[9]

The history of modern parable interpretation undoubtedly begins with Adolf Jülicher (1899), who radically rejected the allegorical interpretation which had been predominant since the Church Fathers, and divided Jesus' parables into a number of categories. The pioneers of form criticism, Martin Dibelius (1919) and Rudolf Bultmann (1921), contributed to our knowledge of the Christian community's motivation and intention in the transmission of the parables, and to a more accurate classification and description of different types of parabolic speech. But it was Charles H. Dodd (1935) and Joachim Jeremias (1947) who substantially advanced the study of the parables by, on the one hand, overcoming the exaggerations of Jülicher's reaction and, on the other hand, studying the parables in the setting of the life of Jesus.

Within the past thirty years a movement has developed called the 'new hermeneutic', one of whose exponents, the post-Bultmannian Ernst Fuchs (1954), studied the parables as 'language-events' in which Jesus revealed his self-understanding. Fuchs's insights on the parables have been developed and applied by two of his students, Eta Linnemann (1961) and Eberhard Jüngel (1967).

While the work of the scholars just mentioned made significant advances in the areas of textual and historical criticism, the situation was very different with respect to literary criticism. This was taken up by Robert Funk (1966), who analysed the parable as metaphor. A somewhat different line was followed by Dan Otto Via (1967), who insisted that parables must be seen as real aesthetic objects and discussed them in terms of three categories: historico-literary criticism, literary-existential analysis, and existential-theological interpretation, his major interest lying in the second category. Another attempt in the same area was pursued by John Dominic Crossan (1973), who studied the parables as poetic metaphor.

Funk, Via, Crossan and others have carried their endeavours further in the SBL Parables Seminar, which devoted itself to a structuralist approach to the parables. Its results have been published in the experimental journal *Semeia*, whose first issue appeared in 1974. Simultaneously, similar approaches were developed in France (semiotics/semiology; e.g., the Entrevernes Group) and in Germany (e.g., E. Güttgemanns, Hans-Josef Klauck, and Hans Weder). These studies have shown beyond any doubt that many of Jülicher's conclusions, several of which are still adhered to by many recent interpreters, are either mistaken or inaccurate — one of the main reasons why this book does not dwell on an exposition of questionable classifications and distinctions. But with the exception of the studies of Klauck and Weder, they have not been equally successful in substantially advancing our understanding of the *gospel* parables.

It has been correctly stated that 'a purely aesthetic treatment of the parables... is a theoretically acceptable, though... unusually injudicious procedure in the case of Jesus' parables'. And in a response given during a structuralist conference, it was said that the structuralist approach does not seem to provide any new solutions, and that when one adds up 'the data supplied by your methods of computation, the answers seem quite precisely the answers I already had'. No doubt, the structuralist approach has made a great impact at the level of literary criticism, but this impact turns out to be disappointing to the (pastorally concerned) interpreter of the parables. A good deal of reading of structuralist studies on the parables has given the author of the present book some interesting insights which, however, are not distinctively structuralist. In the eyes of some he may be guilty of the 'superficial objections and artificial appropriations' discussed in the preface to the American edition of the volume published by the Entrevernes Group.

In 1975 it was stated that 'it is impossible to tell at the moment how important structuralist criticism may become in the interpretation of the parables of Jesus. The SBL Parables Seminar has been devoting a good deal of attention to the subject, but with extremely limited results. The basic problem seems to be a disparity between the parables of Jesus as texts and structuralist criticism as a method... Events may well overtake any prediction that I might make, but as of the Spring of 1975, it does seem that structuralist criticism will have only a limited impact on parable interpretation'.[10] In this author's opinion no such events have occurred up to the present, although he would not go as far as the scholar who, recently referring to a collection of papers on structuralist exegesis, wrote that 'One does not learn much from the volume, and what one can learn from it is not very useful'.[11]

2   The seed growing secretly

(Mk 4:26–29)

This parable is found in Mark alone. While it cannot altogether be excluded that it was not found in the text of Mark used by both Matthew and Luke, it is much more likely that Matthew and Luke knew it, but for some reason omitted it. Matthew apparently preferred to give instead the parable of the weeds (Mt 13:24–30) and its interpretation (Mt 13:36–43). Luke decided to omit the parable altogether. But these omissions are also interpretations. One result of this decision by Matthew and Luke is that we have only one version of the parable and do not have many criteria available to figure out whether and to what extent Mark adapted its formulation to his own theological interests, or, and this is basically the same question, what the parable looked like in the earlier (oral) tradition. The best approach, therefore, seems to be first to read the parable carefully in its present form and to find out what its precise intention is. Then we will try to determine how far this intention can be assigned a situation in life in the ministry of Jesus, or (and) in the life of the post-Easter Church.

A first reading of the parable

> **Verse 26:** And he said, 'The kingdom of God is as if a man should scatter seed upon the ground,

It seems clear that this parable formed a kind of 'twin' parable with the parable of the mustard seed (Mk 4:30–32). The introductory words 'and he said' are not Mark's usual introduction, since Mark himself prefers to use 'he said *to them*', but betray rather the characteristics of his source ('he said'). The first words of the parable itself are an example of the so-called dative introduction. It is found three times in Mark (Mk 4:26, 31; 13:34). Like the other introductions, it should be understood in the following way: 'it is with the kingdom of God as it is with the following case'. We have to find out from the story itself what is the *tertium comparationis*, i.e., the

16

point of the comparison, which relates the picture to the reality for which it is devised.

'As if a man should scatter seed upon the ground' is in the aorist tense in contrast with the following durative present tenses. The best way of rendering the text in English is to use the past tense: a man scattered seed upon the ground. This one action of sowing is all the man did. In what follows it will be stressed that he is not at all involved in the growth of the seed. Thus, already at this stage, it seems that the point of the parable — if one can still speak in this way — begins to emerge.

Attention should also be called to other details of this verse. It is said that the man 'scattered' (or, more literally, 'threw') the seed. Throwing (Greek *ballein*) is, after all, not the normal verb to describe the action of a farmer. Mark could easily have used the verb 'to sow' (Greek *speirein*) which he employs no less than eight times in this same chapter. The man threw the seed 'on the ground' (literally, 'on the earth', as in Mk 4:31). All this sounds very large-scale. It seems that the reality the author is thinking about is already influencing the wording of the parable.

Verse 26b speaks of the man who threw the seed, and the most important feature to be remembered of this introductory verse seems to be that *this is all the man did* regarding the seed. This is in fact the very least the narrator could ascribe to the man, since it could hardly be supposed that the seed found its way to the field all by itself!

Verse 27: and should sleep and rise night and day, and the seed should sprout and grow, he knows not how.

The first part of verse 27 describes the daily life of the same man; the seed is the subject of the main clause, but the last part of the verse shows that attention remains focused on the man. The non-interference of the man is emphatically stressed. He continues his daily life and does not seem to care. Note that it is said that he goes to bed and gets up night and day. We would say: he gets up and goes to bed day and night. But for the Jews the day began at 6:00 p.m., and so the first thing they did was to go to bed and sleep. So the basis and the beginning of the parable is apparently Aramaic.

But let us go back to what seems to be *the* point of this statement. Two words are emphasized in the Greek version of the last clause: *hōs* ('how') at the beginning, and *autos* ('he') at the end. The man does not do anything for the growing seed. He can hardly be expected to cause what 'he does not know how'. And he does not seem to care. This is, quite obviously, not the attitude of a real farmer. It is clear that we have here at least part of the 'point' of the parable.

However, the parable pays no attention to the man's psychology, and so all the insights some commentators claim to derive from the man's alleged patience, or the certainty with which he awaits the harvest, or unbelief in the coming of the harvest, have no foundation in the text.

It has been suggested that 'he knows not how' does not belong to the preceding context, but to the following: 'And the seed should sprout and grow. He does not know how the earth produces by itself...'. But this suggestion has not been accepted by any influential exegete.

Verse 28: The earth produces of itself, first the blade, then the ear, then the full grain in the ear.

Recently proposed arguments against the presence of this verse in the original parable do not seem to carry much weight. The verse describes in detail how 'the earth produces *by itself (automatē)*' all the stages of the seed's growth. This 'automatic' growth is emphasized: during the time of growth the farmer does not do anything in the field; everything happens without his intervention.

The question raised by this verse is whether the quite lengthy description of the growth of the seed is also a *special* point of the story. If so, this should be given great weight in the interpretation of the parable as a whole. Indeed, in that case the idea of the *progressive* and *steady development* would be part of its message. This interpretation was very current in a naively optimistic nineteenth century. Nowadays it is still held by some rather conservative exegetes who think they discover here an indication of the constant progress of the Church (or perhaps even of the constant increase of the *power* of the Church!).

It seems, however, that the description of the seed's growth is only a subordinate element in the parable, for, just like the parable of the mustard seed (at least in the original form found in Mk 4:30–32), the parable of the seed growing secretly is a *contrast*-parable, whose contrast seems to reside in the consecutive actions of the man. In the present composition of the gospel of Mark these two parables form a pair, and therefore their 'point' must be the same.

Verse 29: But when the grain is ripe, at once he puts in the sickle, because the harvest has come.

Some exegetes have contested the authenticity of this verse. Two difficulties are mentioned. Firstly, the citation of Joel 3(4):13, 'put in the sickle, for the harvest is ripe', is said to be out of place: it evokes the image of a judge who comes to 'harvest' the godless (Joel 3[4]:12–16), while we are dealing here with the gathering in of the good grain (cf. Mt 13:30). However, we are not really dealing with a citation, but with a rather free allusion which does not necessarily take over the vengeful aspects of Joel's text. Secondly, the harvester of verse 29 is identified with the man who does not do anything for the growth of the grain. Now if the harvester is God, how can it be said that he does not care for or know about the growth of the seed? This would be a valid objection if we were dealing with an allegorical story, but it does not apply to a parable: even if the conduct of the sower-harvester is intended to explain God's conduct, it is nevertheless described as that of an ordinary man. If God is meant to resemble that man in one respect, this does not mean that he has to resemble him in everything.

In favour of the authenticity of the verse we would say that the description of the seed's growth practically calls for the mention of the harvest. It is true, however, that a certain influence of the Septuagint (the *Greek* text of the Old Testament) on the formula borrowed from Joel may justify some doubt concerning the primitive character of this allusion. The hypothesis of an older form of verse 29 referring to a harvest without clear allusion to Joel 3(4):13 is therefore not altogether to be rejected.

Verse 29 is distinguished from the rest of the parable by the words *de* ('but') and *euthus* ('immediately'). The picture introduced by 'but' clearly expresses the point of contrast: the man who did not do anything while the seed was growing, now at once (*euthus*) hurries to put in the sickle. It is indeed evident that the subject of the main verb is the same person as the one who threw the seed and remained passive while it was growing.

> It seems... impossible to discern Marcan redaction in the parable. Hence Mark reproduces the parable as he found it in the tradition and, with the possible exception of the allusion to Joel 4:13, the parable as a whole has its home in an Aramaic-speaking environment.[12]

Interpretation of the parable

Since this parable has received an amazing variety of interpretations, we give here first a summary of opinions.

The possible centres of attention have been outlined as follows:
(1) The emphasis can be placed either on what happens to the seed, or on the behaviour of the man, or on both.
(2) If one decides for the seed, it is still to be determined whether the growth or the certainty of the harvest should be stressed.

(3) If one decides for the man, should his inactivity during the growth of the seed be stressed, or his sudden activity at the harvest?
(4) The conduct of the man may illustrate either God's conduct in establishing his kingdom, or Jesus' conduct in fulfilling his mission.
(5) The parable may have been intended to exhort the Zealots to patience, or to tell the discouraged disciples not to lose heart.

The 'classical' interpretation, initiated by A. Jülicher, held that the parable speaks of the progressive and irresistible growth of the seed whose inner strength overcomes all obstacles. The parable would call for confidence in the growth of the kingdom in the world.

While A. Schweitzer and other proponents of thorough-going eschatology found in the parable an expression of the expectation of God's final and decisive intervention in history, C. H. Dodd, in the context of his theory of realized eschatology, believed that it teaches that in Jesus' ministry the eschatological harvest is already taking place.

Advocating an eschatology in process of realization, J. Jeremias says that the parable contrasts the patience and waiting of the farmer, on the one hand, and the harvest which is the reward for his waiting on the other hand. It would be a lesson addressed to the disciples who are disturbed by Jesus' unimpressive activity. Agreeing with this interpretation, N. Dahl adds that the parable also says that there is a true relation between the sowing and growing of the seed and the harvest, or between Jesus' ministry and that of the Church.

R. Schnackenburg holds that the ending of the parable determines the meaning of the parable. The figure of the man serves only to enhance the irresistible growth. The parable would stress that God alone establishes the kingdom, which is not discernible in history and cannot be hastened by human activity. J. Gnilka, too, says that the harvest is the outstanding feature of the parable, but, unlike Schnackenburg, he believes that the man occupies the centre of the stage.

While admitting that freedom is not mentioned in the parable, E. Fuchs believes that its core message concerns the freedom of those who share Jesus' certainty of the future which belongs entirely to God. According to H. Kahlefeld, the message of the parable is that the sower of the word is freed from the care for the growth of the seed, since the intrinsic power of God's word is irresistible.

For A. M. Ambrozic the parable should certainly be interpreted from the point of view of the harvest. But this feature should be combined with the statement that the 'earth produces of itself' the grain. The parable proclaims not only the coming of the kingdom but also the manner of its arrival. 'Its coming is, first of all, irresistible and certain... secondly, totally independent of human effort... The parable is basically an appeal... to submit to the only way in which God is setting up his kingdom, i.e., through Jesus.'[13]

According to W. G. Kümmel, it is not the growth and ripening of the seed which is emphasized, but rather that the farmer does not intervene in this growth, that the harvest comes without his assistance. Therefore, the 'point' of the parable is not the growth of the seed, but the certainty of the harvest which nothing can influence. The hidden character of the growth of the kingdom of God should not be allowed to undermine this certainty.

For J. Dupont the parable focuses on the sower, not the seed, and its message is to be found in the contrast between verses 27–28 and verse 29, between the long inactivity and the intense activity of the farmer. Since the conclusion speaks of God's judgment, and the central figure of a parable of the kingdom should normally be God, the farmer symbolizes God. The parable expresses the contrast between the period of Jesus' ministry, during which little is seen of the judgment and harvest announced by John the Baptist (cf. Mt 3:10, 12), and God's actual judgment. But Mk 4:26 implies also continuity, although this aspect seems to be better illustrated by the parable of the mustard seed (Mk 4:30–32).

Since verse 28 allegedly 'creates a major tension in the central image of the parable', John Dominic Crossan suggests that it was secondarily 'inserted into the parable of Mark 4:26, 27, 29 in order to shift the emphasis from the action of the farmer to the fate of the seed; and that this was intended to bring all three parables into a greater unity, with all of them now primarily concerned with what happens to the seed in its growth'.[14] The parable would express the personal religious experience of Jesus.

The original meaning of the parable

It has been noted that verses 26b–27 and 29 have a markedly parallel structure. Both begin by indicating the presupposition (in the aorist) of the principal action: when the seed is thrown on the ground/when the grain is ripe. Then follows the principal datum which concerns the farmer: he sleeps and rises night and day (verse 27a)/at once he puts in the sickle (verse 29b). Finally the activity of the sower finds its explanation in what happens in the field: the seed sprouts and grows, he knows not how (verse 27b)/the harvest has come (verse 29c). We are dealing here with an antithetic parallelism which focuses on the contrast between the two attitudes of the sower: after sowing he does not care for the field/when the grain is ripe he becomes very active.

Verse 28 serves as a transition between 26b–27 and verse 29. With regard to verse 27 it explains that the sower does not have to worry about the seed because the earth does the work by itself; the activity of the earth accounts for the inactivity of the man. At the same time verse 28 prepares for verse 29 by enumerating the stages through which the seed grows from its first sprouting (verse 27b) to full maturity (verse 29a): the blade, the ear, the grain in the ear. Thus verse 28 allows us to pass from the first part of the antithesis to the second. It is, as it were, at the service of the contrast between the conduct of the man after the sowing and his conduct at the harvest.

Indeed, the narrator does not seem to emphasize the contrast between the constant, hidden growth of the seed and the sudden arrival of the harvest. He focuses rather on the contrast between the *inactivity* of the man while the seed grows and his *sudden activity* as soon as the harvest comes. It seems, then, that the extended description of the seed's growth serves only to highlight this inactivity of the man and that it is, therefore, a subordinate feature which should not be interpreted by itself.

The 'point' of the parable is to be found in the contrast constituted by the *laisser aller* of the man during the seed's growth and his sudden activity when the harvest has come. The other details of the story should be regarded as subordinate and should, therefore, be disregarded as long as we are dealing with the story as *parable* in its original form, and not yet with possible allegorical developments.

The structure of the parable can be expressed in the following equation: $a:b = c:d$. In this equation c and d are known, namely the inactivity of the man during the growth of the seed, and his sudden activity as soon as the harvest has come. What is meant by a and b? The best way to handle this question is to begin with b. That means that we should ask ourselves how d (the man's sudden activity at the time of the harvest) should be transposed in the reality the narrator is referring to. What is the saving historical reality signified by d? In other words, what does the parable mean by the harvest?

The harvest, with all its different aspects, is the classical biblical image for the coming of Yahweh, for the fulfilment of saving history (e.g., Isa 9:3[2]; Joel 3[4]:13; Hos 6:11; II Esdras 4:28;[15] Mt 13:30, 39; Gal 6:7ff.; Rev 14:14–19). In fact, Mk 4:29 seems to allude clearly to Joel 3(4):13, the famous text about the day of Yahweh, announcing the divine judgment facing the pagan nations in the valley of Jehoshaphat:

Put in the sickle, for the harvest is ripe.
Go in, tread, for the wine press is full.
The vats overflow, for their wickedness is great.

The last words of the parable echo the words in italics in the citation of Joel. This suggestion is supported by the fact that Joel is cited once more in Rev 14:14–16:

> Then I looked, and lo, a white cloud,
> and seated on the cloud one like a son of man,
> with a golden crown on his head, and a *sharp sickle* in his hand.
> And another angel came out of the temple,
> calling with a loud voice to him who sat upon the cloud,
> *'Put in your sickle, and reap,*
> *for the hour to reap has come,*
> *for the harvest of the earth is fully ripe.'*
> So he who sat upon the cloud swung his sickle on the earth,
> and the earth was reaped.

In the light of Joel 3(4):13 and Rev 14:14–16 there seems to be little doubt that the harvest of which the parable speaks is the eschatological judgment. The only noteworthy difference is that in the Book of Revelation Christ is the eschatological judge, whereas in the parable, as far as we can see, it is God himself, just as in Joel 3(4):13. It remains, of course, possible that the allusion to Joel 3(4):13 is a Christian addition to the original parable. But the theme of the harvest was certainly part of the original parable, and this picture was sufficiently clear, even without reference to Joel. Besides, the whole parable with its description of the growth of the seed leads up to the harvest, just as the sowing and growing of the mustard seed leads up to its contrast picture, the description of the great shrub.

Once it has been established that *b* means that eschatological judgment, we have to determine what *a*, the description of the inactivity of the man while the seed grows, means. Now this man is supposed to be the same person as the one who at once becomes very active when the eschatological judgment has come. That means that this man symbolizes God himself, for every Jew knew that it is God who judges and puts the sickle into the grain. Besides, the parable certainly speaks of the kingdom of God, of how God realizes his rule, and not of what man does in this regard.

The disproportionate importance given by the parable to the seed's time of growth, which is also the time during which the man does not do anything, seems to reflect the actual situation and the problem present in the minds of those for whom the parable was devised.

The parable then apparently deals with the same problem as the following parable of the mustard seed. It is addressed to people who are disappointed because they feel that God is passive, that he does not seem to care. After a first intervention he gives the impression that he lets things follow their own course. If God intervened by sending Jesus, why does he seem to lose interest afterwards? This was a real problem for Jesus' contemporaries, including his disciples. They were scandalized at the fact that nothing extraordinary happened, that Jesus did not show anything of that divine wrath which they had expected for the last days. On the contrary, Jesus showed only goodness and compassion to sinners. How then could he expect them to take his messianic mission seriously? Why did he not immediately give the signal to throw off the yoke of the pagans and to establish the final Israel? Was not the fact that he did not do so an argument against the authenticity of his mission? If we remember that Jesus' disciples were Galileans and that some of them may have been Zealots (cf. Lk 6:12–16), we may have an idea of their bewilderment at Jesus' actual approach in which it was so hard to see that God was at work.

This means that the description of the inactivity of the man during the growth of the seed gives expression to what these disciples were thinking. But their thinking was not correct. God is working all the time, but at present still in a hidden way. Therefore, the disciples mistakenly think that he is not doing anything. Their attitude can be compared with the astonishment of John the Baptist concerning Jesus' conduct (cf. Mt 11:2–6).

In answering their difficulty, Jesus had to start by showing that he understood their problem. He did so by describing the man (=God) as sleeping and apparently not caring. He admits that God indeed does not work the way they think he should. But God has his *kairos*, his opportune time, and the *kairos* of his full manifestation in the last judgment will certainly come. If God gives the impression that he lets things follow their own course, it is because he waits for the opportune time to stage his decisive intervention. Then he will be very active for everybody to see. The meaning of the parable would become much clearer if, in line with the interrogative finale found in several parables (cf. Mk 12:9; Lk 7:42; 10:36; 18:7), one were to insert a question like 'Do you think that the man will never return to his field?' The answer would then be, 'He definitely will when the grain is ripe...'.

With Jesus' ministry the seed has been sown. The kingdom of God to be revealed is already present in a hidden way and developing towards that eschatological day. The attitude of people to this ministry of Jesus will determine their fate when the denouement comes.

The parable on the level of the gospels

After having discovered the meaning of the parable on the level of its earliest existence, we should next ask ourselves what it means on the level of the gospels.

Mark

Since Mark does not seem to have considerably altered the wording of the parable itself to convey the meaning it had for him, the only way to discover the redactional meaning somehow is to study the parable's redactional context, Mk 4:1–34. In this context the parable of the seed growing secretly and the parable of the mustard seed are attached to the Marcan interpretation of the parable of the sower (Mk 4:14–20) which shows a number of Marcan characteristics. The note on *persecution on account of the word* (Mk 4:17) is almost certainly a Marcan addition. And in Mk 4:19 the evangelist speaks of various obstacles to the disciples' perseverance, though in this verse it is not easy to determine exactly what belongs to the Marcan redaction. Anyway, these data alone already indicate that Mark understood the parable in the context of his own situation and that of the Christians he addressed, which was apparently a situation of persecution.

On this level, the period of growth of the seed and of God's seeming inactivity is clearly the period of the Church, and the time of sowing is understood to be the period of Jesus' ministry. Then the man who does not seem to care becomes, of course, Christ, the Lord himself. But, despite appearances, the seed continues to grow. And the sower, Christ himself, will come for the eschatological judgment. Thus the parable becomes first of all a lesson in confidence in the word brought into the world by Jesus, and confidence in the (second) coming of Christ. This confidence is to be preserved in patience and endurance in a time which is characterized, on the one hand, by persecutions and, on the other hand, by a seeming inactivity of Christ (and God).

Matthew

Matthew omitted the parable of the seed growing secretly, but apparently replaced it by the parable of the weeds among the wheat (Mt 13:24–30, 36–43). He certainly knew the former parable because several of its characteristic phrases are found in the latter: 'sleep' — 'grow' — 'the blade' — 'the grain' — 'the harvest'. Why did Matthew prefer the parable of the weeds? Obviously he must have considered this parable more meaningful in the life-situation of his community.

Some scholars hold that Matthew did not really pass over the parable of the seed growing secretly, but that he, or somebody before him, freely edited and expanded Mk 4:26–29, so that it appears now in his gospel in the form of the parable of the weeds. This process would account both for the presence in Mt 13 of the parable of the weeds and for the terminological similarities between Mt 13:24–30 and Mk 4:26–29. But to consider the parable of the weeds as deriving from the parable of the seed growing secretly is to assume an extremely thorough recasting of the latter, and the terminological similarities are due to the fact that both parables deal with the same agricultural realities: sowing, growth, and harvest, rather than to dependence of one on the other. It seems, therefore, that the relationship between the two parables is best accounted for in terms of a substitution made by Matthew because he considered the parable of the seed growing secretly inadequate for his objective.

Throughout the gospel it can be observed that the evangelist's main concern is the difficulties which beset the Church within. It is true that there is no other gospel which gives such a wonderful picture of what the Church should be (see, e.g., Mt 18). But at the same time no other evangelist shows so clearly that he is deeply aware of the presence of 'good and bad' (Mt 13:47–50; 22:10), and that he is disappointed by certain shortcomings and dangers which he observes in the Church of his time. Matthew was much more worried about *internal corruption* than about external assaults by persecutors. In such situation the parable of the enemy who sows bad weeds among the good wheat which Christ had sown obviously became more meaningful than the parable of the seed growing secretly.

Luke

Luke completely omitted the parable of the seed growing secretly. His very personal concerns in this part of his gospel appear clearly in his interpretation of the parable of the sower (Lk 8:11–15). In Lk 8:13 he denounces those who 'believe for a while and in time of temptation fall away (apostasize)'. And in Lk 8:15 he opposes to this group 'those who, hearing the word, hold it fast in an honest and good heart, and bring forth fruit with patience'. Again, in Lk 8:18 there appears a very remarkable Lucan touch. Mk 4:24 says 'Take heed *what* you hear', but Lk 8:18 reads 'Take heed then *how* you hear'. In that same perspective, Luke makes the episode about Jesus' relatives (Lk 8:19–21) the conclusion of this section: the true relatives of Jesus are those who not only 'do the will of God' (so Mk 3:35), but who 'hear the word of God and do it' (Lk 8:21). Throughout this section of his gospel Luke emphasizes the importance of *doing* the word of God. The parable of the seed growing secretly did not fit in this context: the seed grows all by itself! The parable seems to insist on the sole efficacy of God's power, and the uselessness of human effort. Luke probably thought that this could easily be misunderstood. He therefore omitted the parable altogether. But, as stated above, this in itself is already an interpretation.

Reflection

In the optimistic nineteenth century, the parable was generally interpreted as speaking of the steady and irresistible development of the kingdom of God in the world which was more and more identified with a steady progress toward a better world. Such was the faith of the bourgeois Christian of the nineteenth century. This humanistic and anthropocentric interpretation of the parable is, of course, the opposite of the original meaning, which is very far removed from a naively optimistic humanism.

In the meantime there is very little, if anything, left of that nineteenth-century optimism. The principle of agnostic and atheistic humanism led to the other extreme, a philosophy of human despair. It is exactly in this situation that the message of a parable which deals with a different kind of hope gets its full meaning again. J. Weiss dealt a fatal blow to the anthropocentric interpretation of this and many other parables by pointing out the essentially eschatological perspective of the gospel in general and of the parables in particular. This implies the rejection of a merely humanistic, optimistic belief in progress. The parable was and is addressed in the first place to people who live(d) under pressure and persecution, and for whom merely human hope and calculation make little sense. They receive here a different kind of hope.

For a long time this revaluation of the gospel message by J. Weiss remained purely academic. There was still too much false optimism among those who looked upon themselves as model Christians. And those who had no reason for such optimism did not pay any attention to the gospel, because they needed all their energy to stay alive. But now the message of this parable can once more become relevant.

This does not mean that one should entirely accept the eschatological explanation of J. Weiss. He thought of a *merely* eschatological kingdom of God. He did not see that the kingdom of God has already come with the ministry of Jesus and that it is, in fact, growing towards its final fulfilment. The eschatological times have been inaugurated, and our efforts to build a better world have a positive meaning in this context. J. Weiss might be accused of preaching a religion which is the opium of the people, for he certainly gives the impression of looking for an alibi amidst the present distressing problems. The true message of the parable of the seed growing secretly is, however, that we should sail between 'the Scylla of a false human hope and the Charybdis of total dispair'. It invites us to be realists who do not expect too much from human endeavours and ideologies, but never give up either.

> Impatience and 'rushing about' and over-work are the special temptations of many highly educated people today... We think that *all* important problems can be solved by working harder and by sleeping less. But this is not so. A husband and wife do not learn to live together in love by rushing about and working till late at night. A guilty person does not find the peace of God's forgiveness by more work... There was a Nigerian lorry on which was written, 'Let go, let God.' This saying if rightly interpreted, sums up the teaching of this parable... A Christian provides opportunities for growth. We have seen that the parable does not encourage us to be lazy... We are to make opportunities through which God will do his work. We must make opportunities for others and for ourselves.[16]

> This is not the same thing as a facile belief in progress... Yet if such easy optimism was unjustified, equally unwarranted today is the pessimism which proclaims that 'God is dead' and that the world is going to hell of its own momentum.[17]

> We cannot make the seed grow. And because we cannot do it, we should not attempt to do it... The sower, after finishing the task assigned to him, went to sleep. Isn't that carelessness? No! it is faith in the capability of the germination of the word. Psalm 1 talks of the tree that yields its fruit 'in its season.' How much damage has been caused by impatience.
>   What did Mark the evangelist intend to say by this parable? He wanted to clarify the connection between the activity of believers and the coming of the Kingdom of God... just as the sower is himself unable to make the seed grow, even so the follower of Jesus is unable to establish the Kingdom of God by his own power...
>   What does Mark have to say to us today? I am convinced that his message is still extremely timely. In a world in which the opinion is that man is capable of arranging everything, that even

the future is a matter of careful calculation and good planning, the church must take Mark's words to heart. The future of peace and righteousness for our world does not lie in a further extension of human skill and application of power.[18]

The message of this parable is rather clear: The kingdom of God will surely come, but we should continue to work for the fulfilment of that kingdom, the harvest. We need a combination of patience in which we look hopefully to the future which is ultimately God's, and of commitment by which we actively contribute to that future.

It is usually said that we have here a parable of the seed that grows by itself. It seems to me, however, that the decisive factor is precisely the relation of the sower to this work, which is done *without* him ('he sleeps and rises up, night and day'), and the relation is explained in the words: 'without him knowing how.' The relation is one of ignorance: the sower Jesus is confronted with a 'secret,' something 'hidden,' a 'mystery,' namely the underground work accomplished by his practice in the *hearts* of his hearers, where it leads to sterility or to fruitfulness.[19]

3 The mustard seed

(Mk 4:30–32; Mt 13:31–32; Lk 13:18–19)

Methodologically it seems best in this case first to establish the original form of the parable, i.e., to ferret out in what form Jesus himself pronounced it during his ministry, and to determine exactly what is meant on that level. Afterwards the meaning of the parable on the level of the composition of the gospels will be discussed.

The parable on the level of Jesus' ministry

The three canonical versions of the parable

Matthew 13:31–32	*Mark 4:30–32*	*Luke 13:18–19*
Another parable he put before them, saying, 'The kingdom of heaven	And he said, 'With what can we compare the kingdom of God, or what parable shall we use for it?	He said therefore, 'What is the kingdom of God like? And to what shall I compare it?
is like a grain of mustard seed which a man took and sowed in his field; it is the smallest of all seeds, but when it	It is like a grain of mustard seed, which, when sown upon the ground, is the smallest of all the seeds on earth; yet when it is sown	It is like a grain of mustard seed which a man took and sowed in his garden;
has grown it is the greatest of shrubs and becomes a tree,	it grows up and becomes the greatest of all shrubs, and puts forth large branches,	and it grew and became a tree,
so that the birds of the air come and make nests in its branches.'	so that the birds of the air can make nests in its shade.'	and the birds of the air made nests in its branches.'

It is possible that Matthew and Luke derived their versions of the parable from Mark. But there are good reasons to believe that they also used, in whole or in part, a version from their hypothetical common source known as Q. Firstly, there are a number of agreements between Matthew and Luke against Mark, suggesting a non-Marcan source. Secondly, notwithstanding the very different contexts in which Matthew and Luke present the parable of the mustard seed (i.e., the Parable Discourse/the Travel Narrative), it is in both cases immediately followed by a twin, the parable of the leaven, which is not found in Mark. The simplest explanation for this given is that the two parables were already linked in the Q source. Thirdly, the peculiarities of the Matthean version of the parable are best explained by assuming that Matthew combined Mark and Q.

In Mark we find what the Germans call a *Gleichnis* (a similitude). He speaks of a common experience, of what often and usually happens: when the mustard seed is sown upon the ground... when it grows up... when it puts out large branches... This is all something which regularly happens. In Luke, however, we have a real parable, a story about a specific case: the story of a man who once sowed a mustard seed in his garden. As far as this feature is concerned, Matthew has the same form as Luke, a parable, a specific, past story.

But there is more. In Mark there is a strong contrast between the beginning and the end: it is the smallest of all seeds... it grows up and becomes the greatest of all shrubs and puts out large branches. There is no trace of this strong contrast in the parable of Luke. But Matthew, who shares the parable form with Luke, agrees with Mark as far as this contrast is concerned. It appears, therefore, that Matthew has the Lucan form but the Marcan contrast. This does not mean, of course, that Matthew combined the texts of Mark and Luke. Rather, Matthew had the text of Mark and combined it with Q. In other words, Mark represents one form of the tradition and Luke the other (Q).

Two additional versions

In addition to the three accounts mentioned above there is first of all the version found in # 20 of the Coptic *Gospel of Thomas*:[20]

> The disciples said to Jesus:
> 'Tell us what the kingdom of heaven is like.'
> He said to them: 'It is like a grain of mustard seed,
> smaller than all seeds.
> But when it falls on earth which has been cultivated,
> it puts forth a great branch (and)
> becomes a shelter for (the) birds of heaven.'

The fact that this version of the parable has the least evidence of Old Testament phraseology (see below) does not necessarily mean that it is the most primitive, since the *Gospel of Thomas* has also eliminated practically all references to the Old Testament from the parables of the seed growing secretly and the wicked tenants. Unlike the general tendency in the tradition to increase Old Testament references, the *Gospel of Thomas* seems to have moved in the opposite direction.

Moreover, there is also a fifth hypothetical form, i.e., a reconstruction of Q, mentioned above and based on a careful comparison of Matthew and Luke:

> What is the kingdom of God like?
> And to what shall I compare it?
> It is like a grain of mustard seed,
> which a man took and sowed in his field,
> and it grew and became a tree,
> and the birds of the air made nests in its branches.

To determine the primitive form of the parable we should compare Mk 4:31–32, the hypothetical Q version, and to a lesser extent, the *Gospel of Thomas*.

Parable or similitude?

The first question to be solved is which of the two forms is the more original, the similitude form of Mark or the parable form of Luke? Considering the matter closely, one comes to the conclusion that the Q narrative (the parable form) is more original. In Matthew as well as in Luke, we have twin parables (the mustard seed and the leaven), which they apparently found already combined in Q. It has been argued convincingly that neither arguments based on the introductory formula of the parable of the leaven, nor those derived from the fact that Mark records the first parable without the second, nor from a comparative study of the structure of the parable of the mustard seed in Mark and in Luke (Q), nor from the *Gospel of Thomas* where they appear separately, can prove a secondary association which would have made them for the first time into twin parables. Now the parable of the leaven is also a real parable, a narrative about a specific case: a woman took leaven and hid it in three measures of meal. So Q contained first a parable about what a *man* did, and then a parable about what a *woman* did.

The combination of these two parables most probably already existed on an earlier level of the tradition, and may possibly even be traced to Jesus himself. This would be the most acceptable explanation for the fact that we often find such combinations of two parables in the gospel tradition. The same point is illustrated by two different images: the parables of the lost sheep and the lost coin (Lk 15:4–10); the man who builds a tower and the king who prepares for war (Lk 14:28–32); the parables of the hidden treasure and of the precious pearl (Mt 13:44–46); two men who build houses, one on rock and the other on sand (Mt 7:24–27; Lk 6:47–49); the comparison of the ravens and that of the lilies in the field (Lk 12:24–28; Mt 6:26–30). It seems we are dealing here with a pedagogical device which Jesus himself used: to bring a certain lesson home to his audience he expressed the same idea twice in two different images.

Here too, then, it is most logical to accept that the connection between the parable of the mustard seed and the parable of the leaven goes back to the earliest level of the tradition, and that both had the parable-narrative form, one story about a man, another about a woman. It is practically certain, therefore, that the narrative form of Q (as found in Luke and Matthew) is the more original form.

Contrast or no contrast?

Which structure would have the better chance of being the original? The structure of Mark, in which the strong contrast between the small beginning and the great end is expressed? Or the structure of Q, which does not have the contrast? Here we think that the Marcan structure is the more original. Let us consider more closely how strongly Mark expresses this contrast. It is not only expressed in the point of departure (the smallest of the seeds on earth) and the final result (the greatest of all shrubs and large branches), but also in the use of the different tenses: when it *is sown* (one momentary action in the past mentioned twice in the same aorist tense, Mk 4:31, 32),... it *grows up*, and it *becomes* the greatest... and it *puts out* large branches: all these verbs are in the present tense of duration; Mark is describing an ongoing process.

This contrast picture certainly belongs to the more original form of the parable. Luke does not have any trace of this contrast, and therefore in his version it is not clear why the mustard seed is chosen. He could have used any seed; in fact, any other seed would have done better in his version, because the mustard seed does not develop into a tree, as his source said, but only into a bush or shrub, as Mark correctly says.

The smallness of the mustard seed which Mark mentions in this antithesis was proverbial among the Jews of Jesus' time. This can be gathered from sayings like Mt 17:20 (Lk 17:6), 'If you have faith as a grain of mustard seed, you will say to this mountain...'. The rabbis speak of a drop of blood no bigger than the grain of mustard seed. They apparently could not imagine anything smaller. This is obviously a contemporary Palestinian feature. Jesus used it and called attention to the contrast between beginning and end. As already said, in Luke it is not clear why the mustard seed was chosen. It is quite possible that Luke, who was not very familiar with the Palestinian scene, was not aware of this feature. But Mark was acquainted with this Palestinian reality. In fact, attempts to translate the Marcan version of the parable back into Aramaic result in a composition in which a good number of Aramaic word-plays and alliterations are found. We may conclude, therefore, that Mark's contrast structure, like the parable form (Matthew and Luke = Q), belongs to the more original form of the parable of the mustard seed.

The original form of the parable

Further attempts to determine precisely the original form of the parable should concentrate especially on the opening and concluding verses.

The opening verse, which Mark apparently derived from his source ('And he said' in Mk 4:30 is not Marcan), is very elaborate: 'With what can we compare the kingdom of God, or what parable shall we use for it?' This opening clause is thoroughly Jewish. The tautology is one of the introductions occasionally used in rabbinic parables. Besides, the Q form (cf. Lk 13:18) also had it. Mt 13:31 is characteristically Matthean. So it can be said with a fair amount of certainty that the long, tautological introduction belonged to the original form of the parable. It has been suggested that the double question deliberately recalls Isa 40:18, 'To whom then will you liken God, or what likeness compare with him?' Probably Matthew's 'field' follows Q, while Luke's 'garden' seems to reflect the Hellenistic world which considered the mustard a garden plant. Jews grew it exclusively in larger fields.

Turning now to the concluding verse, apparently the most important verse of the parable, another important difference between Mark and Luke will be noticed:

Mk 4:32	Lk 13:19
so that the birds of the air can make nests in its shade.	and the birds of the air made nests in its branches.

The image used here was quite popular in the Bible and in Jewish literature in general. It referred to the protection offered by a king to his subjects. But, as will appear from the text cited below, the image of living under the shade of a tree was more current than the idea of building nests in its branches. In Palestine, the mustard plant can grow to a height of eight to twelve feet. Birds do sit in its branches, but it is unlikely that they actually build their nests in them. Probably this particular feature of the parable should be traced to the influence of Old Testament motifs (e.g., Dan 4:10–12) rather than to what was actually observed in contemporary Palestine. All this leads to the following reconstruction of the original parable:

> With what can we compare the kingdom of God,
> or what parable shall we use for it?
> It is like a mustard seed which a man took
> and sowed in his field,
> and which is the smallest of all seeds on earth.
> And it grows and it becomes the greatest of all the shrubs,
> and it puts out large branches,
> and the birds of the air live in its shade.

The meaning of this parable

What was the meaning of this parable in the context of Jesus' pre-paschal ministry? The parable contains the same equation as the parable of the seed growing secretly: $a:b = c:d$. The relationship between a and b is the same as that between c and d. In this equation c and d are known, namely the smallest of all seeds and the greatest of all shrubs. But what do a and b stand for?

The shrub/tree in which the birds take shelter

As in the parable of the seed growing secretly, it is advisable to start with b, which is found in the final verse to which the whole parable leads, and in which the narrator hints at what he really means: the greatest of all shrubs with large branches, *so that the birds of the air can live in its shade*. It is clear that the reality is somewhat forced by the meaning it is made to express. After all, the birds of the air do not live under the shade of a *mustard* shrub (and they certainly do not make nests in it). But we deal here with a classical image often used in the Bible to symbolize the protection extended by a powerful king to his subjects.

In the apology of Jotham, the thorn bush which represents Abimelech says to the trees: 'If in good faith you are anointing me king over you, then come and *take refuge in my shade*; but if not, let fire come out of the bramble and devour the cedars of Lebanon' (Judg 9:15). Referring to the capture of king Zedekiah, it is said:

'The breath of our nostrils, the Lord's anointed, was taken in their pits, he of whom we said, *"Under his shadow we shall live among the nations"'* (Lam 4:20). The exiled Jews say: 'And the Lord will give us strength, and he will give light to our eyes, and we shall live under the protection (Greek: in the shadow) of Nebuchadnezzar king of Babylon...' (Baruch 1:12). And the Psalmist describes God's loving care for nature as follows: 'By them the *birds of the air* have their habitation; they sing *among the branches*' (Ps 104[103]:12).

The following texts are even closer to the wording of the parable. Ezekiel announces the restoration and future glory of Israel as follows: 'Thus says the Lord God: "I myself will take a sprig from the lofty top of the cedar, and will set it out... on the mountain height of Israel will I plant it, that it may bring forth boughs and bear fruit, and become a noble cedar; and under it will dwell all kinds of beasts; *in the shade of its branches birds of every sort will nest*"' (Ez 17:22–23). The Aramaic Targum transforms this text into a messianic prophecy: 'Thus speaks the Lord God, "I will take from the royal house of David somebody who is comparable to a high cedar, and I will raise him, a child among the sons of his sons, and I shall plant him on the holy mountain of Israel. He will muster an army and come to your rescue. He will become a powerful king, and all the just will rely on him, and *the humble will live beneath his shadow*"'. In an allegorical text prophesying Egypt's ruin by means of the symbol of the felling of a mighty cedar, the same prophet says: 'So it towered high above all the trees of the forest; its boughs grew large and its branches long, from abundant water in its shoots. *All the birds of the air made their nests in its boughs; under its branches* all the beasts of the field brought forth their young; and *under its shadow* dwelt all great nations' (Ez 31:5–6).

Finally, there is the text of Dan 4:12 (Aramaic 4:9), which seems to have exercised some influence on the wording of the last verse of the parable in its Lucan and Matthean versions. The text speaks of Nebuchadnezzar's vision: 'The beasts of the field found *shade* under it (the tree), and *the birds of the air dwelt in its branches*, and all flesh was fed from it'. And the explanation of the vision in Dan 4:21 (Aramaic 4:18) says: '(The tree you saw) whose leaves were fair and its fruit abundant, and in which was food for all; under which beasts of the field found *shade*, and *in whose branches the birds of the air dwelt* — it is you, O king'. In Dan 4:17 Israel's smallness among the nations is cited as evidence that God will set the lowliest over the earth. The image of the great tree, then, belongs to reflection about Israel's insignificance, its great future, and God's rule over all humanity.

It has convincingly been argued that since both in apocalyptic and in rabbinical literature 'the birds of heaven' stand for the Gentile nations, the expression 'the birds of the air' (Mt 13:32) may be a reference to the Gentiles. In this connection it has been pointed out that *kataskēnoō* (Mk 4:32; Mt 13:32; Lk 13:19), meaning 'nesting' and not 'perching', is 'an eschatological technical term for the incorporation of the Gentiles into the people of God'.[21]

Thus the meaning of the imagery is clear. It was firmly fixed in the minds of those who listened to Jesus. It is important to note that its meaning became apparently more and more messianic. It referred to the kingdom of God to come, and to the agent of that kingdom, the messianic king. The last verse of the parable, therefore, confirms the introductory verse which announces a parable of the kingdom of God. It says something about the kingdom of God in its final stage. Thus it has been established what *b*, the second term of the equation, means. What then does *a*, the mustard seed which is the smallest of all seeds, refer to?

The smallest of all seeds

It has already been said that the original content of the parable (as found in Mark) emphasizes the contrast between the beginning and the end, which was already identified as the kingdom of God in its final fulfilment. It is in a sense surprising that the parable did not make use of the image of the cedar (cf. Ez 17:22–23). Its seed was apparently not small enough to convey effectively what Jesus intended to say. The small beginnings of the kingdom, its entirely unexpected modesty, the absence of all the power and glory which Jesus' contemporaries had expected, are very strongly emphasized.

This was obviously also a great problem for Jesus' disciples. It contradicted all their expectations concerning the coming of the Messiah and the eschatological times. Now, when Jesus wants to get across an insight or an idea to his listeners, especially in the parables, he frequently joins them in their impressions and feelings. After showing them that he understands their difficulties, he tries to lead them to a correct appreciation of things. If this is the case in this parable, the smallness of the mustard seed corresponds, in the outlook of Jesus' listeners, to a certain disappointment in the face of a reality which seems to them insignificant, and which is insignificant indeed if it is compared with the impressive images suggested by the thought of the realization of the kingdom of God.

Using the image of the mustard seed, Jesus made it clear that he understood their problem and gauged their sentiments. But then he went on explaining to them the meaning of the situation. Certainly, the beginning looked very small and insignificant, but it was nevertheless the real beginning of the fulfilment of God's great promises. Jesus' ministry was not spectacular by human standards, but that did not mean that it was not the beginning of the eschatological process in which God will finally establish his glorious kingdom. Even nature witnesses to the mysterious power by which small is transformed into great; therefore, the disciples should not be discouraged by the smallness of these beginnings. Moreover, there is a real organic connection between this seemingly insignificant beginning and the glorious completion, the same organic connection as there is between the small mustard seed and the great shrub. The humble beginning of Jesus' ministry should be seen in this light. To reject this beginning amounts to rejecting God's eschatological sovereignty.

> (The parable of the mustard seed) should not be employed to substantiate a wholly present or a wholly future concept of the reign of God but just that polarity between the beginning and the end, between sowing and harvest, between the unobtrusive present and the full future revelation of the glory of God's rule and kingship. There is also a continuous, unbroken relation between 'now' and 'then,' not because of any immanent process due to earthly or human forces but through the intervention of God who manifests in the works of Jesus the kingly role which one day will be shown forth in all its splendor. What happens in the present, despite every failure and opposition, is a promise of the future triumph.[22]

Thus the parable of the mustard seed discloses something not only about the future, but also and even first of all about the present. Its purpose is not to tell the disciples that the kingdom will come very soon, or that Jesus' ministry will soon show its marvellous fruits. It intends to force upon them the *decisive meaning of the present*, i.e., the decisive importance of Jesus' ministry in saving history. Jesus really inaugurates the eschatological kingdom, despite all contrary appearances. This was a decisive message for Jesus' contemporaries. But for us too it is still decisive. Certainly, the time of Jesus' ministry on earth was a privileged period of saving history, because of the divine mission which he fulfilled. But the risen Lord continues the same mission among us. Even after his resurrection the fulfilment of the glorious rule of God has not yet (fully) come. Even now, so long as we can see only in faith, we are still exposed to the same kind of disappointment which Jesus' disciples experienced during his ministry.

It has been suggested that when the parable of the mustard seed is set alongside Ezekiel's vision of the cedar (Ez 17:22–24), the former appears as a burlesque of the latter, or even as a satire in which Jesus describes the disenchanting and disarming way in which the kingdom is breaking in.

> It is not a towering empire, but an unpretentious venture of faith... The parable is full of promise and assurance, but these become available only in the context of what the Kingdom really is, namely, the faith to dwell in the Kingdom... The church, like Israel, is wont to stumble over its hope. It seizes, solidifies, and then takes possession of its hope in the name of divinely certified reality. In so doing, it merely converts the mustard plant back into a towering cedar. As regards that hope and its encapsulation in the tradition, the parable suggests the following items for reflection:
> 1) Whatever the Christian hope is, the form of its realization will come as a surprise to all who think they know what it ought to be.
> 2) The coming of the Kingdom will disappoint the righteous, but be a source of joy to the religiously disinherited...[23]

The parable on the level of the evangelists

Mark

It has already been stated that, in so far as the Marcan text brings to the fore the contrast between beginning and fulfilment, it is very close to the original version. This message was apparently still very relevant in the early Church. The beginning of the Church was very modest and small. Does this mean that the Marcan version still has exactly the same meaning as the original parable? This is very improbable in view of Christ's resurrection and the ensuing emergence of a truly Christian faith, in which the disciples had seen the most striking manifestation of the 'point' of the original parable in Jesus' death and resurrection.

To discover a possible shift in the meaning of the parable on the Marcan level, attention should be paid to the Marcan context of the parable discourse (Mk 4:1–34). Right after the parable of the mustard seed, and as a conclusion to this parable discourse, Mark says that 'with many such parables he spoke the word to them, as they were able to hear it; he did not speak to them without a parable, *but privately to his own disciples he explained everything*' (Mk 4:33–34). But, as it is, Mark does not record any private explanation of the parable of the mustard seed. The only acceptable explanation for this is that he thought he could dispense with it, because he believed that in the context of the parable discourse its meaning should be clear to his readers. This apparently means that to Mark's mind, the elaborate interpretation of the parable of the sower (Mk 4:14–20), to which the parables of the seed growing secretly and the mustard seed are attached, should give his readers a clue to the meaning of all three parables.

According to the interpretation of the parable of the sower (Mk 4:14–20), the seed is the *word*, i.e., the gospel about the risen Lord (Mk 4:14). The mustard seed of the present parable has apparently the same allegorical meaning for Mark. It is the beginning of the gospel about the risen Christ, the beginning of the Christian preaching which is small and seemingly insignificant. And in the overall context of Mark's gospel, this smallness apparently assumes a special flavour.

The proclamation of the gospel is taking place in a situation of oppression. Even the Christ who has manifested his glory to his disciples in the resurrection does not simply crush all opposition, but seems to follow the pattern of his pre-paschal ministry. Referring to this aspect of the spread of the gospel, Mk 4:16–17 reads: 'And these in like manner are the ones sown upon rocky ground, who, when they hear *the word*, immediately receive it with joy; and they have no root in themselves, but endure for a while; then, when tribulation *or persecution* arises *on account of the word*, immediately they fall away'. Mark inserts similar precisions in Mk 8:35, 'for my sake *and the gospel's*', and Mk 10:29, 'for my sake *and for the gospel*'. He is clearly aware of a danger that threatens the faith of the early Christians. They may be scandalized in a similar way to the disciples during Jesus' ministry. They did not expect the present state of affairs. Had not Jesus triumphed over and defeated the opposition to the kingdom? Where was now the power and the glory of the risen Christ?

All such questions were very understandable in a situation in which the early Christians were kept waiting for the glorious (second) coming, the parousia and had not yet given up the idea that this might come very soon. Mark's answer is: certainly, the beginning is small, but the kingdom is growing right now; it is definitely becoming something great, symbolized by the greatest of all shrubs, its putting out large branches, etc.

Luke

Luke does not maintain the strong contrast between the small beginning and the glorious fulfilment which is in the process of coming. He does not mention either the smallness of the seed or the greatness of the tree. Furthermore, all the tenses of the Lucan parable are in the past historical: a man *took* a mustard seed... he *sowed*... and it *grew* and it *became* a tree. The story develops in a straight line without interruption. It seems to be describing a developing process, and Luke seems to be observing this marvellous growth, because he uses the past tense throughout the story. For him the seed has already become a *tree*. Luke speaks about Christianity which in his time was already in full development in the Greco-Roman world. Here we are no longer at the very modest Palestinian beginnings.

This interpretation of the Lucan version of the parable is confirmed by its context. Indeed, in Luke the parable of the mustard seed is found, not after Lk 8:18 but, together with the parable of the leaven, in the context of the Travel Narrative (Lk 9:51 – 19:44). There it follows after the story of the healing of the woman with a spirit of infirmity (Lk 13:10–17). The parable is linked with this pericope by means of the introduction, 'He said *therefore*...' (Lk 13:18). Now in the healing miracle Jesus had cured a poor woman 'who had had a spirit of infirmity for eighteen years', and who 'was bent over and could not fully straighten herself' (Lk 13:11). He had done so on a sabbath. When the ruler of the synagogue protested, he got the following reply: 'You hypocrites! Does not each of you on the sabbath untie his ox or his ass from the manger, and lead it away to water it?' (Lk 13:15, meaning: this woman seems to be less important to you than an animal!). At the end of the story it is said that Jesus' adversaries were put to shame, but that 'all the people rejoiced *at all the glorious things that were done by him*' (Lk 13:17). And then follows as a conclusion the parable of the mustard seed, or maybe one should rather say in this context, the parable of the *tree*: 'He said *therefore*...' (Lk 13:18).

The parable seems to enlarge the perspective of the miracle story. The victory and the glory Jesus has just won in the synagogue is a guarantee and symbol of the greatness of the kingdom which Luke observes in his time. That greatness found its beginning in the glory of Jesus for the benefit of the oppressed, the downtrodden, and the miserable. It was in this miracle that Jesus broke down the narrowmindedness of the Jewish leaders who would have reserved the kingdom, not only to Israel, but even to a particular class within Israel, a class which Luke often refers to as 'the rulers' (Lk 14:1; 18:18; 23:13, 35; 24:20). In this sense this miracle also foreshadowed the breakthrough of the kingdom into the Gentile world which for the Jewish rulers was a doomed world. Luke observed this victory in the expansion of the Church in the Greco-Roman world: this was the tree in which the birds of the air made their nests. In the Lucan version, therefore, attention is no longer focused on the final eschatological fulfilment of the kingdom of God, as was the case in Mark, for whom the different aspects of the history of the Church and the final fulfilment were not yet so clearly distinguished, but on the development of the Church here and now. This is, in fact, Luke's perspective throughout the Gospel and the Acts of the Apostles.

Matthew

Matthew has the narrative form of the parable in common with Luke, but with Mark he shares the contrast between the small beginning and the great fulfilment. Only the distribution of the tenses is different from that in Mark. Mark has, as seen above, an aorist at the beginning, expressing a fact which happened ('when it *is sown*'); all the other verbs are in the present tense: 'it grows up... it becomes... it puts out'. All this is happening now, though in a hidden way.

In Matthew things are different: 'a man *took* it... he *sowed* it... it *has grown*... it *is* the greatest of the shrubs... it *is becoming* a tree'. Just as Luke, he observes the Church in full expansion. It is no longer a hidden process, but something which is already seen. There is, however, one difference from Luke. Luke, as it were, does not explicitly look beyond the situation described ('it *became* a tree'), but Matthew still looks beyond the situation of the mustard seed having become a great shrub, because he adds that 'it becomes a tree', which refers to a process that is still in full development. So Matthew looks back at the past in which there was no more than a small mustard seed, he sees the present as the great shrub, and looks forward to the future when it will be a tree. He refers to three stages in the development of the kingdom.

> (It had become) impossible, from Matthew's standpoint, to say that the presence of the Kingdom in the world was as insignificant as a mustard seed. At the same time, the mustard seed had not yet become a 'tree,'... Although Matthew's Church was certainly still awaiting the final manifestation of the Kingdom of God ('it becomes a tree'), it was none the less even now a conglomerate of both Jews and Gentiles. Hence, while the 'process of growth' was by no means complete, Matthew already sees Old Testament prophecy (v. 32d) being fulfilled.[24]

But we have not yet considered the Matthean context to determine more precisely what the parable means for Matthew. In Mark, the parable is to be interpreted in the light of the interpretation of the parable of the sower (Mk 4:14–20). In Matthew the parable of the mustard seed, together with the parable of the leaven, is found between the parable of the weeds among the wheat (Mt 13:24–30) and its interpretation (Mt 13:36–43). This framework determines the precise meaning of the Matthean parable of the mustard seed. In fact, Matthew clearly connects it with the preceding parable of the weeds among the wheat. Both parables are introduced by an identical formula of Matthew's own: 'Another parable he *put before* them, saying' (Mt 13:24, 31). Both parables are put before the audience to reflect upon them, and to ferret out their deeper meaning, which, as far as the parable of the weeds among the wheat is concerned, is given in the allegorical interpretation of Mt 13:36–43.

This obviously means that in the Matthean context the key to the specifically Matthean meaning of the parable of the mustard seed is also to be found in the interpretation of the parable of the weeds. The man who sowed the mustard seed is, therefore, the Son of man (Mt 13:37). The field (Matthew has *agros*, 'field', not *kēpos*, 'garden', as Luke) is the world (Mt 13:38). The shrub which has grown out of the seed is the kingdom of the Son of man (Mt 13:41). The tree towards which it is growing is most probably the kingdom of the Father (Mt 13:43). The birds which make nests in its branches (cf. Dan 4:9[12], 18[21]) are the sons of the kingdom (Mt 13:38).

The difference from the parable of the weeds, the parable of the net (Mt 13:47–50), and the parable of the wedding feast (Mt 22:1–14) is that in Mt 13:31–32 it is not said that there are also bad seeds and that these are going to be excluded from the final realization of the kingdom. Matthew looks forward to the final fulfilment, but this time he does not stress that this fulfilment will be accompanied by judgment and condemnation.

Reflection

Jesus' disciples and other contemporaries had a hard time believing that while showing only a 'mustard-seed'-sized activity he could nevertheless rightfully claim to be the inaugurator of the 'great shrub' or 'tree' of the kingdom of God. So did the disciples of Mark's (and Matthew's) time. Similarly, many twentieth-century people have a hard time recognizing the 'mustard seed' in our present situation. At one end of the spectrum one finds the 'activists' who are tempted to use 'bulldozer' methods or to undermine the traditional structures to bring about 'the kingdom'. At the other end, the institutional Church is tempted to believe that by organizing solemn, if not pompous Holy and Marian years one may preserve a safe *status quo* and thus strengthen the foundations of 'the kingdom'.

In the light of the parable of the mustard seed, both approaches appear to be *man*-made, or at times *woman*-made 'cedars' which threaten to take away the growth-giving light from *God*'s mustard seed. They appear to be kingdoms of *man/woman* instead of the kingdom of *God*. This goes also for any kind of self-serving promotion in or outside the Church's structures. The kingdom of *God* is not built on ambitions and/or diplomacy, but on the kind of service which Jesus exemplified.

Much is to be said for the interpretation which holds that against the background of the symbol of the mighty cedar found in Ezekiel (and Daniel), 'Jesus has created a light-hearted burlesque of Ezekiel's figure' which 'at second glance, however... takes on the character of serious satire...'. The kingdom 'will erupt out of the power of weakness and refuse to perpetuate itself by the weakness of power... It is not a towering empire, but an unpretentious venture of faith'.[25]

Today, the 'mustard seed' of the kingdom of God is found not so much in pompous functions and institutions as in *true* basic Christian communities. They are communities which spring from a real spirituality of the base rather than from interminable gripe sessions. These basic Christian communities are the real seeds of the final kingdom and as such may be a 'revolutionary' feature in today's established community which may cause that establishment to feel threatened. But then it is good to remember that the establishment of Jesus' time also felt threatened by Jesus and his followers. By remaining silent before the high priest, Pilate and Herod, Jesus communicated that he was not impressed by their pomp. And the present author cannot help but think that Jesus would like his disciples to do likewise. By its ironic power Jesus' parable of the mustard seed made fun of the 'cedars' of his time, as it does today. The kingdom of God belongs to the little ones.

4   The leaven
(Mt 13:33; Lk 13:20–21)

Once the parable of the mustard seed has been interpreted, it is logical to continue with an explanation of the parable of the leaven which immediately follows it both in Matthew and in Luke. It derives from Q and may have been unknown to Mark. It has earlier been said that these two parables already formed a pair in the tradition: one about what a man did, and another about what a woman did. Twin parables are indeed a striking feature of the tradition of the teaching of Jesus, but the pairs are not always the same in different sources (the seed growing secretly and the mustard seed in Mark, the mustard seed and the leaven in Q), so that it is hard to establish whether these particular parables were already pronounced as a pair by Jesus himself. In the *Gospel of Thomas* the parables of the mustard seed and the leaven are separated. As shown in the discussion of the mustard seed, the association of two parables on the same topic most probably belonged to the teaching technique of Jesus. The original twin character of the parables of the mustard seed and the leaven may be supported by the fact that Luke, while removing the parables from the Parable Discourse (Mk 4; Mt 13; Lk 8) and transferring them to the Travel Narrative (Lk 9:51 – 19:44), still presents them as a pair. But strictly speaking, this is only an argument for the connection of the parables in Q.

Matthew 13:33	Luke 13:20–21
He told them another parable.	(20) And again he said, 'To what shall I compare
'The kingdom of heaven is like leaven which a woman took and hid in three measures of meal, till it was all leavened.'	the kingdom of God? (21) It is like leaven which a woman took and hid in three measures of meal, till it was all leavened.'

The parable is also found in a somewhat different form in the *Gospel of Thomas* 96:

The kingdom of the father is like a woman,
who has taken a little leaven
and has hidden it in dough
and has made large loaves of it.

The parable on the level of the tradition (and of Jesus?)

There is practically no difference in the wording of the parable *itself* in Matthew and Luke. The introductions are peculiar to both of them. To determine the meaning of the parable on the level of the tradition (and of Jesus), it should be kept in mind that it probably formed a pair with the parable of the mustard seed from the very beginning of the tradition. Possibly Jesus himself already pronounced the two parables one after the other to get the same 'point' across to his audience in the most effective way. It has been objected that leaven or yeast is used in the Bible most of the time as a symbol of evil and that, therefore, it can hardly be interpreted as referring to the spread of the kingdom of God. But there are other cases in the Bible where the same metaphor is used with opposite meanings; e.g., while Rev 5:5 compares Christ to a lion, I Pet 5:8 uses the same metaphor for the devil. In the present parable the emphasis seems to be on the great effect a little leaven can have. In this respect it can serve as an image parallel to the mustard seed.

On the level of Jesus' ministry, the parable of the mustard seed expressed the contrast between the small beginnings of that ministry and the glorious fulfilment of what he started in this way, namely the fulfilment of the kingdom of God. That Luke's version of the parable of the mustard seed does not make this point is to be ascribed to a later development which had in mind the contemporary expansion of the Church. In the *Gospel of Thomas* the accent falls on the contrast between the 'little leaven' and the 'large loaves', presumably made from a large mass of meal or dough.

In their present form the Matthean and Lucan versions of the parable of the leaven do not express the contrast between the small beginning and the great fulfilment. That means that this is not the original form of the parable. It underwent the same change and adaptation as the Lucan version of the parable of the mustard seed. Originally it expressed the contrast between the small amount of leaven and the huge quantity of dough it leavens. In fact, the end-term of the original contrast is still expressed: three measures of meal is an enormous quantity, about ten gallons. In reality, no woman would prepare such an amount of dough at once. So this feature clearly hints at something else. As in the parable of the mustard seed, the great amount of meal was contrasted with the small amount of leaven in the original parable of the leaven.

It was said earlier that the smallness of the mustard seed was proverbial. It can easily be discovered that the smallness of the amount of leaven needed to leaven a great quantity of dough was also proverbial. This can be seen in I Cor 5:6, 'Do you not know that a little leaven leavens the whole lump', and Gal 5:9, 'a little leaven leavens the whole lump'. The term *holon* ('all', 'whole') found in both Pauline texts is also found as qualification of the end-term in Mt 13:33 and Lk 13:21, 'till it was all leavened'. One can practically be sure, therefore, that originally this parable, which was connected with the parable of the mustard seed, also had the adjective 'small' qualifying 'leaven' (cf. *Gospel of Thomas*). It expressed the contrast between the small, insignificant beginning of Jesus' ministry which scandalized the disciples, and the great final result, the fulfilment of the kingdom of God. It is in this sense that the original parable should be explained.

The second part of the contrast, which is the most important in this kind of parable, and which is described as 'three measures of meal', was not used for the first time by Jesus. It was already a classical image in the Bible. In Gen 18:6, Abraham as the host of three heavenly visitors told his wife to knead three measures of flour. In Judg 6:19 Gideon offered the angel of Yahweh unleavened cakes from an epha of flour (=three measures). And according to I Sam 1:24, Anna went to the temple with an epha (=three measures) of flour to offer her son Samuel. Thus, 'three measures of meal' is associated with the epiphany of or a thanks-offering to the Lord. The immense quantity of three measures, which equal approximately fifty pounds of meal, found in both Matthew and Luke, but absent from the *Gospel of Thomas*, means that we are dealing here with heavenly, eschatological realities. It may be of interest to recall that in Rom 11:16 the people of God is referred to as a mass of dough. The parable insists that 'it was all leavened'. Nothing remains unaffected by the leaven; it causes an upheaval from which nothing is secure. It has also been pointed out that in the Jewish world there was an inseparable relationship between unleavened and holy, and hence between leavened and profane (cf., e.g., Ex 12:17–20). Thus, to speak of the coming kingdom as leavened dough is a reversal.

The small amount of leaven, contrasted with the three measures of meal, symbolizes Jesus' ministry which seemed to be an insignificant reality as compared to the enormous eschatological upheaval which the disciples expected when the kingdom of God would come. In this parable Jesus tells his disciples: in spite of the contrary appearances, my mission is the real beginning of the divine intervention which is going to transform the world. To establish his reign God acts like a housewife who hides a little bit of leaven in a great amount of meal. The kingdom of God was expected to bring about a complete reversal. But Jesus' ministry did not seem to inaugurate any such ́revolutionary change. The parable does not contradict this. It simply states that nothing can be seen when a woman puts a little leaven in a big mass of meal, and yet this action is decisive and initiates the process which will leaven the whole dough. Similarly Jesus' proclamation and the signs which accompany it (cf. Mt 11:2–6; Lk 7:18–23) constitute God's veiled but decisive action which inaugurates a succession of eschatological events which will climax in the coming of his kingdom and the radical change of all things which will accompany it. The kingdom is like what happens when leaven is put into meal and mysteriously transforms the whole mass from within.

It is to be noted that, strangely enough, it is said that the woman *hid* the leaven in the meal. The normal expression would be: *put* the leaven in the meal. Jesus apparently used the term 'hid' to suggest that the present development of the kingdom is hidden by his ministry, although in a mysterious way it also reveals the kingdom. Compared with Luke, Matthew has reinforced the term (*enekrupsen*), indicating that the leaven penetrates the whole mass of dough. The same verb (*kruptō, enkruptō*) is also found in Mt 11:25 (parallel Lk 10:21), 'I thank you, Father... that you have hidden these things from the wise and the understanding', stating among other things that the expected realization of the kingdom of God is in a hidden or veiled way present in Jesus' words and deeds (compare Mk 4:10–11). It is out of this hidden reality that the final glorious kingdom of God will grow. Jesus' audience should know, therefore, that what happens before their eyes is the decisive beginning of the kingdom. Their attitude towards *this* beginning, which is still a veiled reality, will be decisive for their fate when the completion of the kingdom will have come.

Because of the proximity of the terms 'leaven', 'hide', and 'three measures of meal' within this short parable, and the respective connotations of these three phrases (see above), it has been suggested that the parable conveys that the kingdom of God, which does not arrive with observable signs ('hidden'), comes as an inversion of what is considered sacred and profane ('unleavened – leavened'), and has the power and the festive character of an epiphany ('three measures of meal').

The parable on the level of the evangelists

The smallness of the beginning apparently no longer interests the Christian preachers. They concentrate on the encouraging actual situation, the expansion of the Church in the Greco-Roman world.

An irresistible power is at work and the results can already be seen. The parable is also a lesson in confidence for those who can already see what has grown out of Jesus' ministry, after and because of his resurrection.

It is clear that this development could easily lead to complacency, the worst possible result of such a change of perspective, which in itself is acceptable as long as the concentration on God and his activity remains primary. The eschatological perspective should continue to give Christianity that dynamism which flows from awareness that in a sense God's kingdom at present continues to be hidden, not recognized by the world, but nevertheless constantly transforming that world towards its final destiny.

Luke

In Luke the parables of the mustard seed and the leaven (Lk 13:18–21) form the conclusion of the first section of the Travel Narrative (Lk 9:51 – 19:44). In this context, in which Luke has until now mainly dealt with 'following' and the signs of the times (especially Lk 12:54–59; 13:1–9), the twin parables of the mustard seed and the leaven conclude a section, after which our attention is again called to the goal of the journey (Lk 13:22), while the question of entry into the kingdom is also raised (Lk 13:23–30). Similarly, the second and third sections of the Travel Narrative end with an eschatological parable (Lk 17:7–10; 19:11–27). It is clear, then, that both parables are related by Luke to the mission. They promise the worldwide spread of the proclamation of the kingdom. Following his source, Luke deals not so much with the 'growth' as such, as with God's miraculous activity from the tiny beginning (of the kingdom) until the marvellous fulfilment. However, the aspect of growth is also part of the picture, and should be understood in reference to the contemporary Church situation.

Matthew

In the context of the Parable Discourse (Mt 13:1–52), Matthew balances the parables of the mustard seed and the leaven with the two brief parables of the hidden treasure and the precious pearl (Mt 13:44–46). In the parable of the leaven he especially focuses our attention on the 'mystery' (cf. Mt 13:11) of the universal transformation which the kingdom will bring about. He may have understood the parables of the mustard seed and the leaven in contrast with his parable of the weeds among the wheat (Mt 13:24–30). The world (cf. Mt 13:24, 38) is in motion; the kingdom of

God, though still hidden, will make its way successfully until the final fulfilment. The parable of the leaven may also intend to strengthen the Matthean Christians in their conviction that they constitute the eschatological community.

Reflection

In its original form the parable drew attention to the contrast between the small amount of leaven and the exceptionally big amount of dough it leavens. While this contrast feature is basically the same as in the parable of the mustard seed, the present parable insists on the hidden character of the leaven's activity. One would never suspect the presence of the leaven in the dough if it were not for the latter's rising. Strictly speaking, the emphasis does not really fall on (the hiddenness of) the leaven as such, but on the fact that a woman hid the leaven in the meal, that is, her activity is stressed. Hers is a deliberate act. Would this suggest that the kingdom grows through deliberately hidden activity? In our reflection on the parable of the mustard seed we said that the kingdom grows, not through the 'great' manifestations of the established, institutional Church, but through the small-scale activities of basic Christian communities. We may have to add now that the kingdom grows especially through activities that are deliberately 'hidden', as contrasted with well-publicized large-scale ventures. The parable of the leaven may indeed be speaking of the 'politics' of the kingdom. To compare the kingdom of God to the action of leaven in dough is to say that the kingdom will not stop its working in the world 'until it is leavened' (Hosea 7:4), just as the leaven did not cease its activity 'till it was all leavened' (Mt 13:33).

> If one takes seriously leaven's significance as represented in Paul's proverb and the quote from Hosea, then Kingdom will work its way through everything as a moral perversion, undermining normal religious perceptions... By using leaven, the parable announces that the sacred's manifestation is an inversion of expectation. Likewise, since it is hidden, it can be missed and those who would seek Kingdom risk loss of their normal perception of the sacred because it is under another guise...The parable's selection of images demands faith, for it expresses a new vision of Kingdom. To see leaven as compatible with three measures demands faith on the hearer's part. This parable seeks to orient the hearer toward the identification of God within everyday experience. God is at work like leaven, that is, he is undermining the everyday, inverting it. The

religious tradition as predictive of God's locus can no longer serve to demarcate where he is at work. His work is not obvious, but is like moral perversion among the good. It corrupts whatever it touches. So it is with Kingdom. The hearer's faith is severely challenged because the parable articulates such a radical vision of God.[26]

In Luke's gospel, the parables of the mustard seed and the leaven (Lk 13:18–21) which conclude the first section of the Travel Narrative (Lk 9:51 – 13:21) are immediately preceded by a healing of a woman in a synagogue (Lk 13:10–17) who is liberated, 'freed from (her) infirmity' (Lk 13:12). Thus she becomes a beneficiary of the implementation of Jesus' overall liberating approach to all that burdens and oppresses people (Lk 4:18–19). This illustrative act of liberation leads Luke to the broader statement about what the kingdom of God is like. 'He said *therefore*' firmly links Lk 13:10–17 and Lk 13:18–21 together. The leaven of the kingdom is at work wherever true liberation in one of its many forms takes place.

5 The parable of the weeds and its interpretation
(Mt 13:24–30, 36–43)

The texts

Matthew 13:24–30
The kingdom of heaven may be compared to a man who sowed good seed
in his field;
but while men were sleeping,
his enemy came and sowed
weeds among the wheat,
and went away.
So when the plants came up
and bore grain,
then the weeds appeared also.
And the servants of the householder
came and said to him,
'Sir, did you not sow good seed in
your field? How then has it weeds?'
He said to them,
'An enemy has done this.'
The servants said to him,
'Then do you want us to go
and gather them?'

But he said,

'No; lest in gathering the weeds
you root up the wheat
along with them.
Let both grow together until the
harvest; and at harvest time
I will tell the reapers,

Gather the weeds first
and bind them in bundles
to be burned;
but gather the wheat into my barn.'

Gospel of Thomas 57
The kingdom of the Father is
like a man who had (good) seed.

His enemy came by night and sowed
weeds among the seed.

The man did not allow them
to pull up the weeds;
he said to them,
'I am afraid that you will go
intending to pull up the weeds
and pull up the wheat
along with them.'

For on the day of the harvest

the weeds will be plainly visible

and they will be pulled up
and burned.

The shorter version of the parable which is found in the *Gospel of Thomas* looks like a summary of Matthew's text. The dialogue between the householder and the servants is entirely omitted. So, especially, are the important advice, 'let both grow together until the harvest', and the conclusion, 'Gather the wheat into my barn'. Thus the attention is focused almost entirely on the fate of the weeds.

A first reading of the parable

After the parable of the sower (Mt 13:3–8) and its interpretation (Mt 13:18–23), which deal with the *beginning* of the kingdom of heaven, and situated where we would expect Matthew's counterpart of Mk 4:26–29, Mt 13:24–30 offers a parable about its *growth and development*. And, as was somewhat to be expected, here too we get a separate interpretation of the parable (Mt 13:36–43), addressed to the disciples to whom the knowledge of the mysteries of the kingdom is granted (cf. Mt 13:11, 36), and in which Jesus' words are expanded and applied to a new situation.

> **Verse 24:** Another parable he put before them, saying, 'The kingdom of heaven may be compared to a man who sowed good seed in his field;

Verse 24a, 'Another parable he put before them', is Matthew's transitional formula (cf. Mt 13:31, 33). The phrase 'put before them' is striking. The verb *paratithenai* can be used of laying out a banquet, of food being set before somebody (cf. Lk 9:16; 10:8), but also of laws, especially the Mosaic law set before the Israelites, proposed to them to reflect upon (Ex 19:7). Jesus lays the parable before the crowd to reflect upon, to see whether they can ferret out what it says about the kingdom of heaven. Throughout this chapter, Matthew distinguishes between the disciples who are looking for and actually receive an interpretation, and the crowds who do not (want to) understand, and for whom, consequently, the teaching in parables becomes an occasion for further hardening and defection (Mt 13:14–15). Jesus addressed yet 'another parable' to the crowd (cf. Mt 13:2, 36). It is available to whoever is willing to be challenged by it. It is left up to the listeners to decide how they will interpret and internalize the parable.

The formulation of verse 24b is also to quite an extent Matthean ('kingdom of heaven', the dative *anthrōpōi*, and the aorist passive *hōmoiōthē*). It is formally analogous to a number of introductory formulae in special Matthean material. The same special form of dative introduction is found in Mt 18:23, 'The kingdom of heaven may be compared to a king...', and Mt 22:2. 'The kingdom of heaven may be compared to a king...' (entirely different, Lk 14:16). Very similar is Mt 25:1, 'the kingdom of heaven shall be compared to ten maidens...'. Jesus does not say what the kingdom is, but he announces that it can be compared with a human event. The kingdom of *heaven* (or, of *God*) is in some way similar to human events. The aorist passive (*hōmoiōthē*) seems to suggest that from Matthew's vantage point the kingdom of heaven already has a certain history behind it. It seems best then to translate this clause as follows: 'It has been with the kingdom of heaven as with a man...'.

'A man... sowed good seed in his field.' The word *sperma* means 'seed', but it can also denote 'people', as, e.g., in Mt 22:24, 25, where it refers to children. At this stage it is, in a sense, entirely superfluous to say that this man sowed *good* seed. Here Matthew is anticipating verse 25 where we will be told that somebody else sowed *bad* seed. But it receives its full meaning only with the questions of the servants in Mt 13:27–28a, and both elements belong to the same level of the tradition. Matthew uses here *kalos* to describe 'good' things, but the word is synonymous with *agathos* (Mt 7:17–19; 12:33–37) and has the same ethical implications.

It is also remarkable that the seed is said to be sown in *his* field, i.e., the field belonging to the householder (verse 27a). This is stated explicitly because the other one is going to sow in a field which, properly speaking, is not his. In view of the addressees, the 'field' seems to refer to 'Israel', i.e., the people of Israel.

Verse 25: but while men were sleeping, his enemy came and sowed weeds among the wheat, and went away.

The expression 'while men (people) were sleeping' exceeds the setting of the beginning of the parable. We would have expected: 'while the farmer was sleeping'. The narrator depicts a general situation which goes far beyond that of the farmer's field. 'To sleep' (Greek *katheudein*) often has in the New Testament a metaphorical meaning. It refers then to the people's attitude towards the (delayed) parousia (Mt 25:5; Mk 13:36; I Thess 5:6, 7).

Over against the householder, his servants, and the reapers stands 'his enemy', i.e., the personal opponent of the householder. In apocryphal literature, 'the enemy' often refers to the devil (cf. *Test. Dan* 6:3f.; *Apoc Mos* 2.7.25.28, etc.). The only other instance in the New Testament is Lk 10:19, 'Behold, I have given you authority... over all the power of the enemy' (but see also Rev 11:5, 12). In Mt 13:39 the word refers to the devil, the personification of a will opposed to all that Jesus stands for, but who attacks what belongs to Jesus rather than Jesus himself.

The 'weeds' which he sows on top of the wheat (*epespeiren*) are the darnel, a poisonous Palestinian weed botanically related to wheat and hardly distinguishable from it until the plants have grown up. It may be noted here that the enemy and his weeds are taken up in the interpretation (Mt 13:38–39), while 'sleeping' is not mentioned. The final phrase, 'and he went away', creates a certain suspense.

Verse 26: So when the plants came up and bore grain, then the weeds appeared also.

The plants came up and 'made fruit'. Throughout his gospel, Matthew is interested in this theme of fruit-bearing (Mt 3:8, 10; 12:33; 21:34, 41, 43). One should think here especially of Mt 7:20, 'Thus you will know them by their fruits'. Good and bad Christians can be distinguished only on the basis of their fruits. Similarly, the weeds were not discovered before the plants began to bear fruit. There is a clear emphasis on the second part of the verse: 'then the weeds appeared also'. Thus one is confronted by the presence of weeds and wheat in the same field. Verse 26 concludes the first part of the parable. The stage is set for the more important thing, the discussion between the householder and his servants (verses 27–30).

Verse 27: And the servants of the householder came and said to him, 'Sir, did you not sow good seed in your field? How then has it weeds?'

The 'man' of verse 24 is now a 'householder' (Greek *oikodespotēs*), a favourite Matthean term found seven times in the gospel (against once in Mark, and four times in Luke), and applied to God (Mt 20:1, 11; 21:33), as well as to Jesus (Mt 10:25), and even to Christians (Mt 13:52; 24:43). This householder is approached by abruptly introduced 'servants' (Greek *douloi*, 'slaves'). The term *douloi*, which occurs 25 times in Matthew's parables, is almost always used with a religious connotation. A few times it refers to Old Testament prophets (Mt 21:34ff.; 22:3), but usually it indicates apostles, early Christian missionaries, and members of the Church.

The 'servants' are clearly distinguished from the 'reapers' (Mt 13:30) who in Mt 13:39 symbolize angels who will accompany the Son of man on the day of judgment and will act as his agents (Mt 13:39, 41f.; 24:31; 25:31–46). In fact, the servants do not seem to *do* anything (cf. Mt 13:24). It seems that their only role is to ask questions and to receive clarification from the *kurios*.

The servants' two questions reinforce the statement of verse 26b, 'then the weeds appeared also'. The first question clearly ties on to verse 24b with its mention of '*good* seed'. The point of the question refers to the seed, 'Wasn't that seed which you sowed good? How come, then, that the field has weeds?' It should be noted that, strictly speaking, the servants complain about the presence of the weeds, not about their great number. On the other hand, it must be admitted that a total absence of weeds would have been equally surprising!

Verse 28a: He said to them, 'An enemy has done this.'

While the servants' first question refers to verse 24b, the answer ties on to verse 25. The householder does not reply to the first question posed. He does not say, 'Yes, it was good seed'. His answer is directed towards the second question. Given that the seed was good to start with, the fact that there are weeds in the fields is due to an enemy. An outsider, an opponent has been at work here. He sowed in a field which was not his.

Verse 28b: The servants said to him, 'Then do you want us to go and gather them?'

In reply to the householder's revelation that 'an enemy has done this', the servants ask him whether he wants them 'to go and gather' the weeds. They do not ask him whether they should take care of the enemy, but what they should do with the weeds. This is both a question and a suggestion, in other words, the householder is expected to react to a plan of the servants. What is surprising is not so much the question as such, as the use of the term 'gather' (*sullegein*) which is used most of the time for good fruits, not for weeds, although it is true that weeds were often collected, dried, and used for fuel.

It seems that, in contrast to the maturity of the seed in verse 26, verses 28b–30a again deal with the growth of the seed, and with the question (in the present tense) whether the weeds should be gathered *before* the harvest, unless it is accepted that verse 26 means that the grain was 'heading out' and was to be left to ripen.

Verse 29: But he said, 'No; lest in gathering the weeds you root up the wheat along with them.

The answer to the impatient servants who want to put an end to this situation immediately is an unmistakable *no*. The promiscuity of good and bad is, at least for the time being, an inevitable situation. The danger of uprooting the weeds is the danger of losing (some of) the wheat as well. But the time of separation will certainly come at the harvest. The verb 'to root up' (Greek *ekrizoun*) is used in images which speak of a person's destruction by God (cf. Mt 15:13; Jude 12; Wisd 4:4; Sir 3:9).

> **Verse 30:** Let both grow together until the harvest; and at harvest time I will tell the reapers, "Gather the weeds first and bind them in bundles to be burned, but gather the wheat into my barn."'

The parable reaches its climax in the positive part of the householder's answer. Verse 30a, 'let both grow together until the harvest', emphasizes several points. Firstly, it implies a certain passage of time. Secondly, the clause, 'let both grow together', is also a clear assertion that at this stage the wheat and the weeds are not to be irrevocably separated. Thirdly, this separation should wait 'until the harvest'.

Verse 30b then states what will happen to the weeds *and* the wheat at the harvest. They will be irrevocably separated: the weeds will be used as fuel, the wheat will be gathered into the householder's barn.

The reapers are not supposed to root up the weeds just before reaping the wheat, but rather, as they cut the wheat with their sickles, to let the weeds fall, so that they are not gathered into the sheaves. After drying they would then be collected and used for fuel.

The parable, therefore, implies a contrast between the present, in which the weeds and wheat grow side by side, and the time of the harvest, when the two will be separated from each other. It should be noted that although the separation of good from evil is expected at the end, Matthew is not indifferent to the demands of the present. The true and the unbelieving disciples are already differentiated by their doing or not doing the will of the Father (Mt 7:21), by their bearing good or bad fruit (Mt 7:16–20).

Summing up, it appears that three only loosely related combinations of statements can be distinguished. Firstly, from the sowing (verse 24b), through the time of ripening (verse 26), to the harvest (verse 30b). Secondly, the weeds sown by the enemy (verse 25) and the ensuing conversation (verses 27–28a). Thirdly, the question about the uprooting and the negative answer of the householder (verses 28b, 29, 30a).

An attempt to relate the insights gained in the above analysis leads to the following tradition-historical theory:[27]

(1) The oldest form of the parable consists of verse 24b (without the qualification *good* which originated with verses 27, 28a) and

verses 26, 30b. These verses form a consistent narrative which is very similar to the parable of the net (Mt 13:47–50).

the man sows the seed	:	the net is thrown into the sea
wheat and weeds grow together	:	it gathered fish of every kind
the harvest	:	the net is drawn ashore
the weeds are collected, burned	:	bad fish are thrown away
the wheat gathered into a barn	:	good fish put into vessels

This form of the parable can be traced back to Jesus.

(2) On the first level of the early Christian tradition verses 25, 27, 28a, which trace the origin of the weeds to the enemy, entered the parable. Since the 'catalogue' of Mt 13:37–39 (see below) is related to this stage, the two may have originated simultaneously. An earlier form of Mt 13:36 may have served as transition.

(3) On the second level of the early Christian tradition, verses 28b, 29, 30a, which deal with the premature uprooting of the weeds, were inserted.

(4) Matthew himself is responsible for the interpretation found in Mt 13:40–43, the inversion of good and bad in verse 30b (in the interpretation of the net, Mt 13:49–50, as well as in Mt 13:41–43, the bad are mentioned first), and the future recasting of verse 30b ('I will ask'; compare the tenses in Mt 13:40–43). Moreover, by means of the introductory verse 24a he has substituted the parable of the weeds for the parable of the seed growing secretly, has then again followed the Marcan outline (Mt 13:31–35, with insertion of verse 33), and has made the transition to the interpretation by means of Mt 13:36.

(5) The *Gospel of Thomas* (57) does not contain an interpretation (cf. Mt 13:36–43), but it also produces differences which can be explained, on the one hand, as attempts to smoothen and, on the other hand, as attempts to abbreviate the text of Matthew. It is worth noticing that what is related in Mt 13:26, the conversation about the enemy, and the fate of the wheat are absent from the *Gospel of Thomas*.

Explanation of the parable

On the level of Jesus

(24b) The kingdom of heaven may be compared to a man who sowed seed in his field. (26) But when the plants came up and bore grain, the weeds appeared also. (30b) At harvest time the reapers came and gathered the wheat in barns; they gathered the weeds and bound them in bundles to be burned.

In this parable, three 'times' are related to each other: firstly, the time of sowing which forms the foundation for the other two; secondly, the time of fruit-bearing at which the weeds appear; and thirdly, the time of the harvest at which both wheat and weeds reach their destination. The sowing introduces the possibility of wheat and weeds growing up together. But at the same time the certainty arises that they will be separated from each other, for the sowing is definitely followed by a harvest. The kingdom is being proclaimed; it is already bearing fruit. Under the fruit-bearing stalks weeds appear. Both remain together until the harvest, the arrival of the kingdom of God which will bring a time of separation.

The confidence in the certainty of the coming separation keeps one from worrying about the fate of the seed. It sets one free for the ingathering of people into the kingdom of God without any constraint to bring about a 'pure' community of righteous people. The parable speaks of an unconditional invitation, not of the formation of a holy remnant. At the same time it explains Jesus' attitude. It is an invitation insofar as it reminds one that now is the time of sowing, an invitation without worrying whether one will be able to do justice to the kingdom of God. The parable also shows that people are taken seriously since it refers explicitly to the separation of wheat and weeds. God sows the seed, gives it growth, and finally separates what is valuable from what is worthless. We should make room for the word of the kingdom without worrying.

Can one detect a situation in Jesus' life in which it was meaningful to pronounce such a parable? J. Jeremias thinks that Jesus reacted against the puritan movements among such Jewish groups as the Pharisees and the Qumran community. He preached a more humane, tolerant idea of the kingdom of God in which good and bad, at least for the time being, would live together. They should not try to eliminate from the outset the so-called people-of-the-land who did not know the law. This seems to be an acceptable explanation of this level. Nevertheless, it faces a strong objection. This interpretation supposes that in this parable Jesus accepted the categories of the Pharisees, and called the Pharisees the good seed and the simple people the bad seed! This would go against the clear thrust of the whole gospel message, according to which the simple, poor and ignorant people were the good seed, while the Pharisees and their kind were the bad seed. If there is any expression in the gospel tradition in which we hear Jesus' own voice, then it is certainly 'these little ones', and 'these the least of my brothers'.

One should look, therefore, among Jesus' own followers to find a puritanical group which could provoke such reaction on Jesus' part. Now most, if not all, of Jesus' disciples were Galileans. They were a very particular kind of people. They were not very scrupulous about the observance of the law, but they had their own ideas, even strong ideas, about the purity of the kingdom of God. No doubt Judas was not the first follower to leave Jesus. One can easily understand that his Galilean disciples reacted quite ferociously in such cases. They may have lacked many qualities, but they could be loyal to a person and to a cause, especially as long as there was a chance that things might develop in line with their own expectations. It was to them that Jesus spoke about God's patience and about the fundamental paradox of the kingdom: at the present stage it has a humble status and is imperfect. They should not revolt against this situation. They should not anticipate its final, awe-inspiring, and for some even frightening glory. In this perspective the parable was a reply to a fundamental mistake of the disciples, of which they would not be rid before Pentecost. It was the Christians who had to apply, and actually did apply, this teaching to their own situation.

On the level of the Christian communities

On the first community level

> (24b) The kingdom of heaven may be compared to a man who sowed good seed in his field; (25) but while men were sleeping, his enemy came and sowed weeds among the wheat, and went away. (26) But when the plants came up and bore grain, the weeds appeared also. (27) And the servants of the householder came and said to him, 'Sir, did you not sow good seed in your field? How then has it weeds?' (29a) He said to them, 'an enemy has done this'. (30b) At harvest time the reapers came and gathered the wheat in barns; they gathered the weeds and bound them in bundles to be burned.

In view of their own situation the early Christians asked themselves the question whence came the 'sons of the evil one', how to explain that in the world which as a whole was within the reach of the rule of the Son of man, there were also people who did not accept that rule. The community answered this question by establishing that the weeds of the parable were sown by an opponent of the householder (verse 25), and by letting the latter state explicitly that the weeds had their origin in the action of an enemy (verses 27, 28a; in the interpretation, this enemy is identified as the devil). While people sleep,[28] the enemy has a free hand.

As will be shown in the explanation of the interpretation of the parable (Mt 13:36–43), which was added by the same community, this community had an apocalyptic understanding of itself and the world: the Son of man came and formed in the world the 'sons of the kingdom'. But the devil was also active and provided for the 'sons of the evil one'. At the end of time, however, the angels would come and gather the sons of the kingdom into the kingdom (cf. Mk 13:27), while the 'sons of the evil one' would be turned over to the annihilating judgment. This is a clear example of how a parable of Jesus served the community as a means of expressing their understanding of themselves and their situation in the world. Moreover, the parable received a Christological interpretation (the sower is already the Son of man). The question concerning the *when* of the harvest and the proper behaviour until then is not posed.

On the second community level

On this level the parable reached more or less the form it has now in Matthew. The community faced the question whether it should take measures against the weeds in their midst. As time went on and the separation between good and bad was more and more delayed, the question arose whether the servants should take over the task of the reapers (verse 28a). The Lord's answer is clear: such purification of the community is *impossible*, since the sons of the kingdom may be destroyed together with the sons of the evil one, and *untimely*, since the end has not yet come (verses 29, 30a). The right distinction between God and man, reflected in the distinction between servant and reaper, and the distinction between different periods of time allows the community to exist freed from any coercion to separate the good from the bad (verse 30a).

On the level of Matthew

This parable is found in the third of the five typically Matthean discourses, the so-called Parable Discourse (Mt 13:1–52). As is the case for the other Matthean discourses, the composition is topical, not chronological. These seven parables were apparently pronounced on very different occasions, and at very different moments of Jesus' life. It was Matthew who put them together in one chapter, interpreting them as *revelations of the mysteries of the kingdom of heaven*, the knowledge of which was given to the Christian community, but not to outsiders (cf. Mt 13:11ff.). The formation of this discourse had already begun in Mk 4:1–34, and Matthew simply completed the process. Up to Mk 4:32, Matthew is closely parallel with Mark. But he does not have a direct parallel to the Marcan parable of the seed growing secretly (Mk 4:26–29). Matthew has apparently replaced this parable with the parable of the weeds (Mt 13:24–30). Further, Matthew added the parable of the leaven (Mt 13:33, which he may have found attached to the parable of the mustard seed in Q), the interpretation of the parable of the weeds (Mt 13:36–43), the parable of the treasure (Mt 13:44), the parable of the pearl of great price (Mt 13:45–46), the parable of the dragnet (Mt 13:47–48) and its interpretation (Mt 13:49–50), which is but a summary of Mt 13:40b–43. Finally follows the conclusion of the Parable Discourse in Mt 13:51–52, which is in fact a second conclusion, after the first conclusion in Mt 13:34–35.

In the first discourse, the Sermon on the Mount (Mt 5:1 – 7:29) Matthew presents the announcement of the kingdom of heaven *to all* in plain, straight terms. Here in the Parable Discourse (Mt 13:1–52) he gives an exposition of the *nature* of the kingdom (Mt 13:11, 'the secrets of the kingdom'), once it has started among and in people: its growth, its value, and its fulfilment. This exposition is mainly given in parables about sowing and seed, which are interwoven with texts which explain why this subject is dealt with in parables. As a whole, Matthew's text brings out more clearly than the other gospels the beginning of the separation between the crowds, who do not understand this indirect revelation, and the disciples to whom this understanding is given, and who twice receive a separate and more intensive instruction and interpretation (Mt 13:18–23; 13:36–43).

After the parable of the sower (Mt 13:3–8) and its interpretation (Mt 13:18–23), which deal with the *beginning* of the kingdom of heaven, we get here a parable about its *growth and development* (Mt 13:24–30). And, as was to be expected, again a separate interpretation of the parable is addressed to the disciples, to whom the knowledge of the mysteries of the kingdom is granted (Mt 13:36–43).

The denouement of the parable comes with the typically Matthean 'approaching him' (*proselthontes*, Mt 13:27).[29] The disciples ask for a revelation from the Lord concerning the mixture of good and bad Christians in the community. According to their understanding, after the coming of the Messiah, the kingdom should have been entirely pure. Was his victory over evil not complete? Was the Church not supposed to be an immaculate bride? The disciples had still to get used to the idea of a Church in which there were sinners. They had to face the fact that the 'enemy' was still at work within the boundaries of the realization of the kingdom here on earth. Apparently (some of) the disciples were inclined to put an end to this anomalous situation. They felt that an immediate purge was needed. But they are told that this promiscuity of good and evil is, at least for the time being, an inevitable situation. There will always be scandals. The reason for the objection to the proposal is that people will not be able to separate good from bad in the Church. Such a purge might cause more harm than good. The idea is obviously that, though Christians may be able to identify evil in the Church, their knowledge of it will never be deep enough to effectively purge the Church of it. God alone searches the reins and the hearts, and he alone can and will purify his Church of weeds without doing damage to the wheat, the good Christians (cf. I Cor 4:5).

As can easily be noticed, Matthew subscribed to the view expressed on the second community level; but it is not entirely clear whether he was concerned in the first place with the problem of good and bad in the community at present (G. Barth), or with the fate of the bad at the end of time, which he describes in Old Testament language in Mt 13:40–43 (E. Schweizer, H. Weder). The first interpretation depends on texts like Mt 22:1–14, where good and bad enter the wedding hall (although the bad are finally rejected). One could also refer to the parable of the net (Mt 13:47–50). The second interpretation can refer to the 'title' of the interpretation: 'the parable of the weeds of the field' (verse 36). Matthew also changes the original order wheat–weeds (compare Mt 13:48) into weeds–wheat in verse 30b. Moreover, the description of the evil fate of the bad has a paraenetic or exhortatory aim. This interpretation is still strengthened by the fact that Matthew substitutes the parable of the weeds for Mk 4:26–29, which was apparently less suitable for a paraenetic purpose. But the parable is also intended to encourage: the certainty of a judgment which will engulf the whole world, and the shining of the righteous like the sun (verse 43), encourage the community to do the will of the Father without worrying.

The interpretation of the parable of the weeds (Mt 13:36–43)

Mt 13 makes a clear distinction between those to whom the knowledge of the kingdom is given and those to whom it is not given because hearing they do not hear, nor do they understand (Mt 13:10–15). In fact, the expression in Mt 13:24, 'put a parable before them', already hinted that an explanation was going to follow for those who want to hear and understand. Again and again in the parable there is something mysterious which should make the audience raise the question: What is he talking about, what does he really mean? The *crowds*, however, do not raise this question. That is exactly what they are blamed for in Matthew: they do not want to understand! But now in Mt 13:36, the *disciples* approach him and ask him to explain the parable. This explanation is, of course, first of all to be read on the level of the gospel or the underlying Christian tradition.

The interpretation on the level of the gospel

It may be asked whether the separation of the parable from its interpretation is not just a Matthean device to present still another explanation of the parable. It cannot be denied that in the redactional framework of the interpretation (Mt 13:36–37a and 42–43), many Matthean characteristics can be discovered, while in the intermediate verses there are very few. It should also be noted that the interpretation has a very markedly allegorical character. Without joining A. Jülicher in thinking that Jesus could never have spoken in allegorical terms, it should nevertheless be admitted that on the level of *speech* allegory was certainly kept to a minimum; otherwise Jesus would have spoken in riddles. Elaborate allegory was used as a *literary* means to apply Jesus' parables to new and different situations in the early Church.

This allegorization should not necessarily be attributed to Matthew himself. The fact that the strongest Matthean characteristics are found in the initial and final verses seems to indicate that such an allegorization and reinterpretation of the parable already existed on the level of the apostolic tradition. Matthew apparently used a pre-existing interpretation of the parable of the weeds. He did not altogether create the allegorical interpretation. The specific Matthean interest in the allegorization can be observed from the fact that, apart from Mt 13:36–37a and 42–43, most Matthean literary characteristics are found in Mt 13:40–42. This shows that Matthew was especially interested in the eschatological aspect of this interpretation and that he developed this part. It should be kept in mind, then, that Matthew used a pre-existing allegorical interpretation of the parable and expressed his own specific concerns in the second part of the text, particularly Mt 13:40–43.

> **Verse 36:** Then he left the crowds and went into the house. And his disciples came to him, saying, 'Explain to us the parable of the weeds of the field.'

Verse 36 is most probably a Matthean composition. Verse 36a contains a direct reference to Mt 13:1, 'That same day Jesus went out of the house and sat beside the sea'. Verse 36b is patterned after Mt 13:10a, 'then the disciples came and said to him'. And verse 36c is the same as Mt 15:15b, 'explain the parable to us'. Verse 36 is composed to introduce the 'interpretation'.

The function of this verse has already been explained. Attention should be called to the strongly Matthean characteristics of this introduction. The use of the rare verb 'explain' (*diasaphēson*; used only once more, in Mt 18:31) should also be noted. In Dan 2:6 it is used for the explanation of a dream. It has been shown that this apocalyptic book exerted a considerable influence on Mt 13. The verb 'explain' stemming from an apocalyptic setting points to the fact that what had until now been revealed only in images is now going to be explained.

> **Verses 37–39:** He answered (literally: answering he said to them), 'He who sows the good seed is the Son of man; (38) the field is the world; and the good seed means the sons of the kingdom; the weeds are the sons of the evil one, (39) and the enemy who sowed them is the devil; the harvest is the close of the age, and the reapers are angels.'

This is clearly an allegorical glossary which introduces, or would be expected to introduce, the interpretation. But here Matthew is apparently incorporating an existing glossary of which he does not and cannot use many terms. Possibly it was once followed by another continuation in which all the terms explained played an actual role. Now it looks as though somebody had given the cast list of the characters who are supposed to play a part in the following drama, and then the audience discovers that several of these characters never appear in the play itself! Let us have a closer look at this glossary.

Verse 37: The sudden occurrence of the very important, apocalyptic title *Son of man* is striking. It is hard to believe that Matthew himself introduced the title at this point.

Verse 38: The *world* is clearly an editorial term for which there is no Aramaic equivalent. *Kosmos* is found eight times in Matthew, three times in Mark, three times in Luke, and 78 times in John. It witnesses to the growing universality and missionary-mindedness of the early Christian churches. But it cannot be placed in Jesus' own life or in the earliest Christian communities, for the type of universalism which we find in this verse is clearly centrifugal, and not centripetal like that found in the prophets (cf. Isa 2:2f.; 54:7; Mich 4:1). Here the Son of man is going down (in the person of the Christian missionaries) to Samaria, and to the end of the earth (Acts 1:8). In the original parable the field had been Israel alone.

The good seed means the sons of the kingdom. 'The sons of the kingdom' is a remarkable expression found only once more, in Mt 8:12, but then with a completely different meaning. In the latter text it indicates the Jews in so far as they thought themselves to be the

elected members of the kingdom of God. In Mt 13:38 it means the
Christians all over the world, destined for and heirs of the kingdom.
There must have been an intermediate, transitional meaning in
which, on the level of the apostolic tradition in Palestine, the term
indicated the Jewish Christians. In the pre-existing glossary which
Matthew used, the expression may not yet have gone beyond this
meaning. But in Matthew it goes beyond all limitations of a
Palestinian setting and rises to the level of 'sowing the seed in the
world'. At the same time it may express confrontation with and
opposition to the Jews, who are here deprived of their most cherished
title. The latter is a markedly Matthean tendency. Some have
suggested that Matthew may be referring here to Zeph 1:3 and Dan
12:3 in the light of Mal 3:19(4:1).

The weeds are the sons of the evil one. It has been discussed
whether Matthew meant 'the sons of the evil one' (RSV), or in a
more general sense 'the sons of evil'. As far as Matthew himself is
concerned, Mt 13:19 does not seem to leave much room for doubt:
ponēros is a parallel to 'Satan' in Mark, and 'devil' in Luke. And in
Mt 13:39 we read that 'the enemy who sowed them is the devil'. But
what did the expression mean in the pre-existing glossary? The
Aramaic and Hebrew equivalent of *ponēros* never has this personal
meaning, which must be looked for in the Greek tradition. Besides, if
the term had a personal connotation from the beginning, why does
Mt 13:38 not read 'the sons of the devil'? Why should a different term
be used in Mt 13:38 and 39? It seems, therefore, that originally, in
Matthew's source, the expression 'sons of the wicked' was
understood in contrast to 'sons of the kingdom', and that it simply
meant 'the wicked ones'.

Verse 39: *The enemy who sowed them is the devil.* What the
parable (Mt 13:24–30) suggested is made explicit here. It is striking
how impartially this statement is made. In the parable the questions
'who?' and 'then do you want us to go and gather them?' are of
decisive importance. Now, in what is supposed to be the
interpretation of that very same parable, these questions play no role.
This means that the real point is no longer the same as in the parable.
The Christians to whom this interpretation was addressed had other
problems. They no longer needed an answer to the question who did
it or where the weeds came from. At this stage Christendom was no
longer the small elite of the beginning. In a way it may be said that
the masses had begun to enter. Christians were no longer bewildered
at the fact that God's kingdom was not entirely pure, that there was a
mixture of good and bad Christians because of the continuing
influence of the evil one, the devil.

The harvest is the close of the age: *sunteleia aiōnos* is typically

Matthean (five times). Properly speaking it means the fulfilment of a period of time and is not a cosmological but a temporal-historical term. Matthew speaks of the fulfilment and completion of saving history, which essentially means the final divine success, the final realization of the kingdom. For the Jews this coincided with the coming of the Messiah. For the Christians it became clearer all the time that the inauguration was to be distinguished from the fulfilment (Christ's 'first' and 'second' coming). It was exactly this unexpected interregnum which created the problem the parable is talking about.

The reapers are angels. The function of the angels in the eschatological fulfilment derives from the same apocalyptic setting as the 'Son of man' (cf. Mt 24:31). It is here combined with the symbol of the harvest which is again connected with the symbolism of the parable. We go now to the second part of the text.

Verse 40: Just as the weeds are gathered and burned with fire, so will it be at the close of the age.

This sudden transition is rather unexpected. The interpretation of the parable in Mt 13:36–43 was set forth as a real interpretation of Mt 13:24–30, and so the interpretation should really cover the parable. All the elements and the whole action should be explained. But this is not the case. The anomaly was already visible in the allegorical glossary, where only seven terms were explained. There was no word about 'the sleeping of men', the 'blade springing up', the role of the servants, and the 'gathering of the wheat into the barn'. The conversation between the servants and the master which contained the real 'point' of the parable was entirely overlooked. The interpretation leaps at once to the conclusion of the parable in Mt 13:30 and most emphatically to the aspect of the punishment as part of the eschatological fulfilment which is rather extensively elaborated upon (Mt 13:40–42).

Every single expression of Mt 13:40 which does not derive from the parable itself is Matthean. Only a few terms of the parable are allegorized in the glossary. And of those which are mentioned only a few actually play a role in the action of Mt 13:40–43: the Son of man, the angels (who become here the angels of the Son of man), and the close of the age, which is mentioned from the outset in Mt 13:40 as the real topic of the action. No other terms of the glossary play any part. Besides, in Mt 13:40–43 the Matthean characteristics are concentrated: his angels, iniquity, the just, and their father.

There cannot be any doubt, therefore, that in Mt 13:40–43 the Matthean interpretation of the parable is given. The glossary of Mt 13:37–39 existed before, and since it does not even cover the most important terms of the parable, it witnesses to another interpretation of the parable on the level of the apostolic tradition. Matthew uses it only to lead to the point on which all his interest is concentrated, namely the close of the age. In Mt 13:40 the evangelist clearly announces what is going to be the focus of his attention. The first half of the verse refers back to the parable, the second half indicates the subject about which he wants to talk, and on which he is going to elaborate without any further reference to the parable or to the preceding glossary.

30 *I shall say to the reapers,*

   Gather (first)

41 *the Son of man will send his angels* (apocalyptic).
And they will gather. The description is in the indicative, not imperative. 'First' is not mentioned. *Out of his kingdom:* neither the term of the parable (field) nor that of the glossary (world) is mentioned. 'Kingdom' here is an apocalyptic term with obviously universal perspective. It is in the world.

the weeds

The definition of the weeds in the glossary (sons of the evil one) is not used. It is replaced by *all causes of sin and all evildoers.* For this last expression most exegetes refer to Zeph 1:3, but this text seems to have been combined with a text from Mal 3:19(4:1) which contains the expression 'all evildoers'. The same text has influenced Mt 13:43. Besides, Mal 3:20(4:2) refers to the mixture of good and bad, and the burning of the bad on the day of Yahweh. Such combination of one Old Testament text with another is typically Jewish and frequently found in *midrashim.* Since the term 'scandal' is often used by Matthew and 'iniquity' (*anomia*) is exclusively Matthean, it may be concluded that Matthew, the Christian scribe (Mt 13:52), applies Jewish exegetical methods here. The bad ones are no longer just those who do not believe, but those who do not keep the Christian law (*anomia*) and give scandal to their brothers and sisters.

and bind them in bundles to be burned,

42 *and throw them into the furnace of fire* is an allegorical amplification. *There men will weep and gnash their teeth* has no equivalent in the parable. The expression is a Matthean eschatological refrain (cf. Mt 8:12; 13:42, 50; 22:13; 24:51; 25:30). Mt 13:42 as a whole is Matthean and is repeated in Mt 13:50 at the end of the

but gather the wheat into my barn.

parable of the net where, properly speaking, it does not fit at all.

43 *Then the righteous will shine like the sun.* The image of the barn does not occur in the interpretation, which does not use the definition of Mt 13:38 ('the sons of the kingdom') either. 'The just' is a typically Matthean term for those who keep the Christian law. For the rest Mt 13:43 has nothing in common with the parable, nor with any of the allegorical terms given in the glossary of Mt 13:37–39. But the text contains a reference to Dan 12:3 (Theodotion), 'and those who understand (*hoi sunientes*) will shine forth like a light'. Matthew has 'like the sun'. Again the text is combined with Mal 3:20(4:2), 'But for you who fear my name the *sun of righteousness* shall rise, with healing in its wings'. This also explains why Matthew wrote 'the just (righteous)' instead of 'those who understand' of Dan 12:3. The latter text from Daniel, the book which exerted a strong influence on the whole of Mt 13, also explains Matthew's use of the 'furnace of fire' in verse 42. Matthew, however, is speaking of the real furnace of fire to be feared. *In the kingdom of their father* is also a typically Matthean expression. Here he distinguishes the 'kingdom of the father' and 'the kingdom of the Son of man' (Mt 13:41). By the latter expression he seems to refer more directly to the Church before the ultimate fulfilment. *He who has ears, let him hear* is a formula which calls attention to the solemn character of the teaching and to the mystery implied in it (cf. Mt 13:9).

The meaning of the interpretation of the parable on the level of Matthew has thus been established. The focus of attention is certainly the apocalyptic exhortation of Mt 13:40–43. In the first part only the universalistic perspective expressed in the term 'world' (Mt 13:38) and the broad view on the consummation of the history of the world are to be ascribed to Matthean redaction. For the rest the glossary was something Matthew found in the tradition and which he did not entirely adapt to the following drama (Mt 13:40–43) upon which his attention was focused. He just used this glossary to reach the point: an apocalyptic, universalistic exhortation for a Christendom which apparently had a great knowledge of Jewish scriptural arguments.

The real point of the parable itself is simply overlooked. The special interest of the interpretation has certainly something to do with the special life-situation of the author and his readers. For what particular purpose did Matthew want to call attention to the eschatological fulfilment? Did he primarily intend to warn Christians who did not live up to their obligations, or did he want to console Christians who were living with problems and under persecution? The parable focused its attention on the latter in the dialogue between the servants and the master. The servants could not understand why there was still promiscuity between good and bad in the established kingdom of heaven. They were warned against impatience, but at the same time they were also consoled: God will take care of this in the end.

But this conversation between servants and master does not play any part in Mt 13:36–43, which has its real point somewhere else. Besides, while in the parable the kingdom was apparently still limited to Palestine, here it is the world. This presupposes a later development which involved different problems. It is still the mixture of good and bad Christians which occupies the mind of Matthew. The good (just) are those who keep the Christian law, while the bad are those who violate it ('all causes of sin and all evildoers'). This aspect of Christianity is emphasized throughout Matthew's gospel. There cannot be any doubt that the eschatological description in the interpretation of the parable is first of all a *warning* to Christians to observe the Christian law or to face the grave consequences of not doing so. In the parable the warning was addressed to 'impatient' Christians. Here the reaction is against a certain 'patience' and smugness. (Some) Christians are warned that there will come an end to God's patience. At the consummation of world history God will straighten out things.

This development from the perspective of the parable to the perspective of the interpretation of the parable is quite understandable. The interpretation no longer deals with a small Palestinian elite group which was bewildered at the fact that there were also bad Christians. Larger crowds, which did not share the high moral traditions of the Palestinian Jewish Christians, had entered the Church, and consequently the moral standards had gone down considerably. And where these standards go down it is not uncommon for Christians to try to come to terms with the facts and begin to care less about the 'final audit' which seems to be far away. While the interpretation of the parable was adapted to such a situation, its fundamental meaning was not changed. The interpretation is homogeneous. Eschatology always contains a consolation and a threat, depending on the kind of people to whom it is addressed.

The meaning of the interpretation on the level of the tradition

On this level there must have been an allegorical interpretation in which all the allegorical definitions of the glossary (Mt 13:37–39) played a role. In a text which is now lost, the glossary found its real application. While this means that we are involved here in the risky business of saying something about a text we no longer have, we think nevertheless that we can more or less reconstruct the meaning of the pre-Matthean stage. Already on this level several features of the parable were no longer taken up, for the list (*seven* definitions) is apparently complete. In other words, on this pre-Matthean level the point of the text was already no longer the same as that of the original parable, although it was not yet exactly the same point as Matthew now makes in the interpretation of the parable. Apparently that traditional interpretation did not yet have the universalistic outlook which is now found in the Matthean expressions 'the world' and 'the close of the age'. On the level of the tradition, the expression was addressed to Palestinian Christians. It must have been an eschatological warning that their Christian calling was not an absolute guarantee for salvation and that God's judgment would cut right through their ranks, a warning often sounded by the prophets.

The meaning of the interpretation on the level of Jesus

Notwithstanding previous statements to the contrary, it is unwarranted to say that on this level there never was any allegorical interpretation, and that the present distinction between the parable and its interpretation is merely a device of the early Christian community to extend Jesus' teaching to their changing situation. Jewish rabbis used the same method to give first an instruction to a larger audience and next a deeper explanation to a smaller group of insiders. Jesus must certainly have followed the same method. He was looked upon as a rabbi by his contemporaries and, as evidenced from the gospels, he concentrated more and more on a deeper instruction of a smaller group of followers. What did Jesus tell his disciples in this deeper instruction? The only thing which can be said for sure is that the Son of man, the weeds, and the good and bad must have played a role in his explanation, and that this explanation must have been more in line with the parable itself. It explained also those elements which now find no place either on the level of the tradition or on the level of the Matthean redaction. It must, therefore, have been a deeper teaching about the inevitability of the mixture of good and bad in the kingdom of heaven before its final fulfilment.

Reflection

Our natural tendency is to identify with the master's servants. Do they not wish to be of service to their Lord by offering to weed out the tares? For what they see in the wheat is the tares. But they have lost sight of everything else; they are forgetting about the wheat shooting up among the tares. As they see it, the tares are the stronger of the two plants... If they leave them alone, they will get the upper hand and choke the good wheat. They are afraid; they want to act speedily and ruthlessly: weed out those tares. In so doing, they attach less importance to their master than to the enemy. In their eyes, the enemy is stronger; what he has sown will ultimately get the upper hand; perhaps there will be no harvest at all. But, unconsciously, they are thus siding with the enemy and acting *like him*: they are against him in much the same way as he is against their Master; they are attacking the tares, just as the enemy attacked the wheat... Therefore they are making themselves dependent on the enemy and going away from the master: 'Do you want us to go off and weed them out?'

The heart of the parable? Are we advised to let things alone, to be free and easy? Are we dispensed from sturdy action in the world? Of course not. The parable digs deeper: it gets down to the heart of things, to our innermost being whence spring our actions and our involvement. Faith or fear? Faith or the desire to be all-powerful? All depends on the way we look at the world, that field where the good wheat and the tares are intermingled. Do we regard it as the property of Another, who sows life and whose servants we are? Or do we consider ourselves to be solely responsible for our history, for History?[30]

There is a concern with the 'tares' of injustice which is truly inspired by the word of the One to whom the field of the world belongs and which commits itself to the building of the true covenant community where 'there will be no poor among you' (Deut 15:4). But there are also forms of 'commitment' which can become utterly *self*-righteous and *self*-serving, and ultimately arrogant and oppressive.

Some groups or movements are very eager to remove the weeds. But they happen to have a hidden agenda, which is nothing but substituting other weeds for the ones they have removed. In other words, they are eager to 'put down the mighty from their thrones' (Lk 1:52), not in order to remove all thrones from our midst once and for all, but to put others on these thrones. And we are back at square one.

God wants to pull the rich and powerful from their thrones, from their position in society, because the structures of that society are unjust and oppressive. God wants to attack the pyramid, not to invert it, but to do away with it, because in the long run an inverted pyramid may turn out to be more monstrous than the present one. God is on the side of the poor and the oppressed, not to make the poor rich and the rich poor, but for the sake of all humankind. God shows his loving concern for the whole of humankind there where humankind is most threatened: that millions and millions of people are forced to live in subhuman conditions is bad, not only for the poor and the oppressed themselves, but also for the whole of humankind. It is a festering sore which may and will affect the whole human family and bring about its downfall, unless something is done about the global structures of injustice which are responsible for this situation. This will not be without struggle because of the well-known adage *melior est conditio possidentis*, the advantage lies with the possessor. So, for the love of all humankind, we will have to attack the tares, leaving it, however, to the Father to decide who will ultimately sit at his right and left hand (Mt 20:23).

6 The good Samaritan
(Lk 10:25–37)

The general context in Luke

The parable of the Good Samaritan occurs in the first part of Luke's Travel Narrative (Lk 9:51 – 19:44).[31] Anyone who reads this section will be struck by the frequency of references to *comings* and *goings* in the sequence of pericopes or individual passages which make up Lk 9:51 – 10:42: Jesus decides to go to Jerusalem (Lk 9:51); while they are on the road (Lk 9:57); after that, the Lord sent seventy disciples (Lk 10:1); the seventy returned with joy (Lk 10:17); a man went down from Jerusalem to Jericho (Lk 10:30); Jesus was on the road with his disciples (Lk 10:38). After that point phrases or words indicating movement do not occur again until Lk 13:22. And the last reference to a change of place before the Travel Narrative is found in Lk 8:26 (but see also Lk 9:28, 37, though these do not indicate a movement out of an area).

A large number of other verbs of movement are also found in Lk 9:51 – 10:42: send (Lk 9:52; 10:1, 3); enter (Lk 9:52; 10:5, 8, 10, 38); go (Lk 10:7, 30); follow (Lk 9:57, 59, 61); come near (Lk 10:9, 11, 34); descend (Lk 10:30, 31); leave (Lk 10:3, etc.).

The example story of the Good Samaritan seems to fit well in this context, since the verbs of movement found in it represent about 20% of the verbs of movement in all of Lk 9:51 – 10:42. This is very close to the proportion of verses in our pericope to the verses of that context (thirteen to 54). Lk 9:51 – 10:24 and Lk 10:38–42 seem, therefore, to form the immediate context of Lk 10:25–37.

It does not seem to be accidental that the story of the Good Samaritan follows so closely after Lk 9:52–56, which contains a report of a Samaritan refusal of hospitality, but also of Jesus' strong rebuke of James and John who wanted to call down fire upon a Samaritan village. In Luke's other two 'Samaritan' stories, Lk 10:30–36 and 17:11–19, the Samaritan in question is presented in a favourable way. Should Luke's treatment of Samaritans be seen as a preparation for the announcement, and the actual description, of missionary activity in Samaria in Acts 1:8 and 8:1–25 respectively, and the statement that 'Samaria received the word of God' (Acts 8:14; cf. 9:31, 15:3)?

On the other hand, the example story of the Good Samaritan and the pericope of Mary and Martha deal with the same reality: 'to inherit eternal life' (Lk 10:25) and 'the good portion, which shall not be taken away' (Lk 10:42), namely the kingdom. In this connection the former exhorts to 'doing' (Lk 10:25, 28, 37), while the latter emphasizes 'listening, hearing'. These two do not contradict but rather complement each other. 'Listening, hearing' is the presupposition of 'doing' and in 'doing' 'hearing' is made true. By its common theme of 'doing' and 'listening', the combination of pericopes, Lk 10:25–42, becomes a counterpart of Lk 11:27–28. The latter anecdotically summarizes what is extensively narrated in the former. With their common theme, Lk 10:25–42 and Lk 11:27–28 form the framework of Lk 11:1–13, an instruction on prayer, and Lk 11:14–26, an exorcism followed by a controversy.

Lk 10:25–37

While some scholars approach Lk 10:25–37 as one single pericope, a good number of them consider the passage as consisting of two separate pericopes, the lawyer's question (Lk 10:25–28), and the parable of the Good Samaritan (Lk 10:30–37), Lk 10:29 being a transitional verse. In its present setting the parable is a part of a theological dialogue. The relative briefness of the surrounding dialogue should not make us ignore it; otherwise the parable which is framed by it would become merely an ethical lesson or exhortation to reach out to people in need.

Lk 10:25–28

Because Lk 10:25–28 occurs in a different context from Mk 12:28–34 and Mt 22:34–40 — the Travel Narrative instead of Jesus' teaching in Jerusalem after his solemn entry — and because of considerable differences in content, some biblical scholars argue that Lk 10:25–28 is not a Lucan parallel to the text mentioned. But perfectly acceptable explanations have been offered for a possible transfer of the pericope by Luke from its traditional to its present context, and the differences do not seem so important that they can only be explained by postulating two different occasions on which Jesus discussed this matter. Moreover, Lk 10:25–28 contains undeniable reminiscences of Mk 12:28–34, e.g., the fact that he retains the Marcan quartet, 'heart, soul, strength, mind', while the Septuagint had the triad, 'heart, soul, strength'.

In the present study Lk 10:25–28 will be considered a parallel to Mk 12:28–34 and Mt 22:34–40. A careful comparison of the three parallel passages seems to indicate that a pericope containing a question addressed to Jesus and leading to a quotation of Deut 6:5 and Lev 19:18 was found in both Mark and Q. In line with the other similar cases, Matthew seems to have combined the text of Mark and Q, selecting the context of Mark. Luke apparently chose both the text and the context of Q. The existence of a Q version is advocated on the basis of a number of agreements of Matthew and Luke against Mark (cf. Mt 22:35–36 and Lk 10:25–26; lawyer/scribe; to test him/asked him; the address 'teacher'/no formal address; in the law/expression absent in Mark).

Lk 10:29–37

While in Luke the second question of verse 29 leads smoothly from Lk 10:25–28 to the ensuing example story, Lk 10:30–35, no such question or story is found in Mark or Matthew. It should be asked, therefore, whether the unity of Lk 10:25–28, (29), 30–35, (36–37) is to be attributed to Jesus, to the early Christian tradition, or to the Lucan redaction.

Lk 10:29

Picking up the word 'neighbour' from Lk 10:25–28, and using it in the same sense — the object of one's love — the lawyer asked: 'And who is my neighbour?' But at the end of the story the question reads: 'Which of these three, do you think, proved neighbour to the man who fell among the robbers?', i.e., the subject of the action. It seems, then, that 'neighbour' has a double meaning in Lk 10:25–37, or that there is some inconsistency between the meaning of 'neighbour' in Lk 10:27, 29, and Lk 10:36. A similar shift in meaning occurs in the story of the woman who was a sinner (Lk 7:36–50).[32] Lk 10:29 seems to have been formulated to combine Lk 10:25–27 and Lk 10:30–36. The unification of originally separate pericopes was inspired and facilitated by the presence of the word 'neighbour' in both. The threefold *plēsion* ('neighbour') and the fourfold *poiein* ('do') function as cohesive elements.

Lk 10:30–35

The parable proper starts in Lk 10:30 with the phrase 'a (certain) man' (*anthrōpos tis*), which are the initial words of several Lucan parables (cf. Lk 12:16; 15:11; 16:1; 16:19). With the exception of the

parable of the rich fool (Lk 12:16–21), all these parables are
self-contained and not fitted into a larger composition, as is the case
with the two parables of the two debtors and the Good Samaritan in
Lk 7:36–50 and Lk 10:25–37 respectively. Again, it therefore seems
indicated to consider the parable as an originally separate unit. But
was its unification with Lk 10:25–28 effected in the tradition or on the
level of the Lucan redaction? In other words, were they already
united in Q, and was this union then related by Luke (and broken up
by Matthew; cf. Mt 10:5), or did Luke unite them for the first time?
The former seems to be the better hypothesis. The peculiarities of
rabbinical controversy found in the present (combined) composition
fits better into the traditional literary activity than in the Lucan
redaction. One the combination was effected, it is easy to see that
Luke would be inclined to retain it because of his interest in Samaria
and the Samaritans (cf. Lk 9:52; 17:11, 16; Acts 1:8; 8:1, 5, 9, 14, 25;
9:31; 15:3).

Lk 10:36–37

The conclusion of the story consists of a question (verse 36), its
answer (verse 37a), and a commandment/exhortation (verse 37b).
The core of the question, 'which (who)... do you think', occurs
elsewhere in the synoptic tradition only in Matthew, both in parables
(Mt 17:25; 18:12; 21:28) and in controversies (Mt 22:17, 42). In these
parables it occurs either with (Mt 17:25; 21:28) or without an answer
(Mt 18:12). The rhetorical question (i.e., without an answer)
apparently being the more original form, Lk 10:36, in the form of a
rhetorical question, e.g., 'which of these three showed mercy to the
man who fell among the robbers?', seems to have been part of the
original story. Luke partly rewrote this verse by introducing the
second person, 'do you (= the lawyer) think' and the term
'neighbour'.

Since questions and answers conclude the parables in Mk
12:1–9, in Mt 21:28–31, and in Lk 7:41–43, it is possible that Lk
10:37a originally belonged to the parable. However, a study of the
structural balance of Lk 10:25–37 as a whole seems to suggest that
verse 37 is due to the same literary activity which linked Lk 10:25–28
and Lk 10:30–36 by means of verse 29. The structure would look as
follows:

Question (lawyer)	: Lk 10:25	Lk 10:29
Counter-question (Jesus)	: Lk 10:26	Lk 10:30–36
Answer (lawyer)	: Lk 10:27	Lk 10:37a
Counter-answer (Jesus)	: Lk 10:28	Lk 10:37b

Lk 10:25–37 has also been understood as:

> made up of eight speeches that fall into two precise rounds of
> debate. In each round there are two questions and two answers.
> The formal structure of each scene is identical. Shortened to the
> main themes the full dialogue is as follows:

Round One:	A lawyer stood up to put him to the test and said,
(1) Lawyer:	(Question 1) 'What must I *do* to inherit eternal *life*?'
(2) Jesus:	(Question 2) 'What about the law?'
(3) Lawyer:	(Answer to 2) 'Love God and your neighbor.'
(4) Jesus:	(Answer to 1) '*Do* this and *live*.'
Round Two:	He (the lawyer), desiring to *justify himself*, said,
(5) Lawyer:	(Question 3) 'Who is my neighbor?'
(6) Jesus:	(Question 4) 'A certain man went down from Jerusalem. ...Which of these three became a neighbor?'
(7) Lawyer:	(Answer to 4) 'The one who showed mercy on him.'
(8) Jesus:	(Answer to 3) 'Go and continue *doing* likewise.'[33]

But it has been remarked that the unbalance caused by the length of
the example story (Lk 10:30–36) and its difference in content make it
seem unlikely that Luke or the pre-Lucan tradition intended such a
parallel structure, and this would considerably weaken the case
against the originality of verse 37a.

It is even more difficult to determine whether verse 37b did or
did not belong to Luke's source, but its formulation seems to indicate
Lucan redaction (*poreuesthai*, 'to go', 51 times in Luke and 37 times
in Acts, against three times in Mark and 29 times in Matthew; 'doing'
as the way to attain eternal life).

Analysis of the text

> **Verse 25:** And behold, a lawyer stood up to put him to the
> test, saying, 'Teacher, what shall I do to inherit eternal life?'

'And behold' indicates a new beginning which may sound very
Semitic, but which is also very characteristic of Luke (*kai idou* occurs
seventeen times in Lk and six times in Acts), who often imitates the
Semitizing style of the Septuagint.

'A lawyer stood up to put him to the test.' Before looking more
closely at this initial statement of Lk 10:25–37, it is good to remember
the verses which immediately precede it: 'Then turning to the
disciples he said privately, "Blessed are the eyes which see what
you see! For I tell you that many prophets and kings desired to see
what you see, and did not see it, and to hear what you hear, and did

not hear it"' (Lk 10:23–24). What the disciples see is found, on the one hand, in Lk 10:21–22, and, on the other hand, in Lk 10:25ff. The seeing of which Jesus speaks to his disciples has the Hebraic meaning of 'experiencing', belonging to a generation in which the promises will be realized. The prophets and kings wanted to belong to a generation in which God's mercy would become visible in the appearance of Jesus, and in the way he goes. That way started, in a sense, in Lk 4:30, became more definite in Lk 9:51 with the beginning of the Travel Narrative (Lk 9:51 – 19:44), and reaches its decisive phase in Lk 18:31, the way from Jericho to Jerusalem. In fact, it has been argued that Lk 10:21 – 18:30 falls into two parts, Lk 10:21 – 13:20 and Lk 14:1 – 18:30, which loosely correspond to one another in content as well as in sequence, though the latter is an inverted one, or that, in other words, Lk 10:25–37 with its question, 'Teacher, what shall I do to inherit eternal life?', corresponds to Lk 18:18–30, the account of the ruler and his question, 'Teacher, what shall I do to inherit eternal life?'

Luke, in accord with Mt 22:35, uses the term 'lawyer' (*nomikos*), instead of Mark's 'scribe' (*grammateus*, Mk 12:28). The word *nomikos* is found seven times in Luke (once in Matthew, never in Mark). Luke tends to substitute 'lawyer' for 'scribe', which would mean 'secretary' in the Greek world (cf. Acts 19:35), and could therefore easily be misunderstood by Luke's Gentile readers.

The lawyer 'stood up to put him to the test'. A representative of the opposition, those who stand in contrast to the disciples (cf. Lk 10:23), stands up to test Jesus. For the sake of emphasis Luke uses the compound verb *ekpeirazein*, i.e., the lawyer wanted to test Jesus out! The only other instance of *ekpeirazein* in Luke is found in the temptation narrative, where Jesus is referred to as quoting Deut 6:16, 'You shall not tempt the Lord your God' (Lk 4:12), which in turn refers to Ex 17:2 and its mention of the people's dispute with Moses and their testing of the Lord. This whole context may be alluded to when Luke says that the 'lawyer stood up to put him to the test'.

While in Mk 12:28–31, 34, the scribe is presented as asking an honest question which is therefore answered by Jesus, who even praises the scribe as one who is 'not far from the kingdom of God' (Mk 12:34), Luke and Matthew agree that the lawyer's intention is to test Jesus, who therefore, in Luke, replies by a counter-question, so that the material seems to have been arranged in the form of a controversy (cf. Acts 6:9). The lawyer's knowledge of the answer shows that his inquiry was not well intentioned. All these Lucan features intensify the polemical character of the passage.

Moreover, in Luke, the question is very different from that in Mark and Matthew. There is no reference to the 'great' or the 'first' commandment, but 'Teacher, what shall I do to inherit eternal life?' In this form the question was undoubtedly more understandable to Luke's Greek readers, who would have been puzzled by the typically Jewish question about the 'first' or the 'great' commandment. The latter should be understood against the background of the 248 commandments and 365 prohibitions (totalling 613) of the Old Testament. This does not necessarily mean that Luke himself composed the question in its present form. It is thoroughly biblical, and is in fact found in Mk 10:17 (parallel in Mt 19:16; Lk 18:18), in the story of the rich young man/ruler. But it shows Luke's capability of selecting from the traditional material what would be readily understandable for his Greek readers. Moreover, Luke emphasizes the verb *poiein*, 'to do', which occurs in this story four times (Lk 10:24, 28, twice in 37). Elsewhere too Luke stresses the importance of doing, e.g., Lk 3:10, where, in response to John the Baptist's exhortation to repentance, the multitudes asked him, 'What then shall we do?' (see also Lk 3:12, 14; 11:28, 42). In Lk 10:25, doing and inheriting are related more closely than the English text shows. The Greek text has a participle: 'what doing shall I inherit eternal life?'

In the Old Testament the idea of inheritance referred especially to Israel's privilege of inheriting the promised land. Israel did not do anything to deserve this inheritance which was understood as a gift of God. It has been suggested that the 'test' was intended to discover whether Jesus did or did not believe that the inheritance of Israel was available through the keeping of the law. From Lk 18:18–30 it appears that 'inheriting eternal life' (Lk 18:18, 30) is synonymous to 'entering the kingdom of God' (Lk 18:24, 25, 29b).

Verse 26: And he said to him, 'What is written in the law? How do you read?'

Unlike in Mark and Matthew, neither the lawyer nor Jesus raises the question about the first or the most important commandment of the law. This may be due to the redactional intervention of Luke, who throughout his gospel tries to avoid the word 'commandment'.

In the very style of a controversy, Jesus replies with a counter-question which directs his interlocutor to the law of which he is supposed to be an accredited expositor. The double question reflects Jewish methods of discussion, but its precise significance is debated. Some scholars understand it to mean 'How do you expound the law at this point?', while others, especially J. Jeremias, think that the question means 'How do you recite?', i.e., 'what do you recite as part of your regular worship?', which forces the lawyer to answer with the words of the *Shema*, the basic Jewish creed recited twice a day by every orthodox Jew. This may be confirmed by the fact that in the parallel text, Mk 12:29–30, Jesus' answer includes also the previous verse, Deut 6:4, 'Hear, O Israel: the Lord our God, the Lord is one' (although it should also be noted that, strictly speaking, the lawyer recites more than the *Shema*).

By means of this counter-question, Jesus first of all refers to the deeper meaning of the Torah as a guide for life or for practical conduct, but also subjects the lawyer to the judgment of the Torah. Jesus turns the tables on him, first by showing that he already knew the answer to his own question, then, in the example story, by compelling him to measure his own life against the standard which he had been prepared only to use as a weapon in an intellectual sparring match.

> **Verse 27:** And he answered. 'You shall love the Lord your God with all your heart, and with all your soul, and with all your strength, and with all your mind; and your neighbour as yourself.'

In line with the style of a developing controversy, the lawyer, not Jesus (cf. Mk 12:29; Mt 22:37), answers the question. His answer is derived from Deut 6:5 and Lev 19:18, the latter appearing as a separate citation in Mark and Matthew, but in Luke made into a part of the first and only quotation. While for all their closeness the two commandments are nevertheless given a distinct identity in Mark and Matthew, in Luke only one occurrence of 'you shall love' governs the two commandments which are linked together by a simple 'and'. In this way the two commandments become just one.

The Septuagint text of Deut 6:5 speaks of loving God 'with all your heart, with all your soul, and with all your strength'. Luke has the same quadripartite presentation as Mk 12:30, which adds 'with all your mind' (in the third place in Mark, in the fourth in Luke), while Mt 22:37 has a tripartite expression without the phrase 'with all your strength'. It has been duly pointed out that the various parts of the human person mentioned in the quotation should not be diagnosed separately. In a thoroughly Semitic way the verse expresses the totality of one's being, and emphasizes that one should love God with all one's resources. In biblical language the 'heart' is not so much the centre of emotions as what one lives for, one's intention in life. The 'soul' is not purely a spiritual part of our being; the Bible does not know the dualism of body and soul, and Hebrew does not have a separate word for 'body'. 'Soul' refers to the realm of one's consciousness, but means also 'breath', 'desire', and emotions. 'With all your strength' refers to all one's faculties. The expression 'with all your mind', which is part of the citation in all three Synoptics, is not found in Deut 6:5. The word 'mind' or 'understanding' does not often occur in the Torah, but is very common in Wisdom literature and in the Psalms, e.g., the interesting citation from Ps 119(118):34, 'Give me understanding, that I may keep your law, and observe it with my heart'. It has been suggested that the non-Septuagintal 'with all your mind' is not a reflection of the way Jesus himself quoted the text, but rather the result of its use and application in the early Church and by the evangelists.

In the present text, Deut 6:5 and Lev 19:18 are merged into one commandment: one act of love directed towards God and neighbour. By the rules of the developing controversy this perfectly Christian statement is placed on the lips of the lawyer, but it may be safely assumed that the Jewish scribe would never have formulated things this way, unless he intended to refer to Jesus' own way of citing the text, as some scholars suggest. It has also been suggested that the lawyer knew Jesus' position in the matter and quoted it in order to draw it into the discussion. Attempts have been made to support the possibility of such statement by a Jewish scribe by referring to the *Testaments of the Twelve Patriarchs*, more specifically to *Test. Issachar* 5:1; 7:5; *Test. Dan* 5:3, where love of God and love of neighbour are also brought together, but it has often been argued that these texts have undergone Christian influence.

For a Jewish lawyer it would have been extremely difficult to quote these two laws in such a close union. His idea of the exclusive election of Israel made Lev 19:18 an awkward thing to deal with. The idea of neighbour had to be limited, and was in fact increasingly limited. Already in the Old Testament this led to the exclusion of the non-Israelites, at least those living outside Palestine. And in Jesus' time the notion of neighbour was even further restricted. Many religious groups seemed to accept only their own members as brothers and neighbours. This exclusivism was especially strong among the Qumranites, who spoke explicitly of the duty of hating the sons of darkness, i.e., all who did not belong to the community. Matthew, referring to the old law in Mt 5:43, gives a correct description of their views: 'You have heard that it is said, "You shall love your neighbour (countryman) and hate your enemy (foreigner)..."'. At any rate, the Samaritan was definitely excluded by any Jew, and that is exactly the reason why a Samaritan is going to play a major role in the following example story.

Verse 28: And he said to him, 'You have answered right; do this, and you will live.'

This verse, unparalleled in Mark and Matthew, which caps the first phase of the controversy, and to that extent is Semitic in character, may nevertheless in its formulation be due to Lucan editorial activity. This is confirmed in the first part of the verse, 'You have answered right (*orthōs*)', a typically Lucan form of commendation, as seen from Lk 7:43, 'You have judged *rightly*', in reply to the Pharisee's statement in the controversy concerning the woman who was a sinner (Lk 7:36–50; without parallels), and in Lk 20:21, 'you speak and teach *rightly*' (compare the very different formulation in Mk 12:14; Mt 22:16). Elsewhere in the New Testament, *orthōs* occurs only in Mk 7:35, but there with the meaning of speaking 'plainly' (RSV, NEB) or 'clearly' (JB). It may therefore be concluded that Luke recast the traditional material in such a way that, while the lawyer was made to quote the great commandment, the real climax of the first round of the controversy comes in Jesus' statement, 'do this, and you will live' (compare Gen 42:18, 'Do this and you will live'). By means of a reference to Lev 18:5, 'You shall therefore keep my statutes and my ordinances, by *doing* which a man shall *live*', Jesus refers back to the lawyer's initial question and states that the 'commandment' shows the way to life. Jesus' words are also reminiscent of Deut 5:33; 6:24. This emphasis on doing, which anticipates the final exhortation, 'Go and do likewise' (Lk 10:37), is in accord with Lucan doctrine. 'Blessed rather are those who hear the word of God and keep it' (Lk 11:28). The present imperative 'do this' includes the connotation 'continually do this', and indicates that continuous action is the way to life. While Jesus praises the lawyer for having the right theology, his practice is still in question.

Verse 29: But he, desiring to justify himself, said to Jesus, 'And who is my neighbour?'

This is a transitional verse connecting the controversy with the example story. Indeed, it picks up the word 'neighbour' of Lk 10:25–28, and repeats it. The controversial character of the conversation was temporarily subdued by Jesus' commendation of the lawyer, but surfaces again when the latter, possibly in an attempt to remove the edge of Jesus' statement, 'do this and you will live', and perhaps also because of his rabbinic desire for clear definitions, challenges Jesus with a second question which, again, he will be forced to answer himself (Lk 10:36).

The formulation of the introduction with its use of the verb 'justify' is probably Lucan (cf. Lk 16:15, 'you are those who justify yourselves before men'; Lk 18:9–14). The lawyer does not only intend to justify his initial question and thus regain the initiative in the current controversy, but also to justify his hiding behind the commandment of love which is here applied to the 'neighbour'.

One of the key words of Lk 10:25–37, 'neighbour' (*plēsion*; cf. Lk 10:27, 29, 36; the other is *poiein*, 'to do', Lk 10:25, 28, and twice in 37) appears for the second time. The adjective *plēsios* means 'one who is near' and was used in the Septuagint to translate the Hebrew word *rea^c*, a person with whom one has something to do. The Jews currently understood the term to refer to fellow-Jews, but the Pharisees tended to exclude the ordinary people (*^{c}am ha-ares*, literally, 'the people of the land') from their definition, and the Qumran community excluded 'the sons of darkness' (those who did not belong to the community). The lawyer's question should be understood against this background. The commandment speaks of loving one's neighbour, but where are the limits to be set? The lawyer's question implies that there is also a non-neighbour, and that therefore one should ask where the line should be drawn between neighbour and non-neighbour. 'What can be demanded from me?' is the unspoken question which lies behind the lawyer's words.

The lawyer's question is basically individualistic and egocentric; the questioner places himself at the centre and approaches the issue, as it were, in terms of concentric circles, while asking himself how far he should go, or whom he should allow to enter the circle of his 'neighbours'. By means of the following example story Jesus will eventually change the perspective of the question.

> **Verse 30:** Jesus replied, 'A man was going down from Jerusalem to Jericho, and he fell among robbers, who stripped him and beat him, and departed, leaving him half dead.

With the classical Greek expression *hupolabōn* (aorist participle of *hupolambanein*, 'to take up [the question]', 'to take [the floor]'), used only here in the New Testament in the sense of 'to reply', Jesus starts to deal with the lawyer's second question. The example story proper begins with the stereotyped *anthrōpos tis*, 'a certain man' (Lk 13:6; 15:11; 16:1, 19; 18:2; 19:12). He is not identified, and this may imply that the lawyer's question is not going to be solved in terms of nationality or race, but it is presumed that it becomes gradually clearer that he is a Jew. This man 'was going down from Jerusalem to Jericho', along the road which descends about 1,000 metres, from 750 metres above sea level to 250 metres below sea level, over 27 km of winding road bordered by desert and many rocks, and thus an ideal place for ambushes.

At a certain moment he fell (aorist) in the hands of robbers, 'who stripped him and beat him, and departed, leaving him half dead'. The last feature is significant, for it may partly explain why the priest (and the Levite?) passed by. The suggestion that the robbers were Zealots and that the man was an Essene, a member of the sectarian community of Qumran, who enjoyed the favour of Herod the outspoken enemy of the Zealots, and was ignored by both priest and Levite because they belonged to rival religious sects, is interesting, but does not seem to have received much scholarly approval. It seems to narrow the scope of the story down unduly to a lesson condemning the hatred of rival religious sects.

This verse — and the whole story — is clearly told from the point of view of the man who became the victim of the robbers, and thus practically forces the hearers/readers to put themselves in his place. It is almost as if Jesus were saying: Imagine yourself going down from Jerusalem to Jericho...

Verses 31–32: Now by chance a priest was going down that road; and when he saw him he passed by on the other side. (32) So likewise a Levite, when he came to the place and saw him, passed by on the other side.

Although the road was lonely and the man might have lain there a long time before help arrived, 'by chance a priest was going down that road', probably on his way home from his service in the temple. Many priests and Levites lived in Jericho. But when he saw the man who had been maltreated by the robbers, he 'passed by on the other side' of the road. No reason is given for his behaviour or that of the Levite. Some have suggested that the priest thought that the unconscious man was dead (cf. Lk 10:30, 'half dead'), and did not want to defile himself ritually by touching a corpse (cf. Num 19:11–12). Recent studies have shown that while the priest was entitled to pass by for fear of defilement and its consequences, he could have found justification for defiling himself, had he so desired. Most probably the Levite would have felt less bound by ritual requirements than the priest. But probably one is not supposed to speculate about the motives for their failure to assist the man.

The priest and Levite, representatives of the Jewish cult, are opposed to a Samaritan. It has been noticed that the priest and Levite do not merely continue on their way; they pass by on the other side. Although priests and Levites were not exactly representative of contemporary Jewish piety — the Pharisees and scribes were — they were considered the first and privileged class. Their behaviour serves as a foil for that of the Samaritan. By not giving the reason for their refusal to help, Jesus avoids turning the parable into an outright attack on the contemporary religious establishment. Instead he concentrates on the failure to show mercy. 'I desire mercy, and not sacrifice' (Hos 6:6; Mt 9:13; 12:7).

It is tempting to inject a shot of modern anti-clericalism into the story. The audience is then supposed to have reacted with a 'how typical that the priest and the Levite passed by!' But an anti-clerical interpretation only makes sense if it is assumed that the story was told in a context critical of ritual rules and regulations which blind people to the higher reality of love, as seems to be the case in some discussions over healing on the sabbath (Lk 6:6–11; 13:10–17; 14:1–6). But the present story does not demand such an interpretation.

It is possible that the twosome (priest and Levite) has a further meaning in connection with Deut 19:15 and its demand for two witnesses. However, one may also just have here an example of the popular story-telling technique of the rule of three: priest, Levite, Samaritan.

> The aborted sequences with the priest and Levite provide a pattern which causes the listener to anticipate the third traveler and build up tension. Since this threefold pattern is so common in popular story-telling, we also anticipate that the third traveler will be the one who will actually help. Our attention is focused on the third traveler before he arrives, and this heightens the shock when we discover that he neither fits the pattern of cultural expectation nor the pattern of expectation created by the series priest, Levite.[34]

> **Verse 33:** But a Samaritan, as he journeyed, came to where he was, and when he saw him, he had compassion,

It is very clear that the account intends to elaborate on and thus to emphasize the role of the Samaritan. Indeed, with his appearance on the scene there is a new fullness of detail. While the Greek text devotes 46 words to all that precedes the Samaritan's appearance on the scene (Lk 10:30b–32), it uses 60 words to describe the latter's reaction (Lk 10:33–35). The Greek text also stresses the contrast between the priest and the Levite, on the one hand, and the Samaritan, on the other hand, by emphatically placing the word 'Samaritan' (followed by the participle *de*) at the beginning of the sentence. Jesus opposes the Samaritan, the incarnation of his own ideal, to a priest and a Levite, official representatives of Jewish religion, and not just any Jews, thus establishing the opposition between the gospel ideal and the old law (compare Lk 6:27–35; Mt 5:43–48).

In Jewish eyes the Samaritans were bastards, because those who had escaped deportation to Assyria in 722 B.C. had mingled and intermarried with pagans. Since then many conflicts had widened the gap. 'With two nations my soul is vexed, and the third is no nation: Those who live on Mount Seir, and the Philistines, and the foolish people that dwell in Shechem [the Samaritans]' (Sir 50:25–26). Relations were very tense in Jesus' time. 'For Jews have no dealings with Samaritans' (Jn 4:9). *Midrash Mekhilta* on Ex 21:14 says explicitly that Samaritans are not included in one's neighbours.

The Samaritan was journeying (*hodeuōn* occurs only here in the New Testament). In a gospel which invests much theological meaning in the theme of the 'way' (*hodos*) and in references to journeying, a certain importance may be given to this verb, especially at the beginning of the Travel or Journey Narrative.

Like the priest and the Levite, he sees the man, but while the former two move away, the Samaritan 'draws near'. The two movements expressed in 'to pass by' (*antiparerchomai*) and 'drawing near' (*proserchomai*, 'to go to') make the wounded man the centre of the narrative. It is the different relationships to this man which will prove decisive at the end of the account.

While the other two 'passed by on the other side', the Samaritan 'when he saw him, he had compassion' (*esplanchnisthē*; cf. Lk 7:13, 'when the Lord saw her, he had compassion'; 15:20). The root of this verb is *splanchnon*, 'innards', so the Samaritan had a deep 'gut level reaction' to the wounded man. Except in three of Jesus' parables (Mt 18:27; Lk 10:33; 15:20), this expression is always used to describe God's or Jesus' own attitude. But in the three parables of the unforgiving servant (Mt 18:23–35), the prodigal son (Lk 15:11–32), and the Good Samaritan (Lk 10:25–37), it denotes a specific attitude on the part of the men, and in the third parable it appears as the basic and decisive attitude in human and therefore Christian acts. The use of this verb does not seem to be a sufficient ground for claiming a direct Christological reference, but a veiled reference to Christ the Saviour is not to be excluded.

Verses 34–35: and (he) went to him and bound up his wounds, pouring on oil and wine; then he set him on his own beast and brought him to an inn, and took care of him. (35) And the next day he took out two denarii and gave them to the innkeeper, saying 'Take care of him; and whatever more you spend, I will repay you when I come back.'

These verses describing at length everything the Samaritan did for the man who fell among the robbers: he *bound up* his wounds, *poured* oil and wine (to soothe and disinfect the wounds; oil and wine made up a first-aid kit in Jesus' time), *set* him on his own beast, *brought* him to an inn, and *took care* of him. Five verbs to describe his love *in action!*

As the priests and Levites poured out the oil and the wine on the high altar before God, so the Samaritan now pours oil and wine on the man's wounds, thus pouring out the true offering acceptable to God. It has indeed been noted that 'oil and wine' were used in the temple service for the burnt offerings (cf. Rev 6:6), and that in reference to Hos 6:6, 'I desire mercy not sacrifice', the parable would suggest that the Samaritan, not the priest and Levite, offers the right kind of worship to God. Three verses later we read: 'As robbers lie in wait for a man, so the priests are banded together; they murder on the way to Shechem, yea, they commit villainy' (Hos 6:9). Hos 6:1–10 contains more than ten phrases which are echoed in Lk 10:30–35.

The similarity has also been pointed out between Lk 10:34–35 and II Chron 28:8–15, especially 'And the men who have been mentioned by name rose and took the captives, and with the spoil they clothed all that were naked among them; they clothed them, gave them sandals, provided them with food and drink, and anointed them; and carrying all the feeble among them on asses, they brought them to their kinsfolk at Jericho, the city of palm trees. Then they returned to Samaria' (II Chron 28:15).

Since there was almost certainly no inn in the middle of the desert, we are most probably supposed to understand that the Samaritan took the man downhill to an inn in or near Jericho. He thus took the risk of being identified and having to face searching questions and even hostile action. This is the price he is willing to pay to complete his compassionate action.

The Greek word used for 'inn' (*pandocheion*) describes it as 'a place of welcome for all' — and that was practically all that such inns could be called. Actually a shelter for the night, the typical inn consisted of a stockade protected by a stout gate. Porticos along the wall covered the guests, who would sleep on the ground fully dressed, while their mounts were tethered nearby. In Philo and later Jewish literature the 'inn' was portrayed in a rather negative light.

For the rest, the Samaritan did not rely naively on the charity of the inn-keeper, but paid him two denarii (a denarius represented a day's wages) and assured him that he would settle any further accounts upon his return. He took all necessary precautions to assure the well-being of the wounded man.

The return of the Samaritan is expressed by a verb (*epanerches-thai*) which is not found anywhere else in the New Testament, except in Lk 19:15 to designate the return of Christ at the end of time. But again this does not seem to be a sufficient ground for claiming a direct Christological reference.

Verse 36: Which of these three, do you think, proved neighbour to the man who fell among the robbers?'

In line with the controversial character of the Lucan setting of the story, the lawyer is now requested to give an answer and thus to take a stand. Initially he asked 'And who is *my* neighbour?' But by means of the example story the question has undergone a transformation and it now says 'Who proved neighbour to *the man who fell among the robbers*?' It has at times been maintained that

> The alteration in the form of the question hardly conceals a deeper meaning... (that) both Jesus and the scribe are after the same thing: they are not seeking a definition, but the extent of the conception *rea*[c]: the only difference between them is that the scribe is looking at the matter from a theoretical point of view, while Jesus illuminates the question with a practical example.[35]

But many seem to agree that the change in the form of the question corresponds to a change of perspective. The lawyer took the view that his ego was at the centre of the question, while it appears now that it ought to be the 'you' of the person in need. Therefore, the question is turned upside down, or rather, inside out. While the lawyer initially raised the question concerning the limits of love of neighbour (starting from himself as the centre), the example story made it clear that there is no fixed schema. Wherever and whenever I am confronted by the need of a fellow person, I am challenged to act as a neighbour towards that person. The difference between verse 29 and verse 36, and the transformation in verse 36 of the question asked in verse 29, is basically the distance between two religions of which only the second, that of Jesus, has fully understood the primacy and universality of love of neighbour.

> The scribe asks: 'Who is my neighbor?' Jesus does not answer by giving a systematic list of the various classes of men from my fellow-national who is nearest to me to the foreigner who is farthest away... Nor does he reply by extolling the eccentric love of those who are most distant, to which all men are brothers. He

answers the question of the *nomikos* by reversing the question: 'Who is nearest to the one in need of help?' This means that he shatters the older concentric grouping in which the I is at the centre, but maintains the organizing concept of the neighbor, and by means of this concept sets up a new grouping in which the Thou is at the centre. This order, however, is not a system which applies schematically to all men and places. It consists only in absolute concreteness. It is built up from case to case around a man in need.[36]

The story of the Good Samaritan shows that one cannot say in advance who the neighbor is but that the course of life will make this plain enough... One cannot define one's neighbour; one can only be a neighbor.[37]

The lawyer was asking for the *object* of love of neighbour, but is told that the question can be dealt with only by becoming its *subject*, by acting as a neighbour. This is emphasized in the Greek text by the verb *gegonenai*, perfect infinitive of the verb *ginomai*, 'to become'. 'Which of these three... becomes a neighbour to', or 'proved (himself) a neighbour to...' (RSV, JB).

> **Verse 37:** He said, 'The one who showed mercy on him.' And Jesus said to him, 'Go and do likewise.'

Again the lawyer is forced to answer his own question which, however, has been reformulated in the light of the example story. The answer is unavoidable: 'the one who did mercy on him'. Indeed, literally the text says 'The one who *did* mercy', thus taking up again the very first question, 'What shall I *do* to inherit eternal life' (Lk 10:25). It is quite often suggested that the lawyer formulates his answer in this way in order to avoid mentioning the Samaritan by name. He would refuse to give the Samaritan his due explicitly. But it seems more probable that *Luke* formulated the statement in this way to show that becoming a neighbour means showing mercy, i.e., the capacity to identify with the person in need. The Samaritan's assistance is thus described as rooted in his compassion (Lk 10:33) and as an act of mercy (Lk 10:37; cf. Lk 1:78, 'Through the tender mercy of our God').

Capping the controversy, Jesus says 'Go and do likewise'. With these final words, 'Do like the Samaritan', Jesus answers the initial question 'what shall I do to inherit eternal life?' Once more 'doing' is emphasized, and the literal meaning of the text, 'go and do *you* likewise', calls to action all who hear/read the example story. The present imperatives 'go' and 'do' imply that Jesus commands the lawyer (and the listener/reader) to go and put this into effect by following the example of the Samaritan, not by a single act but by lifelong conduct. The concluding verse of the parable makes it clear that the story is now considered an example for Christians to imitate.

Example story or parable?

There seems to be an almost general consensus that in its present unity, Lk 10:25–37, with its culminating admonition, 'go and do likewise' (Lk 10:37b) is an example story which, unlike a parable, does not need any transposition to yield its message, since it is impossible to distinguish between image (e.g., the seed) and the reality intended (e.g., the kingdom of God). It has been shown, however, that this unity is almost certainly not original and that the present composition stems from the early Christian tradition. On the other hand, in virtue of the principle of dissimilarity (the Good Samaritan is very dissimilar from the viewpoint of ancient Judaism as well as from the creativity of the early Church), it is quite generally accepted that Lk 10:30–36 stems from the historical Jesus. It is difficult, however, to determine the precise occasion on which Jesus pronounced this story. Probably one should not try to get more specific than the 'typical' situation in which Jesus defended himself against, and challenged those who were 'scandalized' at his attitude of mercy towards so-called outcasts.

It has been argued that Lk 10:30–36 by itself was not an example story, but a parable. Originally, Jesus did not intend to give an example, but

> that the literal point of the story challenges the hearer to put together two impossible and contradictory words for the same person: Samaritan (10:33) and neighbor (10:36)... The literal point confronted the hearers with the necessity of saying the impossible and having their world turned upside down and radically questioned in its presuppositions. The metaphorical point is that *just so* does the kingdom of God break abruptly into a person's consciousness and demand the overturn of prior values, closed options, set judgments, and established conclusions... if he can accept the literal level and come to say 'Good Samaritan,' then the kingdom of God has come upon him in this experience... tradition encased Lk 10:30–36 in Lk 10:25–37, and scholarly classification followed its lead in terming it an example rather than a parable; a parable of the historical Jesus was 'misinterpreted' by having its literal point taken instead of its metaphorical point and all the more easily in that the former involved a morally excellent action. But the original parabolic

point was the arrival of the kingdom upon the hearers in and through the challenge to utter the unspeakable and to admit another world which was at that very moment placing their own under radical judgment.[38]

How Jesus' listeners could infer from this story, which does not mention the kingdom of God, that this kingdom was upon them and could be experienced in the way mentioned is not immediately clear.

Some have expressed agreement with the view that 'the parable of the Good Samaritan has nothing to do with the question of neighbor'.[39] But others, reminding us that 'the parable is a *metaphor* of the kingdom of *God*', conclude that Lk 10:30–36 'is a metaphor which gives a new meaning to the responsibilities of neighborliness but is not a metaphor of the kingdom of God, and on this ground is not a parable'.[40] Therefore, 'we must go on telling one another seriously, that the Good Samaritan… is an invitation to charity'.[41]

Already for Jesus, then, the story of the Good Samaritan was essentially an example story. But while for Jesus it was a Christological, apologetic, and missionary (i.e., aimed at conversion) example story, for Luke it has become in the first place an example of what it means to love one's neighbour and what is involved in becoming neighbour to the person in need.

Reflection

Like the lawyer, we need to learn that in order to understand and fulfil the true will of God, we must transcend the point of view of our legalistic establishment. Objective standards of behaviour, with the rules as narrowly defined as possible, enable anyone to feel and look like a model of virtue. But love is the only standard, and God alone is in a position to judge. However, like the lawyer, we often look for a more 'reliable' criterion which, once established, protects us against the annoyance of bothersome neighbours and other intrusions on our privacy. Such a criterion also frees us from the nightmare of personal, independent decision-making as well as from the embarrassment of doing more than is required.

To know 'what can be required of me' is like a shell inside which one can live peacefully because everything inside it is familiar. For this purpose it is not so important whether this shell is perhaps too narrow and inconvenient — there existed at the time a large number of very inconvenient precepts! The main thing is the certainty that it gives. The effort to solve to perfection as far as possible even the last questions that remain unanswered is like striving to close even the last doors, so that nothing unusual and uncontrolled can enter. The ideal is to have everything cut and dried, though the demands that are made will be fulfilled seriously and with devotion. The law puts the world in our hands as something perfectly laid out and so basically controlled. One only has to make this control one's own, just as every pupil has to make reading and writing his own, but does not have to invent them.[42]

In all this we try to put the real-life neighbour at a distance. But the example story forces us to put ourselves in the place of the man who fell among the robbers. Put into this position, we experience the approach and passing by of the priest and the Levite, as well as the approach and compassion of the Samaritan. In being asked to make our neighbour's position our own, we find ourselves directed to ourselves, and learn what it means to love our neighbour as ourselves.

> If we are to love our neighbor *as ourselves*, then this commandment opens, as with a master-key, the lock of our self-love and snatches it away from us. Should the commandment to love our neighbor be formulated in another way than by the expression *as thyself*, which can be handled so easily and yet has the tension of all eternity, the commandment could not master our self-love so effectively. The meaning of *as thyself* cannot be twisted and turned; judging man with the insight of eternity, it penetrates the innermost part of his soul, where his egoism resides. It does not allow our egoism to make the least excuse, not to evade it in any way. What a wonderful thing! One might have made longer penetrating speeches about the way man should love his neighbor, but again and again our egoism would have managed to produce excuses and evasions, because the matter would not have been completely exhausted, a certain aspect would have been passed over, a point would not have been described precisely enough or would not have been sufficiently binding in expression. This *as thyself* however — truly, no wrestler could clasp his opponent more firmly or inextricably than this commandment clasps our egoism.[43]

It should not be overlooked that it was their religion which permitted the priest and the Levite, two representatives of organized religion, to get around the half-dead man along the road. As such they are just one example of the way in which religion in any place or time may evade its responsibility for social justice. But the way in which religion and temple are most of the time self-evidently identified is shattered. Instead of leading to the Holy of Holies, the story brings us to the anonymous person lying half-dead along the road. And against the background of the Bible as a whole it should be forcefully stated that passing by the half-dead man on the other side is the same as passing by the God who is on the side of the victims of injustice and oppression.[44] Indeed, in the context of Luke-Acts, in which both the central part of Jesus' ministry (Lk 9:51 – 19:44) and the Christian life (Acts 9:2; 18:25, 26; 19:9, 23; 22:4; 24:14, 22) are described as a *way* or road, more is at stake than literally passing by a victim on the road. The road is everyday life, and indifference towards victims of injustice and oppression is the manifestation of a real godlessness, whether among the adherents of religion or the irreligious.

On the other hand, it should also be seen that

> This story is not about Jews and Samaritans as classes... that the parable does not view people in categories. In practical terms, that also suggests that anyone who is truly compassionate will not respond to others in terms of social or racial classes. Nor is it possible to excuse failure to act with compassion on the grounds that the victim is an enemy, or not of a particular sex, racial or ethnic group. Many of our solutions to such problems of injustice and inequality are unable to avoid intensifying the symbols and boundaries that divide groups of people. But those very divisions can have a backlash in that they make it more difficult for individuals to cross the boundaries and recognize people of the other groups as 'non-enemies,' as objects of the same compassion and generosity that we might show to members of our own families.[45]

> The parable of the Good Samaritan is timeless. Substitute occupations, nationalities, and races for modern equivalents, and nothing has changed since the day Jesus taught the parable. Therefore, the parable is not a story of someone who did a good deed as if he were a member of the Boy Scouts. It is an indictment against anyone who has raised protective barriers in order to live a sheltered life.[46]

> In a way, the parable stands as a timeless example of love in action, and of the command to love one's enemies. Perhaps Luke had no one group in mind. Yet is is not too much to hear a word directed to possessors. The parable claims that love is not words, but deeds. And these deeds involve risks, sacrifices, and

sharing of one's possessions. Any well-off reader cannot avoid the implication with regard to personal wealth... In fact, Luke goes so far as to say that it finally comes down to a matter of life or death to the potential 'good neighbor'. The ringing command of Jesus, twice echoed in the narrative, will not let the reader go: 'Go and do likewise'.[47]

It should be added, however, that the appeal to generous love can be grossly abused. For people in power and class groups this appeal is a proved means of domination. Unfortunately during almost two thousand years of its history the Church has hardly reacted against highly questionable appeals to love. Again and again, and in the name of love, humble patience has been required from people suffering injustice and inhuman situations. Down to the present day, the love command is used with an underlying sense of surrender. Hunger, suffering and oppression are justified by this understanding of love. But does Jesus' demand of love mean a capitulation to injustice? Such misunderstanding of the command of love has made many a Christian unfit for the struggle against injustice and, therefore, for the building of a kingdom of peace and justice.

7 The rich fool
(Lk 12:13–21)

The general context in Luke

At the beginning of Lk 12 the scene changes. After the meal at the house of the Pharisee, during which Jesus strongly attacked the Pharisees and lawyers (Lk 11:37–44), he is now with a gathering of 'many thousands of the multitude', but addresses 'his disciples first' (Lk 12:1). Lk 12:2–12 is an appeal not to fear the hostility of men, probably written with the martyrs of the early Church in view. In Lk 12:13 an incident occurs which provides the opportunity for a series of instructions on earthly goods. First comes a warning against 'covetousness' or greed (Lk 12:15, 21). This negative example is again, for the benefit of the disciples (cf. Lk 12:22), followed by an instruction on anxiety concerning what is necessary for life. This anxiety must give way to a total confidence in God: God can see to it that the disciples do not lack anything (Lk 12:22–32). Lk 12:33–34 form the conclusion of the section begun at Lk 12:13: an appeal to sell one's possessions and give alms in order to have an unfailing treasure in heaven. Lk 12:35 then takes up a new theme: vigilance (Lk 12:35–48).

The unity of Lk 12:13–34 in Luke's redaction is particularly due to the fact that he concludes the example story with a statement (Lk 12:21) which summarily anticipates the conclusion of the whole section (Lk 12:33–34). Instead of storing up riches for oneself (Lk 12:21), through greed (Lk 12:15), the disciples are urged to become 'rich toward God' (Lk 12:21), by distributing their possessions (Lk 12:33). The explanation of the story of the rich fool on the level of the Lucan redaction will have to take into account the totality of the section to which it belongs (Lk 12:13–34).[48] The whole section provides an extended instruction on the proper and improper attitude towards wealth.

The texts

The parable, without its dialogue setting, is also found in the *Gospel of Thomas* 63. We therefore give here the text of the parable proper, Lk 12:16b–20, and its parallel in *Thomas*.

Luke 12:16b–20	Thomas 63
The land of a rich man brought forth plentifully; and he thought to himself, 'What shall I do, for I have nowhere to store my crops?'	There was a rich man who had much money.
And he said, 'I will do this: I will pull down my barns, and build larger ones; and there I will store all my grain and my goods. And I will say to my soul, Soul, you have ample goods laid up for many years; take your ease, eat, drink, be merry.'	He said, 'I shall put my money to use so that I may sow, reap, plant, and fill my storehouse with produce, with the result that I shall lack nothing.' Such were his intentions.
But God said to him, 'Fool! This night your soul is required of you; and the things you have prepared, whose will they be?'	And that night he died.
So is he who lays up treasure for himself, and is not rich toward God.	Let him who has ears hear.

Analysis of the text

> **Verse 13:** One of the multitude said to him, 'Teacher, bid my brother divide the inheritance with me.'

The 'multitude' mentioned in this verse is the same as that found in Lk 12:1. But the connection with Lk 12:1 (and 12:2–12) is most probably to be attributed to Lucan redaction. Lk 12:13–21 is indeed a self-contained unit which has been secondarily fitted between two Q passages (Lk 12:2–12/Mt 10:26–33; 12:32 and Lk 12:22–34/Mt 6:25–33; 6:19–21).

For the sake of continuity the person who appeals to Jesus is described as 'one of the multitude'. It has also been suggested that the expression 'one of the multitude said' refers to public opinion, i.e., how the man in the street thinks and acts. Hence the request would represent the attitude of the multitude as a whole.

The Greek word *didaskalos*, 'teacher', in Luke can be traced to the Hebrew 'rabbi'. There is nothing unusual about this man bringing a 'legal question' before a 'teacher', since rabbis had not only religious but also juridical authority. Most probably the text deals with the younger of two brothers who insists that his elder brother give him his share of the inheritance. The elder brother would rather keep the inheritance undivided, as is mentioned with approval in Ps 133(132):1, 'Behold, how good and pleasant it is when brothers dwell in unity'. In this particular case, however, the younger brother wanted to have his share of the inheritance and to be independent. Therefore, he requests Jesus to pronounce a decision against his brother.

Verse 14: But he said to him, 'Man, who made me a judge or divider over you?'

Jesus' reply is in the form of a (rhetorical) question, as is often the case in controversies. His words, which have a tone of disapproval, are reminiscent of Ex 2:14, 'Who made you a prince and a judge over us?' (cf. Acts 7:27). The address 'Man' often expresses the desire to remain uninvolved in a matter (cf. Lk 22:58, 60; Rom 2:1; 9:20). 'Divider' does not refer to a different function from that of 'judge'; rather, in cases like this the judge was expected to act as a 'divider', i.e., to decide on and to mark out a division of property. It has been pointed out that the Greek word *meristēs*, 'divider', which occurs only here in biblical Greek, is close to *mesitēs*, 'reconciler'. The *Gospel of Thomas* (see below) places even greater emphasis on Jesus' rejection of the role of divider.

Jesus turns down the request by implying that nobody 'appointed' (*kathistēmi*) him to such an office, but that he has a more important mission to fulfil: he has been appointed (by the Father) to proclaim the kingdom. Jesus' refusal to get involved in this inheritance case was retained in the early Christian tradition because it had a paradigmatic significance for his disciples: Jesus did not want to get mixed up in the disputes of the 'haves' about inheritances, etc., and neither should his disciples — especially the leaders of the communities.

Indeed, while the parable of the rich fool is addressed to the multitudes (Lk 12:16), Jesus next addresses himself to the disciples (Lk 12:22), and since the term 'disciples' still remains somewhat ambivalent, it is further elucidated by the phrase 'little flock' (Lk 12:32). And this is again underlined by Peter's question, 'Lord, are you telling this parable for us or for all?' (Lk 12:41). That Luke intends this especially for the apostles (and their 'successors'!) is clear from Jesus' reply, 'who then is the faithful and wise steward (*oikonomos*; Mt 24:45 has *doulos*, 'servant'), whom his master will set over his household...?' (Lk 12:42). Luke uses here the word *oikonomos* which Paul uses specifically for Church leaders (cf. I Cor 4:1–2; Tit 1:7). While this applies in the first place to the theme of watchfulness and faithfulness (Lk 12:35–46), it may also be applied to the rest of Lk 12.

Verse 15: And he said to them, 'Take heed, and beware of all covetousness; for a man's life does not consist in the abundance of his possessions.'

The origin of this verse is much discussed. A first group of exegetes take it to be the traditional conclusion of the episode of the dissatisfied man in verses 13–14. This group is then further divided into those who believe that Lk 12:13–15 describes the occasion on which the example story was pronounced (Lk 12:16–20), and those who maintain that Lk 12:13–15 and 12:16–20 originally constituted two independent passages. A second group divide verse 15 into a first part, which is considered redactional, and a second part, which would be the original introduction to the story of the rich fool (except, maybe, for the expression 'of his possessions', which seems to be Lucan). Finally, the majority of exegetes believe that the verse has been inserted here by Luke. This third group is then again divided into two: some believe that Luke has completely composed the verse, while others think that he used a pre-existent saying. The redactional connections between the beginning of verse 15 and the beginning of verse 16 do not favour the hypothesis of a traditional link between verse 15 and its context. It is difficult to accept that in its present *formulation* verse 15 is older than the Lucan redaction. At any rate, the present *place* of verse 15 is certainly to be attributed to Luke.

We should conclude, therefore, that Lk 12:13–14 was originally an independent piece of tradition, which is in fact found in the *Gospel of Thomas* 72 without verse 15: 'A man said to him, "Tell my brothers to divide my father's possessions with me." He said to him, "O man, who has made me a divider?" He turned to his disciples and said to them, "I am not a divider, am I?"'

Unlike verse 14, which was addressed to the lone petitioner, verse 15 is directed towards 'them', i.e., the multitude. In its present context it reveals the roots of the previously mentioned dispute concerning an inheritance: 'beware of all covetousness!' The classical Greek expression *phulassesthe apo*, 'beware of', which in the New Testament is found only here and in a similar form in I John 5:21 (a warning against idols), is stronger than the more common *prosechete apo* ('beware of'; cf. e.g., Lk 12:1; 20:46). Combined with 'take heed' (*horate*), it expresses a forcible warning against greediness. 'All covetousness' means 'every kind of covetousness' (compare Lk 4:13).

The theme of *pleonexia*, 'covetousness, greediness', occupies an important place in early Christian paraenesis (Mk 7:22: Rom 1:29;

II Cor 9:5; Eph 4:19; 5:3; Col 3:5, '...covetousness, which is idolatry'; II Pet 2:3, 14), and therefore the present verse may be taken to express community interpretation. This may explain the rather muddled state of the text, especially due to the final expression 'of his possessions' (RSV), more literally, 'out of his possessions', which disturbs the flow of the sentence and adds nothing to the thought. Luke does not seem to be composing freely at this point.

Pleonexia, in general, indicates the spirit of those who try to take advantage of their fellows, and is related to over-reaching ambition, rapacity of dishonest officials, injustice and violence. In I Thess 2:5 and II Pet 2:3 it describes the attitude of Church leaders who use their position to take advantage of the people they ought to serve (compare II Cor 9:5). In Lk 12:15 it indicates 'all active striving for the increase of material possessions as a means of security'. 'The original language carries with it the overtones of insatiable desires that make the warning even stronger. The clear implication is that the petitioner will not have his problem solved if his brother *does* grant him his portion of the inheritance.'[49] The idea certainly corresponds to one of Luke's concerns (cf. *philarguroi*, 'lovers of money', in Lk 16:14, a redactional verse).

'A man's life', i.e., a person's natural, earthly life which ends with death (cf. Lk 16:25; Acts 8:33; Lk 12:20 may include the connotation of 'eternal life'), 'does not consist in abundance' (compare Lk 21:4). From the fact that a person has abundance it does not follow that his life consists in his abundant wealth. Others would understand this clause as stating that a person's abundance does not entitle him to consider his life as one of his possessions which he can secure by means of his abundance. The first interpretation seems to be preferable.

The phrase 'of his possessions' (RSV) renders *ek tōn huparchontōn autōi*, an expression which occurs only in Luke-Acts. Lk 8:3 refers to the Galilean women who provided for Jesus and the twelve 'out of their means'. And in a summary description of the life of the Jerusalem community, Acts 4:32 states that 'no one said that any of the things he possessed was his own'. Each time the expression seems to be redactional. Moreover, *ta huparchonta*, with the genitive of possession, is found in Lk 11:21; 12:33; 14:33; 16:1; 19:8. Luke's interest in questions of possessions and renunciation of possessions was inspired by the needs of the Christian communities and pastoral necessity. Lk 12:15 may well be based on negative experience of rich and wealth-hungry people.

Verse 16: And he told them a parable, saying, 'The land of a rich man brought forth plentifully;

As in Lk 10:25–37, the example story follows after a question has been raised by an outsider. The renewed introduction, 'and he told them' (*eipen de... pros autous*, parallel to the beginning of verse 15) is redactional (compare Lk 6:39). The same should be said of the expression *anthrōpou tinos plousiou*, 'a (certain) rich man'.[50] *Anthrōpou tinos plousiou* ('of a certain rich man') is placed emphatically at the beginning of the example story. It is the introduction to the first of five passages in the Travel Narrative which deal with a rich man (Lk 12:16; 16:1; 16:19; 18:23; 19:2). Luke uses the word for the first time in his counterpart of the first beatitude: 'But woe to you that are rich' (Lk 6:24). The verb *euphorēsen*, 'brought forth plentifully', occurs only here in the Greek Bible.

> **Verses 17–18:** and he thought to himself, 'What shall I do, for I have nowhere to store my crops?' And he said, 'I will do this: I will pull down my barns, and build larger ones; and there I will store my grain and my goods.'

There now follows a long soliloquy (compare Lk 12:45; 15:17ff.; 16:3f.; 18:4f., 11, 13; 20:13), which is also often found in rabbinical parables, and is characteristic of popular story-telling. The use of this style results in calling attention to the repeated 'I' and 'my' in the man's words. In this soliloquy the rich man speaks his mind and discusses his thinking and activities (Lk 12:17–19). He poses himself the direct question how to use his ample yield (Lk 12:17), and answers it by means of his plan to build bigger barns to store his harvest (verse 18). In a direct address to his 'soul' he then expresses what he expects from his enterprise (Lk 12:19). These verses effectively expose both the life-style of the rich man and the isolation which it creates. But he does not recognize this as his real problem. 'He obviously has no one else with whom to talk... Thus we begin to get Jesus' picture of the kind of prison that wealth can build. He has the money to buy a vacuum and live in it. Life in this vacuum creates its own realities, and out of this warped perspective we hear him announce his solution.'[51]

The man's problem seems to be that he lacks big warehouses to store his grain for a long time, not just barns where it can be kept until it is threshed. The Jerusalem Bible correctly entitles the story 'on hoarding possessions'. This is confirmed by the expression 'and my goods' (Lk 12:18). 'I will do this' emphatically states his eagerness to set to work (cf. Lk 16:3f., 'What shall I do?... I have decided what to do'). The man decides to destroy whatever storage places he had and build larger ones instead.

Verse 19: 'And I will say to my soul, Soul, you have ample goods laid up for many years; take your ease, eat, drink, be merry.'

Only now do the rich man's basic outlook and main interest become clear. It is striking that the man has no conversation partner; neither God, who has a lot to say about the meaning of life, nor a fellow-man. In his self-centredness he thinks only of 'ample goods' and 'many years'. The man addresses his 'soul' (Greek *psuchē*; Hebrew *nephesh*) which in biblical language means man in his totality, the self (cf. Pss 42:6, 11; 43:5; Lk 1:46). It includes a reference to the seat of desire and satisfaction and sometimes to the principle of life. The phrase 'for many years' is usually related to 'laid up' (RSV and most other English traditions). But it can also refer to 'take your ease...'. His many goods enable him to take it easy, to 'eat, drink, be merry', for many years. The last part of verse 19 recalls Isa 22:13b, 'Let us eat and drink, for tomorrow we die' (quoted in I Cor 15:32; according to Lk 12:20 the man will die the same night!). But as a whole, verses 17–19 are even more reminiscent of Sir 11:18–19, 'There is a man who is rich through his diligence and self-denial, and this is the reward allotted to him: when he says, "I have found rest, and now I shall enjoy my goods!" he does not know how much time will pass until he leaves them to others and dies' (JB translates: 'A man grows rich by his sharpness and grabbing'; see also Ps 49:6–10, 16–20 and Jas 4:13–16).

There is also a very interesting parallel in I Enoch 97:8–10: 'Woe to you who acquire silver and gold unrighteously and say, "We have acquired riches and possessions; we have acquired everything we wanted. Now let's do what we intended, for we have collected silver; we may have many farmers in our houses; our granaries are full to the brim as with water". Yes, like water your lies shall flow away. Your riches will not last but will fly away from you, for you have acquired it all in unrighteousness. You will be handed over to a great curse'.

A striking parallel has also been noted from the *Arabian Nights*: 'A king had gathered together a vast store of gold and other treasures and built himself a great palace reaching the sky... he communed with himself saying, "Soul, you have heaped up for yourself all the good things of the world; now give yourself up to them and enjoy this wealth, these treasures in a long and happy life". Scarcely had he finished when the angel of death came for him'.

The rich man is implicitly described as planning to enjoy his possessions selfishly without giving a thought to God or to his neighbour in need. His mistake consists in having thought only of his 'soul', i.e., himself! He never looked beyond himself, just as it will become clear from the continuation that he never looked beyond this world. The Greek text suggests a word-play between *euphranou*, 'be merry', and *euphorēsen*, 'brought forth plentifully'. Into the state of self-enjoyment of this self-confessed *euphrōn* will penetrate God's judgment: *aphrōn*, 'fool'.

> **Verse 20:** But God said to him, 'Fool! This night your soul is required of you; and the things you have prepared, whose will they be?'

The soliloquy is followed by another scene in which the narration takes a radical turn with the sudden intervention of God. This is a story, and therefore it is beside the point to ask how God spoke to him. The clause 'God said to him' does not introduce direct speech which the man would have heard while thinking of his future dream life. What is meant is rather that God took his life in spite of all his precautions, and how God expresses his view on him.

The statement is certainly inspired by Ps 48:11LXX(=49:10), 'the fool (*aphrōn*) and the stupid alike must perish and leave their wealth to others'. God addresses the man as 'fool' (*aphrōn*; cf. Lk 11:40; 24:25), i.e., a man who lives without taking into account the existence of either God or fellow-man, or a practical atheist (cf. Ps 14[13]:1, 'The fool says in his heart, "There is no God"'). The folly of this man manifests itself specifically in the contrast between his plans devised to live an easy life 'for many years', and the fact that he is going to die 'this (very) night' (emphatically placed at the beginning of God's words). 'No man has the power to retain the spirit, or authority over the day of death' (Eccl 8:8). 'So here, this rich man, who thinks that his *euphoreō* (many things) will produce *euphrōn* (the good life), is in reality *aphrōn* (without mind, spirit, and emotions). His formula for the good life is sheer stupidity.'[52]

His 'soul', i.e., his life, 'is required' (*apaitousin*, literally, 'they require', a Semitic impersonal plural, equivalent to a passive 'is required', a circumlocution for divine activity), meaning that this very night God, or, according to some, 'the angel of death', requires his life. The Greek verb 'is required' is a word that is commonly used for the return of a loan.

The last part of the verse, 'and the things you have prepared, whose will they be?', reminds one of Ps 39:6, 'Surely man goes about as a shadow!... man heaps up, and knows not who will gather!', and Sir 14:15, 'Will you not leave the fruit of your labours to another, and what you acquired by toil to be divided by lot?' The man is also a 'fool' because he has not taken into account that with his death he will lose his riches. Only now does he discover that material goods are not a permanent possession. Because he concentrated exclusively on increasing his material wealth, he now has nothing which he can truly call his own. He has nothing which is not taken away by death. The parable is open-ended. The rich man's silence leaves each listener/reader to answer for him — or for herself.

> **Verse 21:** So is he who lays up treasure for himself, and is not
> rich toward God.'

This verse, which looks like a generalizing paraenetic conclusion (*houtōs*, 'so'), and provides a transition to the discourse which follows (Lk 12:22–34), did not originally belong to the example story. It is an abbreviated anticipation of a recommendation which is found in a more explicit form in Mt 6:19–20, 'Do not lay up for yourself treasures on earth..., but lay up for yourselves treasures in heaven...', which Luke brings in in his own way in Lk 12:33, 'Sell your possessions, and give alms; provide yourselves with purses that do not grow old, with a treasure in the heavens that does not fail, where no thief approaches and no moth destroys'. This means that Luke has interpreted the folly of the rich man in the light of the sentence which constitutes the conclusion of this whole section (Lk 12:33–34). He has thought only of 'laying up for himself treasures on earth' (Mt 6:19); he did not care to provide himself with 'a treasure in the heavens that does not fail' (Lk 12:33), to be 'rich toward God' (Lk 12:21), i.e., to be rich in things that matter with God. For that he should have distributed his possessions (cf. Lk 12:33). Instead of thinking only of enjoying them himself, he should have distributed them to the poor. Thus he would have secured his place before God, before whom one does not possess what one convulsively clings to, but what one has shared with others. That is the only thing death cannot take away.

Parable or example story?

Form-critical analysis reveals that Lk 12:16–21 is not an eschatological parable of judgment. Rather it is a paraenetic illustration, an example story which displays the folly of people who try to determine and secure their identity by means of wealth. Recent attempts to prove that the text was originally a parable metaphorically expressing the disruptive advent of the kingdom, while secondary alterations were responsible for its present form of an example story, are not convincing. For Jesus too this was an example story.

The story appears as a dramatic illustration of the teaching of Wisdom literature on the uselessness of riches in the face of death (cf.

Sir 11:18–19; Ps 49:6ff., etc.). The example story by itself (Lk 12:16–20) intends to show why the rich man deserves the name 'fool' (verse 20). His folly manifests itself in the contrast between his projects planned to assure himself of 'many years' of easy living and the fact that he will die 'this very night'. He who does not take death into account, and believes that he will be able to enjoy his accumulated goods in peace, is a 'fool': he forgets that he will have to abandon everything at his death.

There is no unanimity about the meaning of the story in the context of Jesus' ministry. Some see in it the expression of a general religious truth: the rich man's attitude is not only foolish, but also impious, in that he forgets his dependence on God. But others, more attentive to the actual situation in which Jesus' mission places his hearers, think that the death of the rich man is an image of the catastrophe which threatens those who do not accept the message of the kingdom.

But on the level of Luke's redaction things are certainly different. Here the rich man's folly does not so much consist in that he did not think of death as in that he did not care about what comes after death. He thought only of the immediate advantages of his wealth, and did not understand the advantage he could derive from it with a view to his happiness in the next life (cf. Lk 16:9). Luke's personal viewpoint appears in verse 21 which, irrespective of whether he composed it himself or found it elsewhere, he certainly added in this context. The warning expressed in this verse shifts the emphasis to a demand for the right use of goods: one should not use them egoistically, but try to be 'rich toward God', by sharing one's goods. It betrays a concern that well-to-do Christians might not sufficiently care for their fellow-humans. This concern may have been caused by the experience that in Christian circles too there was a tendency to accumulate riches and a corresponding reluctance to care for others.

Reflection

While at the very beginning of the story one may wonder what is wrong with this rich man, it soon appears that by means of his riches he intends to overcome, and thus to deny, his human limitations. Securing his future becomes for him a calculable factor and is only a question of rationally exploiting the possibilities at his disposal. In this perspective his possessions become the only relevant reality and his life a circular course around his own 'I'. The story shows that such existence is both ungodly and inhuman. The 'fool' forgets that he *receives* his life from day to day, from moment to moment. He ignores that he is God's creature, acts as if he were the master of his life and would therefore have complete control over it. God's intervention shows that man's goal and destiny cannot be found within himself. The man's foolishness consists in failing to recognize this. He reasons with himself because of his attitude towards goods, which he sees as things to be stored away rather than vehicles for relationship. In appearance he is able to plan for the future, but in reality he is locked up in a pathological egoism. His alienation consists in seeing and using things apart from their own meaning, as a consequence of his refusal to see the Other and the others.

Jesus did not see the original questioner's problem as a *bona fide* case of injustice, and therefore his refusal to get involved into it should not be understood as meaning that Jesus himself was not concerned with matters of justice, and that he does not want his followers to get involved in them either. It is indeed important to see that the parable deals with the *accumulation* of additional goods by people who already have enough for their needs. Therefore, it should not be uncritically applied to situations in which people struggle for just wages (cf. Jas 5:4), or other basic human rights. The parable should not be interpreted in such a way, as if the kingdom of God did not include a commitment to justice on earth! One should take into account the whole New Testament, and especially Luke-Acts. If one does so, one will not conclude that Jesus was not interested in how the goods of this earth are shared (cf. Lk 12:21, 33; Acts 2:44–45), or that seeking eternal life can be unrelated to social justice.

> Jesus' cryptic answer warns the reader in two ways. First, with these presuppositions the desire for material things will prove insatiable. Second, the dreams of the abundant life will never be achieved through such an accumulation of surpluses. The insatiable desire for a higher standard of living is widespread in the modern world. The fond hope that LIFE will be the product of more consumption is also very much with us. With the natural resources of the world dwindling and the pressure for more possessions intensifying, some wrestling with the message of this text would seem to be imperative if we are to survive. Again we note a plural, 'he said to them.' The text is meant for all readers/listeners, not just the two brothers... For us the text relates to the very important question of excess profits in a capitalistic society and surplus theories in Marxism... To explore the meaning of all this for a Christian in a capitalistic society would go well beyond the intent and scope of this study. We would only observe in passing that this parable, with its presuppositions, speaks clearly to crucial questions of our own day.[53]

The story can have a broader application than originally intended. Firstly, Jesus warns people to avoid all forms of greed. It could be the greed of a government trying to sell surpluses of grain or rice to the highest bidders while knowing that some poor nations cannot survive. It could be the greed of a corporation piling up oil profits. It could be the greed of people eating so well and so wastefully, knowing that millions starve. Secondly, the people who demand today to be given a share in the inheritance are those who mine tin in Bolivia, diamond and coal in South Africa, those who harvest coffee in Brazil and sugar cane in the Philippines. Their inheritance is the wealth of the earth and the work of their hands. They know now that their poverty is not 'fate', and their protests are like the rumblings of a violent storm. It is clear to whom this piled-up wealth will ultimately go.

8 The wedding feast/great banquet
(Mt 22:1–14; Lk 14:15–24)

The texts

Matthew 22:1–14

(1) And again Jesus spoke to them in parables, saying, (2) 'The kingdom of heaven may be compared to a king who gave a marriage feast for his son,

(3) and sent his servants to call those who were invited to the marriage feast; but they would not come.
(4) Again he sent other servants, saying, "Tell those who are invited, Behold, I have made ready my dinner, my oxen and my fat calves are killed, and everything is ready; come to the marriage feast."
(5) But they made light of it and went off, one to his farm, another to his business,

(6) while the rest seized his servants, treated them shamefully, and killed them.
(7) The king was angry, and he sent his troops and destroyed those murderers and burned their city.

Luke 14:15–24
(15) When one of those who sat at table with him heard this, he said to him, 'Blessed is he who shall eat bread in the kingdom of God!'

(16) But he said to him,
'A man once gave a great banquet and invited many;

(17) and at the time for the banquet he sent his servant to say to those who had been invited,

"Come, for all is now ready."
(18) But they all alike began to make excuses. The first said to him, "I have bought a field, and I must go out and see it; I pray you, have me excused." (19) And another said, "I have bought five yoke of oxen, and I go to examine them; I pray you, have me excused." (20) And another said, "I have married a wife, and therefore I cannot come." (21) So the servant came and reported this to his master.

Then the householder in anger

108

(8) Then he said to his servants, "The wedding is ready, but those invited were not worthy.

said to his servant,

"Go out quickly to the streets and lanes of the city, and bring in the poor and maimed and blind and lame." (22) And the servant said, "Sir, what you commanded has been done, and still there is room." (23) And the master said to the servant,

(9) Go therefore to the thoroughfares, and invite to the marriage feast as many as you find."

"Go out to the highways and hedges, and compel people to come in,

(10) And those servants went out into the streets and gathered all whom they found, both bad and good; so the wedding hall was filled with guests.

(11) But when the king came in to look at the guests, he saw there a man who had no wedding garment; (12) and he said to him, "Friend, how did you get in here without a wedding garment?" And he was speechless. (13) Then the king said to the attendants, "Bind him hand and foot, and cast him into the outer darkness; there men will weep and gnash their teeth."

that my house may be filled.

(14) For many are called, but few are chosen.'

(24) For I tell you, none of those men who were invited shall taste my banquet." '

Gospel of Thomas 64

Jesus said, 'A man had received visitors. And when he had prepared the dinner, he sent his servant to invite the guests. He went to the first one and said to him, "My master invites you." He said, "I have claims against some merchants. They are coming to me this evening. I must go and give them my orders. I ask to be excused from the dinner." He went to another and said to him, "My master has invited you." He said to him, "I have just bought a house and am required for the day. I shall not have any spare time." He went to another and said to him, "My master invites you." He said to him, "My friend is going to get married, and I am to prepare the banquet. I shall not be able to come. I ask to be excused from the dinner." He went to another and said to him, "My master invites you." He said to him, "I have just bought a farm, and I am on my way to collect the rent. I shall not be able to come. I ask to be excused." The servant returned and said to his master, "Those whom you invited to the dinner have asked to be excused." The master said to his servant, "Go outside to the streets and bring back those whom you happen to meet, so that they may dine." Businessmen and merchants will not enter the Places of My Father.'

Lk 14:15–24 is generally agreed to be more primitive than Mt 22:1–10, and the *Gospel of Thomas* has more affinities with Luke's parable than with Matthew's. As a whole, Luke's text seems to have preserved the character of a parable better than Matthew's, in which many allegorical elements occur. Lk 14:15–24 has been called an allegorical parable, while Mt 22:1–14 has been referred to as a historico-theological allegory. The *Gospel of Thomas* expands the invitations and excuses, since it takes the parable to be an illustration of the general truth that 'businessmen and merchants' cannot enter 'the Places of My Father'. This 'moral' understanding assumes that the parable intends to lead people to an aversion from money and possessions. The latter prevent the Gnostic from abandoning the world, and thus exclude him from the true gnosis or knowledge. Thereby the close relation between Jesus' call and the eschaton is lifted and the parable is explained as the illustration of a general truth.

General context of Lk 14:15–24

The parable of the great supper occurs in Luke within the Travel Narrative (Lk 9:51 – 19:44), as part of a table-talk in the house of a Pharisee. The opposition of Israel in its royal house (Lk 13:31–33), its capital city (Lk 13:34–35), and its ruling party (Lk 14:1ff.) forms an introduction to the meal and its conversation. Only Luke records Jesus' meals with Pharisees (Lk 7:36; 11:37; 14:1). They seem to be a setting for anti-Pharisaic speeches (Lk 7:36–50; 11:38–54; 14:2–24).

Lk 14:1–24 is a sequence of pericopes inserted in the framework of a meal, to which three references are made in the course of the account: Lk 14:8, 'when you are invited to a wedding feast'; Lk 14:12, 'when you give a dinner or a banquet'; Lk 14:15, 'eat bread in the kingdom of God'. From where does Luke derive this framework? Hebrew literature contains much information about meals, but while it clarifies the description of Lk 14, it does not plumb the depths of the secret of the internal structure of this chapter.

The section is composed of: (1) an invitation by an important Pharisee (Lk 14:1); (2) the healing of a man with dropsy, tied up with the question of the sabbath (Lk 14:2–6); (3) the 'parable' of the choice of places at table (Lk 14:7–11); (4) the 'parable' of the choice of guests (Lk 14:12–14); (5) the parable of the great supper (or of the discourteous guests, Lk 14:15–24). A change of scene indicates that in Lk 14:25 another section begins.

A single verse suffices to present a vivid picture which immediately places the reader in the context of a meal. It recalls the introduction found in Lk 7:36 and 11:37, but here the description is more precise: the master of the house is a 'ruler who belonged to the Pharisees' and the day is a sabbath. The healing of the man with dropsy may be compared with the healings of the man with the withered hand (Mt 12:9–14; Mk 3:1–6; Lk 6:6–11), and the woman with a spirit of infirmity (Lk 13:10–17). The three parables which follow (Lk 14:7–24) are successively addressed to the guests, the host, and one of the guests.

The banquet atmosphere plays an important role in the composition of Lk 14. It is constantly maintained by the appearance of relevant features: eat, guests, places, invitation, acceptance, refusal. The whole action takes place in the course of a meal. In this connection the redactional formulae have been noted: 'he said also to the man who had invited him' (verse 12), referring to the important Pharisee who invited Jesus (verse 1), and 'one of those who sat at table with him' (verse 15), who should be identified with one of the guests mentioned in verse 7, who are again the same as the people who were at the house of the ruler and watched Jesus (verse 1). The double perspective should also be noted of the meal to which Jesus was invited and the meal of which he spoke in his parables. Luke, who found parables dealing with a meal or a feast in the common tradition and his special source, redactionally placed them in the context of a meal, thus realizing a unity of time and place. He seems to have derived this idea from the Greek symposium literature.

Originally, the symposium was a gathering of cultivated people held after the evening meal. There was drinking, singing, and talking, and it was an ideal occasion for teachers to perfect the instruction of their disciples. These features gave birth to a literary genre determined by set topics, a traditional framework within whose limits each author was free to present the matter of his choice. For Luke too, the symposium genre is only a framework which he uses freely.

In Lk 14, the evangelist chooses the framework of a banquet to introduce three parables concerning a meal. To assure a perfect link of the framework with the parables, Luke regularly inserts a series of link-words in the text: verse 1, 'one *sabbath*'; — verse 3, controversy concerning the *sabbath*; — verse 8, 'when you are *invited*'; — verse 12a, 'he said to the man who had *invited* him' — verse 12b, 'when you *give* a dinner'; — verse 15, 'one of those who *sat at table* with him'; — verse 17, 'he sent his servant to say to those who had been *invited*'. The catch-word in Lk 14:7–24 is *kalein*, 'to invite', found in Lk 14:7, 8 (twice), 9, 10 (twice), 12, 13, 16, 24.

Luke also presents several of the classical characters of the symposium: the master of the house, the guests, the principal guest, and those who are not invited. Even the healing of the man with dropsy seems to fit into the symposium pattern, which very often begins with an incident which provides the occasion for the dialogue. As the principal guest Jesus pronounces a discourse on humility (Lk 14:7–11, reminiscent of Prov 25:6–7). In the symposium genre the host and the guests were of high social rank and their places were carefully assigned (cf. Lk 14:10, 'go up higher'). All these features indicate that Luke may very well have been inspired by the symposium genre for his composition of Lk 14.

The corpus of the chapter is solidly structured and gives an impression of unity, first of all because the first two parables have exactly the same structure:

Lk 14:7–11	*Lk 14:12–14*
Now he told a parable to those who were invited, when he marked how they chose the places of honour, saying to them,	He said also to the man who had invited him,
'When you are invited by any one to a marriage feast,	'When you give a dinner or a banquet,
do not sit down in a place of honour,	do not invite your friends . . .
lest a more eminent man. . .	lest they also invite you. . .
But when you are invited,	But when you give a feast,
go and sit in the lowest place. . .	invite the poor. . .
then you will be honoured. . .	and you will be blessed,
For every one who exalts himself. . .	because they cannot repay you. . .

This impression remains throughout the third parable, especially because of the linking phrase 'the poor, the maimed, the lame, the blind', found in Lk 14:13 and 21. This double procedure gives a strong internal unity to the account, Lk 14:1–24. After a meeting with the crowds in the preceding section (cf. Lk 13:22), we now enter a more polemic section, and Jesus is confronted by the sophisticated rulers who separate themselves from the people (cf. also 13:14, 17).

The orientation of the first two parables is clearly paraenetic. The parable of the great banquet has the same perspective. The first invitees are excluded from the eschatological banquet, not because they were indifferent (cf. Mt 22:5), or unworthy (cf. Mt 22:8), but because their concern with temporal affairs prevents them from accepting the invitation. They should have been prepared to give up everything, rather than let the invitation pass. The parable, then, conveys an instruction on detachment, on the option necessary at the moment of the call to the kingdom. The following section (Lk 14:25-33) confirms this interpretation by presenting the same teaching in a more explicit manner.

Analysis of Lk 14:15-24

Verse 15: When one of those who sat at table with him heard this, he said to him, 'Blessed is he who shall eat bread in the kingdom of God!'

The exclamation by 'one of those who sat at table with him', more literally 'one of those who reclined with him (on couches around the tables)', belonged most probably to the text as Luke received it from the tradition. The words of the anonymous guest take up the macarism pronounced by Jesus in the previous verses, 'But when you give a feast, invite the poor... and you will be blessed' (cf. the use of the link-word *makarios*, 'blessed', in verses 14 and 15). He describes the eschatological salvation ('the resurrection of the just') by the well-known image of the heavenly meal (cf. Isa 25:6-9, where salvation is described in terms of a great banquet given by God for *all the peoples*; Rev 19:9, 'Blessed are those who are invited to the marriage supper of the Lamb'). But Isaiah's idea that the nations would be invited to attend was muted in the Aramaic commentary, the Targum. And according to the Qumran community only the wise, the intelligent, and the perfect will gather with God: 'And then the Messiah of Israel shall come, and the chiefs of the (clans of Israel) shall sit before him, (each) in the order of his dignity, according to (his place) in their camps and marches' (1QSa 2:11). Jesus' opinion has already been expressed in Lk 13:29, 'And men will come from east and west, and from north and south, and sit at table in the kingdom of God'. Lk 13 speaks of a great ingathering and banquet. Some have refused the invitation. Many who expect to be there will be rejected, while the guests come from the four corners of the earth.

The statement of the anonymous guest relates the following parable to the specific situation of the meal in the house of the ruler (cf. the phrase *phagein arton*, literally, 'to eat bread', found in both Lk 14:1 and 15, which is a Hebraism and refers to eating a full meal).

The future tense 'shall eat', and the reference to 'the kingdom of God' indicate that the man is thinking of the final blessing. Indeed this exclamation raises the following parable to an eschatological level.

The blessedness pronounced by Jesus in Lk 14:13–14 cannot fail to provoke a reaction. The context indicates clearly that the words of the anonymous guest do not just carry the theme further, but intend to contradict Jesus' statement. Jesus' reply presupposes that the man's intervention constitutes a criticism of the preceding macarism. The objection should be understood as follows: Inviting the poor and other beggars is not the ground for repayment at the resurrection of the just! Blessed rather is he who will actually participate in the meal of the kingdom of God! To the 'Pharisees' and the 'scribes' it is beyond question who these participants will be. It is clear to them that they themselves eminently and exclusively qualify. Jesus' parable takes up the implicit claim contained in this statement. He does not confirm the man's exclamation, but answers polemically with a parable which exposes the present character of the call. All is ready; the invitation is already issued. Those who do not accept the present invitation, which issues from Jesus' message, will also fail to participate one day in the banquet of the kingdom of God.

A formal parallel for the combination of a macarism with a polemical reply is found in Lk 11:27–28, 'As he said this, a woman in the crowd raised her voice and said to him, "Blessed is the womb that bore you, and the breasts that you sucked!" But he said, "Blessed rather are those who hear the word of God and keep it!"' On the other hand, from the controversies we know the habit of giving a polemical answer in the form of a parable.

> **Verse 16–17:** But he said to him, 'A man once gave a great banquet, and invited many; (17) and at the time for the banquet he sent his servant to say to those who had been invited, "Come; for all is now ready."

'But' (*de*, correctly translated by RSV and JB, but omitted by NEB and NAB) implies that Jesus is opposing the implicit self-complacency of the speaker. Luke's parables often begin with the expression 'a certain man' (*anthrōpos tis*; cf. Lk 10:30; 12:16; 15:11; 16:1, 19). The 'great banquet' is a standard image for eschatological salvation. Luke insists that the man invited 'many', an expression which in biblical literature often designates the community of the elect (cf. Isa 53:11–12; Dan 12:10). But an allegorical interpretation is not unavoidable. The fact that the man invited many simply manifests his generosity, which will be stressed again after the refusal

by those first invited. In Matthew the host is a king who gives a
marriage feast for his son. It is more likely that this is an allegorical
expansion than that Luke omitted these features.

Luke's version of the parable seems to presuppose that,
according to the upper-class customs of the time, the invitation was
extended and accepted several days before the banquet was
scheduled. The guests were reminded at the right time by a servant
specially sent for this purpose. In Matthew the king sends a group of
servants. Some scholars have suggested that Luke reduced the
number to one to make an allegorical reference to Jesus. But, firstly,
it should be noted that the story puts no emphasis on the fact that
only one servant is sent. Moreover, nowhere in the gospels is Jesus
referred to as a (the) servant. Finally, on the supposition that we have
here an allegorical feature, it should remain coherent throughout the
parable; but this does not square with verse 24, which constitutes at
the same time the verdict of the host on the guests and the
condemnation pronounced by Jesus himself.

In the formulation of the invitation, 'Come; for all is now ready',
the phrase 'now' (*ēdē*, 'now', 'already') is to be attributed to Luke.
He adds the word several times, as can be seen especially in Lk
21:30b, 'you... know that the summer is already near' (compare Mk
13:28b; Mt 24:32b; see also Lk 19:37; 23:44). The phrase expresses
Luke's conception of saving history, characterized elsewhere by the
phrase 'today' (*sēmeron*; cf. Lk 2:11; 4:21; 5:26; 19:5, 9; 23:43). The
words of invitation, 'come; for all is now ready', correspond to the
call of Jesus, 'Repent, for the kingdom of heaven is at hand' (cf. Mt
4:17).

> **Verses 18–19:** But they all alike began to make excuses. The
> first said to him, 'I have bought a field, and I must go out and
> see it; I pray you, have me excused.' (19) And another said,
> 'I have bought five yoke of oxen, and I go to examine them; I
> pray you, have me excused.'

In Mt 22:5 the reaction of the invitees is related summarily: 'But they
made light of it and went off, one to his farm, another to his
business'. Luke, however, has three verses (Lk 14:18–20) which
describe the excuses of the invitees, and in which his redactional
activity seems extensive, in the vocabulary (e.g., the thrice-repeated
paraitomai in the sense of 'to make excuses', the only example in the
New Testament; but see Acts 25:11), as well as in the overall
structure of the whole. That 'all alike', i.e., not 'simultaneously', but
'unanimously', decline the invitation is certainly a piece of hyperbole,

and may be intended to prepare the hearers/readers for the reaction of the householder.

A series of legal justifications for the guests' excuses has been suggested; these are, however, far from convincing. The clause 'I must go and see it' affirms that the man's field is of greater importance to him than his relationship to the host. In the East where personal relationships are of unequalled importance, these words mean a break in relationship, which is only partially covered by the request to be excused. The Greek verb *dokimazō*, 'to examine', has the connotation of seeing if they will perform as a pair of yoked oxen or not.

Some have noted a procedure of gradation, analogous to that which Luke has achieved in Lk 20:10–12, describing the ill-treatments inflicted upon the servants of the owner of the vineyard. The verses are also said to be an example of Luke's literary art which enlivens the account by making his characters talk.

Luke's interest in the invitees' excuses may make one wonder whether Luke may not be using this parable to denounce what in the Church of his time constituted the most serious obstacles to conversion. The first two excuses are obviously offered by rich people, and Luke seems to think more specifically of large landowners (cf. the *Gospel of Thomas*, which speaks of somebody who had bought a village!). The first has bought (another) field. The second has bought five yoke of oxen, i.e., ten oxen, which could easily plough 45 hectares of land. Since this is apparently not the first time that he has bought oxen, we are certainly dealing with a large landowner. Luke develops the story in line with concerns with which his whole gospel is occupied, namely, wealth as the great obstacle for entrance into the kingdom, and poverty as a favourable condition (cf. verse 21).

There have been attempts to make the parable look more probable by supposing that the excuses presented in verses 18–19 are not really refusals, but concern a late arrival for the banquet. The invitees would have urgent matters to attend to, which would make it impossible for them to come immediately, but which would occupy them only until evening. But it has rightly been stated that the expressions used do not allow for the toned-down meaning which it was wished to attribute to them.

Verse 20: And another said, 'I have married a wife, and therefore I cannot come.'

While a number of arguments given for the later addition of Lk 14:20 to the original parable may not be very convincing, it is true that the addition of the third excuse is easily understood in the paraenetic use of the parable: the concern for possessions is not the only motive which prevents a positive response to God's invitation. Moreover, the addition creates an improbability in the account: a purchase or acquisition may create an unforeseen obstacle for someone who counted on attending a banquet; but this is not the case for an invitee who is getting married and should know in advance the day of the ceremony.

The third and last excuse, while causing some difficulties, seems to confirm that Luke was concerned with contemporary Church matters. It is improbable on the level of the parable story, but it expresses a concern which Luke also expresses elsewhere (cf. Lk 14:26, where Luke is the only one to have 'and wife'; compare Mt 10:37; and Lk 18:29 where Luke again adds 'or wife'; compare Mk 10:29; Mt 19:29). The motive which prevents the third invitee from accepting the invitation corresponds to the demand Luke formulates in Lk 14:26 and 18:29, and which is found only in his gospel.

It has repeatedly been suggested that these elaborate excuses were modelled on Deut 20:5–7, 'What man is there that has built a new house... let him go back to his house... And what man is there that has planted a vineyard... let him go... And what man is there that has betrothed a wife... let him go back to his house...'. Some even maintain that the last excuse refers more precisely to Deut 24:5. But this is not the case, for the situations are very different. Luke's emphasis is on the involving quality of the excuses. Those invited are so entangled by their acquisitions that they are deaf to the call. Some scholars insist that the grounds for excuses are quite understandable and not at all forced or threadbare, while others insist that they are ludicrous and of very transparent nature.

> **Verse 21:** So the servant came and reported this to his master. Then the householder in anger said to the servant, 'Go out quickly to the streets and lanes of the city, and bring in the poor and maimed and blind and lame.'

The servant reports the refusals and the master breaks out in anger against the invitees. Matthew's expansion of this motif into an account of a punitive action against the guests' city is in accord with his royal setting and is to be attributed to Matthew's redaction.

In Luke the mention of the anger of the host has no function of its own. The emphasis of the text is on the positive action of the master. The people who are destined to take the place of those first invited are divided into two groups. In the present verse the servant is ordered to 'go out quickly to the streets and lanes of the city, and bring in the poor and maimed and blind and lame'. These four groups of invitees allude to the eschatological proclamation of Isa 29:18, 19; 35:5, 6; 61:1. The word 'maimed' (*anapēros*) occurs only in Lk 14:13, 21 in the New Testament. This list of people corresponds exactly to those mentioned in Jesus' recommendation to his host (Lk 14:13). The process of assimilation is undeniable. But verse 13 may have been influenced by verse 21 as well as the reverse; and it has to be admitted that the mention of the 'maimed and blind and lame' fits well in verse 21: the beneficiaries of the eschatological banquet are precisely those whom Judaism excluded from the temple and its service (Lev 21:18–20, 'For no one who has a blemish shall draw near, a man blind or lame...', and II Sam 5:8, 'Therefore it is said, "The blind and the lame shall not come into the house"'). At the eschatological banquet those who were first invited will be replaced by those whom they considered excluded. By including the 'poor' in this list, Luke suggests that the rulers considered them as 'undesirables', on the same footing as the 'maimed and blind and lame'. Although, according to Tobit 2:2, the invitation of a poor man to a meal is considered a good work, a hall full of poor, maimed, blind, and lame must have constituted a challenge to Jesus' audience. These categories stood for the outcasts of Israel who were attracted to and welcomed by Jesus.

> **Verses 22–23:** And the servant said, 'Sir, what you have commanded has been done, and still there is room.' (23) And the master said to the servant, 'Go out to the highways and hedges, and compel people to come in, that my house may be filled.

Suddenly the householder has become the *kurios* (RSV: 'Sir... master'). It should be clear, then, who pronounces the 'for I tell you' in the next verse. Since there is still room, the servant is ordered to 'go out to the highways and hedges' to look for more guests. The majority of interpreters believe that the addition of this second group proceeds from an allegorical intention: Luke would have intended to speak of the calling of the Gentiles. In this perspective it is almost unavoidable to consider these verses as a secondary addition. The following considerations are advanced to support this view. All of them, however, face certain objections.

Firstly, these verses are without parallel in Matthew and the *Gospel of Thomas*. But it could be replied that Luke uses two characteristic expressions which are also found in Matthew. The servant must 'go out to the highways', as Matthew reports that the servants are to 'go to the thoroughfares'; and the master insists that the house be filled, just as in Mt 22:10 it is said that 'the wedding hall was filled with guests'. The first feature is also found in the *Gospel of Thomas*. Moreover, one can speak of Lucan additions only if one is sure that Matthew did not abbreviate the story at this point.

Secondly, it has been said that these verses are superfluous from the point of view of the parable account. But this remark seems to overlook the importance of repetition in the presentation of the parables. The doubling of the servant's mission intends to emphasize the great number of guests and the abundant result which the host envisages. He sends the servant a second time so that his house may be filled.

Thirdly, it has been argued that the probability of the story is not served by this additional mission of the servant sent to the countryside at the moment that the banquet is ready and the hall is already partly filled with guests. But this kind of improbability does not exceed the limits which may be expected in a parable which is at the service of a religious teaching.

Fourthly, the first mission of the servant is motivated by the anger of the host (verse 21); another motive justifies the second mission: the house should be filled (verse 23). Isn't this duality of motives an indication of the adventitious character of the second mission? Suffice it to say that the two motives are also found in Matthew (Mt 22:7 and 10).

Finally, it is said that the intention which prompted the addition can easily be understood: Luke wanted to take into account the situation of the Church at the time of the composition of the gospel, which was characterized by the preaching of the gospel to the Gentiles. But this explanation raises certain difficulties. First, and in general, Luke shows little inclination to an allegorical interpretation of the parables. Secondly, if Luke intended to make an allegorical allusion to the call of the Gentiles, he would be expected to include some indications to this effect in his text.

Summing up, we could say that

> ...Luke may have *understood* the double invitation in an allegorical sense. It accords well with his understanding of the history of salvation. But there is an important difference between allegorical interpretation and the creation of allegory. It is the latter that must be demonstrated in the case of Luke's third invitation, and it is just this demonstration that falls short. The question whether a third invitation, as in Luke's version, belongs to the original form of the parable does not, perhaps, admit of final resolution.[54]

Therefore, that Luke added verses 22–23 is not an inescapable
conclusion. They may very well have stood in the pre-Lucan source to
emphasize the great number of people the host wanted to fill his
house. Luke, then, may have interpreted this allegorically as
referring to the Gentiles. Some scholars, however, exclude any
allegorical interpretation even on the level of the Lucan redaction,
and stress Luke's paraenetic concern, which appears from the context
of the parable and from the emphasis Luke places on the excuses of
the invitees. The parable is then a warning against the danger
incurred by not answering God's call because of concern with worldly
matters. This may very well be in Luke's mind, but does not
necessarily exclude other intentions as, e.g., to present an illustration
of the recommendations mentioned in Lk 14:12–13. In this light,
Luke seems to be concerned with the have-nots 'in and outside the
city'.

The servant must 'compel' (*anankason*) the beggars to enter, just
as Lot 'urged' the angels to receive his hospitality (Gen 19:3), as the
disciples at Emmaus 'constrained' Jesus to stay with them (Lk 24:29),
and as Lydia 'prevailed' upon Paul and his companions to stay with
her (Acts 16:15). The clause perfectly expresses Luke's particular
sensitivity to everything that relates to the duties of hospitality.
Needless to say, Luke is not thinking here of using force. But he
knows that when one invites somebody one must show that one
would really like him to accept the invitation. By insisting, one must
make it possible for the other person to accept the invitation without
offending the rules of courtesy. 'Compel them' constitutes a marked
intensification compared with 'bring them' (Lk 14:21).

It has been suggested that, because the order addressed to the
servant to 'go out to the highways and hedges'... so 'that my house
may be filled' concludes the parable proper, the reader should realize
that this order has not yet been fully executed.

> **Verse 24:** For I tell you, none of those men who were invited
> shall taste my banquet.'

It has been convincingly argued that this verse is the natural
conclusion of the parable and should be considered as original.
Originally, the words will have been spoken by the host. The
expression 'for I tell you' may be a redactional retouch. The plural in
'for I tell *you*' does not agree with the previous statement of the host,
who in verse 23 is addressing one servant. As in Lk 11:8; 15:7, 10;
16:9; 18:8, 14; 19:26, the clause seems to be the introduction to Jesus'
final judgment. The objection that the expression '*my* banquet'
would not allow this interpretation is contradicted by Lk 22:30, 'that

you may eat and drink at *my* table in my kingdom...'. Participation in the banquet in the kingdom of God (verse 15) is participation in 'my banquet' (verse 24). Jesus' table-sharing with religious and social outcasts is already a realization and anticipation of God's rule. It has been suggested that the striking expression 'my banquet' is in line with the ecclesiastical interpretation of an eschatological concept.

General context of Mt 22:1–14

Matthew introduces the parable of the wedding feast into a Marcan setting, i.e., the passion week controversies in which occurs the parable of the wicked tenants (Mk 12:1–12). The theme of conflict with the religious leaders, their rejection of the kingdom and consequent exclusion from it, which is already clearly present in Mark, is further developed by Matthew by means of the two parables of the two sons and the wedding feast, which he inserts into this context.

Indeed, the three parables of the two sons (Mt 21:28–32), the wicked tenants (Mt 21:33–46), and the wedding feast (Mt 22:1–14) seem to have served Matthew as illustrations of one of the most important theological motifs of the gospel, the judgment of Israel. The parable of the wicked tenants is apparently the core around which the other materials have been arranged and to which their form has been to some extent assimilated, giving them a polemical uniformity in their present written form.

Not only these three parables, but also the preceding pericope on the question about authority (Mt 21:23–27) are interrelated. The phrase 'did you not believe him' (Mt 21:25) is literally repeated in the parable of the two sons, 'you did not... believe him' (Mt 21:32, contrast Lk 7:29–30). In this same pericope occurs the (for Matthew) very unusual 'kingdom of *God*' (Mt 21:31), which is unexpectedly repeated in the parable of the wicked tenants, in a verse which is unanimously considered redactional (Mt 21:43, 'the kingdom of God...'). Furthermore, both parables deal with a 'vineyard' (Mt 21:28 and 33). And the second and the third parable are related to each other by means of the two successive phrases, 'he sent his servants' and 'again he sent other servants', found in Mt 21:34, 36 and Mt 22:3, 4, and by the fact that the punishment announced in Mt 21:41 is executed in Mt 22:6–7. This remarkable series of links moulds these pericopes into a strong unity, which seems to suggest that they form a kind of programme for Matthew.

The entry into Jerusalem (Mt 21:1–9), the cleansing of the temple (Mt 21:12–13), and the conversation about faith (Mt 21:20–22) have indicated that the way of Jesus' 'little ones' will separate itself from that of Israel (cf. Mt 21:15). But the case is not yet decided. Even at the end of the 'hearing', Mt 21:23–27, the question about Jesus' authority remains open. But at the end of the parable of the two sons stands the pronouncement, 'tax collectors and harlots believed him;... you did not' (Mt 21:32). In the parable of the wicked tenants follows the meting out of the punishment, 'He will put those wretches to a miserable death...' (Mt 21:41), and the parable of the wedding feast relates the execution of the judgment, 'the king was angry, and he sent his troops and destroyed those murderers and burned their city' (Mt 22:7).

All this had already happened in Matthew's time, but it was not the end, and the evangelist adds four verses to the parable of the wedding feast (Mt 22:11–14), which he addresses to his readers. The final words, 'for many are called, but few are chosen', no longer refer to Israel, but to Jesus' disciples who are warned that what happened to Israel (cf. Mt 21:23 – 22:10) could also happen to them.

This is confirmed by the arrangement of the materials in Mt 22:15 – 25:46. The drama of Israel is presented once more, this time no longer in parables, but in more direct form. The controversies with the leaders of Israel end with the open question who is the 'lord' of David (Mt 22:15–46). In a long series of woes, the following chapter declares the Pharisees and scribes guillty (Mt 23:1–32), and metes out the punishment (Mt 23:33–36). Jesus' departure from the temple and the prophecy of its destruction (Mt 24:1–2) then introduces the eschatological discourse (Mt 24:3 – 25:46), in which we read that the disciple who proves to be an unfaithful servant will be put with the hypocrites, who were so sharply accused in Mt 23 (Mt 24:51). So we have once more the sequence: hearing, pronouncement of guilt, announcement of the sentence and the execution pronounced against Israel, but understood by Matthew as a warning to Jesus' community, who could fare like the 'hypocrites'. It is to them that the thrice-repeated 'weeping and gnashing of teeth' (Mt 22:13; 24:51; 25:30; compare 13:42) is addressed. The section, however, does not end with a condemnation of the unmerciful, but with a reference to those who will go into eternal life (Mt 25:46).

Thus the whole section, Mt 21:1 – 25:46, is ultimately an invitation to life with Jesus, to the wedding feast, to responsible life in the house of the Master, to the kingdom which is prepared for the readers of the gospel 'from the foundation of the world' (Mt 25:34). Thus at the beginning of this section the children in the temple with their acclamations (Mt 21:15) symbolize the 'little ones' or 'the least of my brethren', who are invited to the meal, and with whom Christ will always be, 'to the close of the age' (Mt 28:20).[55]

Analysis of Mt 22:1–14

Verses 1–2a: And again Jesus spoke to them in parables, saying, (2a) 'The kingdom of heaven may be compared to...

These verses connect the parable to the preceding context. The expression 'again... in parables' may mean 'by way of a parable', and may refer in the first place to what Jesus is going to say. But it is also possible that it implies a reference to the two preceding parables of the two sons and the wicked tenants (Mt 21:28–32; 21:33–46). The present parable constitutes the third illustration of the way the Jewish leaders behave toward Jesus' message. Unlike Luke (cf. Lk 14:16; but see 14:15), Matthew introduces the parable by a formula which identifies it explicitly as a parable of the kingdom. 'The kingdom of heaven', a typically Matthean expression, means the irruption, in the person of Jesus, of an altogether new situation for people and for the world. As in Mt 13:24 and 18:23, the kingdom of heaven is here too compared with the whole action which follows (not just with a king).

Verses 2b–3:... a king who gave a marriage feast for his son, (3) and sent his servants to call those who were invited to the marriage feast; but they would not come.

Matthew, or the pre-Matthean tradition, has made the parable into a 'royal' parable. Literally, Matthew writes 'man king' (*anthrōpos basileus*). The same expression is found in Mt 18:23, and similar combinations of *anthrōpos* with another noun are found in Mt 13:52; 20:1 (*anthrōpos oikodespotēs*, 'householder'). It has recently been argued that Jesus himself did not speak of God as a king in his parables.[56] Likewise there are a number of rabbinical parables which only at a later stage in their tradition came to be handed on as 'royal' parables. He who at a later stage of the story sends out an expedition against a city cannot be a simple householder as in Luke. But what about the 'marriage feast' instead of the 'great banquet' of Luke? It is possible that we have here just two translations of the same Aramaic word (*misteh*), but this does not yet explain why Matthew chose *this* translation. Down to Mt 22:10, the parable does not call for a marriage feast, but from that verse on Matthew speaks of a king inspecting guests, and finding one without a *wedding* garment. Since this king inspects wedding guests, Matthew needed a wedding feast. But why a wedding feast 'for his son'? From Hosea onwards the wedding symbolism used for the covenant bond between God and his people played a very important role in the Bible, and it continued to do so in the New Testament in a messianic perspective. The figure of the son apparently derives from the preceding parable of the wicked tenants (cf. Mt 21:37).

Here and in verse 4 Matthew has a group of servants, thus taking up again the presentation he adopted in the preceding parable (Mt 21:34–36), where he has also groups of servants, unlike Mk 12:2–5a and Lk 20:10–12, which mention three missions entrusted to a single servant. The multiplicity of servants corresponds to the fact that the host is a king. Since Matthew transformed the story into a 'royal' parable, it is probable that he is also responsible for the multiplicity of servants.[57] It is quite generally accepted that for Matthew these servants refer to the prophets of the Old Testament, although some have thought of the pre-Easter mission of the disciples. 'Those who were invited (*tous keklēmenous*) to the marriage feast' reject the invitation.

> **Verse 4:** Again he sent other servants, saying, 'Tell those who are invited, Behold, I have made ready my dinner, my oxen and my fat calves are killed, and everything is ready; come to the marriage feast.'

This verse is quite generally considered a Matthean redactional redoubling of the invitation. Notwithstanding the first refusal, another invitation is transmitted by a second group of servants. Although it is not generally accepted, it is probable that for Matthew this second group of servants refers to the apostles and early Christian missionaries. This invitation is more urgent and more detailed. Introduced by 'behold', they must tell the invitees (*tois keklēmenois*): I have made ready my dinner. The perfect tense *hētoimaka* indicates that the preparations are finished: everything is ready. Oxen and fatted calves have been slaughtered for the royal wedding. And then it is said a second time that everything is ready. And again the invitation is formulated: come (*deute*, a typically Matthean term; cf. Mt 4:19; 11:28; 21:38). An Old Testament parallel is found in Wisdom's invitation: 'She has slaughtered her beasts, she has mixed her wine, she has also set her table. She has sent out her maids... "Come, eat of my bread and drink of my wine I have mixed..."' (Prov 9:2–5).

> **Verse 5:** But they made light of it and went off, one to his farm, another to his business,

Following the more urgent and more detailed description of the invitation in verse 4, this verse suggests an even flatter refusal. It is no longer just a matter of not wanting to come (verse 3), but of completely ignoring the invitation. The invitees pay no attention to the servants. They have more important things to do. Some scholars consider this verse to be a summary of the excuses found in Lk 14:18–19, which would allow Matthew to place the emphasis on verse 6.

> **Verses 6–7:** while the rest seized his servants, treated them shamefully, and killed them. (7) The king was angry, and he sent his troops and destroyed those murderers and burned their city.

'While the rest...' is a redactional link. Verse 6, which does not link well with the preceding verses and affects the probability of the account, apparently echoes what the preceding parable of the wicked tenants said of the maltreatments inflicted on the servants (Mt 21:35; cf. Mt 10:17f.). Verse 7 which, except for the mention of anger, is also Matthean, mentions the punishment of the murderers, whom the king 'destroyed' (using the verb *apollumi*, as in Mt 21:41). Verses 6–7, which reflect the well-known prophet-murder motif and cause so much difficulty in the parable, seem therefore to be a kind of repetition of features belonging to the parable of the wicked tenants. Matthew seems to have adapted the parable to the context into which he inserted it.

These verses constitute the most striking difference from Luke's text. They are obviously forcibly inserted into the text, since the transition from Lk 14:21a, 'so the servant came and reported this to his master', to Lk 14:21b, 'then the householder in anger said to his servant, "Go out quickly to the streets and lanes of the city..."' is quite smooth. Moreover, the transition from Mt 22:5 to 22:8 would have been smooth and without a hitch. In fact, verses 6–7 have little logical connection with the parable.

The king gets angry (cf. Mt 18:24) and for a while seems to forget that the dinner was ready (verse 4). He wages a war (cf. Isa 5:24–30), then sends out another group of servants to invite other people to the same meal, which presumably had been on the table all the time! This feature must have been very important to Matthew, otherwise he would not have allowed such a measure of improbability by inserting it.

It is quite generally accepted that Matthew is referring to the destruction of Jerusalem in A.D. 70, as he also does in Mt 21:41 in the preceding parable. This destruction had made an enormous impression, not only on the Jews, but also on the Jewish Christians who had also looked upon Jerusalem as their holy city. Matthew interprets the destruction of Jerusalem (Mt 22:7) as a fulfilment of Jesus' prophecy in Mt 21:41. The opinion that we have here, not a historical reminiscence, but only a well-known Oriental literary *topos* or commonplace has been widely rejected.

> **Verses 8–10:** Then he said to his servants. 'The wedding is ready, but those invited were not worthy. (9) Go therefore to the thoroughfares, and invite to the marriage feast as many as you find.' (10) And those servants went out into the streets and gathered all whom they found, both bad and good; so the wedding hall was filled with guests.

The story, interrupted by the interlude of the punitive action, resumes the theme of the wedding feast. 'The wedding is ready' summarizes what precedes, while the second part of verse 8, 'those invited were not worthy', is a first preparation for Mt 22:11–14. The idea that one must be 'worthy' is typically Matthean (compare, e.g., Mt 10:11, 13, 37, 38 with their parallels). Since the first invitees were not worthy, the servants have to 'go to the thoroughfares'. The expression *diexodous tōn hodōn* refers to the place where the streets of the city turn into country roads, and is probably an allusion to the Gentile mission. The householder insists that they should 'invite to the wedding anyone you can come upon' (NAB).

Verse 10, which is both a closing and an introductory verse, then stresses again that 'they gathered all whom they found, both bad and good'. This antithetic phrase, which intends to express a totality, may emphasize the mercy of God who loves all people (Mt 5:45) and the indiscriminate character of the call into the kingdom. But, like the parables of the weeds (Mt 13:24–30) and the net (Mt 13:47–50; cf. verse 47, they 'gathered fish of every kind'; verse 48, 'good... and... bad'), it also gives a picture of the real condition of the Christian community in Matthew's time. Just as in the case of the fish gathered in the net, a selection will take place; among those who have been gathered are some who are unworthy and who will have to be removed. It does not suffice to have entered the banquet hall, which represents here the Church, to be sure of participation in the banquet of eternal blessedness. As such verse 10 serves also as a preparation for verses 11–13.

> **Verses 11–13:** But when the king came in to look at the guests, he saw there a man who had no wedding garment; (12) and he said to him, 'Friend, how did you get in here without a wedding garment?' And he was speechless. (13) Then the king said to the attendants, 'Bind him hand and

foot, and cast him into the outer darkness; there men will weep and gnash their teeth.'

While it is hard to decide whether we are dealing here with an originally independent (Jesus-)parable, the beginning of which, it has been suggested, may have been the present Mt 22:2, or with a Matthean composition on the basis of traditional material, it is clear that the combination of Mt 22:1–10 and 11–14 should be attributed to Matthew. The transition between the two parables is certainly Matthean. Verses 11–13 have no organic connection with the previous verses, not only because verse 10 marks the denouement of what happens in verses 3–9, but also because the key concept of these verses, the wedding garment, appears abruptly and is an entirely new element. The change of the expression *douloi* ('servants', literally, 'slaves', Mt 22:3, 4, 6, 8, 10) into *diakonoi* further reinforces the independent character of verses 11–13. Anyone who reads these verses at face value is bound to ask how the king who ordered these people to be picked up from the streets could expect them to wear the appropriate garment. (Some say that the 'wedding garment' means here clean, preferably white clothes.) Moreover, the severe punishment inflicted on the one who had no wedding garment seems shocking.

Clearly, these complementary verses do not fit in well with the principal parable. However, their appearance had been somewhat prepared by the king's saying that the first invitees 'were not worthy' (verse 8), and the observation that among the newly invited there were 'bad and good' (verse 10). It is this mixture of good and bad which is ultimately responsible for the addition of verses 11–13. This is typical of Matthew (Mt 13:24–30, 36–43; 13:47–50).

The king addresses the intruder as 'friend', which in Matthew repeatedly implies reproach and disappointment, e.g., to one of the grumbling workers in the vineyard, 'friend, I am doing you no wrong' (Mt 20:13); and to Judas, 'friend, why are you here?' (Mt 26:50). The word *pōs* (RSV translates 'how') may here have the meaning of 'with what right'. In his confusion the man remains silent. The king's reaction is severe. The images used here are also found elsewhere in Matthew and always refer to the ultimate punishment, hell, and cries of despair (darkness: Mt 8:12; 25:30; weeping and gnashing of teeth: Mt 8:12; 13:42, 50; 24:51; 25:30; elsewhere only in Lk 13:28). What was said of the 'sons of the kingdom' in Mt 8:12, is applied here to the one who is found without a wedding garment. Explanations which claim that on such occasions wedding garments were distributed to the guests do not seem to have much ground, notwithstanding references to a much earlier text found at Mari.

Our attention is directed towards a figurative sense: the man was excluded from the wedding feast, and delivered up to despair, because he thought he could enter the kingdom without a wedding garment. In such a context, the wedding garment must also have a figurative meaning. According to some it symbolizes the justice, i.e., a certain way of being and conduct, demanded from those who want to belong to the community of the saved (cf. Isa 61:10; Rev 3:4, 18; according to Rev 19:8, the garment of fine linen, bright and pure, 'is the righteous deeds of the saints'). The requirements of this justice/righteousness are stated in the first place in the Sermon on the Mount (Mt 5:1 – 7:29; cf. the 'heading' of Mt 5:20, 'For I tell you, unless your righteousness exceeds that of the scribes and Pharisees, you will never enter the kingdom of heaven'). Others understand the garment to mean the penance which necessarily accompanies the call. A third group interpret it as a metaphor of the indispensable works of love (cf. Mt 25:35ff.), not in the sense of individual 'good works', but in the sense of complete consistency between confession and deed, faith and life. The third interpretation seems the most likely.

Verse 14: For many are called, but few are chosen.'

In the New Testament this saying is found only here and, according to some manuscripts, in Mt 20:16. It has often been questioned whether this maxim originally belonged here, but it has also been pointed out that except for the doubtful reading in Mt 20:16, it does not fit better anywhere else than here. Mt 22:14 differs from all other New Testament passages in that it distinguishes between 'called' (*klētoi*) and 'chosen' (*eklektoi*). Usually they are equivalent as e.g., in Rev 17:14, 'those with him are called and chosen and faithful'. The statement is connected with the preceding verses by means of the conjunction 'for'. However, there it is said that the call into the kingdom is indiscriminate ('bad and good') and that the number of those who were called into the wedding hall but finally appeared not to have been chosen is only one!

To understand this saying one should bear in mind that neither Hebrew nor Aramaic has a comparative form. The idea of comparison could be expressed in several ways, one of which was to simply put two absolutely opposite forms next to each other. To say that John is taller than Peter, they would simply say 'John is tall and Peter is small', even if the difference was only one millimetre. To say 'many are called, but few are chosen' means therefore that many are called, but less than many, even if only one less, are chosen. Moreover, in Semitic languages 'many' (*polloi*) often has the inclusive meaning of 'all', as can be seen in IV Ezra 8:3, 'many (= all) have been created, but few (= not all) will be saved'. In other words, Mt 22:14 says that the universal call to salvation does not automatically guarantee the total and permanent response of all. Election can never be taken for granted but is subject to God's judgment and grace. There are some who, as the parable shows, receive the invitation and enter the wedding hall, but do not live in a way which is consistent with their initial response.

It has been suggested that the meaning of Mt 22:14 should be derived from all three parables, Mt 21:28–32; 21:33–46; 22:1–13, of which it would be the conclusion. Israel is 'called'. The images of the two sons, the tenants, and the invitees illustrate how Israel reacts to God's invitation. Other tenants (cf. Mt 21:41) will receive the vineyard (compare also Mt 21:43, 'the kingdom of God will be... given to a nation producing the fruits of it'). The king invites many to the marriage feast (Mt 22:3, 4, 8), but they refuse to come. They seize the king's servants, treat them shamefully and kill them (Mt 22:6; compare Mt 21:35). Then follows the destruction of the city (Mt 22:7). But the invitation is repeated (Mt 22:9). Others are called (*klētoi*), but are they also all chosen (*eklektoi*)? No, since the calling can be forfeited, as happens to the man without a wedding garment. Human responsibility plays a part in the doing of God's justice, in the doing of the Father's will (Mt 21:31), in producing the fruits of the kingdom of God (Mt 21:43). Only in practising God's justice is election realized.

Summing up this analysis, it would seem that Matthew has turned the parable of the great banquet into an allegorical account of the history of salvation, as he did also with the parable of the wicked tenants. The first sending of servants suggests the prophets and the rejection of their message (Mt 22:3). The second sending of servants (Mt 22:4) refers to the activity and the suffering and death of apostles and early Christian missionaries (Mt 22:6) in Jerusalem. The destruction of this city (Mt 22:7) is interpreted as a divine punishment for the repeated rejection of the invitation by the Jews. The sending of servants into the thoroughfares to invite as many as they can find (Mt 22:9–10) would then reflect the mission to the Gentiles. But this is not the end of the story, because Matthew has combined it with a second parable (Mt 22:11–13). The inspection of the guests (Mt 22:11) refers to the last judgment and the outer darkness (Mt 22:13) points to hell. So, in this parable Matthew seems to be depicting saving history from the time of the prophets (Old Testament) to the last judgment.

In Matthew this parable in a sense represents a unique case. It has neither a uniform style nor a consistent line of affirmation. Instead it has a double purpose: one polemical, showing the saving-historical failure of Israel, and the ensuing mission to the Gentiles, and another paraenetic, a warning addressed to the members of the Christian community in so far as they do not have the wedding garment, which in Matthew refers to the fruits/works of faithful love. The allegorization of Matthew's text has taken place in two stages, one determined by the paraenetic intent for the community, the other determined by the polemical context.

Lk 14:15–24, Mt 22:1–14, and the underlying tradition

Comparing the Lucan and Matthean redactions, we note the following differences:

Matthew	Luke
(1) the host is a king (verse 2).	(1) the host is a man (verse 16), and a householder (verse 21).
(2) this king invites to the wedding feast of his son (verse 2).	(2) the man invites to a great banquet (verse 16).
(3) two groups of servants are sent successively (verses 3–4).	(3) one servant is sent once (verse 17).
(4) the reasons for the refusal are briefly given by the narrator of the story (verse 5).	(4) the invitees themselves explain the reasons for their refusal at length (verses 18–20).
(5) the second group of servants are treated violently and even killed by some of the invitees, whereupon the king in anger sends his army, destroys the murderers and burns their city (verses 6–7).	(5) no violence against the servant is mentioned, and though the host gets angry, there is no trace of military action (verse 21; except for a reference to anger, Mt 22:6–7 are completely missing in Luke).
(6) after this dramatic turn, he sends once more a group of servants to the crossroads, to invite anybody, bad and good (verses 9–10).	(6) in anger the man sends his servants twice, once to the streets of the city to bring in the poor and maimed and blind and lame (verse 21), and next to the highways to compel people to come in (verse 23).
(7) an inspection of the guests by the king; one man is found without a wedding garment and is thrown out (verses 11–13).	(7) no trace of this inspection in Luke's version.
(8) For many are called, but few are chosen (verse 14).	(8) For I tell you, none of those who were invited shall taste my banquet (verse 24).

A number of scholars think that we are dealing here with a parable which Matthew and Luke received from a common source, Q, and some even feel confident that they can reconstruct the version in Q as follows:

> The kingdom of God may be compared to a man who gave a great banquet, and invited many. And he sent his servant to say

to those who had been invited, 'Come; for all is now ready'. But they made light of it and went off, one to his farm, another to his business. And the servant reported this to his master. Then the householder in anger said to his servant, 'Go out to the highways and invite whomever you find to come in, that my house may be filled'.

However, the parable is so different in its details in Matthew and Luke that a number of scholars think that we are dealing here not with parallels but with two variant versions (M and L) which cannot be reduced to a common basic text. While it is probable that a Q parable underlies the Matthean and Lucan versions, the literary-critical difficulties should make us forgo attempts to reconstruct the Q text. Instead a brief sketch of the conjectural content of the original parable may be attempted as follows:

(1) Introduction
   —a man
   —gives a banquet
   —and invites those (socially) worthy
(2) Development and crisis
   —the banquet is ready
   —he sends a servant for a reminder (Lk once; Mt twice)
   —the guests refuse to come; they offer excuses or go off on pretexts
   (Lk three excuses; Mt two pretexts and the reaction of 'the rest')
(3) Denouement
   —the man is angry
   —he invites those (socially) unworthy (Mt once; Lk twice)
   —the dining room is filled
   —judgment upon those initially invited.

The *pre-Matthean community* expressed its understanding of the connection between Jesus' coming and the eschatological banquet. By means of the 'king' metaphor the community states that God himself offers the banquet that has its beginning in Jesus. The constitutive relation between God and Jesus is expressed in the fact that the king gives a wedding feast (here as in Rev 19:9 understood as the eschatological fulfilment) for his son. The parable's invitation is identified with Jesus' invitation, in the face of which, after Easter, all excuses appear unfit. They are therefore briefly summarized (Mt 22:5). The community understands itself as the guests proleptically participating in the eschatological banquet. Their only 'achievement' is to have accepted the invitation. Therefore, there are 'bad and good' in the festive hall. The parable becomes an expression of the community's self-understanding as a mixed reality (*corpus mixtum*). The post-Easter community adequately handed on Jesus' parable in that they interpreted it Christologically and eschatologically.

Matthew links up with the preceding interpretation in that he describes the invitation even more clearly as the urgent invitation extended by Jesus' post-Easter messengers (Mt 22:4). Added to this is a (saving-)historical interpretation which shows especially in the fact that the negative experience of the Christian missionaries found a place in the parable (verse 6). The parable gets a more *polemical* thrust. Matthew heightens the threadbare character of the refusal to explicit insolence on the part of the first invitees, which provokes God's wrath and leads to the death of the murderers and the destruction of their city. Since Mt 22:7 clearly reflects the events of the Jewish war, Matthew must have understood the first invitees as Jews who had proven themselves unworthy of the invitation (cf. Mt 21:33–43), and the second group of invitees as Gentiles. The parable has thereby become a historical sketch of the transition from the Jewish to the Gentile mission. The latter is justified by the fact that the first invitees were unworthy because they responded with extreme insolence to the urgent invitation. The danger, inherent to this interpretation, of a repeated arrogance and false security is dealt with in verses 11–13, which deal with the question of 'worthiness' and state that the community has still to expect divine judgment. This *paraenetic* accent is underlined by the concluding verse, Mt 22:14, as well as by the insertion of the parable in the present context.

Luke understands the parable in line with post-Easter Christology. Therefore, the original 'man' of the parable becomes the *kurios* (verse 21a), and the original 'point' of the parable now becomes the application (verse 24). Luke understands the repeated invitation as the missionary activity of the community. The call of Jesus is contained in the call of the Christian missionaries. The combination of the parable with verse 15 shows that the gathering of the community is understood as the anticipation of the eschatological banquet. Thus the parable contains references to the historical experience of the community. The qualification of the second group of invitees (verse 21) reflects the missionary experience of the community, while the third invitation (verses 22–23) reflects the transition from the Jewish to the Gentile mission. Jesus' parable becomes a tool for understanding the situation of the community. Whoever seriously considers the connection between Jesus' call and God's banquet must understand it anew now that after Easter the disciples are carrying the call into the whole world.[58]

Luke has taken the parable to be a paraenetic illustration of the point made more directly in Lk 14:12–14 (cf. Lk 14:21). The third invitation (Lk 14:22–23) may originally have meant that the host wanted the banquet hall filled at all cost, and, therefore, did not necessarily have an allegorical meaning. Luke, however, may have read more into it. But, as has been pointed out, there is an important difference between allegorical interpretation and the creation of allegory. Perhaps it is impossible to reach definitive certainty whether the third invitation (Lk 14:23) belongs to the original form of the parable. But, even if it belonged to the original text, Luke may have *interpreted* it allegorically. The second invitation (Lk 14:21) was understood as addressed to the poor, etc., in Israel (cf. 'the city', i.e., Jerusalem), the third to the poor, etc., among the Gentiles, i.e., the Gentile mission which was certainly of great importance to Luke. He seems to be concerned here with the attitude of the Church towards the marginals (Lk 14:12–13, 21) and the Gentiles (Lk 14:23).

The parable on the level of Jesus' ministry

For Jesus as well as for his audience, the 'great banquet' is a metaphor for the great eschatological banquet of joy. On the other hand, 'eating' played an important role in Jesus' life. His meals with the most diverse people, Pharisees, tax collectors and sinners, are a sign of the welcoming love characteristic of the new time of God's rule. His meals are an anticipation of the kingdom. In this context 'all is now ready' is given its full dimension. Now, in Jesus' presence, the time has come in which one is invited to the banquet of the kingdom of God. Now the invitation should be accepted. But the invitees excuse themselves, not because they do not like the host (contrast the story of Bar Ma'jan [see below]), but because they do not understand the importance of the time. It is at this point that Jesus comes to meet the hearers. He tries to make them see that the time for participation in the kingdom has come. Refusing to respond to the call, the first invitees incur a definitive exclusion; their places at the banquet will be occupied by others.

It has been objected that Jesus could not possibly have pronounced a parable in which it is said that because of the refusal of the first invitees others are called to the banquet, people for whom it was at first not intended. This would contradict Jesus' message, which does not teach that the kingdom is given to tax collectors and sinners *because of* the refusal of the just. The God whom Jesus proclaims does not turn to the poor because of the contempt of the rich. It is because God calls the poor to the banquet that the rich stay away, and not the other way around!

The parable does not teach that at first God did not intend to invite the poor; it does not suppose that Jesus turned to sinners as a consequence of the opposition of the just. We are faced rather with Jesus' answer to the just who reproached him with his attitude towards sinners. Jesus granted to his critics that the banquet was prepared for them; but they should not be surprised that their places are given to others. More precisely, the parable invites them to see in the call addressed to the poor and the infirm the sign of their own definitive exclusion, the consequence of their opposition to the message.

The objection mentioned above is based on false presuppositions: firstly, the idea that all the features of a parabolic account must correspond to reality; and secondly, that its teaching must necessarily consist in general and timeless truths rather than an *ad hominem* statement intended for the people whom Jesus addresses.

The lesson of the parable should be derived from the conduct of the man who prepared the banquet. Isn't it normal that the refusal of the guests angers him? Is it wrong that he invites others to take their place? The application is obvious: the conduct of this man should make us understand God's conduct. The parable, therefore, deals with God's way of acting, not in general, but as it is manifested in Jesus' ministry. The situation is that of the parables of mercy: the just are scandalized by the concern Jesus shows for the poor, the publicans and sinners. But, unlike the parables of mercy, Jesus does not try here to make people understand the love God lavishes on the disinherited. He wants to enlighten his opponents on what is for them the terrible meaning of his action on behalf of the poor, sinners and tax collectors: it is a sign of their condemnation.

The invitation addressed to the poor and the infirm symbolizes in the parable the present moment. Those who were invited first either did not care (Matthew), or refused explicitly (Luke). The feature is sufficiently clear for the addressees of the parable to recognize their own attitude: the attitude of people who believe that they have done enough by scrupulously keeping the law to be sure of their share in the eschatological banquet. They are not aware of the new demands of the present hour. While not responding to the message themselves, they are scandalized seeing this message addressed to the people whom they detest: the poor beggars of the parable who represent the masses whom they refer to as 'sinners'. The situation of the parable is clearly that of Jesus' ministry as we find it also, for instance, in the parable of the two sons (Mt 21:28–32).

The reason for the exclusion of the first invitees being their refusal of the divine call transmitted by Jesus, should one conclude that their substitutes were chosen because they were better prepared or better disposed to receive the call? The parable does not give this impression. The only reason given is the anger of the host and his resolution to make his banquet succeed at any cost. God's design will be realized. Luke's 'compel people to come in' is in line with the account, since it underlines that the privilege of the disinherited is due solely to the will of the master of the house, not to the readiness of those who will ultimately participate in the banquet. Their thoughts and personal dispositions are not specially considered. All attention is concentrated on the host and his determination not to let his plan fail. It is useless, therefore, to attribute all kind of virtues, feelings and attitudes to the poor and the maimed, etc. Their role is to manifest God's attitude, his anger because of the behaviour of the parable's addressees, and his compassion with the disinherited. All this fits perfectly in Jesus' proclamation.

Some scholars have stated that Jesus was making use of the story of a rich tax collector Bar Ma'jan and a poor scholar, which occurs in Aramaic in the Palestinian Talmud.[59] It should be pointed out, however, that the only feature which this story really has in common with our parable is that an invitation is declined and the poor called in to the feast. On the other hand, the differences are evident; e.g., Bar Ma'jan's invitation is declined because the invitees consider the host of inferior social rank. While the existence of this story may help us to situate the parable of the banquet in a Palestinian milieu, it is questionable whether Jesus really intended an allusion to the ridiculous misadventure of the tax collector. In the parable, the host should make us understand how God acts, and the lesson is possible only if the audience approves of the conduct of the host. But it would be difficult to achieve this effect if the audience ridiculed the main character of the parable. It is better, therefore, to give up this hypothesis, which falsifies the meaning of the parable.

Reflection

Presumably both types of persons represented in the parable, i.e., the rich and the poor, were in the audience. The former knew that they would go to such a banquet, if the occasion were sufficiently important, if they were invited, and if the social standing of the host were above reproach. They cannot see any reason why they should not be there. But, according to the parable, they decline, and for reasons which they recognize, which they have perhaps advanced on previous occasions, but which they do not like to be publicly scrutinized. And so they resent the parable; they are offended because it appears unbelievable. They do not want to be put down in a way which cannot be ignored, to be ridiculed without recourse. They want to be able to determine for themselves whether or not they will attend.

On the other hand, there were the poor whose mouths watered at the thought of such a banquet. They secretly aspired to be of sufficient social standing to be invited. But could they really hope to ever be included in the list of invitees? Only in fairy tales do beggars sit at kings' tables.

Thus the parable involves both the rich and the poor, though for different reasons. Both groups anticipate a further development and outcome, but neither of them could actually foresee the track the story would follow. It has no surprise ending; in fact, it has no ending at all. This is very upsetting. The conclusion is incorporated in the parable from the very beginning, but it is only temporary. The rich know that they have been excluded and the poor know that they are counted in, although no application has been presented.

On the one hand, the parable constitutes a judgment of the transparent excuses manufactured to cover up the refusal of the invitation. The excuses are not raised to the level of principles; it is not the call of business or other occupations as such that frustrate the messianic banquet. The excuses are important only insofar as they serve the rich as a foundation for their refusal; exactly what they are does not really matter. What matters is that the invitation was not heeded. The rich were too preoccupied with their wealth and business ventures to perceive the gravity of the invitation. They did not grasp the character of the invitation because it came to them veiled in the simplicity of Jesus' proclamation and mission.

On the other hand, the parable is a message of grace. It speaks of an invitation to those who did not expect it, could not have expected it. And they are not merely invited — in that case they might have drawn back before the unsolicited offer of blessedness — but they are hauled into the banquet hall. The outcasts have nothing to hold on to and so, while there is nothing that makes them anticipate the invitation, they are open to it as a free gift when it comes.

It is important to notice that judgment and grace are not spoken of directly. The audience is not alerted in advance that there are two groups. No one is identified. Rather, as the story opens, each hearer is drawn into the tale as he wills. He is allowed to take his place on one side or the other. As the story unfolds, he must make up his mind whether he can unfold with it, i.e., whether he is congenial to its development. If, as the story reaches its turning point, this one or that one draws back, we know who he is! If, as the story comes to its climax, we see a smile pass these lips or those, we have identified him, too! The parable identifies each member of the audience, tells each one who he is, and with that the group is split in two.

Not only are the hearers divided, but those who have received the blunt end of the stick know that they have stood in the dock. They may not care for the judge, or even condescend to acknowledge him, but they have heard the sentence. And those who find themselves unexpectedly favored have at the same time received their invitation. They know themselves to have been invited, indeed compelled. They understand the invitation. They also perceive who it is that gives it. The situation has been qualified, willing or not, by the parable and him who speaks it, although the latter has not appeared for an instant in the picture he is sketching.[60]

9 The three parables of Luke 15

Composition and structure of Luke 15

Lk 15, which is found halfway through the central section of the gospel, the Travel Narrative (Lk 9:51 – 19:44), and hence at its very heart, recalls the structure of the whole work. The mercy of God mentioned repeatedly at the beginning of the gospel (Lk 1:50, 54, 58, 72, 78), and manifested by the sending of the Messiah (Lk 2ff.), precedes the conversion of people narrated in the following chapters. Lk 15 seems to be a parabolic comment on Jesus' saying, 'I have not come to call the righteous, but sinners to repentance' (Lk 5:32).

The whole of Lk 15 is clearly set off from the preceding and following chapters, as indicated by the difference of circumstances and audiences. In its present composition Lk 15 is a closely knit unity. The terms 'sinner' and 'to sin' (*hamartōlos* and *hamartanō*) punctuate the four parts of the chapter, i.e., the introduction (Lk 15:1, 2), and each of the three parables (Lk 15:7, 10, 18, 21). Moreover, the schema of the three parables is always the same and expressed in practically the same words: one element in a hundred, one in ten, and one in two is lost (*apollumai, apollumi*: Lk 15:4a, b, 6, 8, 9; cf. Lk 15:24, 32); it is found (*heuriskomai, heuriskō*: Lk 15:4, 5, 6, 8, 9a, b, 24, 32); the 'owner' rejoices (*chairō, chara*: Lk 15:5, 6, 7, 9, 10, 32), and shares his joy with others: 'rejoice with me' (Lk 15:6, 9), 'let us make merry' (Lk 15:32; cf. 15:24).

The centre of interest of the three parables is not the object lost and found, but the 'owner' of the object or, more precisely, the owner who rejoices in finding what was temporarily lost. In fact, if the application verses (Lk 15:7, 10) are ignored, the first two parables constitute one sentence having as subject the 'man' or the 'woman' of the beginning (Lk 15:4, 8). In the third parable it is the man mentioned at the beginning who has the most important part.

Moreover, the same words are found in the three conclusions: '(have) lost', 'find', 'rejoice' (Lk 15:6, 9, 32). It should be noted that the theme of loss and gain has already appeared in Lk 14:26, 33,

138

while the introduction of the first two parables is strikingly similar to Lk 14:28, 31, '... which of you, desiring... Or what king, going...'.

The scribes and the Pharisees, chief actors of the introductory scene, are referred to explicitly in the first two parables: 'So he told *them*' (Lk 15:3), 'what man of *you*' (Lk 15:4), 'I tell *you*' (Lk 15:7). Their presence is implicitly but clearly affirmed in the third parable.

The author (or final redactor) invites the reader of any part of Lk 15 to refer also to the other parts; particularly, he invites the reader to study each parable with reference to the other two, and all three parables with reference to the introduction. Read in this way, the common elements of the three parables reinforce each other, while the elements present or underlined in only one of them stand out more because of their absence elsewhere. Furthermore, the elements which are not common to all parables may sometimes have to be supplied where they are materially absent. Finally, all three parables receive special clarification from the introduction which is so strongly connected with them.

The structure of the chapter looks as follows:

(1) Introduction (Lk 15:1–3)
(2) First two (twin) parables (Lk 15:4–10)
    (a) the lost sheep found by a man (Lk 15:4–7)
    (b) the lost coin found by a woman (Lk 15:8–10)
(3) The third parable, much longer, connected to the preceding by 'and he said', and itself divided into two parts:
    (a) departure and return of the younger son (Lk 15:11–24)
    (b) resistance of the older son (Lk 15:25–32).

The parallelism of the first two parables is so close that they could be sufficient by themselves and form a whole:

What man of you,	Or what woman,
having a hundred sheep,	having ten silver coins,
if he has lost one of them,	if she loses one coin,
does not leave. . .	does not light. . .
until he finds it?	until she finds it?
And when he has found it,	And when she has found it,
. . .	. . .
he calls together his friends	she calls together her friends
and neighbours, saying to them,	and neighbours, saying,
Rejoice with me,	Rejoice with me,
for I have found my sheep	for I have found the coin
which was lost.	which I had lost.
Just so, I tell you,	Just so, I tell you,
there will be more joy. . .	there is joy. . .
over one sinner who repents. . .	over one sinner who repents.

The third parable is united with the other two by the themes of 'something' lost and found, and of the rejoicing which marks the finding. While there is a thematic unity, there is also a formal duality, the first two parables presenting themselves in one unit as two interrogations, while the third parable is fuller and stands somewhat by itself. This type of composition appears several times in Luke. The remarkable similarity in structure between Lk 15:1–32 and Lk 13:1–9 has been pointed out. After the introduction, 'There were some present at that very time who told him of the Galileans whose blood Pilate mingled with their sacrifices' (Lk 13:1), there follow two parallel references to a disastrous incident, linked by the particle 'or'; both are expressed in the form of a question and are followed by an application:

Do you think that	Or
these Galileans	those eighteen
(cf. 1b: whose blood Pilate	upon whom the tower in Siloam
mingled with their sacrifices)	fell and killed them,
	do you think that they
were worse sinners than	were worse offenders than
all the other Galileans,	all the others who dwelt in
	Jerusalem?
because they suffered thus?	
I tell you, No;	I tell you, No;
but unless you repent	but unless you repent
you will all likewise perish.	you will all likewise perish.

Then follows a somewhat longer narrative, the parable of the fig tree. The entire passage centres on the theme of the urgent need for conversion. A similar structure is found in Lk 13:18–30, where the twin parables of the mustard seed and the leaven are followed by the longer parable of the householder. Although some scholars attribute this structure to Luke's source, it seems more probable that the sections mentioned owe their structure to the evangelist himself.

   To answer the question about the structure of a text composed of several smaller units one should pay special attention to the beginning and the end. The beginning presents Jesus facing two groups, on the one hand, the tax collectors and sinners, and, on the other hand, the Pharisees and the scribes, whereby there is an opposition between the two groups (Lk 15:1–2). The end of the composition presents the father facing two sons, whereby there is opposition between the younger and the elder son. Beginning and end correspond. The narrative structure of the parable of the prodigal son co-determines the structure of Lk 15. Within the composition of Lk 15, the parables of the lost sheep and the lost coin serve as a preamble for the understanding of the parable of the prodigal son which is decisive for the understanding of the whole chapter.

The structure of Lk 15 has made some scholars think of the exercises of classic rhetoric known as *chreiai*, in which a saying of a philosopher or a poet was illustrated by a number of figurative sayings and amplifications. The *chreiai* are of Greek origin but not unknown in Palestine. Oriented to daily practice, they would certainly have been an ideal instrument for the preaching and catechesis of the early Church. But these short parables in interrogative form (Lk 15:4–10) have a number of characteristics which are very similar to those of rabbinic *meshalim*. However, while the *form* of these parables is very similar to rabbinic *meshalim*, their *content*, unlike that of the parables of the kingdom, has no parallels in rabbinic literature. The parables of the lost sheep and the lost coin have all the signs of authenticity which allows one to trace them back to Jesus himself. Most scholars say the same of the parable of the prodigal son.

Analysis of the text

Introduction (Lk 15:1–3)

> **Verses 1–2:** Now the tax collectors and sinners were all drawing near to hear him. (2) And the Pharisees and the scribes murmured, saying 'This man receives sinners and eats with them.'

Verses 1–2 depict a scene which may be considered typical of Jesus' ministry as well as of the objections and judgment which motivated the Pharisees' rejection of Jesus. One has pointed out the many similarities to Lk 5:29–30, which is a Lucan revision of Mk 2:15–16, and of which Lk 15:1–2 may be a free repetition (while Lk 15:7c reaches back to Lk 5:31–32). One is also reminded of Lk 7:29–30, 'When they heard all this the people and the tax collectors justified God... But the Pharisees and the lawyers rejected the purpose of God...'. See also Lk 11:53, 'As he went away from them, the scribes and the Pharisees began to press him hard...'. The two verses constitute a redactional introduction which Luke most probably derived from his source or earlier traditions and retouched for their present purpose as the setting for the following parables.

The Greco-Roman administration collected taxes through 'tax farmers'. An individual bought the right to collect taxes in a certain area from the authorities, to whom he was bound by contract to deliver a certain amount. Whatever he collected beyond this amount he kept. These 'tax farmers' were often Gentiles, who in Jesus' days hired local people to take care of the actual collection. The latter were considered collaborators who co-operated with the occupying power. In the gospel 'tax collectors' are usually linked with equally unpopular groups like 'sinners' (Lk 5:30; 7:34; cf. Mk 2:15; Mt 9:10–11; 11:19), 'adulterers' (Lk 18:11; cf. Mt 21:31–32), and 'Gentiles' (Mt 18:17). The phrase 'sinner' occurs thirteen times in Luke and usually refers to people of low moral character. These people came to Jesus and he welcomed them.

'The Pharisees and the scribes murmured', i.e., they reacted to Jesus in the same way as the people reacted and revolted against Moses in the desert (Ex 15:24; 16:2, 7–8; 17:3; Num 14:2; 16:11). In the New Testament the verb appears only here and in Lk 19:7, both times to describe discontented complaints about Jesus' dealings with sinners and tax collectors. They complain that Jesus receives these people into his fellowship (*prosdechomai*; cf. Mk 9:37; Rom 16:2; Phil 2:29), even to the extent that he 'eats with them', by which he not only defiled himself, but also manifested his total acceptance of them. Because of his dealing thus with people carefully ostracized by the religious establishment, the latter felt threatened. In Luke the verbs *dechomai* and *prosdechomai* often imply hospitality (Lk 9:5, 53; 10:8, 10; 15:2; 16:4, 9; 22:17). To act as a host to sinners would have been a much more serious offence to the Pharisees than merely to eat with sinners or to accept their invitation.

Verse 3: So he told them this parable:

Jesus addressed a parable to 'them', i.e., most probably not the multitudes, the last interlocutors mentioned (Lk 14:25), nor the disciples, the next hearers mentioned (Lk 16:1), but 'the Pharisees and the scribes' of verse 2. Although Jesus proceeds to relate three parables, Luke uses the singular 'parable'. It may designate the parabolic form of discourse (Lk 12:41), or a collection of short parables taken as a unit (cf. Lk 5:36–39; 6:39–41; 12:22–39).

The parable of the lost sheep (Lk 15:4–7)

The parable of the lost sheep is the only one in Lk 15 which has a synoptic parallel, Mt 18:12–14, and is therefore considered to be derived from the Q source. Let us first compare the two synoptic versions of the parable. Then we give also the text of the *Gospel of Thomas*.

Mt 18:12–14	Lk 15:4–7
12 What do you think? If a man has a hundred sheep, and one of them has gone astray, does he not leave the ninety- nine on the hills and go in search of the one that went astray?	4 What man of you, having a hundred sheep, if he has lost one of them, does not leave the ninety-nine in the wilderness, and go after the one which is lost, until he finds it?
13 And if he finds it,	5 And when he has found it, he lays it on his shoulders, rejoicing. 6 And when he comes home, he calls together his friends and his neighbours, saying to them, Rejoice with me, for I have found my sheep which was lost.
truly, I say to you, he rejoices over it more than over the ninety-nine that never went astray. 14 So it is not the will of my Father who is in heaven that one of these little ones should perish.	7 Just so, I tell you, there will be more joy in heaven over one sinner who repents than over ninety-nine righteous persons who need no repentance.

Gospel of Thomas 107

Jesus said, The kingdom is like a shepherd
who had a hundred sheep.
One of them, the largest, went astray.
He left the ninety-nine and looked for that one
until he found it.
When he had gone to such trouble,
he said to the sheep,
I care for you more than the ninety-nine.

The currently accepted opinion that the version found in the *Gospel of Thomas* is a rather late recasting of the parable dependent upon the synoptic recensions has very recently been questioned. That the sheep which strayed was the largest has almost unanimously been interpreted as a Gnostic expansion. But on the basis of a series of rabbinic documents concerning the idea of a census of Israel, which is sometimes cast in the form of a shepherd counting his sheep, and which states that Israel is loved more than the other nations, and is described in superlatives, it has been argued that the 'largest sheep' is Israel. 'Largest' is, then, not a Gnostic, allegorizing element, but an adjective used to identify Israel, which time and again is described as a lost sheep in Old Testament imagery (compare Mt 10:6; 15:24; 18:11).

The parable of the lost sheep may be based on Ez 34:16, which is eschatological. The *Gospel of Thomas* maintains this eschatological character by stating that 'the kingdom is like…', while in Matthew the emphasis is paraenetic, addressed to the (leaders of the) Christian community, and in Luke it is polemic, addressed to the Pharisees and the scribes.

Thomas' version would not be dependent upon the synoptic versions and would even be more primitive than the latter. This conclusion is based on the principle that the shorter version has a better chance of being more primitive, and because of the absence of specific allegorical identifications, the lack of implied or expressed messianism, and the version's faithfulness to the eschatological tone of Ez 34:16.[61]

Comparing the versions of Matthew and Luke, we note the following:

(1) In Matthew, the parable is introduced by the question 'What do you think?' which is a redactional formula of unmistakably Matthean character (cf. Mt 17:25; 21:28; 22:17, 42; 26:66), although some scholars seem to consider it original.

(2) Matthew's 'if a man has a hundred sheep' is said to preserve the original better than Luke's rather strange appeal to the Pharisees' experience as shepherds (a trade which they despised), 'What man of you, having a hundred sheep'.

(3) While Matthew writes that one of the sheep 'went astray', Luke says that the shepherd 'has lost one of them'. A number of scholars favour Matthew over Luke who, they say, has chosen a verb which he could keep throughout the chapter (Lk 15:6, 8, 9, 17, 24, 32). But it should not be overlooked that Matthew too uses the word 'get lost' (*apollumi*, RSV: 'perish') in the application of the parable (Mt 18:14). Matthew makes a distinction between 'go astray' and 'be lost', a distinction which makes little sense in the case of sheep, but is important in speaking of a person. The verb 'went astray', therefore, seems to have been chosen in function of the application in Mt 18:14 and of what will be said of 'straying' church members in Mt 18:15–17.

(4) In Matthew, the incident takes place 'on the hills', while in Luke it is situated 'in the wilderness'. Lk 8:29 reads 'into the desert'

instead of Mk 5:5, 'on the mountains'. *Midrash Rabbah Exodus*
II.2 has been suggested as a possible source for Luke's 'in the
wilderness' (see below, exegesis of verse 5). On the other hand, it
is noted that the change from 'in the wilderness' to 'on the hills' is
more easily imaginable than the opposite. Therefore, many
consider the former original.

(5) According to Matthew, the shepherd 'goes in search (*poreutheis
zētei*) of the one that went astray', while according to Luke, he
'goes after (*poreuetai*) the one which is lost, until he finds it'.
Luke's version is most probably more original than Matthew's
which emphasizes the search, while the original parable deals
with losing and finding.

(6) Verse 5, 'And when he has found it, he lays it on his shoulders,
rejoicing', is found in Luke only. Many think that Matthew
omitted this clause, while others think of a Lucan addition,
pointing out that 'finding' (*heurōn*) is to be attributed to Luke, as
well as the reference to 'rejoicing' (cf. Lk 19:6; Acts 8:39).
Midrash Rabbah Exodus II.2 contains the clause 'he placed the
kid on his shoulders and walked away'.

(7) Verse 6 is also proper to Luke. The vocabulary ('call together',
'rejoice with me', friends', 'neighbours') is very Lucan, and the
scene is similar to that of the birth of John the Baptist (Lk 1:58).
Some say that the verse cannot be traced to a pre-Lucan source,
while others again think of a Matthean abbreviation.

(8) What constitutes the second part of the parabolic account in
Matthew is presented in Luke as the application of the parable
(Lk 15:7). Having the parable without an application, Matthew
may have added the application found in Mt 18:14, while Luke
may have transformed the last part of the parable into an
application. On this occasion Luke would have added the idea of
repentance, which nothing in the parable justifies, but which is
dear to Luke. He also identified the ninety-nine sheep with
'ninety-nine righteous persons who need no repentance'. Lk 15:7
should then be considered as a refashioning of Mt 18:13b. But
others claim that Mt 18:13 is rather an adaptation of Lk 15:7. Lk
15:7c, 'who need no repentance', is most probably Lucan.

(9) Mt 18:14 is apparently redactional. It serves to connect the
parable to the recommendations concerning the 'little ones',
deriving from it a lesson which specifies the teaching of Mt 18:10.

It is very hard to decide which of the two versions, Matthean or
Lucan, is more original. Both Matthean and Lucan originality have
their defenders. Most probably it is better to think in terms of an
adaptation to the situation created by the redactional framework of

each gospel. This is clear for Matthew. Mt 18:14, 'so it is not the will of my Father who is in heaven that one of these little ones should perish', evidently refers to Mt 18:10, 'see that you do not despise one of these little ones', which precedes the parable. But there is also interpretation in Luke's text. While Matthew says 'truly, I say to you, he rejoices over it more than over the ninety-nine that never went astray' (Mt 18:13), this comparison passes in Luke from the description to the conclusion, from the metaphorical account to the real and theological meaning, 'Just so, I tell you, there will be more joy in heaven...' (Lk 15:7 paralleled by Lk 15:10). Moreover, 'one sinner who repents' is understood, not in the sense of one who performs works of expiation, as it would be understood by the Pharisees and scribes, but one who approaches Christ and is accepted by him. Likewise, those 'who need no repentance' are no longer those who keep the law, but those who are already in the kingdom, the members of the community.

The more original form of the parable (Q?) may have looked more or less as follows:

> What man of you,
> who has a hundred sheep and loses one of them,
> does not leave the ninety-nine in the wilderness,
> and go after the one which is lost, until he finds it?
> And when he has found it,
> truly, I tell you,
> he rejoices over it more
> than over the ninety-nine which did not get lost.

It is true that the reconstruction of a form of the parable older than the versions which occur in the gospels does not necessarily take us back to Jesus himself. But in the present case there are no grounds for attributing this parable to the creativity of the early Christian community. Besides, the interpretation given to it by the community indicates rather that we are dealing here with a parable which can be traced to Jesus himself.

The theme of a shepherd searching for lost sheep is very familiar in prophetic literature. The image solely and unambiguously refers to God who requires his lost sheep (thought of in general rather than individually) to be searched for and looked after. Ez 34 deals with the condemnation of the unfaithful shepherds of Israel, and God's own remedial shepherding undoubtedly lies behind the parable of the lost sheep. The image of the Jewish people as lost sheep who have gone astray is found in Ps 119(118):176, 'I have gone astray like a lost sheep; seek your servant...'. It occurs also in Isa 53:6, 'All we like sheep have gone astray; we have turned every one to his own way...'.

> **Verse 4:** What man of you, having a hundred sheep, if he has lost one of them, does not leave the ninety-nine in the wilderness, and go after the one which is lost, until he finds it?

The parable opens with a rhetorical question. The formula 'who among you' (*tis ex humōn*) is found in Lk 11:11; 12:25; 14:24; 15:4; 17:7 (Q and L material). Its effect is to address the listeners personally and urge them to make a decision in what is being told. There are no parallels in contemporary literature (but see Isa 42:23; 50:10) and the expression is therefore quite generally regarded as characteristic of Jesus himself. The word 'man' (*anthrōpos*, also found in Mt 18:12) seems to be superfluous but may have been intended to create a contrast with 'woman' in Lk 15:8. This would then be an indication that the two parables may have formed a pair from the beginning. It has also been suggested that both parables together refer to the Passover with its carrying of the sheep to the temple for slaughter, and the sweeping of the house for any piece of leavened bread. Apparently, the parable refers to a shepherd counting his sheep in the evening and discovering that he has lost one. In Luke, unlike Matthew where the result remains uncertain ('if he finds it'), the search is carried on until it is successful. The parable takes up the theme of God's care for his flock (Ez 34:11–16, 23–24).

Notwithstanding the noble symbol of the shepherd in the Old Testament (Ez 34; Ps 23[22]), a parable about a flesh-and-blood shepherd, who appears in the rabbinic lists of proscribed trades, would be a shock to the Pharisees' sensitivities. Unlike Mt 18:12, where 'one of them has gone astray', Lk 15:4 seems to blame the shepherd for having 'lost one of them'. According to Isa 53:6 all the sheep have gone astray. Apparently the storyteller thinks of the shepherd as leaving the ninety-nine in charge of an assistant while he looks for and brings home the lost sheep. Anyway, the story does not say that he left the ninety-nine totally unprotected; maybe they were driven into an enclosure. The security of *all* the sheep consists in the shepherd's willingness to go in search of any of them which may be lost.

> **Verse 5:** And when he has found it, he lays it on his shoulders, rejoicing.

Placing the sheep on his shoulders, the shepherd performs an action mentioned by Isaiah and Hosea. God himself will take the lost sheep upon his arms (used in the sense of shoulders). There is also the legend in *Midrash Rabbah Exodus* II.1 about Moses who as Jethro's shepherd went in search of a sheep that had gone astray in the wilderness. When he found it he put it on his shoulders and brought it to the flock. This made God decide that Moses would be the man to bring his people out of Egypt.

The key words 'finding' and 'rejoicing' lead to the core of the parable. A lost sheep usually lies down helplessly and refuses to move, so that the shepherd has to carry it over a long distance. It is nevertheless said that the shepherd rejoices. The participle 'rejoicing' (*chairōn*) as description of the situation is found only in Luke-Acts in the New Testament. Since Lk 19:37 adds it to Mk 11:9, and Luke uses the same in Acts 5:41; 8:39, it is probable that in Lk 15:5 and 19:6 it should also be attributed to Lucan redaction. When the shepherd has found the lost sheep, he has still a long way to go. Similarly, when the lost is found the task of restoration has just begun.

> **Verse 6:** And when he comes home, he calls together his friends and his neighbours, saying to them, 'Rejoice with me, for I have found my sheep which was lost.'

The motif of joy is further developed in the shepherd's invitation to his friends and neighbours to share in his joy, which is caused by the restoration of the totality. This feature is lacking from Matthew, but corresponds to the parable of the lost coin. In a sense, verse 6 does not fit well in the parable of the lost sheep, and may well have been derived by Luke (or Q?) from the parable of the lost coin (Lk 15:9). It has been suggested that the lost sheep was most probably owned by the village clan and so, having sustained the loss, they also rejoice together when the sheep is found. But the text says clearly 'I have found *my* sheep'.

> **Verse 7:** Just so, I tell you, there will be more joy in heaven over one sinner who repents than over ninety-nine righteous persons who need no repentance.

The formula 'I tell you' introduces the application of the parable. This application clearly refers to Lk 15:2 ('sinners') and was most probably already attached to the parable in the pre-Lucan tradition. The object of joy is no longer the finding of the sheep, but the return of a repentant sinner (cf. Lk 5:32). The parable, therefore, intends to make understood the joy God experiences when a sinner converts. As so often in biblical language, 'in heaven' is here a circumlocution for God. At the last judgment (this is most probably the meaning of *estai*, 'there will be'), God's joy over one repentant sinner will be greater than over ninety-nine righteous who stayed on the right path (cf. Mt 18:13). Jesus' concern for tax collectors and sinners reveals 'the soteriological joy of God'. In Jesus we see the Father at work (cf. Jn 14:9–10). The words 'righteous persons *who need no repentance*' may be ascribed to Luke, who in Lk 5:32 too adds the word 'repentance' to Mk 2:17. The phrase is often taken to be ironical, but it seems better to understand it as a way of emphasizing the importance God attaches to the repentance of a sinner.

The parable of the lost coin (Lk 15:8–10)

The structure of the parable of the lost coin is almost identical with that of the lost sheep (see above). Most probably the two parables were already told as a pair by Jesus himself. The parable is again in the form of a rhetorical question which, according to some, extends to the end of verse 9, while others place the question mark at the end of verse 8 and consider verse 9 as a statement. In contemporary culture it was certainly revolutionary to present a woman as an image of God's activity.

> **Verse 8:** Or what woman, having ten silver coins, if she loses one coin, does not light a lamp and sweep the house and seek diligently until she finds it?

The word *drachma* occurs only here in the New Testament, but often in the Septuagint (Gen 24:22; Ex 39:2, etc.). It is a 'silver coin' (RSV) of about the same value as the Roman denarius, and worth a day's wages. Living in a small windowless house with a low door, the woman must light a lamp (cf. Lk 11:33), and sweep the house (cf. Lk 11:25), and search diligently (*epimelōs*, 'carefully', cf. Lk 10:34–35; Acts 27:3), until she finds it. The intensity of the search is stressed here more than in the parable of the lost sheep. It has been pointed out that the Aramaic/Hebrew *suzim*, 'drachmae, coins', also means 'those that have moved away, departed', so that one may be dealing here with a word play, which makes the 'coins' an excellent image for people who have departed.

> **Verse 9:** And when she has found it, she calls together her friends and neighbours, saying, 'Rejoice with me, for I have found the coin which I had lost.'

This verse is an almost literal repetition of verse 6 (or is it the other way round?). Here as in verse 6 the emphasis is on the 'joy' which the friends and neighbours are invited to share. Again the joy is caused by the restoration of the totality, or the recovered wholeness.

> **Verse 10:** Just so, I tell you, there is joy before the angels of God over one sinner who repents.

The joy which in verse 7 was described as eschatological ('there will be') is here described as a present reality. 'In the presence of the angels' is again a periphrasis for the name of God. That the name of God is mentioned in the verse is no argument against this interpretation, since in Lk 22:69, Luke also added 'of God' to 'at the right hand of Power', i.e., God (compare Mk 14:62). This time the reference to 'righteous persons' is entirely missing, and the attention is more fully directed towards the repentant sinner.

The parable of the prodigal son (Lk 15:11–32)

Except for a few attempts to prove that the original parable consisted of Lk 15:11–24 and that Lk 15:25–32 was a later addition, possibly composed by the author of the gospel, practically all scholars accept the original unity of the whole parable. Stylistic, as well as juridical, form-critical and redaction-critical arguments are considered not to prove much, if anything, concerning the original unity of the parable.

Since the parable is conformed to Jesus' eschatological message, and compatible with the situation of Jesus' ministry, it is also usually accepted as authentic. Moreover, it has been established that this parable has been only slightly edited by the evangelist.

> **Verses 11–12:** And he said, 'There was a man who had two sons; (12) and the younger of them said to his father, "Father, give me the share of property that falls to me." And he divided his living between them.

Originally, the parable of the prodigal son was most probably not joined to the first two parables of Lk 15, 'and he said' being a very weak linkage. But the association of Lk 15:11–32 with the preceding parables is readily understandable, e.g., on the basis of the common theme 'lost and found' and shared joy. The parable proper begins with the words 'there was a man (*anthrōpos tis*) who had two sons' (compare Lk 16:1, 'there was a rich man who had a steward').

In the face of a number of interpretations which consider Lk 15:25–32 as not belonging to the original story, it should be pointed out that it deals from the beginning with a man who had *two* sons. It is a two-pronged parable in which 'the younger' (Lk 15:12) and 'the 'elder son' (Lk 15:25) refer in their distinction to the common beginning. It can also be said that the father figure gives unity to the parable. He forms the bridge between the two parts of the story. He is present at the beginning (Lk 15:11–12); he welcomes the younger son on his return (Lk 15:20–24); he exhorts the elder son at the end (Lk 15:31–32).

According to Deut 21:17, the elder son would receive two-thirds and the younger son one-third of the inheritance. The younger son, however, does not ask for his 'inheritance' (*klēronomia*; cf. Lk 12:13; 20:14; Acts 7:5; 20:32), which would involve a certain amount of responsibility in the family clan. Instead, he asks for his share of 'property' (in Greek, *ousia*, here alone in the New Testament). *To epiballon meros* ('the share of') is a technical term which occurs only here in the New Testament, but it appears repeatedly in the papyri, as do *ousia, bios, diaireō* ('to divide'), and *sunagō* ('to gather').

The father divided 'his living' between them. *Bios* in the sense of 'living', 'subsistence', is (except for I Jn 2:16; 3:17) found in the New Testament only in Lk 15:12, 30; 21:4 (= Mk 12:44). Luke himself speaks of *ta huparchonta tini* (Lk 8:3; 12:15; Acts 4:32), meaning 'possessions', 'financial means'. *Ousia* and *bios* are used here practically as synonyms.

In the light of Sir 33:19–23, which argues forcefully against giving one's property to anyone during one's lifetime, it is understood that the last moment of life is considered the right time for the kind of distribution requested by the younger son. In fact, his request is two-fold. He asks for the division of the property, which would give him ownership without the right to dispose of his share. But he received also — presumably because he requested it — disposition of his share. To the second, even more than to the first, he had no right until his father's death. Thus, as it were, the younger son treats his father as if he were already dead. It is all the more remarkable that the parable lets the father concur with the request.

The situation has been interpreted as follows: the father gives his part to the younger son, and remains the owner of the rest of his property until his death. The remainder would then go to the elder son alone, for the younger son had decided to remain no longer with his father and no longer to participate in the family enterprise. But there is one difficulty with this interpretation: according to Lk 15:12, the father divides his estate between his two sons and does not just give the younger son his share. The problem, then, does not seem to have received a satisfactory solution. Morever, several commentators have pointed out that the narrator may have had little concern for the juridical accuracy of his story. No matter what one may think of the legal implications of the younger son's demand and the father's reaction, one thing is clear: the parable takes for granted that by his departure the younger son had lost all rights and could not make any demands at his return. It does not intend to teach how the legal aspects of the matter were solved.

> **Verse 13:** Not many days later, the younger son gathered all he had and took his journey into a far country, and there he squandered his property in loose living.

Shortly after (cf. Acts 1:5) he got his share, the younger son 'gathered all he had' (*sunagein*, cf. Lk 3:17; 11:23; 12:17, 18), meaning that he 'turned the whole of his share into cash' (NEB). He 'took his journey', literally, 'he travelled away from his own people' (*apedēmēsen*; cf. Mk 12:1, parallel Mt 21:33 and Lk 20:9; Mt 25:14, 15). The Greek word for 'leaving his own people' can also be understood as a euphemism for 'dying' (cf. Lk 15:24, 32, 'for this my son/your brother was dead'). The expression 'into a far country' (*eis chōran makran*) occurs elsewhere in the New Testament only in Lk 19:12 (compare Mt 25:15, 'he went away'). As in Lk 19:12, here the expression 'into a far country' does not make the son into a type of the pagans, but it makes clear that the younger son is really separated from his father. He 'squandered his property' (*dieskorpisen*, literally, 'scattered'; cf. Lk 1:51; 16:1; Acts 5:37), 'in loose living' (*zōn asōtōs*, literally, 'living without hope of salvation'), i.e., in spendthrift living, or irretrievable squandering. As such the phrase does not specify how he wasted his money (contrast Lk 15:30), but implies that his fault resides mainly in the irremediable loss of the inheritance. One is reminded here of Prov 28:7, 'a companion of gluttons (*hos de poimainei asōtian*) shames his father'. Obtaining his 'share of property', therefore, was only a means; what the younger son was really after was freedom from the 'law of the father'.

> **Verses 14–16:** And when he had spent everything, a great famine arose in that country, and he began to be in want. (15) So he went and joined himself to one of the citizens of that country, who sent him into his fields to feed swine. (16) And he would gladly have fed on the pods that the swine ate; and no one gave him anything.

'A (great) famine arose' (*egeneto limos*; cf. Gen 47:13LXX) is a biblical expression. In a country which suffered ten famines in about 200 years (from 169 B.C. to A.D. 70), famine was a powerful image. As a lone Jew in a far country, without money or friends, the younger son more than others (emphatic *autos*) was in need.

He 'attached himself' (*kollaō*; cf. Lk 10:11; Acts 5:13; 8:29; 9:26; 10:28; 17:34) 'to a citizen', which means not just anybody, but a man of some means and position (cf. Lk 19:14; Acts 21:39). Acts 10:28 shows that such an attachment was reprehensible from the Jewish point of view. Some think that the parable suggests that he 'forced himself on' a citizen, who had not requested his services, and who therefore tried to get rid of him by assigning him a job he was expected to refuse. The Jews considered pigs unclean animals (Lev 11:7). Thus the younger son's 'freedom' ended in the pig sty.

'He desired to be fed' (*epethumei chortasthēnai*; cf. Lk 16:21 where the same is said of Lazarus; cf. also Lk 22:15, literally, 'with desire I have desired to eat this passover'). 'The pods that the swine ate' probably refers not to the Syrian carob (*ceratonia siliqua*), which is sweet and nutritious, and is eaten by many people, but to the bitter berries of the wild carob which are without nourishing value and did not enable him to fill his stomach. And no one was feeding him regularly, so that he was suffering hunger (cf. Lk 15:17).

> **Verses 17–19:** But when he came to himself he said, 'How many of my father's servants have bread enough to spare, but I perish here with hunger! (18) I will arise and go to my father, and I will say to him, "Father, I have sinned against heaven and before you; (19) I am no longer worthy to be called your son; treat me as one of your hired servants."'

These verses recall the Jewish saying, 'When a son (in need in a strange land) goes barefoot, then he remembers the comfort of his Father's house' (*M. Lam* 1:7).

It has sometimes been claimed that 'he came to himself' is not a true expression of repentance and means 'he reconsidered', or 'he changed his mind'. It has also been pointed out that for repentance in the real sense of the word one would expect the verb *metanoiein*. But it has been established beyond any reasonable doubt that the expression 'he came to himself' is in Hebrew and Aramaic an expression of repentance. This is also clear from the continuation, the confession and declaration of unworthiness, and the return home described as 'to go to my father'. He really came to himself and was moved to penitence; the movement by which he returned to his father should be seen from beginning to end as possessing a unity.

'Arising' (*anastas*) often accompanies verbs which mark a movement (cf. Gen 32:23LXX), and should not be given an independent meaning. 'I will arise and go' means 'I will go at once'. The prodigal's planned confession is in harmony with the rabbinic doctrine of repentance which was based on Lam 5:21, 'restore us to yourself, O Lord, that we may be restored', and Mal 3:7, 'return to me, and I will return to you, says the Lord of hosts'.

The formulation of the son's confession should be understood against the background of the Old Testament literary genre of the confession of sins. This genre is always introduced by the admission formula, 'I have sinned', or 'we have sinned', often followed by the name of the person against whom the sin was committed, introduced by the preposition *le*, which the Septuagint translates by a mere dative, or by *eis, enantion*, or *enōpion*, which all mean 'against'. Of special importance for our present text is Ex 10:16, where the Pharaoh addresses Moses and Aaron with the words 'I have sinned against (*enantion*) the Lord your God, and against (*eis*) you'. All this shows clearly that the translation sometimes proposed, 'I have sinned until heaven', i.e., 'my guilt is so great that it reaches up to heaven', is wrong. 'Heaven' here stands for the person of God against whom the sin was committed. Furthermore, there is no theological distinction between 'against (*eis*) heaven' and 'before (*enōpion*) you'. This means also that in Lk 15:18, 21 the sin against the father is considered a real sin which parallels the sin against God. The wording of this verse also indicates that there is no allegorical equation of the father with God. The father's behaviour must represent a real human possibility. Otherwise, one could attribute such forgiveness to God, who is different anyway, while at the same time considering it impossible or not required in the community. It is not fully clear exactly what the prodigal referred to as his sin — his loose and wasteful living, his leaving home, or both — but he certainly believed that he had destroyed his relationship with his father and had thus lost the right of sonship.

The son's conversation with himself begins and ends with the phrase 'hired servants'. The 'hired servant' (*misthios*), or casual labourer, lived in the village. In many ways his existence was more precarious than that of the servants or slaves (*douloi* or *paides*) who belonged to the estate. But, unlike the latter, the 'hired servant' was a free man and could earn his own salary.

> **Verses 20–21:** And he arose and came to his father. But while he was yet at a distance, his father saw him and had compassion, and ran and embraced him and kissed him. (21) And the son said to him, 'Father, I have sinned against heaven and before you; I am no longer worthy to be called your son.'

The son at once carried out his purpose. His father saw him when he was still at a distance (cf. Tob 11:5–6). What would have happened if the father had not seen him? The Greek verbs in this sentence are in a different tense. While the son was yet far away (*apechontos*; present participle; his being far away is a present — and continuous — situation), the father saw him (*eiden*, aorist). The father's seeing is the real act which brings the son near. The word 'yet' indicates that the son could not really do anything to reach his father. By his compassion the father saved him. The father saved him 'while he was yet at a distance', i.e., while he was still hopelessly lost. The whole salvation comes from the father. The son is accepted with no further conditions to fulfil; he has found the freedom which at first he thought he would find by leaving his father.

The actions of the father speak volumes of meaning, surpassing the best of language in communicating his response. Some have understood them as intended to protect the boy from the hostility of the inevitably gathering village crowd. His compassion (cf. Lk 7:13; 10:33) here includes his awareness of what his son will have to go through as he enters the village. Two of the four things that frighten Sirach are 'the slander of a city, the gathering of a mob' (Sir 26:5). First, the father 'ran' down the road (cf. Tob 11:9). An Oriental man of a certain status never runs. Sir 19:30 says that 'a man's manner of walking shows what he is'. The father of this parable, however, forgets about his dignity. Then, he 'embraced him and kissed him' (compare Acts 20:37), or better, 'he kissed him again and again' (*kataphilein*). The father's kisses are not a sign of equality, but rather a sign of reconciliation and forgiveness. Compare especially Gen 33:4, 'But Esau ran to meet him, and embraced him, and fell on his neck and kissed him'.

It should be noted that the father's compassion is not based on the son's appeal. The father had compassion 'while he was yet at a distance', and he hastened to greet him affectionately before he had said a word. Just as Jesus 'receives sinners and eats with them' (Lk 15:2) without first demanding signs of repentance, so the father accepts his son without waiting for him to first prove himself truly repentant and worthy. This feature may correspond to the seeking and searching in the parable of the lost sheep and the lost coin.

Comparing verse 21 with the prepared speech in verses 18–19, one notices that the last part, 'treat me as one of your hired servants', is lacking. It cannot be excluded that we are merely dealing here with a shortened repetition. Traditional exegesis translates the beginning of the verse as '*but* he said', indicating a contrast (see RSV, JB, NEB; different NAB), and generally assumes that the father interrupts his son. It has, however, also been suggested that the son changed his mind in that he gives up 'earning his own way', or offering his own solution. He had been prepared to face the authority of a father who

could forgive him after admission of his fault. But now that he is
confronted by his father's tenderness, which had already forgiven him
before any confession of his fault, he has finally reached the point
where he can forgo pride and accept the gracious love of his father.
Nothing should be added to the words 'I am not worthy'. He did not
speak the last words of his prepared speech because of what he saw of
his father's love which he now accepts without condition.

> **Verses 22–24:** But the father said to the servants, 'Bring
> quickly the best robe, and put it on him; and put a ring on his
> hand, and shoes on his feet; (23) and bring the fatted calf and
> kill it, and let us eat and make merry; (24) for this my son
> was dead, and is alive again; he was lost, and is found.' And
> they began to make merry.

Next the father turned to the servants and ordered them to honour
the prodigal as the son of the house. 'The best robe' (literally, 'the
first robe') will assure the son of respect. There may be an allusion
here to Isa 61:10, 'for he has clothed me with the garments of
salvation, he has covered me with the robe of righteousness' (which
would give the robe eschatological significance). The ring is most
likely a signet ring of the house (cf. Gen 41:42, 'then Pharaoh took
his signet ring from his hand and put it on Joseph's hand, and arrayed
him in garments of fine linen'). This command is a remarkable
expression of the father's trust in his son. The shoes indicate that he is
considered a free man in the house, and by putting these shoes on his
feet, the servants show that they accept him as their master. The
successive acts of the father suggest a complete reintegration of the
younger son into the family.

Some similarities have been noted with a Buddhist story which
begins like the present parable. But when the boy in that story
returns home, he begins to work off his guilt and the penalty for his
previous behaviour by years of service to his father. This illustrates
the difference between the principle of *Karma* and that of grace, free
forgiveness and full restoration of one who is undoubtedly guilty.

Finally, the father ordered the killing of the fatted calf, the grain-
fed animal (*situeton*, derived from *sitos*, 'grain'), kept for a special
occasion (compare I Sam 28:24f.). The killing of the calf indicates
that the celebration is intended for the whole community in a desire
to reconcile the son with that whole community. 'To make merry'
(*euphrainein*) is especially used of the enjoyment of meals (cf. Lk
12:19; 16:19). Both extremities of the prodigal son's situation are
represented by means of eating imagery. In the depths of his misery
he was hungry and would have liked to eat carob-pods, i.e., animal

fodder'; and no one gave him anything to eat. But now, upon his return, the fatted calf is killed for him.

While 'was dead and is alive again' summarizes the story of the younger son, 'he was lost, and is found' summarizes the story of the father. The word *nekros* ('dead') has a religious meaning in Acts 3:15, and the theme of salvation, of a return to life, is frequently found in the New Testament. The section dealing with the younger son ends with a statement which is repeated in practically the same words in verse 32, and functions as a sort of refrain. The parallel use of 'dead' (*nekros*) and 'lost' (*apolōlōs*) is very similar to that in Ps 31(30):13, 'I am totally forgotten as one who is dead (*nekros*), I have become like a lost (*apolōlōs*) object'. The clause 'he was lost and is found' links this parable to the preceding two. The feast is the proclamation of the recovered wholeness. With the clause 'they began to make merry' the parable starts anew and moves towards a second climax.

> **Verses 25–28a:** Now his elder son was in the field; and as he came and drew near to the house, he heard music and dancing. (26) And he called one of the servants and asked what this meant. (27) And he said to him, 'Your brother has come, and your father has killed the fatted calf, because he has received him safe and sound.' (28a) But he was angry and refused to go in.

With verse 25 the second part of the parable begins. The elder brother's attitude affords a very sharp contrast to that of the father. That the elder son was not notified immediately has rightly been considered a 'stage managed' effect. The elder son was outside the house, in the fields, and his home-coming is presented as parallel to the journey of the younger son. As he approached the house he heard music (*sumphōnia*) and dancing. This music would have started while the preparations for the meal were still in progress and the first guests were arriving upon returning from the fields.

He called 'one of the young boys (*paides*)' congregated outside the house, who tried to catch as much as possible of the feast, which was attended only by adults, and asked him a series of questions (imperfect, 'kept asking him'). 'He asked what this meant' (cf. Lk 18:36 where Luke adds to his Marcan source 'he inquired what this meant'). It is also possible that the *paides* (RSV, 'servants') should be identified with the *douloi* (RSV, 'servants') of verse 22.

By refusing to go in, he declines to fulfil his role as elder son at the feast. Instead he will humiliate his father publicly by quarrelling while the guests are present (verses 29–30). This means a break in relationship between the elder son and his father, which is (almost) as serious as the break between the father and the younger son at the beginning of the parable. His refusal to participate in the feast, expressed in the presence of the important people of the village, was a grave insult to the father (cf. Esther 1:12).

> **Verses 28b–30:** His father came out and entreated him, (29) but he answered his father, 'Lo, these many years I have served you, and I never disobeyed your command; yet you never gave me a kid, that I might make merry with my friends. (30) But when this son of yours came, who has devoured your living with harlots, you killed for him the fatted calf!'

Just as the father went out to meet the younger son, so he now comes out and entreats the elder son to join the celebration, thus repeating the same gesture of love.

In contrast to the younger son, the elder reacts to the father's demonstration of unexpected love, not with a confession, but with a complaint and an enumeration of his merits (cf. the Pharisee in Lk 18:11–12, and the rich ruler in Lk 18:21). Omitting all use of a title and demonstrating the attitude of a slave (cf. the verb *douleuō*, literally, 'I slave'), not of a son, he projects an image whose only redeeming feature is that he obeys commands (cf. Deut 26:13, '... I have not transgressed any of your commandments'). He has misunderstood the interpersonal relationship with his father, whom he regards as an employer or master, not as a father. In a clause which, because of the emphatic 'to me' at the beginning, is very egocentric, '*to me* you never gave a kid', he accuses his father of favouritism. There is a clear contrast between 'a kid' and 'the fatted calf', as there is between 'with my friends' and 'with harlots'.

The elder son's fault is that he derives a claim from his performance: he misses *metanoia*, the renunciation of all claims. He believed that his relationship with his father was based on merit and reward. The elder brother's sin 'is not the prideful will to independence and a denial of sonship, but the equally prideful presumption that his sonship was earned, a presumption manifest in his refusal to accept this brother as a brother because the latter had not "earned" his sonship'.[62] The elder son never leaves the house. He is not lost with a loss which permits a return. He does not leave the father by going away; he leaves him, as it were, 'from within'.

To underline the elder son's anger, Luke does not write 'my brother', but 'this son of yours' (*huios sou houtos*). *Houtos* may have here a pejorative sense (cf. Lk 18:11). The elder son reminds the

father that the younger one has squandered his share of the **inheritance**. To the previous description of the younger son's behaviour, the elder adds 'with harlots'. Typically, his objection to his younger brother's celebration is basically selfish, though it is couched in terms of normative morality. Indeed, the underside of much rigid morality is childish selfishness.

> **Verses 31–32:** And he said to him, 'Son, you are always with me, and all that is mine is yours. (32) It was fitting to make merry and be glad, for this your brother was dead, and is alive; he was lost, and is found.'

Using the affectionate and reconciliatory *teknon*, 'child', rather than *huios*, 'son', the father assures him that his rights are not affected by the grace shown to his younger brother: 'all that is mine is yours'. The elder son complained that the father never gave him anything; the father replied that he already had everything. Communion on the level of being entails the communication of having.

> Here in a completely unstudied and spontaneous fashion, Luke has expressed an understanding of possessions which reveals how they can be a symbol of human relationships. When people are together in unity ('you are with me always') they share all possessions ('All that is mine is yours'), and the sharing of possessions signifies that unity. When persons are alienated, the property is divided, and the separation of persons is expressed by each holding 'what is his own.' It cannot go unnoticed how strikingly Lk 15:31 anticipates the language and thought of Acts 4:32ff., particularly in the note that those who are together in unity share all with each other.[63]

The similarity has also been noted between Lk 15:31 and Jn 17:10, 'all mine are thine, and thine are mine'.

To the elder son's 'never' (verse 29), the father opposes 'always'. Then he appeals to him to rejoice at his brother's return. Tactfully, he says 'one should make merry and be glad' not to press his elder son too much. Some say that although the Greek text is ambiguous, and most English translations add 'we', the text seems rather to suggest 'you'. The proximity of 'yours' and 'your' in the preceding and following clauses seems to support this interpretation: 'it was fitting *for you* to make merry', '*you* must make merry'. The return of a brother, more than a good meal with one's cronies, should be an occasion for great joy.

It has been pointed out that the 'refrain' formulated in Lk 15:24

and 32 brings about a truly poetic effect (the same can be said of Lk 15:18 and 21). It links the brothers inseparably to each other and to the father. The father's reply does not contain either an apology for the banquet or a reproach against the elder brother. The gentle reminder 'this (is) your brother' should not be interpreted as an attack. The father's words are rather an urgent plea to understand his offer of grace. The story ends with the elder son still outside. The individual listeners/readers must decide what their response will be.

The concluding clause 'he was lost, and is found' again relates Lk 15:11–32 to the two previous parables and to the broader context of Jesus' ministry (Lk 5:32; 19:10).

The message of Luke 15

The parable of the lost sheep

The parable on the level of Jesus

The starting point for the understanding of the parable on the level of Jesus is the metaphorical meaning of the 'sheep'. In the Old Testament, the Septuagint and early Judaism, the sheep (and the sheepfold) stand for the 'people'. When Jesus spoke of a sheep which got lost from the flock, his hearers must have immediately understood that he referred to someone who went astray from the people of God. Such persons were the tax collectors and sinners, in contrast to the righteous. To the metaphorical world of the 'sheep' also belongs the 'shepherd', who most of the time symbolizes God (sometimes also Moses, the king, or a leader of the people). This context is evoked even if the shepherd is not explicitly mentioned. The proportion of ninety-nine to one intends to emphasize the apparent lack of importance of the one sheep. That it is sought is in the first place due not to its own individual importance, but to the fact that it belongs to the flock. The flock should be complete.

Throughout the parable the shepherd remains the subject, indicating that only *his* conduct matters. The concepts of 'going astray' and 'repenting' are not yet mentioned. The initial question suggests that it is obvious for the shepherd to go after the lost sheep. The hearers are invited to make their own the attitude towards the lost sheep of Israel which is referred to by the parable. This is underlined by the description of the joy which the shepherd experiences at the moment he finds the sheep: he rejoices more over the one sheep than over the ninety-nine which did not get lost. This feature intends to illustrate the joy of the moment, and does not imply an evaluation of the ninety-nine.

In the context of Jesus' ministry this parable will have referred to his attitude towards tax collectors and sinners. He was a 'friend of tax collectors and sinners' (Mt 11:19; Lk 7:34). Taking into account the metaphorical contents of the 'sheep–shepherd' complex, it becomes clear that Jesus legitimates his attitude by means of God's attitude towards sinners; even more, that he sees himself in a function which belongs to God. Jesus' conduct is the actual form in which God's saving intervention appears. In his words and deeds Jesus is now what God was all the time for Israel. God's nearness to the lost materializes in Jesus' nearness to tax collectors and sinners. In this sense the parable is also a self-testimony of Jesus with obvious Christological implications.[64]

The early Christian community

The Christian community noticed the implicit Christological claim of the parable and responded to it by interpreting the shepherd Christology (although the shepherd is not mentioned explicitly — perhaps because the narrator himself is a shepherd?). By the embellishment now found in Lk 15:5, which recalls Isa 40:11; 49:22, it indicates that in Jesus God goes in search of those who are lost in an eschatological sense (see especially Isa 49:22). Moreover, Jesus' conduct is explicitly theologically founded, especially in the pre-Lucan application (Lk 15:7), more specifically by the expression 'in heaven', which is a paraphrase for God. The community has thus preserved the parable as a word of the historical Jesus. This could be done only by interpreting it Christologically. The question must be raised, however, whether by the contrast between 'repenting sinners' and 'righteous who need no repentance' the community is not introducing a legalistic element which was foreign to the original parable and Jesus' conduct. Originally, the reason for joy was not the *repentance* of the sinner, but his having been *found*.

Matthew

Without giving up the reference to Jesus' conduct, Matthew puts the parable into the service of a warning addressed to the community (Mt 18:1–35). Here too the parable ties up with Jesus' conduct and invites the hearers to let Jesus' conduct become once more effective in their own conduct towards erring members of the community. As long as this connection is observed the parable can be understood outside a perspective of law. But as soon as this is no longer the case, Jesus' conduct can receive a merely exemplary character, and so place people under a new commandment. The fact that in Mt 18:12 a change of subject occurs ('you' — 'a man') and that in Mt 18:14 the 'will' of the Father is substituted for 'joy' shows that the danger of 'law abidance' has not been sufficiently perceived and counteracted.[65]

Luke

The same danger, not totally absent in the pre-Lucan community, was counteracted by Luke through the insertion of verse 6, in which he emphasized once more God's joy over the recovered sheep. He concentrated on God as the only subject of the action and thereby avoided the danger of making the acceptance of the sinner depend on the latter's action.

The framework by which Luke sketched a typical situation in Jesus' life (Lk 15:1–2) indicates the aim of the parable. Luke was not particularly interested in the close relationship of the shepherd and the sheep (as in Jn 10), or in the untiring search of the shepherd, but in the contrast between the ninety-nine sheep and the one. This is confirmed by the concluding application: 'Just so God will rejoice more over one sinner who (through Jesus' proclamation and conduct) repents, than over ninety-nine righteous persons who need no repentance' (Lk 15:7). If this statement is to be attributed to Luke, it contains an additional criticism of the Pharisees' understanding of righteousness which Luke expresses at the conclusion of a series of parables (Lk 15:1 – 16:13): 'You are those who justify yourselves before men, but God knows your hearts' (Lk 16:15).

The parable is in the first place concerned with Jesus' conduct towards sinners. By this conduct Jesus has provoked the critique of the Pharisees and the scribes and has challenged their concept of God. In the face of their criticism Jesus claims: My conduct towards sinners (or in the language of the parable: the conduct of the shepherd towards the one sheep) is the same as God's conduct towards sinners (Lk 15:7). In Jesus' conduct, God's concern and liberating, saving activity can be experienced. Jesus is God's interpreter against the entire theological tradition of his time. The parable does not deal with God's future action in a world to come. Jesus is the locus in which God's eschatological love and concern for people can be experienced in the here and now of the nearness of the kingdom.

The parable of the lost coin

On the level of Jesus' ministry

The first part of the parable concentrates on the intensive search by the woman, while the second part expresses the exuberant joy over the recovery of the lost coin. Both parts are important; the intensive search corresponds to the great joy. In contrast to the parable of the lost sheep, in which the leaving of the ninety-nine sheep constitutes a dramatic exaggeration, the search for the lost coin is self-evident. Throughout the parable the woman is the acting subject. The lost coin determines the action only insofar as it is the object of the search and — when found — the ground of the woman's joy. The parable places the hearers in a situation which enables them to understand the woman's search and to agree with her joy experienced in finding the coin.

The parable refers to God as the one who seeks people and who experiences exuberant joy in finding them. The parable may be understood as a parable of the kingdom insofar as the nearness of the kingdom is expressed in the search and the joy. In the parable the kingdom of God comes so close to the hearers that they learn to understand themselves as lost. At the same time they are liberated from an outlook in which they try to overcome their lost condition by their own efforts. They should let themselves be sought and should share in God's joy when they are found. Those who understand themselves as lost in the sense of the parable understand also their belonging to God.

God's search for what is lost has become a reality in Jesus' life. The nearness of the kingdom materializes in Jesus' nearness to people. In the parable Jesus explains his search for people as God's search. He tells people that to be far from God is to be lost, a distance which only God can overcome, or rather, which he has already overcome wherever the parable event has its effect.

On the level of the pre-Lucan community and of Luke

In Lk 15:10 the pre-Lucan community interprets 'being found' as the *metanoia* of the sinner. On the other hand, it emphasizes God's joy so strongly that the danger of understanding *metanoia* as the condition for salvation is sufficiently countered. Possibly for the pre-Lucan community, but certainly for Luke, *metanoia* is closely related to the person of Jesus (Lk 15:1–3). Thereby the theological claim of Jesus' parable becomes explicitly Christological.[66]

The parable of the prodigal son

On the level of Jesus' ministry

The parable speaks of the nearness of God's kingdom as an event of love, and must, therefore, first of all be interpreted in the context of Jesus' life. While he reminds us of God, the father of the parable refers in the first place to Jesus himself. Indeed, the parable does not speak of God's love in general, but it makes God's love into an event. Jesus' call to following and his meal-association with tax collectors and sinners are so many expressions of the love of God. Jesus, therefore, anchors his conduct in the conduct of God. The parable appears, then, as a justification of Jesus' conduct towards tax collectors and sinners. Jesus acts this way because God does so too. Jesus' actual conduct and the parable are very closely related to each other.

Jesus knows himself sent to establish *God's* justice and love among people. But he does not do it the way it is done by world-improvers and prophets of doom who, without admitting it, place themselves above people, and from their elevated viewpoint indicate what goes wrong (interpersonally and structurally), and how things should be. Jesus, however, stands amidst sinners and in solidarity bears their sins and guilt with them, and forgives them. Therefore, he does not offer a definition or an analysis of God, of himself, of sin, repentance, forgiveness and self-righteousness. But the reality of God, of Jesus, of sin, repentance, forgiveness and self-righteousness is constantly present in the parable.

The contents of the parable correspond fully to the life story, the message and praxis of Jesus: on behalf of God Jesus socialized with the outcasts of official religion and society, went in search of what was lost, and spoke of God's joy in finding it. God wants Jesus to act thus on earth: like Father, like son. God's love and mercy for tax collectors and sinners has manifested itself definitively or eschatologically in Jesus. And whoever attacks Jesus, attacks God himself. Therefore, on the level of Jesus' ministry, the parable, as a justification of Jesus against the Pharisees and the scribes, has an eschatological and Christological dimension.

On the level of Luke's redaction

Joy is the password of Luke's gospel. At the announcement of the birth of John the Baptist, the angel says, 'and you will have joy and gladness, and many will rejoice at his birth' (Lk 1:14). The 'narrative of the things which have been accomplished among us' (Lk 1:1) is in Luke's gospel set in a story of joy. The reason, the cause, and the context of this joy is the birth of a son, the 'good news of a great joy which will come to all the people' (Lk 2:10). Joy is also the password of Lk 15, where the joy is caused by the finding of what is lost: the lost sheep, the lost coin, and the lost or prodigal son.

It is interesting to note the sequence of words in the last sentence of the first two parables: 'Rejoice with me, for I have found... which was lost' (Lk 15:6, 9). First there is joy; the reason for this joy is the finding, which in its turn was directed towards the lost. Our attention is drawn, then, not to the sorrow caused by the bereavement, but to the proclamation of joy. This joy serves at the same time as exegesis and interpretation of what God does among men. Lk 15 does not emphasize the sorrow caused by what was lost, but rather that real joy is *shared* joy: 'rejoice with me'. Wherever joy is not the joy of all, of 'all the people' (Lk 2:10), it stagnates and will soon disappear. That is where the danger of sorrow looms; not in the loss of something or somebody, but that there would be somebody who would not participate in the joy. That is what Lk 15 is about; and therefore, in Luke's formulation, joy is given an imperative character; joy is commanded, and rebellion against God now consists in the refusal of this joy.

Joy because of a sinner who repents can be understood only in terms of an act of compassion on God's part. A sinner does not convert *himself*, for what then would 'to be lost' mean? Sin is not a fiction, but it consists in being alienated from our liberator. The joy of which Luke writes is precisely that our liberator is alienably in our midst. This joy is not threatened by the sinner, but by the 'righteous persons who need no repentance'. Will they rejoice when the sinner repents? The question is not whether God will have mercy on the sinner. It is whether, now that God's mercy has appeared in the midst of sinners, whom he receives and with whom he eats (cf. Lk 15:2), the righteous will rejoice, or whether they have something of the devil in that they do not rejoice at the conversion of a sinner.

One thing is sure: we cannot come to the father except because of the sinner who was lost and is found. Together with the person whom we have made the scapegoat we should approach the Father. There is no other joy. But it is the greatest of all joys, as the last verse of Lk 15 indicates: 'it was fitting to make merry and be glad'.

Luke has perceived the connection between Jesus' conduct and the parable at least insofar as he placed the latter in the present context (Lk 15:1–3). The fact that Luke combined the two other parables (Lk 14:4–7 and 8–10), in which he emphasized the joy experienced in finding what was lost (cf. Lk 15:6), with the present parable, may indicate that Luke was especially interested in the invitation to share God's (and Jesus') joy over the repentance of a sinner. How far Luke understands repentance as a condition for salvation is not fully clear from this parable. The parable *itself* states that salvation precedes repentance. It does not teach that the prodigal son must repent, but that the father's love exceeds all ordinary human boundaries and precedes his son's confession.

In the composition of Lk 15 the evangelist places Jesus in a 'unity of action' with God. Lk 15 thus belongs to the **Lucan proclamation of Christ** to his community. They should know how God thinks about the lost, and that through Jesus he extends salvation to all. This proclamation is a warning to take repentance seriously, to let oneself be gathered by Jesus, and to give up all opposition to Christ's universal mediation of salvation, which excludes the oppositionists as lost sons of the Father. Thereby Luke aims also at an ecclesial attitude by which the community searches for the lost, is prepared for reconciliation, and integrates all in the house of the Father. The parable thus also receives a missionary dimension.

The parable is open-ended. It does not tell us whether the elder son eventually joined the celebration or not. The listeners/readers themselves must answer the question whether the elder son will give up his opposition or not. When the parable ends the elder son is still outside, unreconciled with his brother, but the father has affirmed the bond of unity between his son and himself. The father has seen the failures of both sons, but he affirms their relationship anyway. Anybody inclined to be satisfied with the situation as it presents itself at the end of the parable, should ask whether he can live so easily without the elder brother. In the house of the father this is impossible. The elder brother should participate in the celebration. The father shows as much concern for the elder son as for the younger. Lk 15:11–32 is indeed a parable about the lost and to-be-recovered communion of both the sinners and the righteous with God.

Reflection

People become lost in a gradual process of events whereby they feel unwanted and unable to cope with the expectations put upon them by others or by themselves. Countless lives are wasted because of preconceived assumptions and judgments, violence and prejudice. The young, the old, the poor, the unemployed are wasted. Many of them are lost people. Usually they are not explicitly told to 'get lost', but those who are better off do not want to see them, or effectively help them to a better life. Often the problems of people lost in society are not faced because of self-interest. What happens to individuals or certain groups in a given society, happens also to whole peoples and countries.

> Luke's account is a kind of digest: the departure, ruin, and return follow each other in quick succession; but we can actually imagine a long space of time between the different moments of the venture. The son does not return to the father to escape the

phantasms of a hostile world; it is a return to reality, to identity. He is stripped of the alienating factor of his money. He thinks about those who work in his father's house and asks to be a part of this group. The father restores his dignity: he puts him back into his history, into his identity. But nowhere does it say that he restored his lost goods. The relation of the youth to his goods seems turned around. Before, his goods followed him, went with him — he carried his inheritance in his pockets. Afterwards, it is he who goes toward the goods. They are in front of him and against him as a challenge he must accept and must resolve through work... The prodigal had to have this experience of losing everything that was alienating him, preventing him from experiencing the real, in order to find himself again, identifying himself and thus discovering a liberated and liberating love...

We can live our whole life alienated within the power, worth, and possession of the father, in a kind of comfortable casing in which we were born. And this is the highest treason that the middle-class family wreaks upon the children. The price that the rich man immediately pays for the goods he has squirreled away, in prejudice to others, is this: the possibility of leaving an inheritance to his children that will close off the road of life for them. Through a strange irony the rich man accumulates money on the pretext of 'opening up the road' for his children and in reality he does just the opposite.[67]

... the gospel is not an additional power, message, or insight that completes the fabric of little rules within which the individual feels secure — that fabric which convinces him of his competency to judge. Instead, the gospel is a disturbing event involving a radical readjustment of what he understands by right and wrong. In other words, the hearing of the gospel introduces into his life the new justice, which shatters the old... no matter how just the elder brother's claim may appear to be, its plausibility is in doubt because of the complex of anger that motivated it. It does not possess the clear and balanced perspective of righteous anger, typical of a prophetic protest, but is deeply distorted by personal references... in all his insistence upon justice — the one question that must always be put to him and to those who in every age he represents is: How can a man who has no ultimate concern for others really know what justice is? How can he be serious about justice without recognizing that it is precisely in such a concern for others that genuine justice is to be found... And since, moreover, there is no hint of the elder brother's ever being reconciled to the father and to the prodigal, the suggestion will remain that such failure as a form of opposition to the graciousness of God within religion is more dangerous than the escape from God into irreligion. At least the latter in its nakedness may be seen for what it is, while the former remains concealed.[68]

The father's deed is the factual liberation of the elder son from a significant portion of his material legacy and the advantage it gave him over the other son. With his word, the father offers his elder son instead the freedom and liberty of true brotherhood with that marginated and errant younger son. The father *gives to* his younger son in order to offer him the liberation as a son; he *takes from* the elder in order to offer him liberation as a brother. The story does not tell us how either son finally responded. Clearly both were surprised; their human expectations were judged, and a wholly new, unexpected and messianic possibility and promise were offered them. They were presented with a decision; they were offered a freedom and a liberation. The parable is God's word to both; even today it remains to both a word of promised liberation and a call to faithful decision.[69]

One way of describing what happens in this story is to describe it as a 'social drama', a story which plays out some of the tensions inherent in a society. Anthropologists use the term for rituals in which societies diffuse the tensions that build up by dramatizing them. This story is a carefully orchestrated whole, which should never be told without the concluding scene with the elder brother. The Lucan context provides a clue as to what the tension is all about. It is not just an invitation to sinners to repent, though the younger son provides a powerful image for the benefits that can come from repentance. It is also an invitation to the righteous, to the elder brother. Notice how carefully paralleled the two scenes are… The parable asserts the father's unity with the elder in as strong terms as it insists on the appropriateness of his treatment of the younger. By doing so, it leaves open the possibility for the elder to go in and rejoice. Neither son is permitted to score a victory over the other. That lesson is, perhaps, the hardest one we have to apply when we are trying to create our own reconciliations between opposing groups.[70]

The murmuring of the scribes and the Pharisees and the repeated invitations to 'rejoice with me' form a striking contrast. If we overlook the part of the elder son we lose sight of the fact that conflicts exist and that this parable is part of a story full of conflicts. By his attitude towards tax collectors and sinners Jesus tried to get something going but was opposed by the scribes and the Pharisees. Through this parable Jesus tried to change their minds, but the story ends abruptly in Lk 15:32 without any mention of success, and in Lk 22:2 we read that 'the chief priests and the scribes were seeking how to put him to death'. Jesus was not successful with the scribes and the Pharisees. Rather, the elder son — to use the images of the parable — together with his 'friends' (Lk 15:29) killed 'the Father'. Indeed, the narrator of this story was killed, but ultimately rediscovered not in a tomb, but alive and present in his community where his stories are narrated over and over again.

10 The unjust steward
(Lk 16:1–13)

General context

The parable of the unjust steward is again found in the Lucan Travel Narrative (Lk 9:51 – 19:44). Following the parable of the great supper (Lk 14:15–24), the journey theme is resumed in Lk 14:25, 'now great multitudes accompanied him (more literally, travelled with him)', and the next spatial indication will be found in Lk 17:11, 'on the way to Jerusalem he was passing along between Samaria and Galilee'. The immediate context of the parable is Lk 16, which may be considered a literary unity. Between Lk 15:1–32, three parables by which Jesus defends his attitude toward tax collectors and sinners against the scribes and Pharisees, and Lk 17:1–10, a teaching specifically addressed to the disciples, Lk 16 is essentially composed of two parables about riches, both beginning with the words 'there was a rich man' (Lk 16:1, 19). Lk 15 immediately precedes our parable, and there are textual indications that Lk 16:1–13 is tied to the preceding chapter. Firstly, the scene for these parables (lost sheep, lost coin, prodigal son, unjust steward) is set in Lk 15:1–2. There is no new description of the action in Lk 16:1. Secondly, 'he also said...' expresses continuity with what preceded. Thirdly, all four texts share the parable form, and this continuity is emphasized by certain verbal connections, e.g., *anthrōpos tis*, 'a certain man', found in Lk 15:11; 16:1 (and 16:19). Finally, the verb *diaskorpizein*, in the sense of 'squandering other people's property', is found only in Lk 15:13 and 16:1 in the whole New Testament.

While the parable of the unjust steward is related in Lk 16:1–13, Lk 16:19–31 tells the story of the rich man and Lazarus. In the thought of the evangelist these two parables deal with the same theme: the use of money. The example of the unjust steward should teach the disciples (Lk 16:1) a correct use of money; that of the rich man and Lazarus should make the Pharisees (cf. Lk 16:14) understand the danger incurred by using it wrongly (Lk 16:19–31).

170

The subject of riches is very important to Luke, who presents no less than five stories about rich men in his Travel Narrative (Lk 12:13–21; 16:1–13; 16:19–31; 18:18–30; 19:1–10), not to speak of several other passages which deal with possessions (e.g. Lk 12:22–34, etc.).

The two parables are separated by a series of sayings on Pharisaic hypocrisy (Lk 16:14–15), on John the Baptist (Lk 16:16), on the law (Lk 16:17), and on divorce (Lk 16:18). A similar arrangement of two parables separated by a series of sayings is found in Lk 12:13–37, where the parable of the rich fool (Lk 12:13–21) and the parable on watchfulness (Lk 12:35–37) are separated by a series of sayings on anxiety about earthly things. In fact, the story of the unjust steward is an almost perfect antithesis of the parable of the rich fool, especially if one takes into account the commendation of the master, saying that the steward has acted wisely (*phronimōs*; Lk 16:8a), which contrasts with God's reproach, 'Fool!' (*aphrōn*; Lk 12:20). The application found in Lk 16:9 adds a new link, speaking of the moment at which the money will 'fail' (*hotan eklipēi*, recalling the way in which Lk 12:33 speaks of a 'treasure in heaven that does not fail' (*anekleipton*).

There is also an extrinsic connection between the teaching on riches in Lk 16 and the preceding parable of the prodigal son (Lk 15:11–32), which at least in one respect deals with the improper use of possessions. In its present Lucan context, then, the parable of the unjust steward forms part of a group of pericopes dealing with the use of wealth.

Lk 16:16–18 constitutes a little unit composed of three originally unrelated sentences, already grouped before they reached Luke, and attached to the following parable because of the mention of 'the law and the prophets' (Lk 16:16), on the one hand, and 'Moses and the prophets' (Lk 16:29, 31), on the other. Although the role of Lk 16:15 is more difficult to define, it should most probably be attached to verse 14. Thus it becomes clear that, on the level of the Lucan redaction, Lk 16:14–31 is very coherent. In Lk 16:14–15 Jesus denounces the false assurances of the Pharisees, the representatives of Israel (cf. Lk 14:11; 18:14). The self-justifying Pharisees are known by God and they are 'an abomination in the sight of God' (Lk 16:15). Then follows Lk 16:16–18, the only Lucan passage in which Jesus speaks explicitly of the duration of the law. Moreover, Lk 16:16–17 foreshadows the conclusion of the following parable of the rich man and Lazarus by stressing the importance of the law (cf. Lk 16:29, 31). Luke addresses himself to the representatives of Jewish thought, and he intends to speak about the law.

The arrangement of Lk 16:1–31 should be understood in function of Lk 16:14, composed to introduce, not so much the statements found in verses 15–18, as the example story of Lk 16:19–31. In its first part (Lk 16:1–13) the chapter teaches positively how to use one's money; in the second part (Lk 16:19–31) it seeks in the first place to warn against *philarguria*, 'love for money', and its consequences. The role which is thus attributed to Lk 16:14 explains the absence of an introduction at the beginning of the parable of the rich man and Lazarus. Only the particle *de* (usually not translated in English) separates this parable from the statement concerning divorce (Lk 16:18). In the thought of the evangelist, the real introduction of the parable must be found in Lk 16:14. He presents the parable as Jesus' response to the scoffing which was inspired by the Pharisees' love for money. It may be assumed, therefore, that, as far as Luke is concerned, we are dealing here with an instruction against love for money (*philarguria*), which is a grave obstacle to conversion.[71]

Divergences in the interpretation of the parable

It would be better to call this the parable of the astute steward because, whatever explanations of the gospel data are proposed, they seek to attract our attention less to the dishonesty of the steward than to the ability he displays in assuring his threatened future.

The extent of the parable

Firstly, a few scholars see verse 7, just before the *kurios* praises the steward, as the conclusion of the parable.

Secondly, a good number of exegetes see in this praise, expressed in verse 8a, the primitive conclusion of the text. Some of them believe that verses 8b–13 attest three ways in which the early Church used the parable. In the first instance, a lesson in prudence was drawn from it: the sons of this world are more prudent than the sons of light (verses 8b–9); then followed a lesson in trustworthiness (verses 10–12); finally, in verse 13 an exhortation is expressed which does not have much to do with the parable: those who are obsessed by riches cannot serve God, because wealth has become a god for them.

Thirdly, quite a number of interpreters think that verse 8 in its entirety is the original conclusion of the parable. Some of them state further that there should be no hesitation in accepting verse 8b, with its contrast between the sons of this world and the sons of light, since the Dead Sea Scrolls have now familiarized us with this antithesis and show its archaic character. On the other hand, these same interpreters reject verse 9, invoking various arguments.

Finally, just a few commentators agree that the original parable went on to verse 9 inclusively, although it does seem to be prepared by verse 4. 'I have decided what to do, so that people may receive me into their houses when I am put out of the stewardship'.

The interpretation of the parable

Firstly, there are some authors who think that the text can only be understood in an ironical sense.

Secondly, there is the allegorical exegesis which identifies the steward with the religious authorities of Jerusalem, notably the Pharisees in charge of procuring spiritual goods to the people, but unfaithful to their mission.

Thirdly, the eschatological interpretation is usually preferred by those who think that the parable ends with verse 8: time is running out, the catastrophe is imminent; one must show as much ability and spirit of decision as the steward in danger of being dismissed, who acts before disaster strikes.

Fourthly, there is the moral interpretation which is suggested by the text, as well as by the context which does not seem to be eschatological at all. But the moral lesson is not always understood in the same way, mainly (but not only) depending on where one thinks the parable as Jesus pronounced it ended. Those who think the original parable ended with verse 8 believe that it exhorted the sons of light to be as astute in their own sphere as the sons of this world in theirs. Those who include verse 9 in the original parable understand it as a teaching on riches, which is not surprising, since in the parable monetary questions play a capital role.[72]

Analysis of the text

Verse 1: He also said to the disciples, 'There was a rich man who had a steward, and charges were brought to him that this man was wasting his goods.

No change of scene from the previous section is implied, but the disciples are addressed specifically, and are therefore considered the primary audience. The Pharisees are presumably included among the audience, for in verse 14 it is said that they, too, 'heard all this'. Notwithstanding the explicit or implicit assumptions of many scholars, nothing suggests a partner-in-crime status for the rich man. Although the rich man is mentioned first, he is only a secondary figure; the real 'hero' of the story is the steward.

The steward (*oikonomos*; Lk 12:42; 16:1, 3, 8; nowhere else in the gospels) was a member of the household who acted as legal agent of the rich man, who was apparently a landowner. The steward was therefore an estate manager with considerable legal powers. Charges were brought to the master, apparently with hostile intent. The verb *diaballein*, 'to bring charges', seems to suggest some kind of criminal action, but the steward is not called unjust or dishonest before verse 8. The accusation came from others (cf. Lk 16:2, 'what is this that I hear about you?'), perhaps from the other servants as in Mt 18:31? The steward is accused of wasting (*diaskorpizein*; cf. Lk 15:13) the goods of his master. Nothing is said about the precise nature of the accusation; the term 'to waste' does not necessarily indicate criminal malice or injustice.

It has been suggested that the main character of the parable is a steward to indicate to the listeners/readers that they are not the absolute owners of their riches, but that they belong to God whose stewards they are. The terms *oikonomos*/*oikonomia*/*oikonomein* occur six times in Lk 16:1–4, thus apparently emphasizing the idea of stewardship. This opinion is further supported by the fact that in several parables the disciples are presented as being, under different forms, stewards of God or Christ (Lk 19:11–27; Mt 25:14–30; Mt 24:45–51; Lk 12:41–43).

> **Verse 2:** And he called him and said to him, 'What is this that
> I hear about you? Turn in the account of your stewardship,
> for you can no longer be steward.'

The steward is summoned and addressed with the question 'What is this that I hear about you?' The implication is that the rich man has been hearing for a long time, and is still hearing, a steady stream of things about the steward. It is implied that the steward does not know how much his master knows and that he may thus be frightened into volunteering information his master does not yet have. The present steward, however, remains silent and thus shows already something of the 'prudence' for which he will later be commended.

The master then continues, 'turn in the account of your

stewardship', which could mean that the steward is asked either to surrender the account books or to get the accounts in order. It has been argued that the Greek phrase means 'surrender the account books'.

Finally comes the decisive statement, 'for you can no longer be steward'. Does this mean that he is fired right away, or later? In verse 3 the steward says 'my master is taking the stewardship away from me', and in verse 4 he talks about the time 'when I am put out of the stewardship'. Moreover, when dealing with the debtors, the steward acts as if he is not yet fired. While normally speaking the steward would be fired on the spot, in this case the story suggests that he is notified first. His authority is therefore cancelled, but at the same time he has still a short while to manoeuvre until he actually turns in the account books, because word of his dismissal is not yet out, or, while he is dismissed, he still acts as steward until he gets the books in order for his successor.

> **Verses 3–4:** And the steward said to himself, 'What shall I do, since my master is taking the stewardship away from me? I am not strong enough to dig, and I am ashamed to beg. (4) I have decided what to do, so that people may receive me into their houses when I am put out of the stewardship.'

Confronted by the spectre of unemployment, with little or no chance to get another job, the steward, like the rich fool (Lk 12:17–19), the prodigal son (Lk 15:17–19), and the unjust judge (Lk 18:4–5) sets himself to thinking aloud. He evaluates the crisis situation, trying to find a solution. The verb 'to do' (*poiein*, also meaning 'to make', cf. Lk 16:9) becomes decisive in what follows and is, in fact, emphasized throughout Luke's gospel. It is one of the key words of the present parable (Lk 16:3, 4, 8, 9). The question 'what shall I (we) do?' occurs repeatedly in Luke (Lk 3:10, 14; 10:25; 16:3; 18:18). A certain similarity to Lk 10:25–37 may be noticed. There the lawyer initially asked 'What shall I do to inherit eternal life?' (Lk 10:25; compare Lk 18:18). After the lawyer has quoted the commandments of love of God and love of neighbour, Jesus replies, '... do this and you will live' (Lk 10:28), and at the end of the parable of the Good Samaritan again, 'go and do likewise' (Lk 10:37). Here the steward says to himself 'what shall I do?' (Lk 16:3), and 'I have decided what to do' (Lk 16:4), to which Jesus (Luke) replies 'Do/make friends for yourselves... so that they may receive you into the eternal habitations' (Lk 16:9), which may be taken as an equivalent for 'to live'.

The steward first considers two possibilities, digging (*skaptein*;

cf. Lk 6:48; 13:8), and begging (*epaitein*; cf. Lk 18:35), but dismisses them quickly. He considers himself too weak for the first (the expression 'I cannot dig' is found in Aristophanes, *The Birds*, 1432), and ashamed to do the second (see Sir 40:28, 'My son, do not lead the life of a beggar; it is better to die than to beg'). With the dramatic aorist *egnōn* (literally, 'I have known'; but the aorist expresses decision; therefore RSV: 'I have decided'), the listeners/readers are informed about the third possibility he has conceived. He will make the most of his situation by making a number of people indebted to him; the gambler's last throw in an apparently lost situation. The listeners/readers are not told immediately what the steward's plan is. This will be unfolded in the following verses. Like 'to do, to make', the verb *dechesthai*, 'to receive', 'to take', is a key word in the parable (Lk 16:4, 6, 7, 9).

> **Verse 5–7:** So, summoning his master's debtors one by one, he said to the first, 'How much do you owe my master?' (6) He said, 'A hundred measures of oil.' And he said to him, 'Take your bill, and sit down quickly and write fifty.' (7) Then he said to another, 'And how much do you owe?' He said, 'A hundred measures of wheat.' He said to him, 'Take your bill, and write eighty.'

The debtors are apparently tenants who have rented land for which they must pay a fixed portion of the crop. By *summoning* (*proskaleomai*, 'I call to myself', Lk 7:19; 15:26; 18:16; Acts 2:39; 5:40; 6:2; 13:2, 7; 16:10; 23:17, 18, 23) his master's debtors, and asking them how much they owe *his* master, the steward certainly intends to make them think that he is still in authority. The question 'How much do you owe my master?' is not asked in order to get information, since he must have the written statements in front of him. Rather, he is establishing agreement: 'Do you agree that the amount recorded on the bill is an accurate statement of the rent agreement?' That he calls them 'one by one', and insists that they 'sit down quickly and write' suggests that he wants to finish the business before the fraud is discovered. 'A hundred measures of oil' is the produce of about 140 palm trees; 'a hundred measures of wheat' is the harvest of approximately 42 hectares of land. Two samples are considered sufficient for the listeners/readers to become aware of the procedure followed.

It has been stated that, according to contemporary custom in Palestine, a steward was not remunerated and so, when he agreed to lend on his master's goods, he had himself paid in kind, correspondingly increasing the amount on the bill. Fearing for his future, the steward of this parable would then have decided to renounce his interest and reduce the receipts to their real amount. While he had previously inflated the bills to enrich himself, now, in the crisis of his dismissal, he is subtracting his 'cut' from the bill. In so doing he is only sacrificing his own interests and not cheating his master in this instance. This explanation would help to understand how the *kurios* (if he is understood to be the master of the steward) can praise the steward for his astuteness or prudence.

But it has been convincingly argued that the steward was a legal 'agent' for the master, and so acted under the regulations of the Mishnah regulating the activities of such agents. The Mishnah mentions explicitly the fee to be paid by the renter to the agent who draws up the rent contracts. The agent would receive a little something 'under the table', but so long as this did not exceed what was reasonable, it was considered legitimate. But none of this appeared in the accounts. On the other hand, what was recorded on the bills would have been known by the master.

It should be noted that the steward is not collecting the amounts, which are not due until the harvest, but are 'owing' from the day the agreement is signed. He simply makes the debtors rewrite the existing promissory notes, or makes them write new ones. Even after the bills are changed there is no attempt to collect the reduced amounts.

Verse 8a: The master commended the dishonest steward for his prudence;

All scholars agree on the artistic character of Lk 16:1–7. Compared with this, the clumsy expression of verse 8 is striking, the more so because two possible meanings of *ho kurios* have to be considered.

A number of interpreters consider the whole of verse 8 secondary. Others maintain that only verse 8b is secondary, while a third group think that verse 8 is not secondary, but expresses indirectly the original practical application of the parable. Many objections have been levelled against this third interpretation. It has been pointed out that it is very questionable whether the tradition would ever have handed down the practical application of a parable in indirect speech. The alleged parallel in Lk 18:6 is not an indirect rendering of a practical application, since the application follows in direct speech. In any case, as a practical application verse 8 is too general and vague, and too many questions remain unanswered if one follows the hypothesis of indirect speech.

Since the Syriac Peshitta Bible it has been disputed whether *ho kurios* refers to the master of the steward (e.g. Lagrange, Fitzmyer,

Derrett, Schürmann) or to Jesus (e.g., Descamps, Dodd, Jeremias).
If *kurios* refers to the master of the steward, then verse 8a still
belongs to the parable itself. But if *kurios* refers to Jesus, the
evangelist is giving here in his own words Jesus' comment on the man
whose exploits he has just narrated.

The interpreters who understand *ho kurios* to be the master of
the steward advance the following arguments:

(1) The word *kurios* appears several times in the parable (Lk 16:3,
    5), so that one spontaneously thinks in verse 8a, too, of the
    master of the steward.
(2) Since Jesus himself joins the praise of the master by the words
    'but I tell you', verse 8a can refer only to the master.
(3) Only with this understanding of *ho kurios* does the parable have
    its natural climax: it holds up 'prudence' as the *tertium
    comparationis*, the point of comparison.
(4) If *kurios* referred to Jesus, verse 8 would constitute an
    interruption of the direct speech between verses 1–7 and verse 9,
    which one would expect to be clearly indicated.
(5) On the supposition that *kurios* referred to Jesus, verse 8 would
    lack a suitable continuation in verse 9. The evangelist should
    have indicated that while in verse 8 he was speaking about Jesus,
    in verse 9 it is no longer he but Jesus who is speaking.
(6) Jesus could hardly praise the action of the steward.
(7) It is only because of verse 8b that *kurios* in verse 8a is understood
    as referring to Jesus.

The interpretation which understands *ho kurios* as referring to
Jesus is supported by the following arguments:

(1) It would be an offence against faithfulness to the reality of the
    story if the cheated master were made to praise his steward.
(2) It is typical of Luke's style in his narrative material to refer to
    Jesus by means of an absolute *ho kurios* (eighteen out of 21
    times; but the three times it refers to the master of the story are
    all in parables!).
(3) Verse 8b can contain only a judgment of Jesus. Since this is so
    closely related to verse 8a, the latter should also be considered as
    referring to Jesus.
(4) Luke sums up in an indirect way the judgment of Jesus. A
    parallel is found in Lk 18:6, 'And the Lord said, "Hear what the
    unrighteous judge says"'. Here too there follows in Lk 18:8, 'I
    tell you'.
(5) The connection with verse 7 also recommends separating verse 8

from the picture-half (*Bildhälfte*). In the story the master of the
steward is left behind in verse 2, and it is not said that he knows
of the put-up job by the steward. How then can he praise him?[73]

Literary criticism has expressed strong arguments against understanding *kurios* as the master of the steward. The anomalous
character of a parable finale in indirect style is correctly underlined,
but it is explained on the level of Luke's redaction. He would have
found at the end of the parable an application of the usual type, 'You
too should be astute...'. But another application was apparently more
convincing to him, namely the one which he now reports in verse 9.
He did not want to suppress the first application, but by reporting it
in indirect style, he in a sense subordinated it to that of verse 9.
Consequently, while showing his preference for the second
application, Luke attests the traditional character of the first
application, which constitutes now a simple preliminary consideration of the *kurios* Jesus. On the other hand, it has also been argued
that it is the element of success, which belongs to the picaresque
mode (a story about a successful rogue), that suggests that Lk 16:8a
was an original part of the parable, and that the *kurios* was the master
of the steward recognizing the measure of success achieved by the
steward.

The decisive question is how verse 8 becomes part of the whole
of verses 1–7, 9. The main weakness of verse 8 is its stylistic
unevenness. If *ho kurios* is read as the master of the steward,
difficulties arise between verse 8a and 8b, as well as between verses
1–7 and verse 8. If *ho kurios* is read as Jesus, difficulties occur with
the transition from verse 8 to verse 9.

The verb *epēinesen*, 'commended', causes difficulties, irrespective of whether the praise is uttered by the master or by Jesus. In the
mouth of the former it sounds unnatural and not true to life.
Similarly, it is difficult to accept that Jesus praised the steward.
Attempts have been made to lessen the problem by saying that the
verb *epainein* can also mean 'approve of', 'agree to'. In a context
dealing with the settling of accounts the expression would mean 'he
approved of the settlement of the unrighteous steward'. But this
solution has received little approval. Moreover, several scholars have
insisted that in the New Testament the verb often has an
eschatological connotation.

Why is the steward characterized by the depreciating qualification *tēs adikias*, 'of wrongdoing', 'of unrighteousness'? The obvious
answer is because he proved himself to be a cunning, unscrupulous
swindler and forger of documents. This would be especially due to his
manipulation of the accounts (Lk 16:5–7), for which commentators

use expressions like 'forgery', 'crafty expedient', 'fraudulent arrange-ment'. But an important group of scholars consider the steward's settling of accounts correct and morally irreprehensible. The twenty measures of wheat and fifty measures of oil would be the share he had originally allotted to himself and which he is now prepared to forgo. These scholars see the ground for the depreciating qualification in the way the steward had previously handled his stewardship, 'wasting his master's goods' (verse 1). But as we have seen, the verb 'wasting' does not necessarily imply criminal intent. However, the character-ization is the same as that for the unjust judge (Lk 18:6) who in the course of time had established a reputation for being unjust. When he acted on behalf of the widow, he certainly did not commit injustice! In the opinion of both groups of interpreters just mentioned, the steward is called 'unrighteous', while still being praised 'for his prudence'.

Others have tried to explain the qualification 'of unrighteous-ness' as a standing religious category which could apply to the steward as a godless, wicked man, without reference to any particular action as such. On the ground of the Qumran vocabulary the conclusion has been drawn that the qualification 'of unrighteousness' brands the steward as a 'son of this world', one who is totally entangled in this world in which unrighteousness is the leading principle. Consequently, it has been pointed out that renderings like 'unrighteous', 'dishonest', 'deceiving', are inadequate and, in fact, wrong. The steward is presented as typical of 'the sons of this world' who are contrasted to 'the sons of light' in verse 8b.

The steward is praised *hoti phronimōs epoiēsen* (RSV: 'for his prudence', more literally, 'because he acted wisely'). The adverb *phronimōs* does not occur anywhere else in the New Testament, but a number of words belonging to the same family occur frequently. The corresponding Hebrew-Aramaic word would be *ᶜarum*, which can have a positive as well as a negative meaning. In fact, in the Old Testament the ability for good as well as for evil is called wisdom. Semites do not speculate about wisdom in the Greek manner, but regard it as practical *savoir-faire* (cf. Gen 3:1).

There is general agreement that the steward is not praised in general, but only from the point of view of his 'prudent action'. In what respect this prudent action could be praised by Jesus is then further specified. The most generally accepted interpretation is that 'this man was *phronimos* (v. 8a), i.e., he recognized the critical nature of the situation. He did not let things take their course, he acted, unscrupulously no doubt (*tēs adikias*, v. 8), Jesus did not excuse his action, though we are not concerned with that here, but boldly, resolutely, and prudently, with the purpose of making a new life for himself. For you, too, the challenge of the hour demands prudence, everything is at stake!'[74] Jesus' audience must have understood the activity of the steward as a wise, prudent action. A number of scholars have emphasized the eschatological overtones of *phronimōs*, which has even been described by some as 'having grasped the eschatological situation'.

Verse 8b: for the sons of this world are wiser in their own generation than the sons of light.

The expression *huioi tou aiōnos toutou* (RSV: 'the sons of this world') is peculiar to the New Testament, where it is found only here and in Lk 20:34 (RSV: 'sons of this age'). It is absent from rabbinical and Qumran literature. Only Christians who believe that with Jesus the eschatological age has come can use 'sons of this world'. In Jesus' mouth the expression has above all an eschatological meaning: people who have not (or not yet) accepted (or heard) the gospel. A depreciating qualification may be included, but the emphasis is on the eschatological category. The contrast between 'sons of this world' and 'sons of light', as well as the comparison between the two in respect of wisdom or shrewdness, confirm that the speaker is primarily concerned not with negative charactistics, but with the eschatological indication of a category. The meaning of the expression 'sons of light' is thus also clear.

The sons of this world are wiser *eis tēn genean tēn heautōn* (RSV: 'in their own generation'). *Genea* means literally the clan, tribe, kindred descended from one ancestor. In a metaphorical sense it can be used for a group of people who belong together in one or another respect: (1) beings belonging to the same species or race or of the same mind; (2) a series of people living at one time: a generation, contemporaries; (3) as transferred from individuals to a space of time: age, life, duration of a generation.

In our text *genea* is certainly used in a metaphorical sense. The great majority of interpreters understand *genea* here as meaning a group who are of the same mind, and the whole expression as 'towards (*eis*) their own kind'. Others understand *genea* to mean 'contemporaries'. If one takes into account that the word is spoken by Jesus, one should consider the crisis under which he places his generation. *Genea* would then refer to 'their generation', in the sense of the generation of Jesus' contemporaries.

Jesus applies the expression 'this generation' in the first place to the whole people of his contemporaries (e.g., Lk 11:29, 30, 31, 32), who oppose his message. Because of the negative attitude of these contemporaries, the expression has a condemning connotation, without, however, totally supplanting the original meaning of the word as 'the present generation', even when accompanied by qualifications as 'evil' (Lk 11:29), or 'faithless and perverse' (Lk 9:41). All these texts deal with the generation of Jesus' contemporaries, of the evil and faithless generation which Jesus addresses, not a particular group of evil and unfaithful people among his audience.

In the early Christian community, however — and this is important for the possibility of a new actualization of the parable in the Church — the meaning is different, as can be seen in Acts 2:40, 'and he testified with many other words and exhorted them, saying, "Save yourself from this crooked generation"'. The same meaning is found in Phil 2:14–15. 'Do all things without grumbling or questioning, that you may be blameless and innocent, children of God without blemish in the midst of a crooked and perverse generation, among whom you shine as lights in the world'. But, even though in these texts the emphasis is more on the negative qualification, the meaning 'contemporaries' is not entirely extinguished.

The probable meaning of *eis tēn genean tēn heautōn* is then 'in your generation', i.e., in this generation living in a time of decision. The expression, therefore, is probably not intended to limit the scope of 'wiser' or 'shrewder'. The verse does contain a restriction but this is rather to be found in the expressions 'sons of this world' and 'sons of light'.

It is not explicitly said what is meant by 'wiser' or 'shrewder'. According to many scholars the expression *eis tēn genean tēn heautōn* specifies and limits the scope of the comparison between the wisdom of the sons of this world and that of the sons of light. The sons of this world are wiser than the sons of light, not in general, but only in a certain respect.

In what are the 'sons of the world' wiser? This is said in the parable which in the person of the steward shows how a 'son of this world' is wise or astute in the face of a serious threat to the foundations of his existence. The sons of light are less astute in handling the crisis that faces their generation. The ironical praise which Jesus addresses to the 'sons of this world' is, in fact, blame for the 'sons of light'. It should be noted once more that the two 'wisdoms' are compared only in as far as they represent examples of astuteness in the Semitic sense.[75]

> **Verse 9:** And I tell you, make friends for yourselves by means of unrighteous mammon, so that when it fails they may receive you into the eternal habitations.

In this application of the parable, three key words return: to do/to make (*poiein*), to receive/to take (*dechesthai*), and houses/tents.

Interpreters do not agree on the function of the introduction to verse 9, 'And I tell you'. The majority see in it a solemn conclusion formula. It constitutes an emphatic connection with verse 8 and the preceding parable: 'I too tell you', or even stronger, 'and so I tell you'. Many understand it in an adversative sense and read: 'I, on the other hand, tell you'. Some take it rather as a transitional formula leading to a new theme. Which of these possibilities should be preferred depends on how one judges the connection between verse 9 and the preceding as well as the following context.

No longer addressed to an indifferent crowd but to Jesus' disciples, to the Christians for whom the gospel is written, the parable of the unjust steward has, in the eyes of the evangelist, its real conclusion in verse 9. The formula, 'and I tell you', is calculated to underline the importance of this verse.

It is not explicitly said what the listeners/readers of the parable should do to make friends (who would receive them), but it has generally been accepted as a summons to share one's wealth with the poor. Surprisingly, this verse seems to say that the poor have heaven at their disposal for the benefit of their benefactors. But is this so surprising after all? Did not Jesus declare himself the advocate of the poor and identify himself with them (cf. Mt 25:34–45)? Some, however, are not satisfied with this plain explanation and try to specify things further.

Some stress the active role of the 'friends', and point out that the text does not say 'so that you may be received because of them', but 'so that they may receive you'. Others emphasize that the 'friends' are not explicitly identified, that the verb 'to receive' is here used in the impersonal sense, and so would refer to God, Christ or the angels (compare Lk 12:20, which reads 'they will require your soul'). The 'friends', then, would not do anything else but pray for their benefactors, or welcome them at the moment they enter heaven. But the way 'to receive' is used in verse 9 is not more impersonal than in verse 4, and its subject is in both cases those who are 'indebted' to their benefactors. In general it may be said that the subtleties advanced by this group of interpreters do not do justice to the text.

How does one know, however, that the use of the unrighteous mammon which makes friends for eternity is by sharing *with the poor*? There are three arguments. Firstly, the parable of the rich man and Lazarus teaches the necessity of sharing with the poor in order to be received into the bosom of Abraham. Secondly, the parallel with Lk 12:33, 'Sell your possessions, and give alms;... a treasure in the heavens that does not fail'. Thirdly, the general treatment of riches in Luke-Acts.

The Greek word *mamōnas* is derived from the Aramaic substantive *mamon* which, according to the majority of exegetes, is derived from the root *'mn*, in the causative form: 'to trust in'. *Mamōnas* would then mean 'that in which one trusts', 'deposited money', 'what one has put in safety'. It is generally used to refer to possessions, wealth, especially money.

The word does not occur in the Hebrew Bible, but it is often found in the Targums, in the Mishnah and the Talmud, and in the writings of Qumran. In the New Testament, *mamōnas* occurs only four times: three in the present text (Lk 16:9, 11, 13) and once in Mt 6:24, which is the parallel to Lk 16:13. Twice it is accompanied by an adjectival expression: *mamōnas tēs adikias* (Lk 16:9, 'mammon of unrighteousness'), and *adikos mamōnas* (Lk 16:11, 'unrighteous mammon'). In the third use too it has a definitely negative meaning, as appears from the contrast between the service of God and the service of mammon (Lk 16:13).

The expression 'unrighteous mammon' is often understood to refer to possessions or wealth which have been acquired unjustly. But this interpretation is difficult to reconcile with the broad demand of Jesus (Lk 16:9), unless it is accepted that Jesus addressed himself only to those who possess unjustly acquired possessions, e.g. tax collectors (cf. Lk 19:8), but this is highly improbable. The opinions on the matter can be summed up as follows:

(1) Many interpreters think that Jesus qualifies mammon negatively because he is referring to the injustice committed in the acquisition, possession and use of mammon, irrespective of whether the present owner contributed to the injustice or not.
(2) Others say that mammon is thus qualified because the accumulation of superfluous possessions instead of sharing them with the poor is an injustice before God.
(3) Again, others maintain that mammon is called unrighteous because the owner unjustly considers it his property, while in fact he is only its steward on God's behalf.
(4) A fourth group of scholars state that wealth is 'unrighteous mammon' because it is a deceptive and unreliable possession which disappoints and ultimately leaves its owner in the lurch.
(5) Another group of exegetes consider the alluring character and the incentive to evil which are particular to wealth the decisive reasons why Jesus calls it 'unrighteous mammon'.
(6) In reference to Lk 16:13, '... you cannot serve God and mammon', mammon appears as a counter-god, the personification of the prince of this world. As such, wealth is called 'unrighteous mammon'.
(7) Jesus calls wealth 'unrighteous mammon' as a religious appraisal of one of the prominent elements of this world which is

commonly referred to as 'unrighteous'. In the same line the expression 'unrighteous mammon' has been related to Jesus' general attitude towards wealth, and it has been stressed that this also expresses the way of thinking of the *anawim*, the poor who are totally dependent on God's righteousness.[76]

A number of contemporary scholars see in the expression *māmōn disqār* of the Targum and rabbinic literature a legitimate parallel to *mamōnas tēs adikias*. There is no doubt that in the former expression the depreciating by-meaning originates in the dishonest acquisition of the wealth referred to. But it seems that in order to trace the exact meaning which this statement must have had for Jesus, it should be taken into account that Jesus did not share the Old Testament and Pharisaic optimism about riches. Because of the basically different stance towards wealth, Jesus most probably also called mammon unrighteous for another motive, which was his religious appraisal of wealth, insofar as it constitutes one of the most important motive powers of a world opposed to God. This attitude of Jesus is reflected in passages like Lk 16:13; 18:24–25; 12:13–21.

Why does Lk 16:9 call riches 'mammon of unrighteousness'? This expression corresponds to 'steward of unrighteousness' (Lk 16:8). Later, the parable of the judge and the widow will deal with a 'judge of unrighteousness' (Lk 18:6). The two are so called because they have committed injustice, the first towards his master (and presumably previously also towards the tenants), the second towards his clients. It is certainly tempting to interpret 'mammon of unrighteousness' in the same way, especially if it is true that we are dealing here with a personification of wealth. It may be true that riches are not declared unjust in themselves, but it is certainly not sufficient either to say that riches are unjust only when they are the result of fraudulent dealings, or when they are not shared with the poor. It seems right to add that the personified mammon is considered to cause evil by itself, and that it does so in the first place to those who consider themselves as its absolute owners, while in reality becoming its slaves. In this connection one may refer to the description of Judas' reward as *misthos tēs adikias* (Acts 1:18), which is often translated as 'the reward for his unrighteousness', but the genitive noun is better taken as the equivalent of an adjective, suggesting that the reward has in itself the character of 'unrighteous mammon'.

The sharing of mammon is urged in view of the situation prevailing 'when it fails'. The basic meaning of *ekleipein*, which in the New Testament is used only intransitively, is 'to go out', 'to be exhausted', 'to be at an end'. Secondarily, when dealing with life that comes to an end, it can also mean 'to die'. Three interpretations have been suggested. The first interpretation says that the expression means the loss or giving away of wealth during the owner's life. But the great majority of interpreters understand the expression as an allusion to death which in the early Church, because of the delay of the parousia, takes over for the individual Christian many of the aspects of what was originally attributed to the day of the Lord. Some of those who adhere to this interpretation refer to Lk 12:20, 33. According to a third group of scholars, the meaning is to be found in an allusion to the eschatological eclipse of the present world (*aiōn houtos*). It should be noted that the second and third interpretations do not necessarily exclude each other.

The verb *ekleipein* recalls the corresponding adjective introduced by Luke into the statement also found in Mt 6:19–20, to which he gives the following form: 'provide yourselves with purses that do not grow old, with a treasure in the heavens that does not fail (*anekleipton*), where no thief approaches and no moth destroys' (Lk 12:33). The thought context is the same. According to the traditional wisdom theme expressed, e.g., in Ps 49(48), money accumulated on earth will fail at the moment of death. At that moment it is good to have a 'treasure in heaven', or, in other words, to have friends in heaven, in order to be introduced by them into the eternal habitations.

The expression 'eternal habitations' or 'eternal tents' is not found anywhere else in the Bible or in rabbinical literature. It occurs, however, in II Esdras 2:11, an apocryphal text, where it is almost certainly dependent on Lk 16:9. The plural *skēnai* occurs in Mk 9:5 ('booths, tents'), and in Heb 11:9 ('tents'), but in neither of these two passages does the word refer to eschatological dwellings for the faithful. The singular 'tent' is used metaphorically for heaven in Heb 8:2, 9:11; Rev 21:3.

The interpretations go in two directions. The first and most widely accepted takes the expression 'into the eternal habitations' as a whole and understands it as the eschatological gift, eternal life. The second tries to solve the question by interpreting the terms 'eternal' and 'habitations' separately.

In the first attempt three nuances are distinguished:

(1) The more general explanation from the Church Fathers to the present day understands reception into the eternal habitations as reception into heaven. This interpretation does not distinguish clearly between later Christian eschatology and that of Jesus' contemporaries, and thus shifts the accent from the parousia to the death of the individual with subsequent reception into heaven.

(2) A smaller group of interpreters gives more weight to more precise considerations of the eschatological understanding of Jesus' time. They therefore interpret the image to mean the eschatological fulfilment of the kingdom of God.

(3) In between the two previous interpretations may be placed those allegorical interpretations which understand the image as the Church. The dismissal of the steward symbolizes the end of the Old Covenant, while the 'eternal habitations' represent the institution of the New Covenant, the Church. This interpretation is no longer found in contemporary parable study.

The second, non-eschatological, interpretation thinks that the text speaks of a lasting hospitable reception. This is the interpretation of those who understand the parable as a summons of Jesus to his disciples to secure for themselves a hospitable reception by friends during times of persecution.[77]

The insertion of verse 9 in the context and the boundaries of this context are disputed. The introductory formula 'and I tell you' as well as the striking similarity with verse 4, i.e., 'make friends for yourselves... so that they may receive you into the eternal habitations' with 'I have decided what to do, so that people may receive me into their houses', give the impression that we have here the conclusion or so-called practical application of the parable.

Since in verse 9, abruptly and in a way which is easily misunderstood, Jesus recommends unrighteous mammon as a means of making friends, without explaining exactly how this is meant, it is assumed that this verse can hardly be the end of Jesus' statement, but that his thoughts must be further clarified in a speech, the core of which would be found in verses 10–13. This teaching reaches its climax and conclusion in the words 'you cannot serve God and mammon' (verse 13b).

Critical study immediately questioned the spontaneous assumption of the unity of Lk 16:1–13. The first reason for this questioning was found in Lk 16:13, which occurs in almost the same form in Mt 6:24 in a totally different context. As exegesis gradually discovered the loose connections between many gospel logia or sayings of Jesus, it was more and more doubted whether Lk 16:13 was the original place of this logion. Next it was wondered whether verses 10–12 belonged to the original parable. Modern parable exegesis looked for the point of the parable, and so verse 9 as its practical application was also put into question. As the point of the parable scholars almost invariably recognize the cleverness (prudence) and determination with which the steward grasped and overcame the critical situation in which he found himself.

This point is made explicit in the expression 'by means of unrighteous mammon' and so restricted to a smaller area of activity. This led to the suspicion that verse 9 was not the original practical conclusion of the parable but a later addition. So far as anything of an original application is still traceable, it should be found in verse 8.

The majority of the scholars who separate verse 9 from the parable nevertheless consider it an authentic saying of Jesus. Some ascribe it to the early Christian community, while still others express the conjecture that Luke formulated verse 9 and attached it to the parable. A few even express the firm conviction that only Luke can have formulated it, but their arguments do not seem to prove more than that Luke *could* have formulated the verse.

It has been suggested that verse 9 originated from another context which is no longer known. As such it could have been originally pronounced by Jesus himself. In fact, the statement is easily thinkable in the context of Jesus' proclamation. Nevertheless it has a very specific emphasis. This appeal to almsgiving is not motivated by a reward for the good work, but by the danger of being excluded from the kingdom of God. And this reflects exactly the point of the parable transferred to the religious level.

But then it seems that the concept of *mammon* in verse 9 cannot be derived from the parable of the steward. This concept which appears unexpectedly in verse 9 remains the main theme until verse 13. Moreover, verses 9–13 form a unity which is separated from verses 1–8 by the formula 'but I tell you'. Finally, the objection has been raised that verse 9 and verse 1a are addressed to a different audience, but it is not entirely excluded that verse 9 was originally addressed to the disciples (cf. Lk 16:1a).

Verses 10–12: He who is faithful in a very little is faithful also in much; and he who is dishonest in a very little is dishonest also in much. (11) If then you have not been faithful in the unrighteous mammon, who will entrust to you the true riches? (12) And if you have not been faithful in that which is another's, who will give you that which is your own?

These three verses should undoubtedly be considered a whole, held together by means of the catchword *pistos*, 'faithful', which echoes the fuller expression in Lk 12:42, 'the faithful and wise steward'. Verse 10 contains a statement derived from general experience in the style of a wisdom saying, from which a deduction is drawn in verses 11–12 by means of 'then' (*oun*). According to form these propositions stand in strict parallelism. Consequently, throughout the three verses there appear two series of parallel features which

oppose each other. The first series consists of: little (twice), unrighteous mammon, that which is another's; the second of: much (twice), faithful, your own.

The theme of these statements is easily recognized as trustworthiness in taking care of the goods indicated by the first series of features as proof of worthiness to receive the goods indicated by the second series. Thus the thought moves in the sphere of the theme of the parable of the talents. The words 'faithful, little, much' constitute a verbal connection with Mt 25:21, 23, 'well done, good and faithful servant; you have been faithful over a little, I will set you over much...', and Lk 19:17, 'well done, good servant! Because you have been faithful in a very little, you shall have authority over ten cities'. Nothwithstanding these contacts, Lk 16:10–12 cannot have been formulated in connection with the parable of the talents/ pounds. The formulation of Lk 16:10–12 may also have been influenced by the thought of the faithful servant who is considered worthy to be put in charge of the household (Mt 24:45–50; Lk 12:42–46). The meaning of this image for the early Church can be gathered from I Tim 3:1–10; 5:17; Titus 1:5–11, where it refers to Church officials. This seems to be the background of 'if then you have not been faithful in the unrighteous mammon, who will entrust to you the true riches?' (Lk 16:11). The negatively formulated rhetorical question strongly emphasizes the need for proving one's worthiness to be entrusted with the true riches by the way one deals with the unrighteous mammon. By themselves, verses 10–11 could have originated in such a situation. However, verse 12, which is closely related to verses 10–11, makes it difficult to maintain this.

The expression *to alēthinon* (literally, 'the true [thing]') is a vague reference to something that should be identified on the basis of the context. *Alēthinos* refers to what is characteristic of the new age and, therefore, real. Here it may refer to the gospel, the spiritual goods of the Christian message (cf. Eph 1:13, '... the word of truth, the gospel of your salvation').

To solve the question whether verses 10–12 may have had an independent existence as a saying of Jesus, the following consideration is important. The statement in verses 11–12 is too vague to have existed as an independent saying. One has to figure out what is meant by 'unrighteous mammon' and 'that which is another's' (*allotrios*, only here in Luke), on the one hand, and by 'the true (thing)' and 'your own', on the other hand. Moreover, the two series of parallel features in verses 10–12 are too heterogeneous for it to be possible to show that they all refer to the same reality. By itself the expression 'unrighteous mammon' is not synonymous with 'that which is another's'. The same is true for 'the true (thing)' and 'that which is your own'. Only the reality they all refer to allows one to place the two expressions in parallel. Therefore, it is improbable that Lk 16:10–12 was formulated independently of a particular context.

It has been noted that verse 12 borrows the image of a son who must first prove that his own inheritance can be entrusted to him by acting as steward of another's possessions. This and similar images have their *Sitz im Leben* in the paraenesis of the Christian community. Looking for a proper context for verses 10–12 we notice that the most specific expression of the paragraph, 'unrighteous mammon', appears in practically the same form in verse 9. Moreover, we find in verse 9 and verses 10–12 practically the same opposition, while verse 10 connects with verse 9 without any transition.

Summing up, we may say that we are probably dealing here with the creation of an early Christian teacher (compare Acts 13:1) who, intentionally using the ideas of the parable of the talents and considerations concerning Church officials (cf. Mt 24:45–50; Lk 12:42–46), developed the thought of verse 9 in a definite sense, which he and his readers accepted as obvious.

It is generally accepted that the first series of synonyms, 'very little, the unrighteous mammon, that which is another's', refer to riches or earthly goods. This series links up with verse 9a, 'make friends for yourselves by means of unrighteous mammon'. It is not immediately clear what is meant by the second series of synonyms, 'much, the true (thing), that which is your own'. Verse 10 does not have a specifically religious sense, so that only 'the true (thing)' and 'that which is your own' remain to determine the meaning of the paragraph. Because of the fairly unequivocal meaning of the first series (earthly goods, a treasure on earth, cf. Mt 6:19), and because of the opposition of the two series, it seems probable that it is dealing with another, opposite treasure, i.e., 'a treasure in heaven'. This then seems to link up with verse 9b, and 'making friends for yourselves by means of unrighteous mammon' with 'laying up for oneself treasure in heaven'. Laying up treasures by means of unrighteous mammon means, then, to share one's wealth with the poor, to share what one possesses in earthly goods which are ultimately not lasting, but only something over which one has received (temporary) stewardship, a talent which the Christians should administer faithfully and so convert into a true treasure. This is to be wise with the wisdom of the sons of light in their relations to their brothers and sisters.

The whole admonition is directed towards trustworthiness, as expressed in verse 10, 'he who is faithful (trustworthy) in a very little is faithful also in much...'. It stresses the aspect of stewardship in 'very little' as well as in 'much'. But since we are dealing here with a wisdom saying, which the author of the paragraph was not the first to formulate, it is possible that he used it only as a premiss for his thoughts. He refers to the faithfulness in very little, the unrighteous mammon, and that which is another's, considered as a kind of stewardship in which to prove faithfulness, and thereby worthiness to receive the 'true riches'.

From the parallel arrangements of verses 11–12 in the narrowest, verses 10–12 in the less narrow, and verses 9–12 in the wider sense, which constitute two series of parallel statements, it may be concluded that the particular expressions of both opposite series mean the same things: one series refers to earthly riches, the other to the treasure in heaven. Earthly riches should be shared with the poor in order to become worthy of the heavenly treasure which the Christian claims his own. If this is so, the meaning of the individual expressions should not be specified or pressed.

If the proposed interpretation of verses 10–12 is correct, the original purpose of this addition did not consist in giving a new meaning to the parable, or protecting it from misinterpretation, but in expressly inculcating the contemporary understanding of the parable. This is a paraenetic aim which fits very well in the catechesis of the early Christian community.

Verses 10–12, therefore, are a later addition to the parable which never existed independently but originated from a paraenetic need of the community, namely to impress on the early Christians the sense in which verses 8b–9, and that means the whole parable, were understood. There are no decisive indications that Luke was the first to create this addition, rather than any teacher in the community.[78]

> **Verse 13:** No servant can serve two masters; for either he will hate the one and love the other, or he will be devoted to the one and despise the other. You cannot serve God and mammon.'

This verse had its origin in Jesus' proclamation rather than in the catechesis of the early Christian community, although in the latter too it could have been expressed with approval. But the stand against mammon is typical of Jesus. It may be accepted beyond any doubt that verse 13 and the parable of the steward belong to the same *Sitz im Leben*, and, considering that riches are characterized as mammon in no other gospel passage, they may even have originated on the same occasion. In both texts the word 'mammon' is so essential that it can hardly have been introduced secondarily in one of the texts under the influence of the other.

Nevertheless it is rather improbable that from the beginning verse 13 was transmitted together with Lk 16:1–9. Firstly, except for the word *oiketēs*, 'servant', the text is exactly the same in Lk 16:13 and Mt 6:24. Secondly, a certain shift in meaning from that of the parable has taken place. Jesus addressed it to the disciples to invite them to liberate themselves from mammon to be free for the proclamation of the gospel. In the understanding of the early Church the disciples should free themselves spiritually from riches to manage them as stewards and put them at the service of the poor. Verse 13 is no longer closely related to this understanding of the parable. Thirdly, the form of verse 13 makes it very suitable for independent tradition.

Therefore, it is probable that the statement was handed on independently and thus reached Matthew and Luke, who both inserted it in what appeared to them a suitable context. Luke probably inserted the logion in its present context because it was the only one that contained the word 'mammon'. Moreover, in its apodictic, absolute form it was very suitable as the conclusion of a composition on the theme of mammon. This new context also made Luke change the vague 'nobody' (Mt 6:24) into 'no servant'. To serve God means now to be faithful in very little, in the unrighteous mammon, to make friends by sharing it with the poor. To serve mammon is: to be unfaithful in this, to use wealth selfishly, to gather it there 'where moth and rust consume and thieves break in', instead of 'laying up for oneself treasure in heaven'. No Christian can do both at the same time.[79]

Mammon is here personified as an idol, the service of whom amounts to the rejection of God. The way people deal with possessions is not irrelevant to their response to God, but indicates in a very tangible way the quality of that response.

Tradition history of the parable

The original parable (Lk 16:1–8a)

Verse 8a was the original conclusion of the parable. As such, the parable does not warn of the danger of riches or encourage the disciples to give alms. Neither is it to be understood as a polemic against the Jewish authorities, more specifically the Pharisees, 'stewards' in the metaphorical sense. The parable has an eschatological meaning. Just as the steward faced by a decisive crisis assessed the situation, considered the different possibilities, chose the one that would assure his future, and acted upon it, so should Jesus' audience act in the face of the crisis brought about by Jesus' proclamation of the kingdom. This proclamation has created a situation which calls for immediate decision. Lk 16:1–8a is, therefore, a crisis parable. It is the steward's ability to deal with a crisis which is the point of the story, the reason for the master's commendation, and the example for the disciples. This is the message of the original parable, which is obscured if the added comments and applications (Lk 16:8b–13) are used immediately as a key to the understanding of Lk 16:1–8a.

Early comment (Lk 16:8b)

Verse 8b is an early secondary addition (cf. the double *hoti*, 'for', in verse 8a–b). The phrase 'wiser' (*phronimōteroi*) has the same root as 'prudence'; verse 8a says literally 'for he acted wisely/prudently' (*phronimōs*). The verse is a comment which tries to clarify the cryptic ending of the original parable, and particularly the fact that Jesus chose a man like the steward as the hero of his parable. The steward and his likes, 'the sons of this world', prove to be astute in their dealing with each other. The disciples, 'the sons of light', should prove equally astute in dealing with what really matters to them.

First application (Lk 16:9)

Verse 9 is clearly formulated in reference to verse 4. Moreover, the phrase 'unrighteous mammon' links up with 'dishonest steward' in verse 8a, for the Greek phrases are literally 'mammon of unrighteousness' and 'steward of unrighteousness'. The verse constitutes a kind of wisdom saying or proverb (*mashal*) which, on the one hand, draws from the parable a practical application which can be understood only against the background of that same parable, while, on the other hand, it cannot be excluded that it renders an originally independent logion (addressed, e.g., to tax collectors?) into which Luke may have inserted only 'when it fails' to make it refer to the moment of death (cf. Lk 12:33, *anekleipton*, 'that never fails'). Several elements of the text (e.g., 'unrighteous mammon', 'eternal habitations/tents') indeed suggest a Jewish-Christian milieu.

Luke understands the statement as an advice to make friends by sharing one's wealth with the poor, so as to be welcomed (by the poor, by Christ, by God?) into the kingdom. 'Unrighteous mammon' refers not only to clearly unjustly acquired wealth, but to wealth as such, inasmuch as it is usually connected with injustice (Sir 27:1, 'Many have committed sin for a trifle, and whoever seeks to get rich will avert his eyes') and often unjustly used.

Second application (Lk 16:10–12)

This application is linked with Lk 16:1, which mentioned that the steward wasted his master's goods. These verses, composed of an antithetically arranged proverb (verse 10), followed by a double application to mammon and true riches (verses 11–12), are linked to verse 9 by means of the phrase 'mammon' and 'unrighteous/ dishonest'. Since they view mammon from another point of view — its stewardship requires faithfulness and reliability — they were not formulated by Luke who, however, attached them to the parable. Sharing one's wealth is not tantamount to 'wasting his goods' (cf. Lk 16:1). In this respect the steward is not a model but a deterring example, a warning of what not to do.

The disciples should be 'faithful' in their dealings with mammon, i.e., they should share it; then God will give them the 'true riches'. Found in between Lk 16:9 and 16:19–31, the only faithfulness verses 10–12 can be talking about is sharing the 'unrighteous mammon' with those in need. The disciples should be reliable in using what does not really belong to them; then they will receive from God what is their own. The 'true riches' (verse 11) do not refer to heaven, but to the task of stewardship which Jesus will entrust to the disciples (cf. Lk 12:42, 48b). Carrying the thought further, verse 12 then states that those who are faithful in dealing with another's goods entrusted to them will receive their reward in the kingdom.

Third application (Lk 16:13)

Verse 13 is linked to verse 11 through the word 'mammon' and to the parable, Lk 16:1–8a, through the word 'servant' (*oiketēs*, which is related to the word *oikonomos*, 'steward'). In a blunt either/or, this concluding logion sets the service of God and the service of the mammon against each other. It does not speak of (self-)confirmation through dealing with money, but rather of the impossibility of serving both God and mammon. Piling up wealth is not only depriving the poor of what rightfully belongs to them; it leads also to idolatry, to serving mammon. Those who allow mammon to control them render service to it and thereby exclude service of God. But he who 'seeks' the kingdom of God will receive what he needs (Lk 12:31).[80]

Conclusion

The original parable is confined to Lk 16:1–8a, while Lk 16:8b–13 consists of a comment and three practical applications of the original parable. These have been likened to 'the notes of an early church preacher or teacher who used the parable for Christian exhortation' (F. C. Grant), or 'notes for three separate sermons on the parable as text' (C. H. Dodd). What was originally a parable addressed by Jesus to the crowds has been turned by Luke into a parable for the disciples (cf. Lk 16:1). Though Jesus' parable dealt originally with the need for decisive action in view of the impending crisis. Luke, by appending verses 9–13 to it, has made it into a parable concerned with the right use of money in the light of the coming parousia.

Reflection

There are basically two reasons why this parable is not exactly the most popular one for preachers and teachers. The first is the urgency which Jesus teaches here and which is difficult to translate into modern terms. In the face of the crisis with which Jesus' message confronts people they should act now, and act decisively. But how does one say this to people who have been members of the Church since they were born? Secondly, how can a contemporary homilist actualize the example of a criminal who, when uncovered, tries to cover up the embezzlement by tampering with the accounts? On the one hand, not a few people in his audience may consider his homily improper and risqué. On the other hand, it is clear that Jesus used the daily experience and interest of his audience to express the meaning of his coming for their lives. Criminal activity has always fascinated people. The number of successful crime series on TV shows that this is still true today. Crooks and criminals work hard for their ends and act decisively when the occasion warrants. Can Christians match their grim determination when it comes to acting decisively here and now for the realization of the kingdom of God?

Parables are open-ended stories for people of any time to finish them. They have a remarkable way of challenging people and carrying them far beyond the story line. In view of the uncertainty and crisis that face people everywhere, what is our crisis plan? The real question is not 'what is going to happen?' but 'what are we going to do?' (cf. Lk 3:10). This question should be asked again and again. And again and again Christians everywhere and at all times should try to come up with basically the same and yet always new, creative gospel answers realized in inexhaustible, creative action. Today's crisis appears largely in the challenge posed by the poor to the rich, by the poor nations to the rich nations. What then shall we do?

Looking at management today, it can be said that managers and business leaders operate on the premiss that 'anything goes'. In a society where profit and mass production are the great values, it appears that management is often irresponsible and inhuman. It is irresponsible in that it works without the aid of good and lasting principles. It appears not to be as concerned about persons, the quality of life or environmental questions as it is about how the ledgers and budgets look at the end of the month. It is high time for people to look at management in a new, refreshing way, not as it is, but as it should be. As managers, as stewards of God's good gifts, people are called today to use these gifts to build up the kingdom of God, not the kingdom of man. In doing this, they must find for themselves a new understanding of faithfulness and responsibility. Today they are called to be faithful to the plan of God, not the plan of man, to see themselves as co-workers in carrying out his plan. Similarly, their responsibility lies in inviting others to join in this great act of helping all people rediscover the presence of the Lord in their lives. Their responsibility lies not in accumulating goods and making great profits, but in living in such a way that others are called to join them in service to the human community. In the face of a society which is incapable of looking beyond profit and competition, Christians are called to listen to a different voice which tells them about life, about God's great plan for creation. This voice speaks about joy, understanding and giving.

In the many things they do for money, people hurt others and themselves in the process, today more than ever before, physically, psychologically, and spiritually. The problem with money is one of means and ends. Money of itself is only good to be spent and shared. But people easily think that banknotes are valuable of themselves. The ironic quip 'in gold we trust' for the 'in God we trust' found (of all places) on US dollar bills, could be used to formulate a modern version of Lk 16:13c, 'You cannot trust in God and in the gold mammon'.

According to the Bible there is no legitimate fashion of acquiring differentiating wealth. Unless this moral thesis of economics is supposed, the punishment of the rich *in quantum* rich will be altogether incomprehensible. All these texts imply that only by illicit means it is possible to reach a higher economic level than that of the majority of the population. It is evident that 'illicit' does *not* mean: by transgressing the positive laws currently in force. The fact of legislation of nations authorizing means of acquiring wealth does not make these means to *be* licit, does not *make* these means licit. If there is anything of value in the Christian intellectual tradition it is that the criterion of good and evil does not depend on current laws or decrees or customs...

The condemnation of differentiating wealth is the most solid and inescapable documentary datum in the Bible. This is why Jesus of Nazareth calls money the 'money of iniquity' (Luke 16:9, 11), adopting the expression of the Jewish Book of Henoch 63:10, which is a faithful continuation of the Old Testament tradition. Saint Jerome comments, 'And wisely he said "with unjust money," for all riches derive from injustice, and unless one loses the other cannot gain. Therefore it is clear to me that the familiar proverb is eminently true: "The rich is either unjust, or heir of one unjust"' (PL 22:984). It should not be thought that we are inventing a new interpretation of the Bible here. Before the church associated itself for all future centuries with the exploiters, all the fathers of the church understood the Bible as we have... And hence it is that Augustine says, 'To succor the needy is justice' (PL 52:1046). And Ambrose, 'You are not giving the poor person the gift of a part of what is yours; you are returning to him something of what is his' (PL 14:747). Chrysostom: 'Do not say, "I am spending what is mine, I am enjoying what is mine." It is not actually yours, it is someone else's' (PG 61:86). Basil: 'It is the hungry one's bread you keep, the naked one's covering you have locked in your closet, the barefoot one's footwear putrefying in your power, the needy one's money that you have buried' (PG 31:277). That the holy fathers are serious about this may be seen from Jerome's phrase quoted above: 'All riches derive from injustice.'... All differentiating wealth is acquired by exploiting and despoiling the rest of the population.[81]

11 The rich man and Lazarus
(Lk 16:19–31)

Similar ancient accounts

Striking similarities have been pointed out between our parable and the Egyptian story of Setne or Satme and his son Si-Osiris.[82] When, after witnessing the burial of a rich and a poor man, the father commented that the rich man was much better off than the poor, his son took him to the underworld and showed him the rich man in torment and the poor man in luxury. The story illustrates two things: on the one hand, the contrast between the human condition on earth and hereafter, and, on the other hand, the affirmation of retribution beyond the grave.

Several forms of a similar account, certainly dependent on the Egyptian story, possibly via Alexandrian Jews, are found in Jewish literature. The oldest of them seems to be that found in the Palestinian Talmud Hagigah, the story of the deaths of a rich publican Bar Ma'jan and a poor scribe, which, according to some, may also have provided the inspiration for the parable of the great supper (Lk 14:15–24). The Egyptian and Jewish stories have the same basic schema, but unlike the former, the latter story concentrates on proving God's justice in all details, even in the difference between the two burials. Lk 16:19–31, on the other hand, seems to stress that after death it is 'too late'. There is a widespread agreement that Lk 16:19–31 was inspired by the rabbinic story, although in some respects it seems to be closer to the Egyptian story. Analysis of the points at which Lk 16:19–31 departs from its parallels shows that it expresses that what one does now with one's life is done before God and as such has eternal implications. The emphasis is on the present, on life, not on what happens after death.

Among those who doubt whether this Egyptian/Jewish story underlies our parable some have referred to another Jewish legend which tells of a rich godless couple. The woman went to hell. A boy who journeyed to hell to see her was sent back with an urgent message for her husband to repent. Deeply moved, the husband repented.

General context

Like the rich man of Lk 12:16–21, the one in Lk 16:19–31 is a fool and, in this respect, his conduct contrasts with that of the unjust steward, whom Lk 16:9 invites us to follow as an example. Before it is too late, make sure to use your money wisely: share it with the poor, who will then be your friends at the moment that money will no longer have any value for you, the moment you will have to leave this world. Money accumulated for oneself brings disaster; it is 'mammon of unrighteousness', but shared with the poor it becomes a guarantee of happiness shared in the eternal habitations. As the context shows, the parable is for Luke the climax of Jesus' speech against mammon.

The story presents two typical characters whose example illustrates God's judgment on people. It does not contain any explicit application. Apparently it was considered unnecessary to add anything to the statements of Abraham, sufficiently clear by themselves, and from the context. The two statements of verses 25 and 26 boil down to saying that the pitiful condition of the rich man is unavoidable, while verses 29 and 31 state that the brothers of the rich man could avoid his fate by listening to 'Moses and the prophets'. These statements divide the story into two parts: the first, Lk 16:19–26, shows what fate awaits the rich man in the hereafter; the second, Lk 16:27–31, answers the question what the rich should do *now* to avoid such a fate.[83]

Analysis of the text

Verse 19: There was a rich man, who was clothed in purple and fine linen and who feasted sumptuously every day.

Luke's redactional intervention in the description of the rich man is very extensive. The initial expression, *anthrōpos de tis*, 'certain man', is his. Sometimes the rich man is called Dives, but this is simply the Latin for 'rich man'. The phrase 'named Neues', found in some manuscripts, and certainly secondary, has given rise to some very ingenious but entirely hypothetical interpretations. The description of the cloths witnesses to the attention of the evangelist for a person's dress and the prestige that goes with it: 'he was clothed in purple and fine linen'. These materials would have been imported from abroad (Egypt or India). In Luke's thought this purple mantle is not just expensive, but above all 'glorious' (*endoxos*, cf. Lk 7:25), assuring esteem to the one who wears it (compare Lk 9:29; 23:11; 24:4; Acts 12:21).

The clause 'who feasted sumptuously every day' is entirely Lucan and expresses the evangelist's interest in festive meals (*euphrainein*: Lk 12:19; 15:23; cf. Acts 14:17). The rich man's attitude to life is well expressed in Lk 12:19, '... you have ample goods laid up for many years; take your ease, eat, drink, be merry'. The rich man's feasting is certainly intended to contrast with the description of the hungry Lazarus, which also contains a number of redactional elements (Lk 16:21; compare the similar contrast between Lk 15:16 and 15:23). It has been noted that the text does not say anything about unrestrained waste or ruthless exploitation, but rather about the total lack of concern with which the rich man enjoys his wealth. He belongs to the generation of the flood, 'in the days of Noah' (cf. Lk 17:26–27), unaware of the impending catastrophe.

> **Verses 20–21:** And at his gate lay a poor man named Lazarus, full of sores, (21) who desired to be fed with what fell from the rich man's table; moreover the dogs came and licked his sores.

Here follows the description of the miserable situation of the poor man (*ptōchos*; ten times in Luke, six of these without parallel), named Lazarus (*Lazaros*, i.e., *El'azar, Eleazar*, 'he whom God helps'). This is the only instance of a name being given to a character in the parables of Jesus. The occurrence of a proper name may be due to the fact that the later conversation between the rich man and Lazarus calls for one (cf. Lk 16:24, 25, 27), and in view of its etymology the name Lazarus is very fitting. But it has also been suggested that the use of the proper name indicates that the poor man is not just 'anyone': God knows him and is aware of his need. His name is written in heaven (cf. Lk 10:20). One would have expected the rich man to have a name and the poor man to be anonymous, but here the opposite is true. That Lazarus lay at the rich man's gate does not necessarily imply that he was paralysed, but rather intends to give a realistic description of an (ancient) Oriental street scene.

A possible link has repeatedly been suggested between our parable and the account of the raising of Lazarus in Jn 11. Some scholars have proposed that Jesus himself made the allusion to the miracle in his parable. It has been said, e.g., that Jesus told the parable after he and his disciples had received the news of Lazarus' illness, and later his death, and his disciples speculated about the possible favourable reaction to Jesus if he raised Lazarus from the dead: 'neither will they be convinced if some one should rise from the dead' (Lk 16:31). Other scholars believe that the allusion is due to Luke's redaction, e.g., to explain why the risen Christ did not appear to everybody, but only to his disciples. Finally, a few scholars have considered the hypothesis that Jn 11 is a development of the parable. Some of these suggestions and hypotheses are rather far-fetched. It should be noted that the name Lazarus/Eleazar was very common, and therefore could very well have been used independently in Lk 16 and Jn 11.

In contrast to the rich man, clothed in purple and fine linen, Lazarus was covered with sores (cf. Job 2:7), just as in contrast to the rich man's feasting, he 'desired to be fed' (cf. Lk 15:16) 'with what fell from the rich man's table' — either crumbs which fell from the rich man's table and were normally eaten by dogs (cf. Mt 15:27), or the pieces of bread used to wipe one's hands and then thrown on the floor. Some manuscripts add here: 'and no one gave him anything', which is apparently borrowed from Lk 15:16. And worst of all (*alla kai*), 'the dogs came and licked his sores'. It has been suggested that this clause may be intended to show that animals are more compassionate than people. But the formula which introduces this clause, *alla kai* (RSV, 'moreover'), makes this hypothesis impossible, and shows that the clause intends to reinforce the description of Lazarus' misery: he had only dogs for his company. He was so defenceless that he could not even ward off the dogs, which were considered to be unclean animals. Thus the evangelist describes the extreme misery, the outcast condition of Lazarus.

Lazarus did not do anything especially good; he was just poor. This seems a foil to the rich man, who does not do anything bad, except for enjoying his riches while Lazarus was going hungry. One should indeed underline the total absence of any religious or moral note: neither patience or resignation, nor piety or confidence in God are mentioned. The text describes only Lazarus' extreme poverty. The rich man's indifference to Lazarus' situation was apparently determined by clan-mentality and social distinctions. He certainly did not heed the admonition to 'invite the poor, the maimed, the lame, the blind' (Lk 14:13, 21). But the text does not explicitly mention either the 'crimes' of the rich man, or any 'merits' of the poor man. It simply underlines the revolting juxtaposition of extreme wealth and abject poverty, in which the rich man couldn't care less about entering into communion with the poor. In fact, we have here the exact opposite of the conduct demanded of the rich in the parable of the dishonest steward.

In the first three verses literally nothing happens, while everything indicates that something is going to happen.

Verse 22: The poor man died and was carried by the angels to Abraham's bosom. The rich man also died and was buried;

Literally the verse begins: 'It happened, however, that...' (*egeneto de*). The real story starts here. The decisive turning point of the account comes with the death of both Lazarus and the rich man. This brings about a radical reversal, foreshadowed in the fact that they are now mentioned in reversed order (compare Lk 16:19–20). 'The poor man died and was carried by the angels' (cf. Targum on Cant 4:12, saying that the souls of the righteous are carried to paradise by angels) 'to Abraham's bosom'. This expression corresponds to a number of Old Testament expressions (cf. Gen 15:15; 47:30; Deut 31:16; Judg 2:10). It has been suggested that the linking of Abraham and Lazarus recalls Gen 15, where Abraham laments that *Eliezer* of Damascus will be his heir; but this may be far-fetched. 'Abraham's bosom' is not a synonym for paradise, but to rest in Abraham's bosom suggests that Lazarus is in paradise since Abraham is there. The expression presents Lazarus as a guest of honour, being close to the host of a banquet (cf. Jn 13:23; see also Lk 13:29). He is taken out of his isolation and led into full communion of life.

The rich man's fate is abruptly mentioned: he 'also died'. Unlike Lazarus' case, the rich man's funeral is mentioned: he 'was buried'. And no doubt he got a first-class burial! But this was the very last respect people could pay him — or to his riches. The rich man was taken out of society and transferred to a limitless loneliness.

It has correctly been remarked that this story is not a 'tourist guide' to the next world. It makes use of traditional images and does not give any precise information on what heaven or hell is like. Moreover, there is no indication whatsoever that the story intends to describe an intermediate state between a particular judgment immediately after death and a final, universal judgment. One should resist the temptation to read later theological speculation into the biblical text.

Verse 23: and in Hades, being in torment, he lifted up his eyes, and saw Abraham far off and Lazarus in his bosom.

Hades (Lk 10:15; Acts 2:27, 31; Hebrew *sheol*) often refers to the place where all the departed stay; but in the New Testament it seems to be especially the place of punishment (cf. 'being in torment'), and to have become synonymous with *Gehenna* (cf. Lk 12:5). Gehenna is derived from the name of the valley of Ge-Hinnom, which was south-west of Jerusalem. It was believed that in ancient times infants had been sacrificed there to the god Moloch. The Jews looked upon it as a place of abomination, and used it as a garbage dump where fires were kept constantly burning, whence the derived meaning of Gehenna as 'hell'. Striking parallels to the imagery of this parable have been found in Enoch traditions which were very popular in Jesus' time. In Enoch 22, Sheol is described as having two compartments where the good and evil can see each other. It should be noted that in the New Testament times there was a multiplicity of images and symbols which could be used even by one and the same author, without any concern for consistency or logic. Therefore, the details of the picture cannot be insisted upon.

That the rich man 'lifted up his eyes' does not necessarily imply that Lazarus was above him (cf. Lk 6:20; 18:13). But it is certainly true that the rich man is suddenly forced to look at things from a new angle since he is no longer 'on top'. He 'saw Abraham far off' (*apo makrothen*; cf. the 'great chasm' in Lk 16:26), and 'Lazarus in his bosom', enjoying his happiness. 'For though the Lord is high, he regards the lowly; but the haughty he knows from afar' (*apo makrothen*, Ps 138[137]:6).

> **Verse 24:** And he called out, 'Father Abraham, have mercy upon me, and send Lazarus to dip the end of his finger in water and cool my tongue; for I am in anguish in this flame.'

With this verse begins a dialogue in direct speech which will continue until verse 31, and which, since the speakers remain the same, should be taken as a whole. One can, however, distinguish two parts, introduced by 'Father Abraham... send Lazarus...' (verse 24) and 'then I beg you, father, to send him...' (verse 27), so that verses 24–26 and 27–31 can be understood as two segments of one and the same sequence. From the point of view of the story, verse 24 has a double function. Firstly, in contrast with the rich man's previous sumptuous feasting, it now specifically describes his sufferings. The antithesis would have been more exact if the story had referred to hunger (as in the second woe, Lk 6:25); but here the more terrible suffering of thirst is substituted for it, possibly because of the mention of fire. Secondly, the verse leads to Abraham's answer.

As a faithful Jew the rich man addresses Abraham as his 'father', which is exactly what John the Baptist had warned the unrepentant against (Lk 3:8; cf. 1:73; 13:16; 19:9). The rich man calls for 'mercy' (cf. Lk 17:13; 18:38f.), i.e., gracious help in need. But for the sake of the story the help is actually expected from Lazarus. Thus the two main characters of the story face each other again. The water into which the rich man expects Lazarus to dip his finger belongs to another image of heavenly happiness, that of paradise, a well-irrigated garden in which the existence of a source or a river is mentioned (cf. Enoch 22, 2). Water is also constantly mentioned in association with Osiris, the chief Egyptian god, e.g., on sepulchral inscriptions found in Italy from imperial times: 'May Osiris give you the cold water'. The water of paradise contrasts with the fire of Gehenna. The flames enveloping the rich man are traditional and symbolic and are not to be taken literally.

> **Verse 25:** But Abraham said, 'Son, remember that you in your lifetime received your good things, and Lazarus in like manner evil things; but now he is comforted here, and you are in anguish.

Luke's redactional intervention is considerable. It is impossible to overlook the close relationship to the first woe, 'But woe to you that are rich, for you have received your consolation' (Lk 6:24). This last word, 'consolation' (*paraklēsis*), seems to have been inspired by the beatitude which, in reference to Isa 61:2, promises the mourners that they will be 'consoled' or 'comforted'. This beatitude is echoed in Lk 16:25; Lazarus is 'consoled' or 'comforted'. In this verse the general resemblance of the parable to the beatitudes (and woes) becomes clear to the extent that it may be considered a Lucan paraphrase of the first 'woe'. It seems that for Luke the decisive answer is given in verse 25, and there is therefore good reason to look here for the evangelist's own thought. Perhaps one may even discover here the deeper meaning of the beatitudes and the woes. One should also refer to the repeated use of the adverb 'now' in Luke's version of the beatitudes and woes (Lk 6:21, 25, altogether four times) and here. The 'now' of the hereafter is contrasted with the 'now' of the earthly existence of both rich and poor.

The second part of the Magnificat has also been cited, especially Lk 1:53, 'he has filled the hungry with good things, and the rich he has sent empty away', but since the 'rich' here are not clearly distinguished from the 'proud' of Lk 1:51 and the 'mighty' of Lk 1:52, the perspective cannot be said to be the same as in Lk 6:24; 16:25, and it may be better not to use Lk 1:53 too directly in the interpretation of Lk 16:25.

It is obvious that Abraham is thought of here as the mouthpiece of God. But it does not seem to be necessary to state that he must be a Jewish substitute for the pagan god Osiris. It is not clear how far

Abraham's use of the address 'son' (*teknon*, literally, 'child') is a recognition of the kinship claimed by the rich man (cf. 'Father Abraham'). Abraham invites him to 'remember' (cf. Lk 23:42) that in his lifetime he had received his 'good things' (*ta agatha*; cf. Lk 12:18), which are contrasted here with the 'bad things' which Lazarus received. The verse intends to make the rich man understand that what happens to him is right. Each person has his share of good and bad. The rich man had chosen 'his' (cf. 'your') good things — he had what he chose: purple and fine linen and daily feasting — while the 'evil things' (without 'his') were not Lazarus' choice. Eternity assures a compensation for what one has not received during one's earthly life. The strongly redactional character of Lk 16:25 shows that Luke was especially interested in this statement.

On the one hand, this verse presents life hereafter as a reversal of the earthly conditions. This affirmation does not pose the question of retribution; it only proclaims the privilege of the poor, as do the beatitudes (Lk 6:20–21) and the corresponding woes (Lk 6:24–25), and, to some extent, the Magnificat (Lk 1:52–53). On the other hand, a second point is added: death fixes the fate of the person for ever (Lk 16:26). Once death has come, it is too late for changes. Lazarus cannot reach the former rich man; neither can the latter reach Lazarus. Their fate is fixed irrevocably.

Abraham plays the part of a kind of superintendent of the heavenly goods, while Lazarus fulfils the role of steward, corresponding to what in the parable of the dishonest steward is said of the poor who had been made friends by means of unrighteous mammon. Abraham's words should not be understood as if he were simply saying: everyone in his turn. They mean rather: when you and Lazarus were on earth, you were immersed in your shameless luxury and he in his need. There was no communication whatsoever between you. You lived radically separated lives. The wealth which you regarded as your absolute property and practically the goal of your existence (although you may have taken part in some religious practices) has never been used to enter into a relationship with Lazarus and befriend him (cf. Lk 16:9). Now this absence of sharing and communion is perpetuated. Lazarus, who is now in happiness, cannot enter into any form of communion with you to alleviate your suffering; and it is not his fault.

Verse 26: And besides all this, between us and you a great chasm has been fixed, in order that those who would pass from here to you may not be able, and none may cross from there to us.'

Except for the expression 'and besides all this' (*kai en pasi toutois*; cf. Isa 9:11LXX[=9:12]; Lk 24:21), nothing in this verse can with certainty be attributed to Lucan redaction. Nevertheless some scholars think that this verse has been composed to serve as a transition to the second part of the story, which must therefore have taken place before the Lucan redaction. The image of the 'great chasm', found only here in the Greek Bible, and which is said to make the passage 'from here' to there and vice versa impossible, indicates the finality of the verdict. Abraham cannot help, even if he would like to. One should not try to find anything like a 'topography of hell' in this text. It does not say anything about purgatory either. One could possibly speculate that this 'chasm' is of the rich man's own making: the artificial distance which he maintained between himself and the poor man during their life on earth has been finalized, and the step is irreversible. The gate of the rich man's house could still be passed; the chasm which now separates the rich and the poor man is unbridgeable. Rather than a simple symbol of the impossibility for the elect as well as for the damned to change their destiny, it is the opposite of the ideal of sharing and communion described in Lk 16:9. A chasm fixed between persons signifies their definitive separation, and not just the immutability of their respective destinies.

The basic significance of the first part of the parable is that by closing their hearts to any true feeling of mercy and compassion, by deliberately barricading themselves in a world of their own which tries to ignore the plight and suffering of the poor, the rich themselves prepare their downfall (possibly already here on earth, but certainly) in the hereafter. Contrary to Lk 16:9, where the poor who have entered the kingdom welcome those who have shared their wealth with them, the eternal loss of the rich is here conceived as a total absence of communion, which results from a deliberate refusal of all fraternal communion here on earth. Divine judgment and punishment is not purely extrinsically added to human action: if people do not bear fruits of communion, they bear fruits of separation from God and man.

Verses 27–28: And he said, 'Then I beg you, father, to send him to my father's house, (28) for I have five brothers, so that he may warn them, lest they also come into this place of torment.'

With the second request of the rich man the story takes a new direction. For the benefit of the living, the second part intends to state precisely the significance of the fact affirmed in the first part.

The question considered is what the rich should do to escape the terrible fate just described. Luke's redactional intervention is again extensive and testifies to the interest he had in these last verses, which however should not entirely be attributed to him.

Verses 27–28, which have not been essentially altered by Luke's redaction, describe the rich man's intercession for his brothers. It does not make sense to question the probability of such an expression of charity by a condemned man. We are dealing here with a literary device which permits the story to return to the living and their conduct. The only purpose of the rich man's request is to introduce Abraham's answer which constitutes the second climax and lesson of the story.

The man requests Abraham to 'send' (*pempō*; cf. Lk 16:24; also used of the sending of Elijah, Lk 4:26, and the sending of the servants and the son of the vineyard, Lk 20:11, 12, 13) Lazarus to 'warn' (*diamarturesthai*, literally, 'to witness', found ten times in Acts) the five brothers. The thought is that if they know that their present lifestyle will lead them into torment, as testified by a witness from the dead, they will change their ways. He wants a kind of visible demonstration which will take away all unknowns from people in this world, and make conversion something dictated by a person's intelligence. 'Five' is doubtless a round number. Attempts to find here an allusion to the Herod family or to the unbelieving half of Israel's twelve tribes (one plus five = six brothers!) are ill-directed.

Verse 29: But Abraham said, 'They have Moses and the prophets; let them hear them.'

It has been stated above that the present parable is addressed to the Pharisees who 'mocked' (cf. Lk 23:35) Jesus for what he said about the use of money. They should recognize their own conduct in that of the rich man. Through Abraham's words, Jesus addresses himself now to the people who have 'Moses and the prophets' (Lk 16:29, 31), which is Luke's transcription of the Jewish expression 'the law and the prophets', which again indicates the Scriptures (cf. Lk 24:27, 44; Acts 26:22; 28:23). If they listen to them they will know what to do to avoid the terrible fate of the rich man, more precisely, they will 'repent' (Lk 16:30). Perhaps the parable with its underlying demand for mercy (cf. Isa 58:7, 'is it not to share your bread with the hungry, and bring the homeless poor into your house') may be understood as an answer to the question of the new interpretation of the law.

The verb 'to hear' (Lk 16:29, 31) seems to refer to the synagogue service (cf. Lk 4:16–21). 'Hearing' means 'repenting' (Lk 16:30), while 'not hearing' means 'not being convinced' (Lk 16:31). This recalls Jesus' saying that no sign will be given to this generation except the sign of Jonah — that is, someone who calls people to repentance. The people of Niniveh repented at the preaching of Jonah, and now someone greater than Jonah is here (Lk 11:29–32).

> **Verse 30:** And he said, 'No, father Abraham; but if some one goes to them from the dead, they will repent.'

The rich man contradicts Abraham: Moses and the prophets are not enough! He insists on a miraculous proof which will make the decision easier. If somebody returned from the dead, his brothers might repent. It is the same demand for a sensational sign which the Jews addressed to Jesus (Lk 11:16, 29), and which many people still make today.

> **Verse 31:** He said to him, 'If they do not hear Moses and the prophets, neither will they be convinced if some one should rise from the dead.'

The word of God, which the rich recognize within the scope of their nominal religion but have no real interest in obeying ('hearing'), should be sufficient. If they do not listen to 'Moses and the prophets', even the resurrection of a dead person will not 'convince' them (*peithomai*; Lk 20:6, and eight times in Acts; absent from Mark and Matthew). Their situation is pictured as hopeless. Those who reject Jesus (Lk 16:14) are themselves rejected (cf. Jn 5:45–46). The words 'if some one should rise from the dead' echo the formulation of the Christian faith after Easter and are therefore possibly a post-Easter allusion to Jesus' resurrection. This resurrection did not 'convince' the rich whom 'Moses and the prophets' had not managed to 'convert'. *Metanoiein* and *metanoia* are characteristic of Luke's vocabulary (*metanoiein*: five times in Matthew; twice in Mark; nine times in Luke; *metanoia*: twice in Matthew; once in Mark; five times in Luke).

Originally, the words about rising from the dead may have referred to Jesus' ministry, during which the Pharisees had 'sought from him a sign from heaven' (Lk 11:16), and had rejected him, notwithstanding the fact that, according to Luke's account, Jesus raised several people from the dead (Lk 7:14–15, 22; 8:53–55). But it seems probable that Luke writes this final clause having in mind the resurrection of Jesus, which had so little influence on the Pharisees and Israel. (Although the fact that some manuscripts read 'if some one should *go* from the dead' may suggest that the verse has not always been taken to refer to the resurrection.) It has been pointed out that Lk 16:31 and 24:46 use the same verb to refer to resurrection. This resurrection can convince only those who listen to 'Moses and the prophets', i.e., not just what the Old Testament says about responsibility towards the poor, but the witness it gives to the gospel, its appeal to conversion and faith in Jesus. Attempts to link the parable to the raising of Lazarus (Jn 11) are not convincing.

A miracle will not change those who make no use of the (ordinary) means which God has placed at their disposal. Thus the story ends with the admonition to seek salvation by the 'normal' way, and not to slacken in obedience to the word of God. In the concluding dialogue a traditional story climactically receives a powerful thrust. An account which deals with the reversal of fortunes in the afterlife is made to witness to the basis of faith as against a false understanding of the miraculous. Faith itself is the miracle.

According to Acts, the gospel preached by the apostles is first and foremost a gospel of someone who has risen from the dead. And one of the themes of Acts is that this gospel is the culmination of the best Judaism had to offer, and that in rejecting it the Jews are rejecting the essence of their own faith. The final words of the parable of the rich man and Lazarus may then be a comment on the early Church's missionary experience. On the one hand, it sounds pessimistic, but, on the other hand, it resolves to some extent the mystery of unbelief.

It has repeatedly been asked why the parable gives us such unexpected details in verses 27–31. Why does it attribute to a damned man such a vivid concern for his relatives? The story of the relations of Lazarus and the rich man is in reality finished; why then this extra last part which seems to jeopardize the unity of the parable? Usually it is said that verses 27–31 are subordinated to the first part of the parable and serve only to confirm its teaching. But there is more. The final verses of this parable seem to tackle a very precise question. The ideas concerning riches expressed in Lk 16:1–13, and confirmed by an example *a contrario* in the parable of the rich man and Lazarus, are new and not found in the Old Testament as such. Hence the possible objection: can the rich man be condemned for not having taken into account a doctrine which he did not know? The answer to this objection is given by Abraham: the law of Moses and the prophets were sufficient to instruct people on the good use of riches (Lk 16:29, 31). So many passages recommend sharing one's wealth with the poor (e.g., Ex 22:25; Deut 24:6, 10–13; Amos 6:4–7; 8:4–8; Isa 58:7, etc.). This explanation is suggested by Lk 16:14–18, which, as we saw, introduces Lk 16:19–31, and which can be summarized as follows: Jesus brought a new economy of salvation (Lk 16:16), which far surpasses the old one. Nevertheless, his teaching, particularly his teaching on riches, which provoked the scoffing of the Pharisees (Lk 16:14), was already prepared by the law and the prophets (Lk 16:16).

Jesus or Luke?

The meaning of the parable for Luke

Addressing the parable to the Pharisees (Lk 16:14), Luke indicates that it deals with a message which concerns Israel. And the second point of the parable (Lk 16:29) shows that the conversion of this people is at stake: the law and the prophets (the Scriptures) contain all the light necessary to find the way to salvation. Miracles are only secondary signs, ineffective for those who refuse to accept the message of the Scriptures.

The first part of the parable (Lk 16:19–26) indicates that this conversion is urgent: death comes and fixes a person's lot. Afterwards it is too late to change one's fate. Luke is too sensitive to the privilege of the poor and the dangers of wealth (cf. Lk 16:1–13) not to pay here special attention to the fate of the rich and the poor. But, while the Egyptian story and its rabbinic adaptations explain this fate by referring to the retribution for earthly merits, Luke in no way presents their happiness or torment hereafter as a sanction (Lk 16:25). This does not mean that he denies that God's judgment is founded on people's actions (cf. Lk 3:9; 12:35–48; 13:1–5, 23–27; 14:14; 16:10–12; 19:12–26; 21:34–36). But he wants to emphasize first of all the grace of salvation, the privilege of the poor, and in addition to it the dangers of wealth.

The parable in the preaching of Jesus

The parable of the rich man and Lazarus is found only in Luke. It is so strongly marked by his style and favourite themes that it may be asked whether it is possible to reach beyond Luke towards Jesus' own thought.

Several exegetes have maintained that the two parts of the parable (Lk 16:19–26 and 27–31), so different because of their theme as well as their pre-history in the tradition, cannot both be attributed to Jesus. The majority of this group trace the first part of the parable to Jesus, because it describes the fate of rich and poor in a way similar to the beatitudes and the woes, using an old traditional story. But the second part has no foundation in ancient Jewish tradition. It deals with very different subjects: conversion, the signs which may lead to it, the inefficacy of a resurrection to inspire it. Would not this be a composition of the early Church — possibly of Luke — reflecting on Israel's refusal to believe in Jesus' resurrection?

Many contemporary exegetes nevertheless opt for the primitive unity of the parable and its attribution to Jesus. They insist especially on the complementarity of the two parts of the parable, on the originality of its ideas, and on the support which they find in the message of Jesus. In fact, the first part is very different from the Egyptian story and its rabbinic adaptations in its refusal to pose the question of retribution. This corresponds very well to the announcement of salvation for the poor, so characteristic of Jesus' message. The second part illustrates concern for the conversion of Israel (cf. Lk 13:1–5), the refusal of exceptional signs requested by the Jews (cf. Mt 12:38; 16:1), insistence on the value of the Scriptures. All this corresponds well to Jesus' thought. Finally, the second part completes the first by suggesting that if the rich man is lost, it is not only because he is rich, but because he did not convert in conformity with the message of the Scriptures. This idea too can be traced to Jesus (cf. Mt 11:21–24 and parallels; Lk 13:1–5).

The most striking difference which can be perceived between Jesus' thought and its presentation by Luke consists in their respective eschatological imagery. Luke is a Greek preoccupied with the individual fate of a person. Jesus, as well as the whole biblical tradition, is before anything else attentive to the salvation of his people, which he describes most of the time in communitarian images: the kingdom, the earth, the banquet, the marriage feast, the reconstitution of the twelve tribes, the gathering of the elect. It is probable that by using the old story of the rich and the poor man in the hereafter, he intended to speak only of God's judgment, without any distinction between a particular judgment at the death of the individual, and a general judgment at the end of history. Luke may have interpreted this in the perspective of an individual eschatology.[84]

This difference between Luke and Jesus is secondary and constitutes a case of traditional interpretation. For Jesus as for Luke, the urgency of the conversion to which the people are invited is essential. The people of God have in their tradition all that is necessary to recognize the way of salvation. They should not ask for exceptional signs. For, of all the signs which God gives to his people, his Word is the greatest.[85]

Reflection

The issue which at this point will probably confront us is whether the story is vulnerable to the charge that the comfort it affords the poor may be described as an opiate of the people. On this basis, the parable would assure the beggars of the best in the world to come. With thisassurance, they may endure their plight in the world of the present. At the same time, it would assure them of the final punishment of the rich, which would sublimate the anger they would otherwise direct at the rich. Interpreted in such a manner, the parable becomes a most effective propaganda weapon of the rich, and more deceptive and captivating of the mind and heart than any other means at their disposal. For even though they are not persuaded of the religion the parable represents, it is to their advantage from this point of view to promote it. For the more beggars persuaded of good things to come in the world beyond, the less trouble they will cause for their masters now. But this is not the purpose of the parable.[86]

The story of the rich man and Lazarus does not assert that it is good to have a miserable life here on earth, that it is right for society not to fight poverty, and that it is the Church's task to console people in need by referring to heaven. Neither is it a projection of the fantasies and hostilities of the poor. To read such ideas into the parable would be equally wrong. It starts from the fact that in the world some have abundance, while others suffer lack. Either our relation to God shows itself in our relation to our fellow human beings, especially to the poor and the oppressed, or it is an illusion.

The parable emphasizes the seriousness of the present. What really matters is what we do right now. The story calls us to a real sense of responsibility for the poor and the oppressed. And all this in reference to God's judgment and criterion. The parable pictures the rich man as an example of the many rich who, no matter what happens, do not seem to understand the situation, and then pathetically try to salvage the situation once it has been lost.

In other words, his problem is the same as that of the wealthy everywhere... They are surprised by, and as unprepared for, the historical antecedents of hell and judgment as they will be for the ultimate form of these, which is integral to the biblical understanding of destiny.[87]

One is not guilty only when one commits evil, but also when one does not act. The rich man's sin consists in the fact that he has not shown any concern, that he has been blind to the plight of the poor. It is of paramount importance to see Lazarus, and to know how to relate to him. He does not have to lie at the gate or under the window. The world has become so small that one cannot ignore what happens in Africa, Asia, or South America. The question is whether we commit ourselves to the cause of the poor, or whether we remain indifferent, whether we can go on revelling, knowing that others live in hunger.

In Lk 16:19–31 the condemnation does not fall on wealth as such. The description of the rich man and Lazarus is a description of the way things are. But the condemnation falls on the lack of community created by barriers of wealth. This recalls Isa 5:8, 'Woe to those who join house to house, who add field to field, until there is no more room, and you are made to dwell alone in the midst of the land'. These barriers of wealth are protected, confirmed, and fortified by the concerted actions of the rich. 'How hard it is for those who have riches to enter the kingdom of God!' (Lk 18:24). The parable is a threatening lesson addressed to the rich who refuse to share their wealth with the poor, and thus to do their share in building a fraternal community (cf. Lk 16:9). Although the word is not mentioned in Lk 16, the whole chapter is nevertheless dominated by the reality of 'communion' (*koinōnia*) which is given so much attention at the beginning of the Acts of the Apostles.

Many efforts have been made so that the rich may see. But the initiatives remain ultimately insufficient, because they do not succeed in making the rich *as a group* aware of the inequality of their existence as rich and the existence of the poor as poor. In the parable the rich man and Lazarus are not just individual characters. Each of them also represents a collective human reality. The parable is not an incidental story pertaining only to a particular case, but a parable of history. While the rich man represents upper-class affluence, Lazarus dramatizes the social poverty of the masses.

The story speaks of the whole human world of which part will be found 'in the bosom of Abraham', while the other part will be outside. All those who have not become aware of an inequality contrary to the will of God, and have acquiesced in it — while perhaps being prepared to make it less glaring by accepting a few poor at their gate — will be outside. Things may become clearer if one has a look at how the help to developing countries is conceived: one practises 'aid'. Even when disinterested, this aid does not change the inequality. It renders it apparently less insupportable. It is exactly in the same terms that relations between rich and poor people, between rich and poor classes are lived. As soon as these relations are given the dimension of the world with its problem of development, the insufficiency of all this is evident. Aid does not express a real solidarity; it is not a real sharing; it does not establish real justice in relationships; it does not make the rich see. And they remain exposed to the real danger of not being found 'in the bosom of Abraham'.

A pastoral ministry which tries to tackle this problem and in doing so emphasizes social categories is often misunderstood. Some well-meaning people deplore that it does not give sufficient attention to persons, and that it does not think in terms of the relation of such and such rich person to such and such poor. It is true that the person is a value which should not be ignored. But persons should be approached in their actual life context, amidst the group whose preoccupations and mentality they share. This approach by social categories demands that one accept the rich as they are, while insisting that they open their eyes and become aware of what as a group they tend to ignore. This is more difficult than convincing individual rich people to care for a few poor, while it is also slower and less spectacular than stigmatizing the rich from the heights of the pulpit. But it is a concrete attempt to get the rich involved in something more than 'repairs' in building a just world, closer to what God wants us to make it.

> ...the parable does concentrate on the social/economic discrepancies and not moral ones. God's justice and compassion for the poor as poor, apart from their individual piety and his verdict against the rich as rich, is clearly present. Yet, there is more. For how could anyone hear the vivid descriptions of the gross discrepancy in social conditions as anything other than a devastating critique against the rich who exploit the poor and live in selfish luxury, unmindful of the dying beggars at their gate?... The central focus of the parable is the issue of wealth and poverty and the related theme of justice. The Old Testament is affirmed as the norm for justice which the six brothers have violated (cf. 16:17). Their extravagant wealth and Lazarus' dire poverty is the condition of inequality which needs rectification. God himself will make things right in the end. That is comfort to the poor and warning to the rich. Yet there is still opportunity for the violators of God's justice to hear Moses and the prophets and to repent. That is the note on which the parable ends. Without repentance, however, the fate of the rich is sealed.[88]

12   The judge and the widow
(Lk 18:1–8)

General context

The present pericope belongs to the great Lucan Travel Narrative (Lk 9:51 – 19:44). Its more immediate context is Lk 17:11 – 18:34, a coherent series of pericopes with a single theme: the coming of the kingdom of God and the consequences which people who want to have part in it should draw.

In Lk 17:11–19 Jesus is presented as the one who brings near the kingdom of God. He has the power to heal lepers. Both the raising of the dead and the healing of lepers were considered as signs of dawning of the kingdom of God. Jesus thus appears as the eschatological bringer of salvation (cf. Lk 17:19, 'your faith has made you well' [*sesōken se* = 'saved you']).

Luke's first eschatological discourse (Lk 17:20–37) logically follows the miracle story. The healing of the lepers leads naturally to the Pharisees' question 'when the kingdom of God was coming' (Lk 17:20a), which in turn leads to the eschatological instruction, first briefly addressed to the Pharisees (Lk 17:20b–21), then to the disciples (Lk 17:21–37). This prophetic discourse concerning 'the day of the son of man' (Lk 17:22, 24, 26, 30) warns against attempts to calculate when the end will come, against reading off the end from certain signs, and against false certainty: the end will come suddenly.

From Lk 18:1 on, Luke deals in more detail with the consequences and the attitudes the Christians should pay attention to in virtue of the preceding eschatological instruction. As first and most important Luke mentions prayer (Lk 18:1–14), which, according to the evangelist, constitutes the most important 'eschatological attitude' of the Christian.

The parable of the judge and the widow (Lk 18:1–8) emphasizes the necessity of *continued* prayer (Lk 18:1, '… they ought always to pray'). The special connection with the general theme of the section (and with the preceding discourse, Lk 17:20–37), is achieved by means of the redactionally added verse 8b, which deals with 'the coming of the Son of man' (cf. Lk 17:24, 30), and with the faith

215

expected from people: 'Nevertheless, when the Son of man comes, will he find faith on earth?' Thus Luke uses this parable as a culmination of his first apocalypse (Lk 17:20 – 18:8) in reply to the Pharisees' question when the kingdom will come (Lk 17:20). The evangelist repeatedly concludes a discourse with a parable (Lk 6:20–49; 10:1–37; 11:37 – 12:21, etc.).

The parable of the Pharisee and the tax collector (Lk 18:9–14) in its Lucan context also deals with prayer. As the two frame-verses (Lk 18:9 and 14b) show, it is concerned with the right kind of prayer, *humble* prayer, which alone justifies a person before God. By this example story the evangelist wants to illustrate how one should pray. The two consecutive parables have a rather different aim (compare Lk 18:1 and 9), but they are related by their genre and by the theme of prayer.

From Lk 18:15 on, Luke resumes the order of themes found in Mark (compare Mk 10:13–34). So he introduces next in Lk 18:15–17 the pericope of the blessing of the children (compare Mk 10:13–16), then the story of the 'rich man' (Lk 18:18–27; compare Mk 10:17–27), further Peter's 'reward question' (Lk 18:28–30; compare Mk 10:28–31), and finally the third prophecy of the passion (Lk 18:31–34; compare Mk 10:32–34). These pericopes too deal with the same theme: after prayer, other basic eschatological attitudes, derived from Lk 17:20ff., are enumerated. Thus Lk 18:17 demands that one be 'small' with regard to the kingdom of God. Then Luke refers to the importance of imitation of Christ, which is an imitation 'in poverty' (Lk 18:22, 25, 29f.). Jesus has shown the way in his passion (cf. Lk 18:31–34).

Old and New Testament parables

An Old Testament prototype

In Sir 35:14–18 we have a text in which the similarities with our parable are so numerous that it is very attractive to assume with several scholars that there is conscious borrowing:

> He will not ignore the supplication of the fatherless, nor the widow when she pours out her story.
> Do not the tears of the widow run down her cheek as she cries out against him who has caused them to fall?
> He whose service is pleasing to the Lord will be accepted, and his prayer will reach to the clouds.
> The prayer of the humble pierces the clouds, and he will not be consoled until it reaches the Lord; he will not desist until the

Most High visits him, and does justice for the righteous, and
executes judgment.
And the Lord will not delay, neither will he be patient with
them, till he crushes the loins of the unmerciful and repays
vengeance on the nations.

It has been shown that in this text we find points of complete
similarity, as well as points of similarity (but with a difference), and
points of complete dissimilarity.[89]

A Lucan parallel

The similarity between Lk 18:2–5 and Lk 11:5b–8 has repeatedly
been pointed out. Some have even spoken of twin parables, which
Luke found together in his source, but which he separated to use at
different stages of his gospel. The similarity of the two passages is
indeed striking:

2 In a certain city there was a
  judge who neither feared God
  nor regarded man;
3 and there was a widow in that
  city who kept coming to him
  and saying,
  Vindicate me
  against my adversary.

4 For a while he refused;

but afterward he said to himself,

Though
I neither fear God
nor regard man,
5 yet because this widow bothers
  me, I will vindicate her,
  or she will wear me out
  by her continual coming.

5b Which of you who has a friend

will go to him at midnight
and say to him,
Friend, lend me three loaves,
6 for a friend of mine has arrived
  on a journey, and I have nothing
  to set before him.
7 and he will answer from within,
  Do not bother me; the door
  is now shut, and my children are with
  me in bed; I cannot get up and give you
  anything.

8 I tell you,
  though
  he will not get up and give him
  anything because he is his friend,
  yet because of his importunity he will
  rise and give him whatever he needs.

Just as Lk 18:2–5 begins by focusing attention on the judge, who is
also centre stage in the parable's finale, so Lk 11:5b–8 focuses on the
friend, and concludes with an observation about this friend. In both
parables, therefore, the main character was originally the one
petitioned, not the petitioner. This means that the main point of

these parables was originally not (persevering) prayer, but rather that the one petitioned — God — will certainly listen. In both passages the central concept of 'bothering' or acting importunately is expressed by the same Greek verb (*parechein*, Lk 11:7; 18:5; four times in Luke and five times in Acts, against once in Mark and Matthew). It is only because of the pre-Lucan or Lucan arrangement of the texts (Lk 18:1 in the case of the parable of the judge and the widow, and the insertion of the parable of the friend at midnight in between the Lord's Prayer, Lk 11:2–4, and the admonition about asking, seeking, and knocking, Lk 11:8–9) that attention goes now primarily to the petitioner. It is not necessary to accept the opinion that the two parables originally formed a pair and that Luke or the pre-Lucan tradition separated them to use Lk 18:2–5 in its present context. But it may be interesting to note that Lk 11:1–13 and 18:1–14 seem to occupy parallel positions in the Travel Narrative.[90]

Analysis of the text

Verse 1: And he told them a parable, to the effect that they ought always to pray and not lose heart.

The introductory verse contains a number of Lucan stylistic features and has at least been edited by the evangelist. The expression *legein parabolēn*, 'to tell a parable', is used by Luke alone (Lk 12:41; 13:6; 14:7; 18:1; 20:9). In the context, the personal pronoun 'them' must refer to the disciples, who were already addressed in Lk 17:22–37. The parable thus appears as a paraenetic application of the preceding eschatological discourse (similarly, Lk 21:34–36 following Lk 21:8–33). They must always pray. Where God is 'assailed' by persistent prayer for the fulfilment of a request, Luke does not use the phrase 'always' (*pantote*), but 'earnestly' (*ektenōs*), as, for instance, Jesus' prayer at the Mount of Olives, 'and being in an agony he prayed more earnestly' (Lk 22:44), and the community's prayer for Peter in prison, 'but earnest prayer for him was made to God by the church' (Acts 12:5). 'Always' (*pantote*), on the other hand, does not signify *duration* of time. It does not give an answer to the question 'how long', but 'when', and means, therefore, 'at all times' (cf. Mk 14:7, 'For you always have the poor with you... but you will not always have me'), while the answer to the question 'how long' would be 'to the end' (*eis telos*; Lk 18:5).

It is a well-known fact that Luke emphasizes prayer, both Jesus' own prayer, mentioning eight instances on which Jesus prayed not found in the other gospels (Lk 3:21; 5:16; 6:12; 9:18; 11:1; 22:32; 23:34, 46), and his teaching about prayer (Lk 11:1–13; 18:1–14;

21:36). Prayer is also frequently referred to in Acts. The present statement is dealing with prayer throughout the period until the parousia, as is confirmed by the phrase 'and not lose heart' (*enkakein*) which, just like 'to pray', depends on 'ought' (*dei*): They must always pray and not give up. They must not become weary or tired; they must not 'lose heart' in the midst of difficulties; they must not give up before reaching the goal: the coming of the Son of man. It should be clear, then, that this parable is not (in the first place) concerned with untiring prayer with a view to obtaining personal favours from God.

The purport of the parable is seen here neither in the certainty of being heard, nor in the duration of the prayer, but in the necessity to pray always. To this corresponds in Lk 18:8b that the Son of man will find faith when he comes. The faith which he is supposed to 'find' is apparently shown in the prayer of the disciples. They ought to pray for the coming of the kingdom (Lk 11:2). In the apparently long period separating the departure of Jesus and his return (cf. Lk 19:12), 'they ought always to pray and not lose heart'.

Verse 2: He said, 'In a certain city there was a judge who neither feared God nor regarded man;

In the usual style of biblical example stories the parable proper begins with the presentation of the characters. First the judge, who is the principal character, the only one mentioned in the application (cf. verse 6). He lives 'in a certain city', whose name and other details are not important. The judge is described as one 'who neither feared God nor regarded man', i.e., he was corrupt. As such, the judge who in Israel was regarded as appointed to carry out God's own justice among the people, did not take the judgment of God seriously, and defied public opinion. This description is underlined by its repetition in verse 4, this time in the judge's own words. Attention has been drawn to the fact that this is one of the rare instances in Jesus' parables where the word 'God' is mentioned (Lk 18:2, 5; cf. 18:7), and that this may be one of the clues to the parable's meaning.

It has been pointed out that Lk 18:2–8 and Wisd 1 – 5 have a number of elements in common. In both texts juridical practice is described in terms of righteousness or unrighteousness (Wisd 1:1, 5, 8; 5:6; Lk 18:6). In both passages the unrighteous lack eschatological awareness of God's judgment (Wisd 2:1–5; Lk 18:2, 4). In both the widow is presented as the victim of injustice (Wisd 2:10; Lk 18:3, 5). In both passages the same verb, 'to regard' (*entrepein*) is used to describe (legal) oppression (Wisd 2:10; Lk 18:2, 4). In both there is a reference to plotting, either in soliloquy or in collective conversation

(Wisd 2:1–5, 9–12; Lk 8:4–5). In both passages the case of God's 'elect' is taken up (Wisd 2:18; Lk 18:7). It seems, then, that the judge and the widow are typical characters according to a standard pattern.

In Lk 20:13, we find the same verb *entrepein*, 'to regard', in the context of the parable of the wicked tenants, 'I will send my beloved son; it may be they *will respect* him'. So the last part of verse 2 may be translated: 'he did not respect anybody'. But the meaning 'to feel shame before...' has also been suggested for both Lk 18:2 and 20:13. This would give the meaning, 'the judge did not feel shame before men' (cf. Jer 8:12).

In the light of Deut 1:17; 16:19, and especially Ex 23:3 and Lev 19:15, taken up again in Sir 35, attempts have been made to give the phrase 'not regarding man' a positive sense, and to understand it as 'impartial'. But the judge's unfavourable treatment of the widow and his ultimate act of justice, seen as a conscious infringement of his usual behaviour, militate against this interpretation. Moreover, the fact that 'not regarding man' is paired with 'not fearing God' necessarily implies a negative meaning.

In verse 6, the judge will be described as 'unrighteous'. He was of a type that was very common in Israel (cf. Amos 2:6–7; 5:7, 10–13; Isa 1:23, 'every one loves a bribe... and the widow's cause does not come to them'). A judge was accountable to the Lord. 'Consider what you do, for you judge not for man but for the Lord; he is with you in giving judgment. Now then, let the fear of the Lord be upon you; take heed what you do, for there is no perversion of justice with the Lord our God, or partiality, or taking bribes' (II Chron 19:6–7). Luke's description is paralleled in non-Christian literature, e.g., Livy, who speaks of a Roman consul who was 'fearful neither of the laws nor the senatorial majesty, and not even of the gods'. It is even more similar to Josephus' description of king Jehoiakim as 'neither religious towards God nor kind towards men'.

Verse 3: and there was a widow in that city who kept coming
to him and saying, 'Vindicate me against my adversary.'

The other character is a widow, who is evidently the victim of injustice, probably because of a rich and influential man. Widows are very often referred to in the Old Testament as the symbol of helplessness and defencelessness. The Old Testament often denounces those who oppress widows (Ex 22:22; Deut 10:18; Isa 1:17; Jer 22:3). Sir 35:12–15 describes God's role as judge on behalf of widows. See also I Tim 5:5, 'She who is a real widow, and is left all alone, has set her hope on God and continues in supplications and prayers night and day'. The widow of the parable 'kept coming' (the imperfect indicates her persistence) to the judge. The parable implies that the widow had right on her side, but the judge did not care about the rights of a penniless widow and preferred to favour her adversary.

The verb 'to vindicate' (*ekdikeō*), the vindication of a just cause against an opponent, is the key word of the parable (Lk 18:3, 5, 7, 8). The appeal for vindication, finally heard notwithstanding delay, assures the unity of the whole pericope. 'To vindicate' refers either to securing the rights of a wronged person, for instance, by the payment of a compensation, or to punishing the offender (Acts 7:24). Here apparently the former is intended. The fact that the widow is said to bring her case before a single judge seems to suggest that it was a money matter which, according to the Mishnah, could be settled by a single judge.

The situation in which the judge and the widow are involved has been clarified by pointing out that since the Ptolemaic-Seleucid period, there had been two juridical systems in Palestine: the customary courts run on lines laid down by the Torah, and an administrative jurisdiction run by the occupying power, similar to that found in the state of Egypt. In many cases the latter was more efficient, and even pious people would not hesitate to go to a secular court if it would be to their advantage. This situation and the habit of taking a case from one court to another is said to underlie the parable of reconciliation with one's adversary (Lk 12:58–59; Mt 5:25–26). The adversary has no role of his own in the present parable; what is important is what happens between the judge and the widow.

Verses 4–5: For a while he refused; but afterward he said to himself, 'Though I neither fear God nor regard man, (5) yet because this widow bothers me, I will vindicate her, or she will wear me out by her continual coming.'

Just as the widow 'kept coming', so the judge 'kept refusing' to settle her case (imperfect tense). He did not want to do anything for quite some time. The indication of time 'for a while' (*epi chronon*) is important for the further development of the story. It explains the 'continual coming' of the widow. But it is especially important in contrast to 'speedily' (*en tachei*) in the application of the parable (verse 8a). The soliloquy, which is very frequent in the parables peculiar to Luke (Lk 12:17–19; 15:17–19; 16:3–4), is nothing like a psychological analysis, but constitutes a classical parabolic feature to explain the action. The description of the judge's character given in verse 2 is almost literally repeated, though not without modalizing the sequences: '*Though* I neither fear God... *yet* because of this widow... I will vindicate her'. So the parable leaves no doubt about what kind of a judge he is. He does not care for the traditional exhortations to give the widow right (Ex 22:22; Deut 27:19), not to oppress her (Jer 7:6; Zech 7:10; Mal 3:5), to render justice to her (Isa 1:17, 23).

There is no question of remorse. Nevertheless he decides to do the widow right. But if he changes his mind, it is certainly not because of a sense of justice. He gives in because of the widow's importunity (compare Lk 11:8). So, while on the one hand, the widow achieves a certain measure of success, on the other hand, the judge did not act with conviction, and so there is no assurance that there will be a general restoration of justice. 'This widow' may carry a depreciatory overtone, like 'this son of yours' in Lk 15:30. The judge is afraid that she might 'wear him out', literally, 'hit him under the eye', 'give him a black eye'. This expression is probably to be understood metaphorically, although some have understood it as suggesting that the judge fears the widow might in the end resort to violence. She might give him a bad name; and he wants to be left in peace. As translations have been proposed: 'or she will blacken my face', with all the connotations this expression has in the East; or, if one wants to take into account that the judge was described as being without shame, 'she will give me a headache'. She will do so 'by her continual coming'. The Greek expression *eis telos* (RSV: 'continual') implies a will to go on forever. It is ironical that the widow, a model of helplessness in her society, should turn out to be a figure of power.

> **Verses 6–7:** And the Lord said, 'Hear what the unrighteous judge says. (7) And will not God vindicate his elect, who cry to him day and night? Will he delay long over them?

'And the Lord said' is considered a Lucan linking formula. The Greek expression *eipen de* (plural: *eipan de*) is found 59 times in Luke and fifteen times in Acts, but only twice elsewhere in the New Testament (Jn 8:11; 12:6). In the narrative parts of the gospels, the expression 'the Lord' is, outside Luke where it occurs sixteen times, used of Jesus only five more times, namely in the Fourth Gospel. Here in Lk 18:6 it marks the transition from the parable to the interpretation. The exalted Lord applies the parable to the actual situation of the Church.

The summons 'hear' recalls the summons at the beginning of the parable of the sower (Mk 4:3), and the eschatological exhortation at its end (Mk 4:9; compare Lk 8:8). The imperative 'hear' underlies the importance of the judge's words for the following application of the parable.

The Lord calls attention to what is said by the 'unrighteous judge', literally, 'judge of unrighteousness' (cf. Lk 16:8, 'dishonest steward', literally, 'steward of unrighteousness'). In both cases we are dealing with a characterizing genitive which, in Lk 18:6, describes the judge, either as one who perverts justice, or as one who, like the dishonest steward, belongs to 'the sons of this world', opposed to 'the sons of light' (Lk 16:8), and thus stands in strong contrast to God.

If the linking phrase, 'and the Lord said', and verse 8, which may have to be attributed to Luke as shown below, are omitted, one retains the application of the parable which Luke found in his source. Indeed, except for the elements just mentioned, no Lucan redaction can be identified with any degree of certainty, and so the pre-Lucan application can still be recognized in verses 6–7.

This application culminates in the emphatic question of verse 7, in which the granting of the widow's request (verse 6) is contrasted with the much more certain vindication of the elect. Perseverance in prayer, which in the core of the parable (verses 2–5) occupied an important place, now plays only a subordinate role of an obvious accepted presupposition for vindication, whose certainty becomes now the point of the parable. The parable says: the unjust judge ultimately vindicates the widow, notwithstanding the initial hopelessness of her request. The listeners should now draw the conclusion *a minori ad maius*: how much more will God vindicate his elect, since they enjoy his favour from the very beginning. The *minus* is not the unjust judge (to whom God would be opposed as *maius*). Rather, the hopeless situation of the widow before the unjust judge is the *minus* in contrast to the favourable situation of the elect before God as *maius*. The conclusion runs: If even the unjust judge does a widow right for whom he does not care — a case, therefore, in which the chances for a positive outcome are very slim — how much more will God respond to the unceasing crying of his elect, since, in contrast to the judge, he listens favourably to them. The negative phrasing of the *a fortiori* argument, 'and will not God vindicate his elect', calls for a positive response (compare Lk 11:13).

The term 'elect' (*hoi eklektoi*) is found elsewhere in the synoptic tradition only in the so-called synoptic apocalypse (Mk 13:20, 22, 27; Mt 24:22, 24, 31; but see also Mt 20:16[in some MSS]; 22:14). The only other Lucan use of 'elect' or 'chosen' is in Lk 23:35, as used by the Jewish leaders to designate the Messiah. In Lk 18:7 the phrase should be attributed to the tradition (cf. Acts 13:17; 15:7). The 'ecclesial' concept of 'the elect', which occurs only here in Luke, does not belong to Jesus' preaching. The elect are those who hope for God's eschatological intervention, and to whom applies God's saving promise. He will grant satisfaction to those who 'cry' (*boan*, the cry of distress of the oppressed) to him. 'Night and day' refers not so much to a protracted period of time as to urgency and intensity, or, viewed chronologically, 'all the time' (cf. Mk 5:5; Acts 9:24; I Thess 2:9; 3:10).

Verses 6–7 contain three contrasts which oppose to each other the situation of the widow of the parable and the elect, on which the conclusion *a minori ad maius* is based. The first contrasting pair is clearly stated: the unjust judge and God. The second antithesis consists in 'the elect' contrasted with the widow: the widow does not mean anything to the judge, while God has a lively interest in the elect. The third: the judge hardly wants to listen to the widow; God, on the other hand, is always prepared to listen to the elect whose cries rise to him: *kai makrothumei ep' autois* (RSV: 'will he delay long over them?', NEB: 'while he listens patiently to them'). As can be seen from these translations, the meaning of this short clause is not at all clear.

The verb *makrothumein* and related words, when applied to people, speak of forbearance, patience, perseverance; applied to God, they refer to his merciful forbearance notwithstanding the sinfulness of individuals or the people (cf. e.g., Sir 5:4–7). Many exegetes refer to the assurance given in Sir 35:14 – 36:17 to the widow and the pious Israelite, who wait in prayer and supplication for the vindicating intervention of God against their oppressors. Linguistically this text is indeed close to Lk 18:1–8, but while in the Old Testament text God is said to take the defence of his people without further delay, Jesus, comparing God with the unjust judge, admits that he lingers with regard to his elect. This means a considerable difference in perspective; and so the Old Testament text cannot solve any of the questions raised by Lk 18:1–8. But already in the Old Testament the granting of a period for repentance is not the only motive for God's patience. The verb does not just mean a waiting game played by God's wrath, but a gracious keeping back of his wrath, a grace-ful mercy instead of a deserved punishing intervention.

What meaning does the verb *makrothumein* have in Lk 18:7? The divergence of opinions concerning this clause is due to the difficulty of its grammatical construction. The opinions can be grouped in three categories.[91]

Firstly, a considerable number of scholars read the phrase as a continuation of the question 'will God not vindicate his elect who cry to him day and night?' Under the influence of Sir 35:18, 'and the Lord will not delay, neither will he be patient (*makrothumēsei*) with them', it is translated: 'and will he delay (his help) long over them?' But the present indicative *makrothumei* excludes this interpretation, since it would call for an aorist subjunctive or a future indicative (as in Sir 35:18!). Lk 18:7c can certainly not be interpreted as simply borrowed from Sir 35:18.

A second group of exegetes interpret Lk 18:7c as a concessive clause, translating, e.g., 'even when he delays to help them'. This interpretation concedes a delay on God's part. But this delay is only an *apparent* failure to listen to the cries of the community. In reality it is nothing but a demonstration of God's grace, even though it seems to be the opposite. Most proponents of this interpretation explain that the delay is a necessary respite of grace, a sign of God's mercy on the weakness of the elect, who know that they are not excluded from God's judgment. In this connection II Pet 3:9 has often been cited: 'The Lord is not slow about his promise as some count slowness, but is forbearing toward you, not wishing that any should perish, but that all should reach repentance'. For this text the delay of the parousia is an *aporia*, a serious problem. But this overlooks the fact that Luke rejects the question about the moment of the parousia, which is pushed by him into an indefinite future. Moreover, grammatically Lk 18:7c is not a concessive clause.

The third group takes Lk 18:7c as a concluding clause to '(those) who cry to him', proposing the following translation: 'to whom he listens graciously, if they cry to him'. But this interpretation runs into insurmountable difficulties because of the construction of the Greek text, even if the latter is considered a translation from the Aramaic.

In verse 7 one can distinguish two syntactic units which are both related to 'his elect' (*tōn eklektōn autou*): a participle construction, 'who cry to him day and night', which should be taken as an attribute to 'the elect', and an independent clause, *kai makrothumei ep' autois*, which contains a statement about God, of which verse 7a, 'will not God vindicate his elect', already speaks, and of whom it is said that he is merciful on them. In what grammatical connection does *kai makrothumei ep' autois* stand to 'his elect', on the one hand, and to 'who cry to him...', on the other? The answer to the first question is that our clause fulfils the function of a relative clause, 'and to whom he listens patiently'. On the other hand, 'who cry to him...' is also an attribute of 'his elect'. So, we have in the second half of verse 7, 'who cry... over them', two grammatical independent attributes connected by *kai* ('and', not rendered here by RSV). The main clause *makrothumei...* is co-ordinate to the expression 'who cry to him', and characterizes the elect as people who cry out day and night to God who has mercy on them: Will God not vindicate his elect who cry to him day and night, *and to whom he shows mercy?*

This translation/interpretation also fits the context. It opposes God's dealing with his elect to the judge's dealings with the widow:

while the judge (at first) does not listen to the widow's request, God always readily gives ear to the cries of the elect. The latter do not, like the widow with the judge, have to force God by their persistence. Their prayer always meets a favourable hearing. That the elect — like the widow — call day and night, is not a demand, but is reported as a self-evident fact. Lk 18:6–7 does not deal with a demand for persistent prayer, but exposes in an *a minori ad maius* conclusion the certain result of such prayer. No obstacle obstructs the prayer of the elect. Their persistence, however, is sustained not by their own will power, but by God's grace. Therefore, their steadfast calling definitely reaches God, who does not close his ears, but listens mercifully.

Verse 8a: I tell you, he will vindicate them speedily.

It has been suggested that verse 8a, in a somewhat different form, i.e., 'he (the judge) will vindicate her (the widow) speedily', was part of the original parable, but it seems preferable to follow the opinion that verse 8a should be entirely attributed to Luke. It is an answer to the preceding question, introduced by the emphatic, assuring 'I tell you' (cf. Lk 18:14a). The phrase is an appeal to the Lord's authority: what Jesus is going to say must be believed, notwithstanding all misleading appearances. But to what exactly is the verse an answer? Attemps to consider it as an answer to the latter part of verse 7 fail, since 'will he delay long over them' is not a question, as seen above. And to the main question of verse 7, 'and will not God vindicate his elect', no answer is expected. In Lk 18:7 a conclusion *a minori ad maius* is presented in the form of a rhetorical question which includes its answer. Any answer to it is superfluous and weakens the import of the rhetorical question. This is clear if verses 6–7 are read first for themselves, and then once more together with the 'answer' in verse 8a. Some scholars hold that verses 7c and 8a form one thought unit, and support this by a reference to Bar 4:25, 'My children, endure with patience (*makrothumēsate*) the wrath that has come upon you from God. Your enemy has overtaken you, but you will soon (*en tachei*) see their destruction and will tread upon their necks'. But it should be noted that while in Lk 18:7 the verb *makrothumein* is used of God, in Bar 4:25 it refers to the patient waiting of the pious.

That the 'question' in the latter part of verse 7 does not call for an 'answer' is also confirmed by the fact that in the parables and proverbs of the New Testament which are formulated as questions, only in Lk 11:8 and Mk 2:19 does an answer follow the question; but even in these cases they cannot be considered adequate and conclusive answers. It is, therefore, improbable that our parable (including its application) ever ended with verse 8a, as is often said. Rather, verse 8a has been attached to the parable together with verse 8b. Thus our text is no longer concluded by an 'answer' to verse 7. Verse 8a is rather a summarizing introduction to verse 8b, which therefore becomes important for the understanding of the whole pericope on its Lucan level, and is no longer a mere appendage that does not have to be considered in the interpretation of the pericope, Lk 18:1–7, and especially verse 1.

Two further considerations support the Lucan character of verse 8a. Firstly, the phrase 'I tell you' without any addition is found in Luke alone (fourteen times, several of which are certainly Lucan redaction). Secondly, the final expression 'speedily' (*en tachei*) is found only here in the gospels, but also three times in Acts (12:7; 22:18; 25:4). It is therefore characteristic of Luke. Some have proposed to translate the expression by 'suddenly, unexpectedly', because this meaning is attested in the Septuagint (Deut 11:17; Jos 8:18–19), and especially because Luke reacts several times against the expectation of an imminent parousia (Lk 17:23; 19:11; 21:8–9). The latter observation is correct, but in all three passages from Acts the expression means 'quickly'. To understand the expression in the same way here would not take away the uncertainty of the hour (Lk 12:35–40; Acts 1:7). Especially on linguistic grounds, the translation 'suddenly' should be rejected. 'Speedily', then, should not be interpreted in the sense of the apocalyptic expectation of an imminent parousia, but rather in a personal sense: it is Jesus who guarantees this affirmation with his own person.

The central part of verse 8a is composed by means of words borrowed from verse 7, 'he will vindicate them', and should not be expected to contain Lucan characteristics, even if it is a Lucan composition.

Verse 8a clearly indicates that Luke wants the *a minori ad maius* conclusion of verses 6–7 to be understood eschatologically, i.e., expressing, not the certainty that the prayer of the faithful will be heard, but the certainty of God's intervention, of judgment and parousia. And this will happen *en tachei* (RSV: 'speedily'). It has often been stated that 'he will vindicate them speedily' does not predict a speedy arrival of the end. It is a pointed summary of verses 6–7 (or even of verses 2–7), and a transition to verse 8b. The 'question' formulated in verse 7 does not call for an answer, and verse 8a is the point of departure for the warning question of verse 8b. The 'question' of verse 7, then, no longer has a meaning of its own, and becomes also an introduction to Lk 18:8b. A parable which in an *a minori ad maius* conclusion deals with the effect of untiring prayer is thus transformed into a warning to be prepared for the arrival of the

Son of man, i.e., to pray for it. But the idea that by their prayer the community could accelerate God's action and thus shorten the period of waiting is not contained in this verse.

The emphasis on the sudden character of the vindication with which Lk 18:7 was concerned is now summed up in verse 8a, which forms the basis for a new affirmation: the original assurance that God will so much more vindicate his elect, becomes a menacing reference to the unavoidable breaking-in of the vindication. In this way the parable, Lk 18:2–7, which is reinterpreted by verse 8a (and verse 8b, introduced as it is by verse 8a) can be incorporated into Lucan eschatology without inconsistency. For Luke, the parousia is no longer near. This leads to an increased emphasis on the suddenness of its arrival, and the necessity of preparedness despite the long wait.

Verse 8b: Nevertheless, when the Son of man comes, will he find faith on earth?'

It is practically certain that Luke has given this clause its present place, irrespective of whether he composed it himself, or found it as an isolated saying somewhere in the tradition and inserted it here. It may contain an allusion to Eccl 7:20, 'Surely there is not a righteous man on earth who does good and never sins', but the real source of the thought is undoubtedly Prov 20:6, 'Many a man proclaims his own loyalty, but a faithful man who can find?'

Much can be said for the redactional character of this clause. Firstly, 'nevertheless' (*plēn*, used as a conjunction) is a favourite term of Luke found fourteen times in the gospel and once in Acts. In Lk 6:24; 10:11; 19:27; 22:21, 22, 42, *plēn* is probably redactional. Secondly, in view of Lk 17:22; 21:36; 22:48; 24:7, the possibility that Luke has composed Son of man sayings cannot be excluded. Thirdly, the verb *heuriskein*, 'to find', is a favourite word of Luke, found 45 times in the gospel and 35 times in Acts (against 27 times in Matthew and eleven in Mark). Fourthly, for *pistis*, 'faith', with a definite article Lk 17:19 should be cited: 'your faith has made you well' (literally, '*the* faith of you'). Our present clause has a parallel in Lk 12:43, speaking of what the Lord will *find* at the parousia. Compare also Lk 12:37–38 (see also Lk 13:6–7; 22:45). Fifthly, the expression 'on earth' (*epi tēs gēs*) occurs so often that statistical data do not lead to any conclusion. But if one considers the redactional insertion of the expression in the parousia texts, Lk 21:25, 35, it becomes probable that in Lk 18:8b it should also be attributed to the evangelist. These arguments indicate that verse 8b comes probably from the evangelist, although some support its pre-Lucan character. The present reference to 'faith' almost certainly constitutes an inclusion or framing repetition with Lk 17:5, 'Increase our faith'.

While the long watch may give rise to the thought that God does not listen to his community (cf. Lk 18:4a, 'for a while he refused'), the danger exists that God's intervention will not find his community prepared for his decisive action. Verse 8b warns of this danger. In the Greek, the particle *ara* indicates how uncertain the answer to the question is. The Vulgate has rendered this nuance well by translating *ara* by *putas*: 'when the Son of man comes, *do you think that* he will find faith on earth?'

The use of *pistis*, 'faith', with a definite article and without any further qualification occurs elsewhere in the gospels only in Mt 23:23, where it means 'fidelity'. Luke uses it several times in Acts to designate the gospel message (Acts 6:7; cf. 15:9), and especially the lived adherence to the message (Acts 13:8; 14:22; 16:5). The latter is also expressed by the absolute use of the verb *pisteuein*, 'to believe' (Lk 8:12, 13; Acts 2:44; 4:4, 32, etc.). Luke refers to a commitment to the Lord, lived in the practical fidelity of witness of life. According to Lk 18:1, the evangelist may think here particularly of steadfastness in prayer. The parable has promised that God will not fail to vindicate his elect tested in the world. But will they themselves remain faithful to the end, in prayer (cf. Lk 21:34–36)? The structure of the question seems to suggest that at his coming the Son of man will find little faith, that many will have lost heart.

The message of the parable

Jesus

In Jesus' own proclamation the parable dealt with the kingdom which God was going to establish soon. The parable was based on great trust and confidence in God's help and assistance. The same confidence is found in the parables of growth: the beginning may be small and insignificant as a mustard seed, but the mustard seed grows into a great shrub (Mk 4:30–32; compare Lk 13:18f.; Mt 13:31f.). At the time of sowing the situation may seem unfavourable; but at the harvest the field bears a rich harvest (Mk 4:3–8; compare Lk 8:4–8; Mt 13:3–9). So, by the parable of the judge and the widow (Lk 18:2–5), Jesus reveals God's dispositions: he does not so much tell people how they should behave towards God, but how God behaves towards them.

Jesus could be so straightforward in his assurance that God hears the cry of his people because he took seriously the action of God in his own life and ministry. He was deeply convinced of God's acting in and through his actions, in the history of Israel and the world around him. In this light one should understand what Jesus said about his contemporaries' failure to discern the signs of the times (Lk 12:54–56). The signs of the times had to do with evidence of the action of God, which, according to biblical tradition, is evident in history, more particularly in the history of God's own people. In order to be encouraged the elect had to acquire a new awareness of the active presence of God.

The early Christian tradition

In the early Christian community the interpretation of the parable is introduced with the words 'and the Lord said', and the summons to 'listen'. The description of the judge as 'judge of unrighteousness' shows that he is opposed to God. Thus we get an *a minori ad maius* conclusion: If even the judge will do the widow right, how much more will God vindicate his elect, who in their oppression call to him day and night, even when it may seem that God delays his judgment. The formulation of this statement may have been influenced by Sir 35:11–20, but it is determined by the condition of the community which described its situation in words derived from Sirach. It is the situation of an oppressed and persecuted Church which placed its trust and confidence in God, but which also needed the exhortation that this trust and confidence are not in vain. God will come to the rescue of his elect and will save them from their adversaries.

Luke

Possibly the parable was already combined with the preceding eschatological discourse (Lk 17:20–37) in the pre-Lucan tradition, and formed its conclusion, as the Sermon (on the Mount) in Q also ended with a parable (Mt 7:24–27; Lk 6:47–49). Luke felt that the basic tendency of the parable was exhortation to continual prayer. He expressed this in his introduction (Lk 18:1). Although Luke does not overlook the original meaning of the parable (cf. Lk 18:8b), by combining it with the parable of the Pharisee and the tax collector, which is concerned with prayer and not with the parousia, he showed that he prefers to place this section under the heading 'prayer', rather than 'parousia'. But for Luke the two are not mutually exclusive. How can they be reconciled? To answer this question, one should understand what led Luke to the redactional statements in verses 1 and 8b. It does not suffice to say *that* verse 8b is not an original part of the parable but, across the parable, looks back to Lk 17:22–37. It should also be asked *why* verse 8b looks back to the preceding section, the eschatological discourse. If the parable as Luke found it in his source (Lk 18:2–8a) was already combined with the eschatological discourse whose conclusion it formed, then he may have intended to restore this connection, which he had himself loosened with his introductory statement (Lk 18:1).

On the other hand, the statement about the elect in verse 7 ('crying day and night') was related to the theme of prayer, just like the following parable of the Pharisee and the tax collector (Lk 18:10–14a). By the combination of this theme with the retrospect on the eschatological discourse, the evangelist wanted to express that he was not just concerned with a general reference to continual prayer, but with prayer in the eschatological situation of his community. In contrast to Lk 21:5–36, Lk 17:22–37 does not directly mention prayer, and so it is not coincidental that in the immediately following context (Lk 18:1–8), Luke insists on the necessity of continual prayer (verse 1: 'they ought always to pray'). The question 'nevertheless, when the Son of man comes, will he find faith on earth?' (Lk 18:8b) refers back to Lk 17:22–27, which speaks of the coming of the Son of man. One should answer: If the waiting for the Son of man is accompanied and supported by continual prayer, then — and only then — the Son of man will find faith on earth at his coming. Thus understood, the statement does not have a pessimistic ring, while it intends to express the same idea as the concluding verse of the second eschatological discourse (Lk 21:36). The preparation for the coming of the Son of man takes place in continual prayer which gives the Christian protection, strength and help. One should not exaggerate the 'tension' between verse 1, which situates the 'point' of the parable in perseverance in prayer, and verses 6–8, according to which the 'point' of the parable is not so much perseverance as the presupposition for being heard, as the certainty that those who cry day and night will be heard. As seen above, these two perspectives can quite easily be reconciled.

Reflection

This can be considered a parable about today's bureaucracy and red tape, bribery of people in administration and venality of judges. The widow is simply the injured party in our society, the person who cannot succeed because he or she lacks the things which give people a real chance: money and connections, influence and power, health and charm.

Scripture never speaks of God without a certain commitment. Even if apparently it describes only an act of God, people are at stake as well. Saying what God is like is at the same time saying how people should be. Everything that people affirm of God should also be a task they shoulder. When, therefore, it is said: a 'father of the fatherless and protector of widows is God' (Ps 68:5), and that 'he will not ignore the supplication of the fatherless, nor the widow when she pours out her story' (Sir 35:14), one cannot fail to hear also: '...cease to do evil, learn to do good; seek justice, correct oppression; defend the fatherless, plead for the widow' (Isa 1:16–17; in the Old Testament, 'widows and orphans' is a standard phrase for 'the poor and the oppressed'). God takes the part of those whose rights are not respected and he expects people to do the same.

Exegesis discusses the question whether the parable focuses mainly on the judge or on the widow. The faithful reader, however, can learn from the judge as well as from the widow. The widow keeps asking for justice; just so, the faithful should not lose courage. They should keep facing the unjust judges of this world and insist that justice be done. But the figure of the judge too is in his own way instructive for Christians. Via this judge, Jesus and Luke refer to God: if this unjust judge finally gave in to the request of the widow, how much more will God... But does this text speak only of God? In the light of what was said above, here again a task for the faithful is discovered. Those who say they believe in this God cannot remain indifferent or neutral when they hear people cry out for justice; they should commit themselves to the cause of justice.

The clause, 'nevertheless, when the Son of man comes, will he find faith on earth?', by which Luke concludes the parable, shows to full advantage only in the wider context. The statement forms the conclusion of the whole discourse about the coming of the kingdom which begins in Lk 17:20. In this discourse, Luke particularly refers to two dangers to which the faithful are exposed.

Firstly, just as the Son of man suffered because of his liberating message, so will his followers (Lk 17:22–25). The proclamation of 'release of the captives' and the efforts 'to set at liberty those who are oppressed' (Lk 4:18) will face violence, and everything possible will be done to silence exacting Christians. But they should not let themselves be intimidated, for they should listen to God rather than to man, like Peter called to account before the authorities (Acts 4:18–19).

Luke also indicates a second danger that threatens the faithful. 'As it was in the days of Noah, so will it be in the days of the Son of man... they bought, they sold, they planted, they built' (Lk 17:26–28). Money and truth are hardly compatible with each other. Christian witness is most effectively paralysed by the fear for the loss of one's established position. Possessions and self-interest tie people's tongues and hands. Therefore, Luke ends the parable with the warning question 'when the Son of man comes, will he find faith on earth?' (Lk 18:8b).

God takes the side of the victims of injustice. If we take this seriously a hard task is awaiting us. And since it is better to start in one's own home, we should stand for justice in the Church and among the churches. We should allow all people in the Church to be themselves and respect their opinions, rather than use the pressure principle, 'he who pays the piper, calls the tune'.

For the great men and women of this earth and for all who have an interest in maintaining exploitation and oppression, Christians should be exacting people. There is an urgent need for people who even at the risk of their own lives dare to insist on justice. Jesus showed the way. 'Whoever seeks to gain his life will lose it, but whoever loses his life will preserve it' (Lk 17:33). Therefore, one should expect to find the real Christians on the side of the victims of exploitation and oppression.

13   The Pharisee and the tax collector
(Lk 18:9–14)

General context

To those who determine the extent of Luke's Travel Narrative on the basis of the use of sources, this parable concludes the central section, since in 18:15 Luke takes up again his Marcan source. Lk 18:1–14 contains two parables about prayer, which were already attached to each other in the pre-Lucan tradition. While Lk 18:2–8 deals with the 'vindication' (Lk 18:5, *ekdikēsis*, 'rendering of justice') of the pious, Lk 18:10–14 is concerned with the necessary presuppositions of justification (Lk 18:14a, *dedikaiōmenos*) by God. In connection with the parable of the unjust judge (Lk 18:2–8), the example story of the Pharisee and the tax collector functions as a kind of correction: the disciples should not so much cry for justification/vindication against their adversaries by divine judgment, as confess before God that they are sinners, and pray for God's mercy (Lk 18:13). Then they will be 'justified' (Lk 18:14a).

It is possible that Jesus himself did not intend this story as an illustration of true and false piety, but as a defence of his attitude towards tax collectors and sinners, by pronouncing God's judgment on the Pharisee and the tax collector (Lk 18:14a). This judgment of Jesus stands in sharp contrast to the ideas of the scribes and Pharisees.

Luke has 'framed' the example story (Lk 18:10–14a) by identifying the addressees in verse 9, and explicitly stating the 'grounds' for the justification of the tax collector in verse 14b. Notwithstanding the indication that Jesus addressed his story to people 'who trusted in themselves that they were righteous', it is not intended so much for the Pharisees as such, as for disciples who pray like Pharisees (cf. Lk 14:11). The disciples should pray like the tax collector. However, Lk 18:14b does not refer to the manner in which one should pray, but deals in a more general and basic way with the attitude of the disciple who should 'humble himself', so that (in the end) he will be 'exalted' by God. 'Humility' is closely related to faith in God's promise (cf. Lk 1:45, 48, 52). Since in Lk 18:8b too the need for faith is stressed, the redactional clauses in Lk 18:8b and 18:14b correspond to each other. By mentioning self-righteous pious people 'who despise others', the story is for Luke at the same time a warning not to despise the (repentant) sinners in the community (compare Lk 5:29–32; 7:36–50).

The parable of the Pharisee and the tax collector is immediately followed by the episode of the blessing of the children (Lk 18:15–17; parallel Mk 10:13–16). The story directly connects with the statement which Luke has made into the conclusion of the parable: 'every one who exalts himself will be humbled, but he who humbles himself will be exalted' (Lk 18:14b). The meaning is obviously that, like the tax collector, the children illustrate the humility recommended to the disciples of Jesus: to enter into the kingdom one should become like a child. The rich ruler is unwilling to show this childlike trust (Lk 18:18–30), but it is demonstrated by the blind man near Jericho (Lk 18:35–43), and the same can be said of Zaccheus (Lk 19:1–10).

Analysis of the text

Verse 9: He also told a parable to some who trusted in themselves that they were righteous and despised others:

In a way which is characteristic of Luke (cf. Lk 18:1; 19:11) this verse explains the purpose of the parable. It is addressed to (*pros*, possibly to be translated as 'against', cf. Lk 20:19), 'some who trusted in themselves that they were righteous', i.e., the Pharisees and the like. But Luke does not mention them here explicitly, possibly because he wants to address it to the 'Pharisees' of all times. More specifically, the evangelist seems to intend to include the disciples (cf. Lk 17:22, 18:1) in the audience of the parable. So Luke's target may be the paragons of virtue in his community, who think that they have the monopoly of holiness.

The description of the addressees is apparently drawn from the parable itself. In the Pharisee's 'thankfulness' for his good deeds, Luke finds his 'trust in himself' manifested. His dissociation from 'other men... unjust (unrighteous)' is diagnosed as his self-confidence as 'righteous'. His attitude towards the tax collector is referred to as 'despising others'. It is possible that one should understand that they 'trusted in themselves' rather than in God (cf. II Cor 1:9) *because* 'they were righteous', or considered themselves righteous. 'Righteous' (*dikaios*, cf. Lk 1:6) qualifies the conduct of one who is acceptable to God. Apparently the parable is then addressed to people who are convinced that the reason for their acceptability before God is to be found in themselves. Self-confidence is a basic

flaw of Jewish — and much other — piety: those who correctly fulfil
the stipulations of the law are absolutely sure of their salvation. This
kind of self-confidence supplants trust in God. The pendant of such a
presumptuous attitude before God is arrogance towards people, i.e.,
'all the rest' (*hoi loipoi*). 'They (utterly) despised (*exouthenein*, cf. Lk
23:11; Acts 4:11) all the rest.' The people who are addressed in this
parable certainly do not consider themselves 'unworthy servants' (cf.
Lk 17:10).

> **Verse 10:** 'Two men went up into the temple to pray, one a
> Pharisee, and the other a tax collector.

With this verse the parable proper begins. The temple of Jerusalem
was the centre of Jewish religion and the place *par excellence* for
worship and prayer (Lk 1:10; Acts 3:1). Since Jerusalem was situated
on a hill, and the temple itself lay higher than the rest of the city, 'to
go up' became the verb currently used for visits to the temple. The
two men went up 'to pray', possibly at the regular hours for public
worship, i.e., 9 a.m. or 3 p.m., or at any given time of the day for
private prayer. 'Prayer' (*proseuchē*) and 'to pray' (*proseuchesthai*)
are favourite Lucan terms (Lk: nineteen and three times respectively;
Acts: sixteen and nine times respectively).

The two men represent two extremes in Jewish society. 'One a
Pharisee', the paragon of piety and meticulous law-abiding, and 'the
other a tax-collector', who by common opinion was outside the law
and whose name was the equivalent of a sinner (cf. the expression
'tax collectors and sinners', Lk 5:30; 7:34; 15:1). The Pharisees were
national heroes, protectors of national identity, while the tax
collectors were a national disgrace, undesirables. Both men stand in a
'vertical' relation to God. The 'horizontal' relation of the two men to
each other is expressed only in terms suggesting opposition. In most
of his sermons on this text, Martin Luther saw the whole of mankind
represented in the Pharisee and the tax collector as either arrogant or
repentant sinners.

> **Verses 11-12:** The Pharisee stood and prayed thus with
> himself, 'God, I thank you that I am not like other men,
> extortioners, unjust, adulterers, or even like this tax
> collector. (12) I fast twice a week, I give tithes of all that I
> get.'

These verses contain an illustration of three practices of piety: the
Pharisee went up to the temple to pray (Lk 18:10), he thanks God not
only for his observance of the commandments (Lk 18:11), but also

because he fasts twice a week and gives tithes on all that he gets (Lk 18:12). This man, therefore, is not satisfied with doing what is prescribed by the law; he goes beyond it, by praying, fasting, and giving gifts which were not obligatory (compare Mt 6:2–4, 5–6, 16–18).

The Pharisee 'stood' (*statheis*; cf. Lk 18:40; 19:8; Acts 2:14; 5:20, etc.), which is an expression proper to Luke to characterize the attitude of a person who takes the floor. Standing was also the normal posture for prayer, but it may here indicate the conscious adoption of an attitude or of a conspicuous place (contrast verse 13, *hestōs*, 'standing').

He prayed 'with himself', perhaps silently, but more probably quietly (cf. I Sam 1:13), since it was Jewish practice to pray aloud. Some prefer to attach 'by himself' to the verb 'stood', so that one should read: 'The Pharisee stood by himself and prayed thus'. But it has been pointed out that in this case the Greek expression would most probably be different (*kath' heauton* instead of *pros heauton*). Recently, however, no less than seven arguments have been given to support the meaning 'he stood by himself', i.e., apart from the rest of the worshippers about him.[92]

The suggestion that the Pharisee prayed 'to himself', rather than to God has been judged too farfetched by some scholars, but it is not excluded that the expression 'with himself' intends to indicate that this prayer does not reach its goal. He thinks that he is talking with God, but in fact he conducts only a monologue. Indeed, if the initial words 'God, I thank you' are omitted, one gets a simple monologue.

The Pharisee forgoes all form of petition. His 'thanksgiving' (*eucharistein*, cf. Lk 17:16) , which is offered without any conscious hypocrisy, is in fact all but a real prayer. It has been suggested that the narrator — Jesus — intentionally presented a caricature to his audience, but it seems that the prayer is taken from life, as can be seen from a very similar prayer that dates from the first century A.D. and is found in the Talmud.[93] Such prayers were not necessarily manifestations of *individual* pride.

Only in form can Lk 18:11–12 be considered a thanksgiving; in reality it looks more like an expression of self-congratulation. Indeed, after the initial address, 'God', he says 'I' five times! First he enumerates the sins from which he has refrained (verse 11b), and then his good works (verse 12). He 'thanks' God for not being like other people, i.e., for being much better than 'extortioners' (cf. Isa 10:1–2; Mt 7:15; I Cor 5:10–11; 6:10), 'unjust' (*adikos*, cf. Luke 16:10 twice, 11; Acts 24:15), i.e., swindlers (cf. I Cor 6:9), and 'adulterers' (cf. Lk 16:18; I Cor 6:9), and 'for that matter, like this tax collector'. The latter stands, as it were for 'other men', better, 'all the rest'. The mere juxtaposition of the two men develops into a qualified relationship: the Pharisee compares himself with the tax collector and dissociates himself from him as well as from other men. The house of self-righteousness is a house without doors and windows; it allows no outlook on God and the real situation of the neighbour.

The Pharisee goes on 'thanking' God for the fact that he has done more than the law required. As a Pharisee of the strict observance he voluntarily fasted twice a week, i.e., on Monday and Thursday, instead of the required annual fast. He also gave tithes, i.e., a tenth of all that he got, i.e., bought, although on many of these products the producers would already have paid tithes. The text may intend to refer to the fact that he paid ten per cent on his total income. This recalls Deut 26:12–15: 'When you have finished paying all the tithe of your produce...then you shall say before the Lord your God, "I have removed the sacred portion out of my house, and moreover I have given it to the Levite... I have not transgressed any of your commandments, neither have I forgotten them; I have not eaten of the tithe while I was mourning... I have obeyed the voice of the Lord my God, I have done according to all that you have commanded me"...'. The description of the elder son who 'served' his father with a fidelity which lasted 'for many years', and whose service was characterized by his extreme care never to 'disobey' a single 'command' (Lk 15:29), is a nearly perfect description of the religious ideal of the Pharisees. They took for granted that their observance of the law gave them rights, and that these rights were unjustly misjudged by the favours accorded to people whom they disapproved of, 'like this tax collector' (cf. Lk 15:30, 'this son of yours').

The parable does not blame the Pharisee for any lack of sincerity when he thanks God for not being 'like other men'. And he is not accused of lying, when he says 'I fast twice a week, I give tithes of all that I get'. On the basis of conventional standards, the Pharisee was a good man. There is no reason for thinking that his appraisal of his achievements was not correct. With such qualifications, his modern counterpart would be welcomed into any respectable circle, religious or social, and given a responsible position. There is no doubt that this man is 'just', and yet, Jesus explains, God prefers the tax collector to him!

The phrase 'or even like this tax collector' is the key to the whole text. In the fact that the Pharisee compares himself with the tax collector, and that he dissociates himself from him, resides the negative character of his prayer, which causes him to go home without being justified. He is not justified, not because he is a Pharisee, not because he thanks God for not being like notorious sinners, not because he mentions his religious achievements, but because he compares himself with the tax collector and dissociates himself from him, because he considers himself better. This dissociation is not a simple separation from the tax collector, an expression of abhorrence from sinfulness. It does not only seclude the Pharisee from the tax collector, but also intends to exclude the tax collector from God's salvation. In the past as in the present, any form of religious monopoly functions in practice as a means of separation which prevents the recognition of any significant action of God and his Spirit elsewhere.

> **Verse 13:** But the tax collector, standing far off, would not even lift up his eyes to heaven, but beat his breast, saying, 'God, be merciful on me a sinner!'

In contrast to the Pharisee, the tax collector stood at a distance in an inconspicuous place, far from the Pharisee. It has been pointed out that the indications of place have 'semantic relevance'. The tax collector, 'standing far off', has taken the 'lowest place' (Lk 14:10), i.e., he leaves it to God to assign the places. Aware of his condition, he did not dare (*thelein*, cf. Lk 18:4) to 'lift up his eyes' (*epairein*, cf. Lk 6:20; 16:23) to heaven, as praying Jews used to do (cf. Mk 6:41; 7:34; Jn 11:41; 17:1). He did not hold up his hands to heaven (cf. I Tim 2:8), but kept beating his breast (cf. Lk 23:48) as a sign of contrition. The prayers of the Pharisee and the tax collector also form a striking contrast in length. In words which recall Ps 51:1, 17 the tax collector's short prayer expresses the meaning of his gesture. Here is no comparison with others, but concentration on his position before God. He admits before God that he is a sinner and asks for mercy. He does not hesitate to apply to himself the label pinned on him by the Pharisee – sinner. It has been said that what is noteworthy is not so much the content of the prayer as such, as the fact that it is pronounced by the tax collector.

The tax collector is an example of – to use a Matthean expression – the 'poor in spirit': a sinner who knows that he can present himself before God only with empty hands, without any righteousness of his own, without actions of piety to refer to. The Pharisee, on the other hand, did not consider himself poor before God, and he had the impression that he could present himself before God with full hands. The poor whom Jesus proclaims blessed are, among others, the tax collectors and sinners with whom he associated in meals (cf. Lk 7:29), and who came to him in great numbers (cf. Lk 15:1).

The tax collector's words, *hilasthēti moi*, have been commonly translated as 'have mercy on me'. But in Lk 18:38, the blind man cries out *eleēson me*, which means 'have mercy on me'. What then do the tax collector's words mean? The verb *hilaskomai* occurs only here and in Heb 2:17. The noun *hilastērion* appears in Rom 3:25; Heb 9:5, and *hilasmos* in I Jn 2:2; 4:10. Both clearly refer to the atonement sacrifice. The tax collector, therefore, does not offer a generalized prayer for God's mercy, but expresses his longing for the benefits of an atonement.

> It is important, however, not to misconstrue the nature of the tax collector's confession as if it were a preoccupation with sin comparable to that of the Pharisee with piety. For it is possible to do all that the Pharisee did, but in a negative manner, praying his prayer in reverse and as strongly depreciating oneself as he exalted himself. The degree of egotism would be the same, but its direction would be opposite. Under these circumstances the spiritual significance of such self-depreciation—still an egotistical confession—would be remarkably similar to that of the Pharisee's self-exaltation. . . The significance of the tax collector's prayer would be perverted if in the slightest degree such pride were regarded as secretly motivating him. . . All we know is that a man who throws himself upon the mercy of God in such an unconditional manner, and therefore without presumptions of pleasing him and of winning his favour, is by the grace of God accepted by him. We know this not because of a law, rule, or principle applicable to each situation to determine how God will act but because of the twofold testimony of the Spirit and the Scriptures to the faithfulness of God, who does not despise a broken and contrite heart.[94]

Verse 14a: I tell you, this man went down to his house justified rather than the other;

The phrase 'I tell you' introduces an important statement uttered with authority (cf. Lk 7:26, 28; 9:27; 10:12, 24, etc.). The speaker claims that he knows God's standards better than his opponents. It is possible that '*this man*' looks back to the contemptuous '*this tax collector*' in verse 11. 'This despised man went down to his house justified before God.' The phrases 'went down to his house' and 'went up into the temple' form the framework of the story. This stresses that Jesus' judgment does not originate from basic considerations about *the* Pharisees and tax collectors as such, but rests on what happened to the two men between their ascent to the temple and their return to their house. This is still more underlined by the switch from the plural (verse 10, 'two men went up') to the singular (verse 14a, 'this man went down'). The neutral juxtaposition, 'the one. . . the other' (verse 10), is replaced by the qualitative subordination 'this man. . . rather than the other' (verse 14a). It is also noteworthy that the two protagonists are now mentioned in reversed order (compare the rich man and Lazarus; Lk 16:19 and 22).

The tax collector went down—the temple lay on a hill—'justified', i.e., as a righteous man. What distinguishes the tax collector from the Pharisee are his confession of guilt, the knowledge that he cannot be justified on account of his works, i.e., that he has no claim before God, and the absence of all comparison with others. All human rank and value-scales fail in the new situation created by God through Jesus. The crucial distinction between the Pharisee and the tax collector is not at this point determined by conventional standards of morality but by what has happened or not happened in the heart of each man in relation to God.

It has been pointed out that the word 'justified' forms an inclusion with the beginning of the pericope, 'He also told this parable to some who trusted in themselves that they were righteous/just'. Therefore, this verse expresses one of the core elements of the parable. The tax collector was 'justified', i.e., obtained justice, found justice, favour, grace before God. The teaching of the parables in Lk 15, 'there is joy before the angels of God over one sinner who repents' (Lk 15:7, 10) is here confirmed. Together, 'I tell you' and the passive 'justified' suggest that this statement is made with divine authority.

This is the only passage in the gospels in which the verb 'to justify—to be justified' (*dikaioun/dikaiousthai*) is used in a sense similar to that in which Paul uses it, although it should not be understood in a strictly Pauline sense. This verse certainly shows that Paul's teaching on justification takes up and interprets Jesus' own teaching.

The expression 'justified rather than the other' is an attempt to translate an Aramaic *min*, used as a substitute for both comparative and superlative, which do not exist in Semitic grammar. One might, therefore, translate: 'more justified than the other'. But since the Aramaic *min* is often used with an exclusive sense, one should prefer the translation: 'God extended his favour to him, not to the other'. God did not accept the Pharisee's prayer. Just as in his prayer the Pharisee dissociated himself from the tax collector (*houtos*, 'this'), so now Jesus dissociates the same tax collector (*houtos*) from the Pharisee (*par' ekeinon*). The prayer of the man who wanted to exclude others, among whom was the tax collector, from God's favour, results in his own exclusion, i.e. non-justification.

Verse 14b: for every one who exalts himself will be humbled, but he who humbles himself will be exalted.'

This second conclusion is a generalization which in a sense weakens the parable and can hardly be original. It has been pointed out that this 'conclusion' does not perfectly square with the meaning of the parable itself, which illustrates the opposition between 'considering oneself just' and 'justified by God', and not the contrast between 'exalted' and 'humbled'. But to this remark it has been replied that this distinction seems to overlook the content of the tax collector's prayer.

The statement definitely deals with being exalted in relation to God, which here as in the Old Testament is practically synonymous with 'to deliver' or 'to redeem'. The same statement, 'for everyone who exalts himself. . .', is found at the end of the parable concerning the choice of places at table (Lk 14:11). In Matthew it is applied to the arrogant Pharisees (Mt 23:12), and in somewhat different terms to the disciples asking themselves who is the greatest in the kingdom of Heaven (Mt 18:4). It seems, therefore, that we are dealing here with an isolated, 'floating' logion, which was attached to the parable by the early Christian tradition or the Lucan redaction. This final comment also paves the way for Lk 18:15–17, the blessing of the children, especially if one takes into account the statement found in Mt 18:4.

Some have felt that the isolated logion has the form of a proverbial statement, applicable in various situations, rather than that of an eschatological prediction. But it cannot be denied that in an antithetical parallelism the verse shows that God (the passive verb is a circumlocution for divine action) will act at the judgment (future tense). Because of the context this allusion to the final judgment is evident.

It is generally accepted that Luke (or the tradition before Luke?) has attached this parable to that of the unjust judge. The latter too ends with a secondary conclusion whose eschatological bearing cannot be doubted: 'when the Son of man comes, will he find faith on earth' (Lk 18:8b). On the level of the final redaction, then, Lk 18:9–14 makes a definite contribution to the section Lk 17:20 – 18:14.

Lk 18:14b has rightly been understood as a call to humility. But the meaning of humility is ambiguous and susceptible to misinterpretation. It has many meanings, some of which are very derogatory to Jesus and to the faith of his followers. The failure to recognize this often leads to the dubious assumption that any exhortation to be humble is self-explanatory to the hearer. It is of great importance to recall the reference in respect to which humbling oneself should occur, for it is possible to be humbled in respect to many things, e.g. one's opinion of oneself or the expectations of the community. The only true reference point of Christian humility is God himself and his judgment (as indicated by the passive 'will be humbled... will be exalted'). This is not the false humility which listens when the powerful sound their trumpet, or steps aside when they push themselves forward, but a creative power in the life of any person, involving a reorientation of one's motives and a shattering of false securities in the interest of true freedom.

The message of the parable

Jesus

The authenticity of Lk 18:10–14a is almost generally accepted. What did the parable convey in the context of Jesus' teaching? It does not take the field against the Pharisees, nor does it promote the tax collectors. It does not deal with the tax collectors as objects of hate, but with *this* tax collector who puts his trust in God's mercy. The listeners should identify themselves, not with the tax collector as tax collector, but with the tax collector as sinner who trusts in God. The parable tries to persuade the listeners to accept the narrator's verdict (verse 14a) that the sinner who trusts in God's mercy finds God's favour, whereas the righteous man who excludes notorious sinners from salvation does not find God's justification because of this attitude of his.

Such a verdict can easily be situated in the context of Jesus' message. Jesus proclaims a God who does not exclude sinners who trust in his mercy, but receives them (cf. Lk 7:36–50; 15:1–32; 19:1–10). If Jesus proclaims a God who does not exclude sinners from salvation, then it is to be assumed in virtue of the context of the whole gospel that these two characters are deliberately chosen. Jesus' theological controversy with the Pharisees concerning the salvation of the tax collectors belongs to the core of his proclamation.

This permits an answer to the question of the parable's audience. Corresponding to the twofold possibility for the listeners to identify themselves either with the tax collector or with the Pharisee, the parable addresses itself to sinners and righteous. To the sinners Jesus says that they should commit themselves in full confidence to God's mercy, while righteous people who want to exclude sinners from salvation are told that their thinking contradicts that of God and that, therefore, they cannot enjoy God's favour. The Pharisees, therefore, were included among the addressees of the parable. Jesus tried to open their eyes by warning them not to limit God's mercy, and by trying to convince them that sinners too enjoy God's favour.

The early Christian tradition

Verse 9, which Luke probably found in his source, was almost certainly created for the story by one of those who transmitted it. The clause 'some who trusted in themselves that they were righteous' refers to people who are convinced that God's verdict on them is favourable. The description fits the Pharisees who, as we saw, were at least part of Jesus' original audience. The paraphrase may have been chosen because Pharisaic behaviour is not confined to the past. The followers of Jesus too can fall into it. The parable is passed on to exhort them and to warn them.

Luke

The parable has been given an application in verse 14b, originally an independent saying of Jesus, which is also found in Lk 14:11 and Mt 23:12. By inserting it here Luke supplied his commentary on Jesus' parable. He apparently understood it as a warning against pride and an exhortation to humility. It was as such that he passed it on to his Church and addressed it to the disciples: they should pray like the tax collector.

But verse 14b is not only applicable to prayer. It speaks in a more general and fundamental sense of the attitude of the disciple who should 'humble himself', so that (in the end) he 'will be exalted' by God. Jesus' parable was, however, more than a warning and an exhortation, and to that extent Luke's interpretation does not do full justice to its original meaning. But it fits well in Luke's favourite theme of eschatological reversal (cf. Lk 1:51–53; 6:20–26; 16:19–31).

Reflection

The eschatological rule of God which is inaugurated by Jesus involves a fundamentally new offer of salvation addressed in like manner to sinners and righteous. Fulfilment of the commandments does not suffice as foundation for justification before God. Justification can only be *received* from God, not *achieved* by one's piety. Since God does not measure with the familiar standards of piety, any derogatory comparison with other people, any arrogance towards others is not in accordance with the new situation. Jesus announces authoritatively the insufficiency of hitherto accepted standards in the new situation. He reveals God's new offer of salvation to man; his word announces God's new attitude towards people.

Originally Lk 18:10–14a did not deal in the first place with 'moral' categories, with moral virtues and vices, such as pride and haughtiness, or awareness of sin and repentance, but with basic attitudes before God. In the prayer of the two men the parable described the attitude of two people before God. Their prayer attitude reflected their image of God. Lk 18:10–14a, therefore, shows two images of God, and by saying that one man went home justified while the other did not, it also passes judgment on both images of God. Consequently, it is first of all proclamation and revelation of God. It may rightly be said, then, that the parable seeks to illustrate and teach what God's grace is.

In the Pharisee and the tax collector the narrator depicts two attitudes and invites us to make a choice. In so doing he makes it very clear which attitude he prefers. In fact, he tries his utmost to make us reject the attitude of the Pharisee and to adopt that of the tax collector. From the very different behaviour of these two people appear two totally different images of God. The Pharisee does not have any idea of God's greatness: he stands before God with his head raised high. He thanks God, but strictly speaking he thinks he can manage all by himself. According to the Pharisee God knows how to appreciate achievements and respects and confirms the current code of ethics and acquired privileges. God functions as the keystone of an established order in which the Pharisee himself is lord and master.

The attitude of the tax collector reveals a very different image of God. Sinful as he is he can only bend down before the holy and mighty God. This God does not stick to the boundaries which people draw and the judgments they pronounce in his name. From our limited point of view he seems at times unpredictable, but this is only an 'optical illusion'. In our narrowmindedness we underestimate his real greatness: a mercy from which nobody is excluded and to which nobody appeals in vain. Such magnanimity will always confuse people who barely meet the demands of justice. Therefore, this parable will never become self-evident.

Originating from two different images of God,

the righteousness of the tax collector and the righteousness of the Pharisee cannot be brought under a common heading: the righteousness which the Pharisee can show is unthinkable without an order of precedence, a scale on which in distinction from others, he can be acknowledged as the righteous one. The righteousness which the tax collector is given through God's forgiveness cannot be classified in any order of precedence, however arranged. Nor is it possible to understand it as an exception which breaks the rule. Every man who has been bowed down by the burden of guilt knows for sure that here not just *something* but *everything*, in fact he himself, has been called in question. If a man realizes what it means to need forgiveness, and that here the whole of his existence is exposed to a radical challenge, how could it occur to him to classify forgiveness as an exception? The result is that in the Pharisee's order of precedence there is no room for a 'righteous tax collector', but in the place where the tax collector stands, before God who forgives him, the sinner, the Pharisee's order of precedence loses its meaning.

An inescapable choice of alternatives comes to light here. . . When man is at one with himself and can stand before what he has set himself as a standard, he makes this standard the final court of appeal. But when his conscience declares him guilty, and when the world gives its verdict against his right to exist, he relies on something that can transcend it; he asks for a final court that can annul this verdict without denying it. . . A basic decision is therefore inevitable. Each of Jesus' listeners must make it for himself, by deciding what he wants to count as the final court of appeal.[95]

The actualization of this parable is not as obvious as is often thought. Nowadays self-righteousness is no longer the domain of the devout who would despise sinners. There is in intellectual circles a radically impious self-righteousness which at times asserts itself very consciously.

The present parable resists hurried attempts at identification. What we are told here is not easily arranged according to groups: here the pious, there the enlightened; here the progressives, there the reactionaries. The denunciation of others, with whom we do not want to have any dealings, whom we despise or secretly fear, this beloved perennial attitude of self-affirming accusation of others, shows the Pharisee in our own heart. The parable holds up a mirror to us, pious and impious, progressives and reactionaries, Marxists and capitalists. All without exception we are placed by Jesus in God's own presence; that is why he situates this scene in the temple. And he asks us which righteousness, which justice we want to choose: our own, which allegedly entitles us to denounce and despise others, or the altogether different, real righteousness.

While several modern salvation theories abolish all sense of guilt, at no other time does there seem to have been so much denunciation and condemnation. Groups and parties level massive accusations at each other. The theatrical scene has been turned into a permanent 'tribunal'. Nothing surpasses the critique of society, and the self-righteous is always a potential public persecutor of his fellow human being. The story of the Pharisee and the tax collector repeats itself time and again in constantly new forms. People appeal to their own achievement and righteousness and condemn others whom they consider as to be written off. The number of cleaning-up actions or purges in the name of higher ideals is interminable.

The parable asks us which righteousness/justice we want. This choice does not happen just once in a lifetime, but has to be made again and again. The Pharisee is present in each of us. We are proud of our achievements and so easily condemn others. In many ways people like the desperate tax collector are rather unsympathetic. If we look at things closely, we will realize that the provocation, the scandal of Jesus' proclamation is as great now as when he told the story of the Pharisee and the tax collector for the first time.

Of course, the Pharisee's prayer raises another difficult issue. Religious symbols can be used to foster such inequality even when they were certainly not intended to create such divisions. Does a person who is going to make the sacrifices that the Pharisee does require someone who is clearly 'unrighteous', clearly a sinner? In other words, does the presence of certain socially despised persons reinforce the values and ethical commitments of the rest of a society? There are many examples in which the despised, the good-for-nothings, etc., do play such a role.[96]

Conclusion
Preaching the parables

At the end of the film *Ship of Fools*, the dwarf comes down the gangway, stops and stares at the cinema audience while saying, 'I suppose you are wondering, "What does all this have to do with me?" ' Then with a knowing smile, he walks away. Some readers, especially those who decided to read this book in the hope of finding here some enlightenment concerning the homiletical or catechetical use of the parables, may have asked the same question at various stages of their reading. The writer had these concerns in mind throughout the research for, and the actual delivery of, the lectures and sessions in which these parables were first explained, as well as during the redaction of this book. But his first intention was to do justice to modern parable research and to inform the reader about its most interesting results. In the process it may have become clear that a number of things the scholars are telling us run counter to interpretations of the parables which for a long time have been dear to homilists and catechists.

Faced with this reality, some may feel like consigning all of their old homilies or catechetical instructions to the waste-paper basket, while others may be inclined to ignore the results of this research under the pretext that this may be an interesting pastime for scholars, but does not concern people in the actual ministry. The first reaction may lead to the discard of a number of things which have an authentic spiritual value of their own, while the second attitude is a sin against the fuller light which God offers us through the work of biblical scholars of our time. The Pontifical Biblical Commission's *Instruction on the Historical Truth of the Gospels* (1964) states: 'Unless the exegete pays attention to all these things which pertain to the origin and composition of the gospels and makes use of all the laudable achievements of recent research, he will not fulfil his task of probing into what the sacred writers intended and what they really said' (paragraph X).

This does not mean, of course, that the homilist and catechists should pass on to their audiences all that the scholars tell them. Very often the result of scholarly research should determine not so much

248

what one is going to say, and even less *how* to say it, as what one should certainly *not* or *no longer* say. In other words, scholars may quite often provide us with negative rather than with positive guidelines.

Having said this, let us now look at the three main approaches to the parables which have been proposed in the course of the centuries.

(1) *Arbitrary* allegorizing should be strictly avoided. But this does not necessarily mean that *any* form or amount of allegorizing is excluded. While there may have been few allegorical elements in Jesus' parables, they were certainly not completely absent. Therefore, the present-day exegete or homilist should avoid eliminating all allegorical features in an ill-advised attempt to trim the texts into 'pure parables'. Features which either in the Old Testament or in current rabbinic theology had a more or less generally accepted symbolical meaning, should be so interpreted. But one should never allegorize to a point which would obscure the basic thrust of the parable.

(2) During the last hundred years, the most common approach to the parables has been the moralizing one. Following Adolf Jülicher, many who have rejected all forms of allegorization try to draw from each parable one, and in the worst case two or three moral lessons. All too often it appears that this type of exegesis and the ensuing homily miss the point of the parable, and make Jesus moralize about issues which have little or no connection with the real message of the parable. Does this mean a total embargo on all moralizing of the parables? It has been said that 'total abstinence here would be a counsel of perfection, and that what we ought to aim at is rather temperance' (A. M. Hunter). In some instances, a certain amount of moralizing is practically unavoidable, but *indiscriminate* moralizing should be shunned.

(3) Sound preaching based on the parables should as far as possible begin with the meaning the parable had when Jesus first pronounced it, or at least with the meaning the parable had for the evangelist, whose version of a given parable we start from. One should be first of all concerned with the original thrust. Then, and only then, should one proceed to the translation of the parable's message into contemporary terms. While this book is mainly devoted to the first phase, attempts at actualization and contemporary application can be found especially in the 'Reflection' sections.

While keeping in mind what has already been said, the homilist or catechist should also take into account the following considerations:

(1) The context in which the parable is placed in a particular gospel (e.g. Luke's parable of the great supper in the Travel Narrative, and Matthew's parable of the wedding feast between the entry into Jerusalem and Jesus' death) will often give an indication of the meaning it is intended to convey.

(2) The homilist or catechist must resist the temptation to give meaning to details which cannot be closely related to the central theme, or cluster of themes, of the parable. One should never attempt to decide the meaning of any (allegorical) detail in a parable in abstraction from the whole parable. In deciding what any feature might stand for, one must first of all take into account its relation to other details and to the whole parable.

(3) In interpreting the parables one must recognize that they have an 'elasticity' which enables them to fit the manifold and developing situations of the Church in every generation and in every culture. It may be quite legitimate, therefore, to give different interpretations to a particular detail, or even to a whole parable.

Notes

1 For a more detailed treatment of these distinctions, see, e.g., E. Linnemann, *Parables of Jesus. Introduction and Exposition* (New York: Harper & Row, 1966/London: SPCK, 1971), pp. 3–47; M. I. Boucher, *The Parables* (New Testament Message 7; Wilmington, Del.: Michael Glazier/Dublin: Veritas, 1981), pp. 11–50; P. Perkins, *Hearing the Parables of Jesus* (Ramsey, N.J.: Paulist Press, 1981), pp. 1–34.

2 The considerations that follow are based especially on J. Dupont, *Pourquoi des paraboles? La Méthode parabolique de Jésus* (Lire la Bible 46; Paris: Éditions du Cerf, 1977).

3 A recent study on the nature of the parables (which forms the first part of a projected study on the rabbinic parables and Jesus as parable narrator), however, emphasizes that the realism of the rabbinic and therefore also of Jesus' parables is only apparent (*scheinbar*). Both their material contents and their format would thus be highly stereotyped and fixed in nature. See D. Flusser, *Die rabbinische Gleichnisse und der Gleichniserzähler Jesus*, 1. Teil: *Das Wesen der Gleichnisse* (Berne/Frankfurt am Main/Las Vegas: P. Lang, 1981), pp. 31–47.

4 M. I. Boucher, *The Parables*, p. 58.

5 The reflections that follow are based on S. Lamberigts, 'Jezus sprak verhalenderwijs, in gelijkenissen en parabels', *Rond de Tafel* 35 (1980), 154–162.

6 See, e.g., H. Hendrickx, *The Story Behind the Gospels* (Manila: Communication Foundation for Asia, 1977), pp. 3–61; J. W. Miller, *Step by Step Through the Parables* (New York: Paulist Press, 1981), pp. 8–14.

7 K. E. Bailey, *Through Peasant Eyes. More Lucan Parables, Their Culture and Style* (Grand Rapids: Eerdmans, 1980), p. x.

8 C. W. F. Smith, *The Jesus of the Parables* (revised edition; Philadelphia: United Church Press, 1975), pp. 212–213.

9 For a history of the interpretation of the parables, see W. S. Kissinger, *The Parables of Jesus. A History of Interpretation and Bibliography* (Metuchen, N.J.: The Scarecrow Press, 1979), pp. 1–230.

10 N. Perrin, *Jesus and the Language of the Kingdom. Symbol and Metaphor in New Testament Interpretation* (Philadelphia: Fortress Press, 1976), pp. 204–205.

11 D. Flusser, *Die rabbinische Gleichnisse*, p. 15 note 6 (my translation).

12 A. M. Ambrozic, *The Hidden Kingdom. A Redaction-Critical Study of*

the *References to the Kingdom of God in Mark's Gospel* (Washington, D.C.: The Catholic Biblical Association of America, 1972), p. 108.

13   A. M. Ambrozic, *ibid.*, pp. 117–120.

14   J. D. Crossan, 'The Seed Parables of Jesus', *Journal of Biblical Literature* 92 (1973), 251–252.

15   'The treatise identified in Latin manuscripts as 4 Ezra comprises chapters 3–14 of an expanded form of the book traditionally included among the Apocrypha of English Bibles under the title 2 Esdras. This expanded form includes a Christian framework, comprising chapters 1f. and 15f., commonly called 2 and 5 Esdras in the later Latin manuscripts': J. H. Charlesworth (ed.), *The Old Testament Pseudepigrapha*, I: *Apocalyptic Literature and Testaments* (Garden City, N.Y.: Doubleday/London: Darton, Longman and Todd, 1983), p. 517.

16   J. Hargreaves, *A Guide to the Parables* (TEF Study Guide 1; London: SPCK, 1968), pp. 15–16.

17   A. M. Hunter, *The Parables Then and Now* (London: SCM Press, 1971), p. 41.

18   Mennonite World Conference, *Parables of the Kingdom* (Napannee, Ind.: Evangel Press, 1978), pp. 37–38.

19   F. Belo, *A Materialist Reading of the Gospel of Mark* (Maryknoll, N.Y.: Orbis Books, 1981), p. 123.

20   The *Gospel according to Thomas*, one of the thirteen manuscripts discovered in 1945 in a Gnostic library at Nag-Hammadi, Upper Egypt, is not a gospel in the true sense, since it says hardly anything about the life of Jesus. It is a collection of 114 teachings, about half of which are parallel to Jesus' teachings in the gospels, and among which are twelve parables. See, e.g., R. M. Grant and D. N. Freedman, *The Secret Sayings of Jesus* (Fontana Books; London: Collins/Garden City, N.Y.: Doubleday, 1960); J. M. Robinson (general editor), *The Nag Hammadi Library* (New York: Harper and Row, 1977), pp. 117–130.

21   J. Jeremias, *The Parables of Jesus* (New York: Scribner's/London: SCM Press, 1963), p. 147.

22   R. Schnackenburg, *God's Rule and Kingdom* (New York: Herder and Herder, 1963), p. 159.

23   R. W. Funk, 'The Looking-Glass Tree is for the Birds (Ezekiel 17:22–24; Mark 4:30–32)', *Interpretation* 27 (1973), 7–9 *passim*.

24   J. D. Kingsbury, *The Parables of Jesus in Matthew 13* (London: SPCK, 1969), p. 82.

25   R. W. Funk, 'The Looking-Glass Tree', 7.

26   B. B. Scott, *Jesus, Symbol-Maker for the Kingdom* (Philadelphia: Fortress Press, 1981), p. 76.

27   For the considerations that follow we are greatly indebted to H. Weder, *Die Gleichnisse Jesu als Metaphern* (Göttingen: Vandenhoeck & Ruprecht, 1978), pp. 123–125.

28   We should keep in mind the metaphorical meaning of the verb 'to sleep'; see especially Mk 13:36; I Thess 5:6, 7 and, in contrast, 5:10.

29   *Proserchesthai* occurs 52 times in Matthew, against five times in Mark and ten in Luke. RSV translates it here as 'came'.

30 P. Bacq, 'Reading a Parable: the Good Wheat and the Tares (Mt 13)', *Lumen Vitae* 39 (1984), 193–194.
31 While all scholars agree on the beginning of the Travel Narrative, there is no such agreement about its end (Lk 18:14, 19:10, 19:27, 19:44 or 19:48). For an extensive study see H. L. Egelkraut, *Jesus' Mission to Jerusalem. A Redaction-Critical Study of the Travel Narrative in the Gospel of Luke, Lk 9:51 – 19:48* (Frankfurt am Main: P. Lang, 1976). For a brief history of research, see pp. 30–61.
32 Is the woman's love the cause or the result of Jesus' forgiveness? This is not immediately clear (compare Lk 7:47a and 47b). It is also worth noting the similarity of the questions in Lk 7:42 and 10:36.
33 Cf. K. E. Bailey, *Poet and Peasant. A Literary-Cultural Approach to the Parables in Luke* (Grand Rapids: Eerdmans, 1976), pp. 73–74 note 53, and *Through Peasant Eyes*, p. 34.
34 R. C. Tannehill, 'Comments on the articles of Daniel Patte and John Dominic Crossan', *Semeia* 2 (*The Good Samaritan*: 1974), 115.
35 J. Jeremias, *The Parables of Jesus*, p. 205.
36 E. Stauffer, '*agapaō, agapē, agapētos*' in *Theological Dictionary of the New Testament* I (ed. G. Kittel; Grand Rapids: Eerdmans/London, SCM Press, 1964), p. 46.
37 H. Greeven, '*plēsion*' in *Theological Dictionary of the New Testament* VI (ed. G. Friedrich; Grand Rapids: Eerdmans/London, SCM Press, 1968), p. 317.
38 J. D. Crossan, 'Parable and Example in the Teaching of Jesus', *Semeia* 1 (1974), 76–77 *passim*.
39 R. W. Funk, 'Critical Note', *Semeia* 1 (1974), 189.
40 D. O. Via, Jr, 'Parable and Example Story: A Literary-Structuralist Approach', *Semeia* 1 (1974), 118–119.
41 D. O. Via, Jr, 'A Response to Crossan, Funk, and Petersen', *Semeia* 1 (1974), 225.
42 E. Linnemann, *Parables of Jesus*, p. 52.
43 S. Kierkegaard, *Leben und Walten der Liebe*, pp. 19f., as quoted in G. Bornkamm, *Jesus of Nazareth* (New York: Harper and Row/London: Hodder and Stoughton, 1960), pp. 113–114.
44 Cf. H. Hendrickx, *The Bible on Justice* (Quezon City: JMC Press, 1978).
45 P. Perkins, *Hearing the Parables of Jesus*, pp. 120–122.
46 S. Kistemaker, *The Parables of Jesus* (Grand Rapids: Baker, 1980), p. 174.
47 W. E. Pilgrim, *Good News to the Poor. Wealth and Poverty in Luke-Acts* (Minneapolis: Augsburg Publishing House, 1981), p. 143.
48 See J. Dupont, *Les Béatitudes*, III: *Les Évangélistes* (Paris: J. Gabalda, 1973), pp. 113–118, 183–185.
49 K. E. Bailey, *Through Peasant Eyes*, p. 62.
50 *Anthrōpos tis* occurs eight times in Luke, against once in Matthew. A substantive followed by *tis* occurs 101 times in Luke, once in Matthew; twice in Mark. The adjective *plousios*, 'rich', occurs eleven times in Luke, twice in Mark, three times in Matthew.
51 K. E. Bailey, *Through Peasant Eyes*, p. 65.

52   K. E. Bailey, *ibid.*, p. 76.

53   K. E. Bailey, *ibid.*, pp. 63–64.

54   R. W. Funk, *Language, Hermeneutic, and the Word of God* (New York/London: Harper and Row, 1966), p. 185.

55   See E. Schweizer, *Matthäus und seine Gemeinde* (Stuttgarter Bibelstudien 71; Stuttgart: Katholisches Bibelwerk, 1974), pp. 116–125.

56   D. Flusser, *Die rabbinische Gleichnisse*, p. 67.

57   A. Weiser, *Die Knechtsgleichnisse der synoptischen Evangelien* (Munich: Kösel Verlag, 1971), pp. 60–63.

58   See H. Weder, *Die Gleichnisse Jesu als Metaphern*, pp. 190–193.

59   J. Jeremias, *The Parables of Jesus*, pp. 178–179.

60   See R. W. Funk, *Language, Hermeneutic, and the Word of God*, pp. 191–193.

61   W. L. Petersen, 'The Parable of the Lost Sheep in the Gospel of Thomas and the Synoptics', *Novum Testamentum* 23 (1981), 128–147.

62   R. T. Osborn, 'The Father and His Two Sons: A Parable of Liberation', *Dialog* 19 (1980), 206.

63   L. T. Johnson, *The Literary Function of Possessions in Luke-Acts* (SBL Dissertation Series 39; Missoula, Mont.: Scholars Press, 1977), p. 161.

64   For a fuller development of this last point, see J. Dupont, 'Les implications christologiques de la parabole de la brebis perdue' in *Jésus aux origines de la Christologie* (ed. J. Dupont; Louvain: Leuven University Press, 1975), pp. 331–350.

65   See H. Weder, *Die Gleichnisse Jesu als Metaphern*, pp. 173–176.

66   See H. Weder, *ibid.*, pp. 250–252.

67   A. Paoli, *Meditations on Saint Luke* (Maryknoll, N.Y.: Orbis Books, 1977), pp. 107–113 *passim*.

68   J. S. Glen, *The Parables of Conflict in Luke* (Philadelphia: Westminster Press, 1962), pp. 36–39 *passim*.

69   R. T. Osborn, 'The Father and His Two Sons', 208.

70   P. Perkins, *Love Commands in the New Testament* (Ramsey, N.J.: Paulist Press, 1982), pp. 55, 57.

71   See J. Dupont, *Les Béatitudes*, III: *Les Évangélistes*, pp. 163–173; L. J. Topel, 'On the Injustice of the Unjust Steward: Lk 16:1–13', *The Catholic Biblical Quarterly* 37 (1975), 221–223.

72   For a detailed exposition of the various opinions concerning this parable, see M. Krämer, *Das Rätsel der Parabel vom ungerechten Verwalter* (Zürich: Pas-Verlag, 1972), pp. 15–74.

73   M. Krämer, *ibid.*, pp. 140–144.

74   J. Jeremias, *The Parables of Jesus*, p. 182.

75   M. Krämer, *Das Rätsel der Parabel vom ungerechten Verwalter*, pp. 156–163; J. W. Taeger, *Der Mensch und sein Heil* (Gütersloh: Gerd Mohn, 1982), pp. 49–56.

76   M. Krämer, *Das Rätsel der Parabel vom ungerechten Verwalter*, pp. 85–91.

77   M. Krämer, *ibid.*, pp. 100–105.

78   M. Krämer, *ibid.*, pp. 212–224.

79   M. Krämer, *ibid.*, pp. 226–232.

80 Compare J. Reumann, *Jesus in the Church's Gospels* (Philadelphia, Fortress Press, 1968/London: SPCK, 1970), pp. 189–198.
81 J. P. Miranda, *Communism in the Bible* (Maryknoll, N.Y.: Orbis Books, 1981/London: SCM Press, 1982), pp. 24–25, 50–51.
82 This story seems to have originated in the sixth century B.C., but was possibly contaminated later by foreign elements. The extant manuscript is dated A.D. 50–100.
83 For further considerations on the place of this parable in Lk 16 and in the wider Lucan context, see the beginning of Chapter 10.
84 See J. Dupont, 'Die individuelle Eschatologie im Lukas-Evangelium und in der Apostelgeschichte' in *Orientierung an Jesus* (ed. P. Hoffmann; Freiburg: Herder, 1973), pp. 34–37.
85 See A. George, 'La parabole du riche et de Lazare (Lc 16, 19–31)', *Assemblées du Seigneur* 57 (1971), 80–93, especially 90–93.
86 J. S. Glen, *The Parables of Conflict in Luke*, pp. 68–69.
87 J. S. Glen, *ibid.*, pp. 70–71.
88 W. E. Pilgrim, *Good News to the Poor*, pp. 116–119 *passim*.
89 K. E. Bailey, *Through Peasant Eyes*, p. 128.
90 K. E. Bailey, *Poet and Peasant*, pp. 79–82.
91 See W. Ott, *Gebet und Heil. Die Bedeutung der Gebetsparänese in der lukanischen Theologie* (Munich: Kösel Verlag, 1965), pp. 44–63.
92 K. E. Bailey, *Through Peasant Eyes*, pp. 147–148.
93 See J. Jeremias, *The Parables of Jesus*, p. 142.
94 J. S. Glen, *The Parables of Conflict in Luke*, pp. 57–58, 61.
95 E. Linnemann, *Parables of Jesus*, pp. 61–62.
96 P. Perkins, *Hearing the Parables of Jesus*, p. 174.

Further Reading

Boucher, M. I., *The Parables* (New Testament Message 7; Wilmington, Del.: Michael Glazier/Dublin: Veritas, 1981).

Dodd, C. H., *The Parables of the Kingdom* (Fontana Books; London: Collins, 1969).

Flood, E., *Parables of Jesus* (New York: Paulist Press, 1971).

Flood, E., *Parables for Now* (London: Darton, Longman and Todd, 1981).

Flood, E., *More Parables for Now* (London: Darton, Longman and Todd, 1981).

Granskou, D. M., *Preaching on the Parables* (Philadelphia: Fortress Press, 1972).

Hargreaves, J., *A Guide to the Parables* (TEF Study Guide 1; London: SPCK, 1968).

Harrington, W. J., *A Key to the Parables* (Deus Books; New York: Paulist Press, 1964).

Harrington, W. J., *Parables Told by Jesus. A Contemporary Approach* (New York: Alba House, 1974).

Hunter, A. M., *Interpreting the Parables* (London: SCM Press, 1969).

Hunter, A. M., *The Parables Then and Now* (London: SCM Press, 1971).

Jeremias, J., *Rediscovering the Parables* (London: SCM Press, 1966).

Jones, G.V., *The Art and Truth of the Parables. A Study in Their Literary Form and Modern Interpretation* (London: SPCK, 1964).

Linnemann, E., *Parables of Jesus. Introduction and Exposition* (New York: Harper & Row, 1966/London: SPCK, 1971).

Miller, J. W., *Step by Step Through the Parables* (New York: Paulist Press, 1981).

Mussner, F., *The Use of Parables in Catechetics* (Notre Dame: University Press, 1965).

Perkins, P., *Hearing the Parables of Jesus* (Ramsey, N.J.: Paulist Press, 1981).

Perrin, N., *Jesus and the Language of the Kingdom: Symbol and*

Metaphor in New Testament Interpretation (Philadelphia: Fortress Press, 1976).

Stein, R. H., *An Introduction to the Parables of Jesus* (Philadelphia: The Westminster Press, 1981).

Via, D. O., Jr, *The Parables. Their Literary and Existential Dimension* (Philadelphia: Fortress Press, 1967).

Bibliography

I. On the parables in general

Adams, D., 'Informing Liturgies with Parables', *Modern Liturgy* 8 (3; 1981), 4–5, 17.

Adams, D., and Adams, M., 'Linking Parables to our Lives', *Modern Liturgy* 8 (3; 1981), 8–9.

Albers, R. H., 'Perspectives on the Parables – Glimpses of the Kingdom of God', *Word World* 4 (1984), 437–454.

Alexandre, J., 'Note sur l'esprit des paraboles en réponse à P. Ricoeur', *Études Théologiques et Religieuses* 51 (1976), 367–372.

Almeida, Y., *L'Opérativité sémantique des récits-paraboles* (Louvain: Éditions Peeters, 1978).

Ambrozic, A. M., 'Mark's Concept of the Parable', *Catholic Biblical Quarterly* 29 (1967), 220–227.

Arens, E., 'Gleichnisse als kommunikative Handlungen Jesu. Überlegungen zu einer pragmatischen Gleichnistheorie', *Theologie und Philosophie* 56 (1981), 47–69.

Arens, E., *Kommunikative Handlungen: Die paradigmatische Bedeutung der Gleichnisse Jesu für ein Handlungstheorie* (Düsseldorf: Patmos Verlag, 1982).

Arens, E., 'The Parables as Communicative Acts', *Theology Digest* 31 (Spring 1984), 43–46.

Aurelio, T., *Disclosures in den Gleichnissen Jesu* (Regensburger Studien zur Theologie 8; Frankfurt am Main: P. Lang, 1977).

Aussems, A., 'Re-writing the Parables in Terms of Modern Life', *Lumen Vitae* 14 (March 1959), 64–68.

Bailey, K. E., *Poet and Peasant. A Literary-Cultural Approach to the Parables in Luke* (Grand Rapids: Eerdmans, 1976).

Bailey, K. E., *Through Peasant Eyes. More Lucan Parables, Their Culture and Style* (Grand Rapids: Eerdmans, 1980).

Barclay, W., *And Jesus Said. A Handbook on the Parables of Jesus* (Philadelphia: The Westminster Press/Edinburgh: The St Andrew Press, 1970).

Barr, D. L., 'Speaking of Parables: A Survey of Recent Research', *TSF Bulletin* 6 (5; 1983), 8–10.

Bauckham, R., 'Synoptic Parousia Parables and the Apocalypse', *New Testament Studies* 23 (1976–77), 162–176.

Bauckham, R., 'Synoptic Parousia Parables Again', *New Testament Studies* 29 (1983), 129–143.

Bauer, J. B., 'Gleichnisse Jesu und Gleichnisse der Rabbinen', *Theologisch-praktische Quartalschrift* 119 (1971), 297–307.

Beardslee, W. A. 'Uses of the Proverb in the Synoptic Gospels', *Interpretation* 24 (1970), 61–73.

Beardslee, W. A., 'Parable Interpretation and the World Disclosed by the Parable', *Perspectives in Religious Studies* 3 (1976), 123–139.

Beardslee, W. A., 'Parable, Proverb, and Koan', *Semeia* 12 (1978), 151–177.

Berger, K., 'Materialen zu Form und Überlieferungsgeschichte neutestamentlicher Gleichnisse', *Novum Testamentum* 15 (1973), 1–37.

Berger, K., 'Zur Frage des traditionsgeschichtlichen Wertes apokrypher Gleichnisse', *Novum Testamentum* 17 (1975), 58–76.

Bergmann, W., *Die zehn Gleichnisse vom Reich der Himmel* (Dinglinger Taschenbücher 700; Lahr-Dinglingen: Verlag der St. Johannis-Druckerei C. Schweickhardt, 1976).

Beyer, D., *Parables for Christian Living. Seeing Ourselves as Jesus Sees Us – Parables from Luke* (Valley Forge, Pa.: Judson Press, 1985).

Biser, E., *Die Gleichnisse Jesu. Versuch einer Deutung* (Munich: Kösel Verlag, 1965).

Biser, E., 'Das Gottesreich als Sinn und Thema der Gleichnisse', *Hochland* 58 (1966), 556–560.

Blackman, E. C., 'New Methods of Parable Interpretation', *Canadian Journal of Theology* 15 (1969), 3–13.

Blank, J., 'Marginalien zur Gleichnisauslegung', *Bibel und Leben* 6 (1965), 50–60.

Blomberg, C. L., 'New Horizons in Parable Research', *Trinity Journal* 3 (1982), 3–17.

Blomberg, C. L. 'Preaching the Parables: Preserving Three Main Points', *Perspectives in Religious Studies* 11 (1984), 31–41.

Blomberg, C. L., 'When is a Parallel Really a Parallel? A Test Case: The Lucan Parables', *Westminster Theological Journal* 46 (1984), 78–103.

Bonnard, P., 'Où en est la question des paraboles évangeliques. De Jülicher (1888) a Jeremias (1947)', *Foi et Vie* 66 (1967), 36–49.

Boobyer, G. H., 'The Redaction of Mark IV.1–34', *New Testament Studies* 8 (1961–62), 59–70.

Borsch, F. H., 'Who Has Ears', *Anglican Theological Review* 52 (1970), 131–141.

Boucher, M., *The Mysterious Parable. A Literary Study* (Washington, D.C.: Catholic Biblical Association, 1977).

Bourbeck, C., *Gleichnisse aus altem und neuem Testament* (Stuttgart: E. Klotz Verlag, 1971).

Bouttier, M., 'Les paraboles du maître dans la tradition synoptique', *Études Théologiques et Religieuses* 48 (1973), 176–195.

Bowker, J. W., 'Mystery and Parable', *Journal of Theological Studies* 25 (1974), 300–317.

Boys, M. C., 'Parabolic Ways of Teaching', *Biblical Theology Bulletin* 13 (1983), 82–89.

Breech, E., 'Kingdom of God and the Parables of Jesus', *Semeia* 12 (1978), 15–40.

Breech, J., *The Silence of Jesus: The Authentic Voice of the Historical Man* (Philadelphia: Fortress Press, 1983).

Brown, R. E., 'Parable and Allegory Reconsidered', *Novum Testamentum* 5 (1962), 36–45.

Brown, R. E., *The Parables of the Gospels* (Doctrinal Pamphlet Series; Glen Rock, N.J.: Paulist Press, 1963).

Brown, S., '"The Secret of the Kingdom of God" (Mark 4:11)', *Journal of Biblical Literature* 92 (1973), 60–74.

Carlston, C. E., 'Changing Fashions in Interpreting the Parables', *Andover Newton Quarterly* 14 (1974), 227–233.

Carlston, C. E., *The Parables of the Triple Tradition* (Philadelphia: Fortress Press, 1975).

Carlston, C. E., 'Proverbs, Maxims, and the Historical Jesus', *Journal of Biblical Literature* 99 (1980), 87–105.

Carlston, C. E., 'Parable and Allegory Revisited: An Interpretative Review', *Catholic Biblical Quarterly* 43 (1981), 228–242.

Cave, C. H., 'The Parables and the Scriptures', *New Testament Studies* 11 (1964–65), 374–387.

Cerfaux, L., *The Treasure of the Parables* (De Pere, Wisc.: St Norbert's Abbey Press, 1968).

Cerfaux, L., and Garitte, G., 'Les Paraboles du Royaume dans l'Évangile de Thomas', *Le Muséon* 70 (1957), 307–327.

Coates, T., *The Parables for Today* (St Louis/London: Concordia Publishing House, 1971).

Congar, Y. M. J. 'The Parables as God's Revelation', *Cross and Crown* 20 (1968), 10–25.

Crossan, J. D., 'Parable and Example in the Teaching of Jesus', *New Testament Studies* 18 (1971–72), 285–307.

Crossan, J. D., *In Parables. The Challenge of the Historical Jesus* (New York: Harper and Row, 1973).

Crossan, J. D., 'Parables as Religious and Poetic Experience', *Journal of Religion* 53 (1973), 330–358.

Crossan, J. D., 'The Seed Parables of Jesus', *Journal of Biblical Literature* 92 (1973), 244–266.

Crossan, J. D., 'The Servant Parables of Jesus', *Semeia* 1 (1974), 17–62.

Crossan, J. D., 'Structuralist Analysis and the Parables of Jesus', *Semeia* 1 (1974), 192–221.

Crossan, J. D., 'A Basic Bibliography for Parable Research', *Semeia* 1 (1974), 236–274.

Crossan, J. D., *Raid on the Articulate: Comic Eschatology in Jesus and Borges* (New York/London: Harper and Row, 1976).

Crossan, J. D., 'Parable, Allegory, and Paradox' in *Semiology and Parables* (ed. D. Patte; Pittsburgh: Pickwick Press, 1976), pp. 247–281.

Crossan, J. D., 'Waking the Bible. Biblical Hermeneutic and Literary Imagination', *Interpretation* 32 (1978), 269–285.

Crossan, J. D., 'Paradox Gives Rise to Metaphor: Paul Ricoeur's Hermeneutics and the Parables of Jesus', *Biblical Research* 24–25 (1979–80), 20–37.

Crossan, J. D., *Cliffs of Fall: Paradox and Polyvalence in the Parables of*

Jesus (New York: Seabury Press, 1980).

Culbertson, P., 'The Pharisaic Jesus and His Gospel Parables', *Christian Century* 102 (1985), 74–77.

Daalen, D. H. van, *The Kingdom of God is Like This* (London: Epworth Press, 1976).

Deever, P. O., *Lending the Parables Our Ears: Toward a Meaningful Experience with the Gospel Parables* (Nashville: Tidings, 1975).

Deever, P. O., *The Kingdom Is. . .* (Nashville: Tidings, 1976).

Dehandschutter, B., 'Les paraboles de l'Évangile selon Thomas: la parabole du Trésor caché (log. 109)', *Ephemerides Theologicae Lovanienses* 47 (1971), 199–219.

Detweiler, R., *Story, Sign, and Self. Phenomenology and Structuralism as Literary Critical Method* (SBL Semeia Supplements; Missoula, Mont.: Scholars Press, 1978).

Dewey, K. E., '*Paroimiai* in the Gospel of John', *Semeia* 17 (1980), 81–99.

Diamond, P., 'Reflexions upon Recent Developments in the Study of the Parables in Luke', *Australian Biblical Review* 29 (1981), 1–9.

Doerksen, V. D., 'The Interpretation of Parables', *Grace Journal* 11 (1979), 3–20.

Doty, W. G., 'The Parables of Jesus, Kafka, Borges and Others, with Structural Observations', *Semeia* 2 (1974), 152–193.

Drury, J., 'The Sower, the Vineyard, and the Place of Allegory in the Interpretation of Mark's Parables', *Journal of Theological Studies* 24 (1973), 367–374.

Drury, J., *The Parables in the Gospels. History and Allegory* (London: SPCK, 1985).

Duling, D. C., 'Norman Perrin and the Kingdom of God: Review and Response', *Journal of Religion* 64 (1984), 468–483.

Dumas, A., 'De l'archétype à la parabole', *La Vie Spirituelle Supplément* 92 (1970), 28–46.

Dupont, J., 'Le chapitre des paraboles', *Nouvelle Revue Théologique* 89 (1967), 800–820.

Dupont, J., 'Le point de vue de Matthieu dans le chapitre des paraboles' in *L'Évangile de Matthieu* (ed. M. Didier *et al.*; Gembloux: J. Duculot, 1972), pp. 221–259.

Dupont, J., *Pourquoi des paraboles? La méthode parabolique de Jésus* (Lire la Bible 46; Paris: Éditions du Cerf, 1977).

Dupont, J., 'Actualiteit van der parabelmethode van Jezus' in *Parabels Meerstemmig* (Antwerp: Patmos, 1980), pp. 151–175.

Eichholz, G., *Gleichnisse der Evangelien. Form, Überlieferung, Auslegung* (Neukirchen-Vluyn: Neukirchener Verlag, 1971).

Ellena, D., 'Thematische Analyse der Wachstumsgleichnisse', *Linguistica Biblica* 23 (1973), 48–62.

Entrevernes Group, *Signs and Parables. Semiotics and Gospel Texts* (Pittsburgh Theological Monograph Series 23; Pittsburgh: Pickwick Press, 1978).

Faluse, G. K., 'Jesus' Use of the Parables in Mark with Special Reference to Mark 4:10–12', *The Indian Journal of Theology* 31 (1982), 35–46.

Flood, E., 'Jesus in the Parables', *The Sower* 5 (1981), 21–25.

Flusser, D., *Die rabbinische Gleichnisse und der Gleichniserzähler Jesus*, 1. Teil: *Das Wesen der Gleichnisse* (Judaica et Christiana 4; Frankfurt am Main: P. Lang, 1981).

Frankemölle, H., 'Hat Jesus sich selbst verkündet? Christologische Implikationen in den vor-markinischen Parabeln', *Bibel und Leben* 13 (1972), 184–207.

Frankemölle, H., *In Gleichnissen Gott erfahren* (Stuttgart: Katholisches Bibelwerk, 1977).

Frankemölle, H., 'Kommunikatives Handeln in Gleichnissen Jesu. Historisch-kritische und pragmatische Exegese. Eine kritische Sichtung', *New Testament Studies* 28 (1982), 61–90.

Fuchs, E., *Studies of the Historical Jesus* (SBT 42; London: SCM Press, 1964).

Funk, R. W., *Language, Hermeneutic, and the Word of God* (New York/London: Harper and Row, 1966).

Funk, R. W., 'The Parables' in *Jesus and Man's Hope* II (ed. D. G. Miller and D. Y. Hadidian; A Perspective Book; Pittsburgh: Pittsburgh Theological Seminary, 1971), pp. 287–303.

Funk, R. W., 'The Looking-Glass Tree is for the Birds', *Interpretation* 27 (1973), 3–9.

Funk, R. W., 'Structure in the Narrative Parables of Jesus', *Semeia* 2 (1974), 51–73.

Funk, R. W., 'The Narrative Parables: The Birth of a Language Tradition' in *God's Christ and His People* (ed. J. Jervell; Oslo: Universitets-forlaget, 1977), pp. 43–50.

Funk, R. W., *Parables and Presence* (Philadelphia: Fortress Press, 1982).

Gaeddert, J., *Parables of Jesus* (Newton, Kan.: Faith and Life Press, 1978).

Galloway, C. J., 'The Point of Parable', *The Bible Today* no. 28 (February 1967), 1952–1960.

George, A., 'Les paraboles', *Lumière et Vie* 23 (119; 1974), 35–48.

Gerhardsson, B., 'The Seven Parables in Matthew XIII', *New Testament Studies* 19 (1972–73), 16–37.

Glen, J. S., *The Parables of Conflict in Luke* (Philadelphia: The Westminster Press, 1962).

Goulder, M. D., 'Characteristics of the Parables in the Several Gospels', *Journal of Theological Studies* 19 (1968), 51–69.

Grassi, J. A., 'Drama from Real Life: Teaching through Stories and Parables' in *Jesus as Teacher. A New Testament Guide to Learning 'The Way'* (Winona, Minn.: St Mary's College Press, 1978), pp. 65–68.

Güttgemanns, E., 'Die linguistisch-didaktische Methodik der Gleichnisse Jesu' in *Studia Linguistica Neotestamentica. Aufsätze...* (Munich: Kaiser Verlag, 1971), pp. 99–183.

Güttgemanns, E., 'Narrative Analyse synoptischer Texte', *Linguistica Biblica* 25/26 (1973), 50–73.

Güttgemanns, E., 'Narrative Analysis of Synoptic Texts', *Semeia* 6 (1976), 127–179.

Gutbrod, K., *Ein Weg zu den Gleichnissen Jesu* (Stuttgart: Calwer-Verlag, 1973).

Hanko, H. C., *The Mysteries of the Kingdom: An Exposition of the Parables* (Grand Rapids: Reformed Free Pub. Assoc., 1975).

Harnisch, W., 'Die Ironie als Stilmittel in Gleichnissen Jesu', *Evangelische Theologie* 32 (1972), 421–436.

Harnisch, W., 'Die Sprachkraft der Analogie. These vom "argumentativen Character" der Gleichnisse Jesu', *Studia Theologica* 28 (1974), 1–20.

Harnisch, W., 'Die Metaphor als heuristisches Prinzip. Neuerscheinungen zur Hermeneutik der Gleichnisreden Jesu', *Verkündigung und Forschung* 24 (1979), 53–89.

Harnisch, W. (ed.), *Gleichnisse Jesu. Positionen der Auslegung von A. Jülicher bis zur Formgeschichte* (Wege der Forschung; Darmstadt: Wissenschaftliche Buchgesellschaft, 1982).

Harnisch, W. (ed.), *Die neutestamentliche Gleichnisforschung im Horizont von Hermeneutik und Literaturwissenschaft* (Darmstadt: Wissenschaftliche Buchgesellschaft, 1982).

Harrington, W. J., 'The Parables in Recent Study, 1960–1971', *Biblical Theology Bulletin* 2 (1972), 219–241.

Harrington, W. J., 'The Parables: Recent Explorations', *Doctrine and Life* 22 (1972), 395–404.

Harrington, W. J., 'Hidden Treasure', *The Furrow* 26 (1975), 523–529.

Haufe, G., 'Erwägungen zum Ursprung der sogenannter Parabeltheorie Mk 4, 11–12', *Evangelische Theologie* 32 (1972), 413–421.

Hedrick, C. W., 'Kingdom Sayings and Parables of Jesus in the Apocryphon of James: Tradition and Redaction', *New Testament Studies* 29 (1983), 1–24.

Heyer, H., *Denket um. Überlegungen zu Worten und Gleichnissen Jesu* (Munich: Don Bosco Verlag, 1970).

Hoffman, J. C., 'Story as Mythoparabolic Medium: Reflections on Crossan's Interpretation of Jesus' Parables', *Union Seminary Quarterly Review* 37 (1983), 323–333.

Hubbard, D. A., *Parables Jesus Told* (Downers Grove, Ill.: InterVarsity, 1981).

Huffman, N. A., 'Atypical Features in the Parables of Jesus', *Journal of Biblical Literature* 97 (1978), 207–220.

Hurley, N., 'Jesus' Parables as Strategic Fiction', *Review for Religious* 31 (1972), 756–760.

Irwin, K. M., 'MEDIAting Parables', *Modern Liturgy* 8 (3; 1980), 18–19.

Javelet, R., *The Gospel Paradox* (New York: Herder and Herder, 1966).

Jeremias, J., *Die Gleichnisse Jesu* (Göttingen: Vandenhoeck & Ruprecht, 1956; 1970).

Jeremias, J., *The Parables of Jesus* (New York: Scribner's/London: SCM Press, 1963; translation of the preceding).

Jones, I. H., 'Recent Work on the Parables', *Epworth Review* 12 (1985), 89–96.

Jones, P. R., 'The Modern Study of Parables', *Southwestern Journal of Theology* 22 (1980), 7–22.

Jüchen, A. von, *Die Kampfgleichnisse Jesu* (Munich: Kaiser Verlag, 1981).

Jülicher, A., *Die Gleichnisreden Jesu* (Darmstadt: Wissenschaftliche Buchgesellschaft, 1963).

Kahlefeld, H., *Gleichnisse und Lehrstücke im Evangelium* (Frankfurt am Main: Knecht, 1981).

Kemmer, A., *Gleichnisse Jesu. Wie man sie lesen und verstehen soll* (Herderbücherei 875; Freiburg: Herder, 1981).

Kingsbury, J. D., *The Parables of Jesus in Matthew 13* (London: SPCK/Richmond, Va.: John Knox Press, 1969).

Kingsbury, J. D., 'Ernst Fuchs' Existentialist Interpretation of the Parables', *Lutheran Quarterly* 22 (1970), 380–395.

Kingsbury, J. D., 'Major Trends in Parable Interpretation', *Concordia Theological Monthly* 42 (1971), 579–596.

Kingsbury, J. D., 'The Parables of Jesus in Current Research', *Dialog* 11 (1972), 101–107.

Kirkland, J. R., 'The Earliest Understanding of Jesus' Use of the Parables: Mark IV,10–12 in Context', *Novum Testamentum* 19 (1977), 1–21.

Kissinger, W. S., *The Parables of Jesus. A History of Interpretation and Bibliography* (ATLA Bibliography Series 4; Metuchen, N.J.: The Scarecrow Press/The American Theological Library Association, 1979).

Kistemaker, S. J., *The Parables of Jesus* (Grand Rapids: Baker, 1980).

Klauck, H.-J., 'Neue Beiträge zur Gleichnisforschung', *Bibel und Leben* 13 (1972), 214–230.

Klauck, H.-J., *Allegorie und Allegorese in synoptischen Gleichnistexten* (Neutestamentliche Abhandlungen 13; Münster: Aschendorff, 1978).

Klemm, H. G., 'Die Gleichnisauslegung Adolf Jülichers im Bannkreis der Fabeltheories Lessings', *Zeitschrift für die neutestamentliche Wissenschaft* 60 (1969), 153–174.

Knibb, M. A., 'The Date of the Parables of Enoch: A Critical Review', *New Testament Studies* 25 (1978–79), 345–359.

Knoch, O., *Wer Ohren hat, der höre. Die Botschaft der Gleichnisse Jesu. Ein Werkbuch zur Bibel* (Stuttgart: Katholisches Bibelwerk, 1983).

Kümmel, W. G., 'Jesusforschung seit 1965. IV. Bergpredigt—Gleichnisse— Wunderberichte', *Theologische Rundschau* 43 (1978), 105–161, 233– 265.

Lamberigts, S., 'Jezus sprak verhalenderwijs, in gelijkenissen en parabels', *Rond de Tafel* 35 (1980), 154–162.

Lambrecht, J., *Parables of Jesus. Insight and Challenge* (Bangalore: Theological Publications in India, 1978).

Lambrecht, J., *Once More Astonished. The Parables of Jesus* (New York: Crossroad Publishing Company, 1981).

Linton, O., 'Coordinated Sayings and Parables in the Synoptic Gospels. Analysis Contra Theories', *New Testament Studies* 26 (1979–80), 139–163.

Little, J. C., 'Parable Research in the Twentieth Century. I. The Predecessors of J. Jeremias', *Expository Times* 87 (1976), 356–360.

Little, J. C., 'Parable Research in the Twentieth Century. II. The Contribution of J. Jeremias', *Expository Times* 88 (1976), 40–44.

Little, J. C., 'Parable Research in the Twentieth Century. Developments since J. Jeremias', *Expository Times* 88 (1976), 71–75.

Lohse, E., 'Die Gottesherrschaft in den Gleichnissen Jesu', *Evangelische*

Theologie 18 (1958), 147–157 [= *Einheit im Neuen Testament* (Göttingen: Vandenhoeck & Ruprecht, 1973), 49–61].

Lührmann, D., 'Der Verweis auf die Erfahrung und die Frage nach der Gerechtigkeit' in *Jesus Christus in Historie und Theologie. Neutestamentliche Festschrift für H. Conzelmann* (ed. G. Strecker; Tübingen: J. C. B. Mohr, 1975), pp. 185–196.

McFague, S., 'Conversion: Life on the Edge of the Raft', *Interpretation* 32 (1978), 255–268.

MacPhail, J. R., *The Parables of Jesus. King and Teacher* (Madras: Christian Literature Society, 1976).

Magass, W., 'Zur Semiotik der signifikanten Orte in der Gleichnisse Jesu', *Linguistica Biblica* 15 (1972), 3–21.

Magass, W., 'Die magistralen Schlussignale der Gleichnisse Jesu', *Linguistica Biblica* 36 (1975), 1–20.

Magass, W., 'Bemerkungen zur Gleichnisauslegung', *Kairos* 20 (1978), 40–52.

Maillot, A., *Les Paraboles de Jésus aujourd'hui* (Geneva: Ed. Labor et Fides, 1973).

Maillot, A., 'Introduction aux paraboles', *Foi et Vie* 75 (5–6; 1975), 6–12.

Manek, J.,. . . *und brachte Frucht. Die Gleichnisse Jesu. Ein Arbeitsbuch für die Aus- und Weiterbildung kirchlicher Mitarbeiter* (Stuttgart; Calwer-Verlag, 1977).

Mearns, C. L., 'Dating the Similitudes of Enoch', *New Testament Studies* 25 (1978–79), 360–369.

Mees, M., 'Die moderne Deutung der Parabeln und ihre Probleme', *Vetera Christianorum* 11 (1974), 416–433.

Mellon, C., 'La Parabole. Manière de parler, manière d'entendre', *Recherches de Science Religieuse* 61 (1973), 49–63.

Miller, J. W., 'Jesus' Personality as Reflected in His Parables' in *The New Way of Jesus. Essays Presented to Howard Charles* (Newton, Kan.: Faith and Life Press, 1980), pp. 56–72.

Montefiore, H. W., 'A Comparison of the Parables of the Gospel According to Thomas and the Synoptic Gospels', *New Testament Studies* 7 (1960–61), 220–248.

Moule, C. F. D., 'The Use of Parables and Sayings as Illustrative Material in Early Christian Catechesis' in *Essays in New Testament Interpretation* (Cambridge: Cambridge University Press, 1982), pp. 50–53.

Nelson, B. A., *Hustle Won't Bring the Kingdom of God. Jesus' Parables Interpreted for Today* (St Louis: Bethany Press, 1978).

Nichols, A., 'Parables for Primaries; A Way to Teach Little Children', *Religion Teacher's Journal* 9 (May–June 1975), 13–15.

Nicoll, M., *De nieuwe mens. Een interpretatie van enige gelijkenissen en wonderen van Christus* (Wassenaar: Servire, 1970).

Osborn, E., 'Parable and Exposition', *Australian Biblical Review* 22 (1974), 11–22.

Osten-Sacken, P. von der, 'Streitgespräch und Parabel als Formen markinischen Christologie' in *Jesus Christus in Historie und Theologie. Neutestamentliche Festschrift für H. Conzelmann* (ed. G. Strecker; Tübingen: J. C. B. Mohr, 1975), pp. 375–394.

Patte, D. (ed.), *Semiology and Parables* (Pittsburgh: The Pickwick Press, 1976).

Patten, P., 'The Form and Function of Parable in Select Apocalyptic Literature and Their Significance for Parables in the Gospel of Mark', *New Testament Studies* 29 (1983), 246–258.

Payne, P. B., 'The Authenticity of the Parables of Jesus' in *Gospel Perspectives. Studies of History and Tradition in the Four Gospels* (ed. R. T. France and D. Wenham; 2 vols, Sheffield: JSOT Press, 1980–81), vol. 2, pp. 329–344.

Pentecost, J. D., *The Parables of Jesus* (Grand Rapids: Zondervan, 1982).

Perkins, P., 'Metaphor and Community', *American Ecclesiastical Review* 69 (1975), 270–281.

Perkins, P., 'Interpreting the Parables; the Bible and the Humanities' in *Emerging Issues in Religious Education* (ed. Gloria Durka and Joanmarie Smith; New York: Paulist Press, 1976), pp. 149–172.

Perrin, N., 'The Parables of Jesus as Parables, as Metaphors, and as Aesthetic Objects: A Review Article', *Journal of Religion* 47 (1967), 340–346.

Perrin, N., 'Biblical Scholarship in a New Vein. Review of Dan Via, Jr. The Parables: Their Literary and Existential Dimension', *Interpretation* 21 (1967), 465–469.

Perrin, N., 'The Modern Interpretation of the Parables of Jesus and the Problem of Hermeneutics', *Interpretation* 25 (1971), 131–148.

Perrin, N., 'Historical Criticism, Literary Criticism, and Hermeneutics. The Interpretation of the Parables of Jesus and the Gospel of Mark Today', *Journal of Religion* 52 (1972), 361–375.

Perrin, N., 'The Evangelists' Interpretation of Jesus' Parables', *Theology Digest* 21 (1973), 146–149.

Pesch, R., and Kratz, R., *So liest man synoptisch. Anleitung und Kommentar zum Studium der synoptischen Evangelien. IV: Gleichnisse und Bildreden. Aus der dreifachen Überlieferung* (Frankfurt: J. Knecht, 1978).

Pesch, R., and Kratz, R., *So liest man synoptisch. . . V. Gleichnisse und Bildreden. Aus der zweifachen Überlieferung* (Frankfurt: J. Knecht, 1978).

Petersen, N., 'On the Notion of Genre in Via's "Parable and Example Story: A Literary-Structuralist Approach"', *Semeia* 1 (1974), 134–181.

Petuchowski, J. J., 'The Theological Significance of the Parable in Rabbinic Literature and the New Testament', *Christian News from Israel* 23 (1972), 76–86.

Petzoldt, M., *Gleichnisse Jesu und christliche Dogmatik* (Göttingen: Vandenhoeck & Ruprecht, 1984).

Polk, T., 'Paradigms, Parables, and Meshalim: On Reading the Mashal in Scripture', *Catholic Biblical Quarterly* 45 (1983), 564–583.

Poovey, W. A., *Mustard Seeds and Wine Skins. Dramas and Meditations on Seven Parables* (Minneapolis: Augsburg Publishing House, 1972).

Popkes, W., 'Die Funktion der Sendschreiben in der Johannes-Apokalypse. Zugleich ein Beitrag zur Spätgeschichte der neutestamentlichen

Gleichnisse', *Zeitschrift für die neutestamentliche Wissenschaft* 74 (1983), 90–107.

Pryor, J. W., 'Markan Parable Theory: An Inquiry in Mark's Principles of Redaction', *Expository Times* 83 (1972), 242–245.

Purdy, J. C., *Parables at Work* (Philadelphia: The Westminster Press, 1985).

Radl, W., 'Zur Struktur der eschatologischen Gleichnisse Jesu', *Trierer Theologische Zeitschrift* 92 (1983), 122–133.

Ragaz, L., *Die Gleichnisse Jesu* (Stundenbücher 99; Hamburg: Furche-Verlag, 1971).

Reese, J., 'Responding to the Parables', *Catholic Charismatic* 1 (October–November 1976), 10–13.

Reese, J., 'Parables Reveal the Kingdom', in *Jesus, His Word and Work* (New York: Pueblo Publishing Company, 1978), pp. 68–80.

Reese, J., 'The Parables in Matthew's Gospel', *The Bible Today* 19 (January 1981), 30–35.

Ricoeur, P., 'Listening to the Parables. Once More Astonished', *Christianity and Christ* 34 (6 January 1975), 304–308.

Ricoeur, P., 'Biblical Hermeneutics', *Semeia* 4 (1975), 29–148.

Ricoeur, P., 'Le "Royaume" dans les paraboles de Jésus', *Études Théologiques et Religieuses* 51 (1976), 15–19.

Ricoeur, P., 'The "Kingdom" in the Parables of Jesus', *Anglican Theological Review* 63 (1981), 165–169.

Riegert, E. R., 'Parabolic Sermons', *Lutheran Quarterly* 26 (February 1974), 24–31.

Riesenfeld, H., 'The Parables in the Synoptic and Johannine Traditions' in *The Gospel Tradition. Essays* (Philadelphia: Fortress Press, 1970), pp. 139–169.

Ripoll, F., 'The Parabolic Teaching of Jesus on the Kingdom Based on Mt 13', *BibleBhashyam* 6 (1980), 207–212.

Robinson, J. M., 'Jesus' Parables as God Happening' in *Jesus and the Historian. In Honor of E. C. Colwell* (ed. T. Trotter; Philadelphia: The Westminster Press, 1968), pp. 134–150.

Robinson, J. M., 'Les paraboles comme avènement de Dieu', *Le Point Théologique* 3 (1972), 33–62.

Röhr, H., 'Buddha und Jesus in ihren Gleichnissen', *Neue Zeitschrift für systematische Theologie und Religionsphilosophie* 15 (1973), 65–86.

Roguet, A.-M., 'Paraboles oubliées', *Vie Spirituelle* 135 (644–645; 1981), 334–360.

Sabourin, L., 'The Parables of the Kingdom', *Biblical Theology Bulletin* 6 (1976), 115–160.

Satake, A., 'Zwei Typen von Menschenbildern in den Gleichnissen Jesu', *Annual of the Japanese Biblical Institute* 4 (1978), 45–84.

Schoedel, W. R., 'Parables in the Gospel of Thomas. Oral Tradition or Gnostic Exegesis?', *Concordia Theological Monthly* 43 (1972), 548–560.

Scholz, G., *Gleichnisaussage und Existenzstruktur. Das Gleichnis der neueren Hermeneutik unter besonderer Berücksichtigung der christlichen Existenzstruktur in den Gleichnissen des lukanischen Sonderguts* (Europäische Hochschulschriften Reihe XXIII. Theologie 214; Frankfurt am Main: P. Lang, 1983).

Schweizer, E., 'Zur Sondertradition der Gleichnisse bei Matthäus' in *Matthäus und seine Gemeinde* (SBS 71; Stuttgart: Katholisches Bibelwerk, 1974), pp. 98–105.

Scott, B., 'Parables of Growth Revisited: Notes on the Current State of Parable Research', *Biblical Theology Bulletin* 11 (1981), 3–9.

Seagren, D. R., *The Parables* (Wheaton, Ill.: Tyndale House, 1978).

Segalla, G., 'Cristologia implicita nelle parabole di Gesù', *Teologia* 1 (1976), 297–337.

Sellin, G., 'Gleichnisstrukturen', *Linguistica Biblica* 31 (1974), 89–115.

Sellin, G., 'Luke as Parable Narrator', *Theology Digest* 25 (1977), 53–60.

Sellin, G., 'Allegorie und "Gleichnis". Zur Formenlehre der synoptischen Gleichnisse', *Zeitschrift für Theologie und Kirche* 75 (1978), 281–335.

Sider, J. W., 'The Meaning of *Parabolē* in the Usage of the Synoptic Gospels', *Biblica* 62 (1981), 453–470.

Sider, J. W., 'Rediscovering the Parables: The Logic of the Jeremias Tradition', *Journal of Biblical Literature* 102 (1983), 61–83.

Slee, N., 'Parables and Women's Experience', *Modern Churchman* 26 (1983–84), 20–31.

Smith, C. W. F., *The Jesus of the Parables* (A Pilgrim Press Book; revised edition; Philadelphia: United Church Press, 1975).

Snodgrass, K., *The Parable of the Wicked Tenants: An Inquiry in Parable Interpretation* (WUNT 27; Tübingen: J. C. B. Mohr, 1983).

Sorger, K., *Die Gleichnisse im Unterricht. Grundsätzliche Überlegungen* (Essen: Hans Driewer Verlag, 1972).

Steinmetz, F.-J., 'Vom Geheimnis der Gleichnisse', *Geist und Leben* 49 (1976), 161–166.

Sturch, R. L., 'Jeremiah and John: Parables in the Fourth Gospel', *Expository Times* 89 (1978), 235–238.

Sunden, H., 'Exegesis and the Psychology of Religion. Some Remarks on the Interpretation of the Parables of the Kingdom', *Temenos* 11 (1975), 148–162.

Suter, D. W., *Tradition and Composition in the Parables of Enoch* (SBL Dissertation Series 47; Missoula, Mont.: Scholars Press, 1979).

Suter, D. W., '*Masal* in the Similitudes of Enoch', *Journal of Biblical Literature* 100 (1981), 193–212.

Täubl, A., *Gleichnisse Jesu. Ein theologischer Kurs im Medienverband* (Projekte zur theologischen Erwachsenenbildung 5; Mainz: Grünewald, 1977).

TeSelle, S. M., 'Trial Run; Parable, Poem, and Autobiographical Story', *Andover Newton Quarterly* 13 (1973), 277–287.

TeSelle, S. M., 'Parable, Metaphor, and Theology', *Journal of the American Academy of Religion* 42 (1974), 630–645.

TeSelle, S. M., *Speaking in Parables. A Study in Metaphor and Theology* (Philadelphia: Fortress Press/London: SCM Press, 1975).

TeSelle, S. M., 'Learning for the Whole Person: A Model from the Parables of Jesus', *Religion in Life* 45 (1976), 161–173.

Tinsley, E. J., 'Parable and Allegory; Some Literary Criteria for the Interpretation of the Parables of Christ', *Church Quarterly* 3 (July 1970), 32–39.

Tinsley, E. J., 'The Parables and the Self-Awareness of Jesus', *Church Quarterly* 4 (1971), 18–27.

Tolbert, M. A., *Perspectives on the Parables. An Approach to Multiple Interpretations* (Philadelphia: Fortress Press, 1979).

Topel, J., 'On Being "Parabled"', *The Bible Today* no. 87 (1976), 1010–1017.

Trinquet, J., *Les paraboles de jugement* (Paris: Ligue Catholique de l'Évangile, 1967).

Truchon, R., *Aujourd'hui les Paraboles* (Lac Beauport-Quebec: Éditions Anne Sigier, 1980).

Verbeeck, L., *et al.*, *Parabels Meerstemmig. Verslagboek van de Vlieberg Sencie Leergang. Afdelingen Catechese en Bijbel. Augustus 1979* (Antwerp: Patmos, 1981).

Via, D. O., Jr, 'Matthew and the Understanding of the Parables', *Journal of Biblical Literature* 84 (1965), 430–432.

Via, D. O., Jr, 'Parable and Example Story: A Literary-Structuralist Approach', *Semeia* 1 (1974), 105–133.

Via, D. O., Jr, 'A Response to Crossan, Funk, and Petersen', *Semeia* 1 (1974), 222–235.

Via, D. O., Jr, 'Religion and Story: Of Time and Reality', *Journal of Religion* 56 (1976), 392–399.

Waelkens, R., 'L'analyse structurale des paraboles. Deux essais: Luc 15, 1–32 et Matthieu 13, 44–46', *Revue Théologique de Louvain* 8 (1977), 160–178.

Wanner, W., *Werkbuch Gleichnisse. Praktische Bibelarbeit* (Giessen: Brunner-Verlag, 1977).

Weder, H., *Die Gleichnisse Jesu als Metaphern. Traditions- und redaktionsgeschichtliche Analysen und Interpretationen* (FRLANT 120; Göttingen: Vandenhoeck & Ruprecht, 1978).

Weiser, A., *Die Knechtsgleichnisse der synoptischen Evangelien* (Studien zum Alten und Neuen Testament 29; Munich: Kösel Verlag, 1971).

Weiser, A., 'Die Gleichnisse in der Verkündigung Jesu', *Bibel und Kirche* 33 (1978), 48–52.

Westermann, C., 'Die Vorgeschichte der Gleichnisse Jesu im Alten Testament' in *Erträge der Forschung am Alten Testament. Gesammelte Studien* III (ed. R. Albertz; Munich: Chr. Kaiser, 1984), pp. 185–197.

Westermann, C., *Vergleiche und Gleichnisse im Alten und Neuen Testament* (Calwer theologische Monographien A14; Stuttgart: Calwer-Verlag, 1984).

Weyers, K., *Von Perlen, Salz und einen falschen Schlips: Nachdenkliches zu Bildern der Bibel* (Berlin: Morus-Verlag, 1975).

Wierbse, W., 'Preaching from the Parables', *Moody Monthly* 78 (1977), 107–109.

Wilder, A. N., *Early Christian Rhetoric: The Language of the Gospel* (Cambridge, Mass.: Harvard University Press, 1971).

Wilder, A. N., *Jesus' Parables and the War of Myths* (Philadelphia: Fortress Press, 1981).

Williamson, R., 'Expressionist Art and the Parables of Jesus', *Theology* 78 (663; 1975), 474–481.

270   *The Parables of Jesus*

Wimmer, G., *Die grosse Überraschung. Für einen lebendigen Umgang mit den Gleichnissen Jesu* (Freiburg: Herder, 1982).
Wink, W., 'Letting Parables Live', *Christian Century* 97 (1980), 1062–1064.
Wittig, S., 'Meaning and Modes of Signification: Toward a Semiotic of the Parable' in *Semiology and Parables* (ed. D. Patte; Pittsburgh: Pickwick Press, 1976), pp. 319–374.

II. On particular parables

1. The parable of the seed growing secretly (Mk 4:26–29)

Ambrozic, A. M., *The Hidden Kingdom. A Redaction-Critical Study of the References to the Kingdom of God in Mark's Gospel* (Washington, D.C.: The Catholic Biblical Association of America, 1972), pp. 106–122.
Baltensweiler, H., 'Das Gleichnis von der selbstwachsenden Saat (Markus 4, 26–29) und die theologische Konzeption des Markusevangelisten' in *Oikonomia. Heilsgeschichte als Thema der Theologie. Festschrift O. Cullmann* (ed. F. Christ; Hamburg: H. Reich, 1967), pp. 69–75.
Carlston, C. E., *The Parables of the Triple Tradition* (Philadelphia: Fortress Press, 1975), pp. 202–210.
Crossan, J. D., 'The Seed Parables of Jesus', *Journal of Biblical Literature* 92 (1973), 244–266, especially 251–253.
Dahl, N., 'The Parables of Growth' in *Jesus in the Memory of the Early Church* (Minneapolis: Augsburg, 1976), pp. 141–166.
Dupont, J., 'La parabole de la semence qui pousse toute seule (Marc 4, 26–29)', *Recherches de Science Religieuse* 55 (1967), 367–392.
Dupont, J., 'Encore la parabole de la semence qui pousse toute seule (Mc 4, 26–29)' in *Jesus und Paulus. Festschrift für W. G. Kümmel zum 70. Geburtstag* (Göttingen: Vandenhoeck & Ruprecht, 1975), pp. 96–108.
Harder, G., 'Das Gleichnis von der selbstwachsenden Saat: Mark. 4, 26–29', *Theologia Viatorum* (1948–49), 51–70.
Kümmel, W. G., *Promise and Fulfilment. The Eschatological Message of Jesus* (Studies in Biblical Theology, first series 23: London: SCM Press, 1961), pp. 127–129.
Kümmel, W. G., 'Noch einmal: Das Gleichnis von der selbstwachsenden Saat. Bemerkungen zur neuesten Diskussion um die Auslegung der Gleichnisse Jesu' in *Orientierung an Jesus* (ed. P. Hoffmann; Freiburg: Herder, 1973), pp. 220–237.
Mussner, F., 'Gleichnisauslegung und Heilsgeschichte dargetan am Gleichnis von der selbstwachsenden Saat', *Trierer Theologische Zeitschrift* 64 (1955), 257–266.
Sahlin, H., 'Zum Verständnis von drei Stellen des Markus-Evangeliums (Mk 4:26–29; 7:18f.; 15:34)', *Biblica* 33 (1952), 53–66, especially 53–58.
Stuhlmann, R., 'Beobachtungen und Überlegungen zu Markus IV. 26–29', *New Testament Studies* 19 (1972–73), 153–162.

2. The parable of the mustard seed (Mk 4:30–32 and parallels)

Ambrozic, A. M., *The Hidden Kingdom* (Washington, D.C.: The Catholic Biblical Association of America, 1972), pp. 122–134.
Bartsch, H. W., 'Eine bisher übersehene Zitierung der LXX in Mk 4, 30', *Theologische Zeitschrift* 15 (1959), 126–128.

Bergmann, W., *Die Zehn Gleichnisse vom Reich der Himmel* (Lahr-Dinglingen: St. Johannis Druckerei, 1976), pp. 28–32.

Casalegno, A., 'La parabola del granello di senape', *Rivista Biblica* 26 (1978), 139–161.

Crossan, J. D., 'The Seed Parables of Jesus', *Journal of Biblical Literature* 92 (1973), 244–266, especially 253–259.

Didier, M., 'Les paraboles du grain de sénevé et du levain', *Revue Diocésaine de Namur* 15 (1961), 385–394.

Dupont, J., 'Les paraboles du sénevé et du levain', *Nouvelle Revue Théologique* 99 (1967), 897–913.

Dupont, J., 'Le couple parabolique du sénevé et du levain (Mt 13, 31–33; Lc 13, 18–21)' in *Jesus Christus in Historie und Theologie. Neutestamentliche Festschrift für H. Conzelmann* (ed. G. Strecker; Tübingen: J. C. B. Mohr, 1975), pp. 331–345.

Frankemölle, H., *In Gleichnissen Gott erfahren* (Stuttgart: Katholisches Bibelwerk, 1977), pp. 46–50.

Funk, R. W., 'The Looking-Glass Tree is for the Birds. Ezekiel 17:22–24; Mark 4:30–32', *Interpretation* 27 (1973), 3–9.

Granata, G., 'Some more information about mustard and the Gospel', *Bibbia e Oriente* 25 (1983), 105–106.

Hertzsch, K. P., 'Jésus herméneute: Une étude de Marc 4, 30–32', *Cahiers Bibliques* (May 1971, special issue), 117–125.

Klauck, H.-J., *Allegorie und Allegorese in Synoptischen Gleichnistexten* (Münster: Aschendorff, 1978), pp. 210–218.

Kuss, O., 'Zur Senfkornparabel' in *Auslegung und Verkündigung* I (Regensburg: Pustet Verlag, 1963), pp. 78–84.

Kuss, O., 'Zum Sinngehalt des Doppelgleichnisses vom Senfkorn und Sauerteig' in *Auslegung und Verkündigung* I (Regensburg: Pustet Verlag, 1963), pp. 85–97.

Laufen, R., '*Basileia* und *ekklēsia*: Eine traditions- und redaktionsgeschichtliche Untersuchung des Gleichnis vom Senfkorn' in *Begegnung mit dem Wort. Festschrift für H. Zimmermann* (ed. J. Zmijewski and E. Nellessen; Bonn: P. Hanstein, 1980), pp. 105–140.

McArthur, H. K., 'The Parable of the Mustard Seed', *Catholic Biblical Quarterly* 33 (1971), 198–210.

Schultze, B., 'Die ekklesiologische Bedeutung des Gleichnisses vom Senfkorn (Matth 13, 31–32; Mk 4, 30–32; Lk 13, 18–19)', *Orientalia Christiana Periodica* 27 (1961), 362–386.

Sproule, A., 'The Problem of the Mustard Seed', *Grace Theological Journal* 1 (1980), 37–42.

Weder, H., *Die Gleichnisse Jesu als Metaphern* (Göttingen: Vandenhoeck & Ruprecht, 1978), pp. 128–138.

Zingg, P., *Das Wachsen der Kirche* (Orbis Biblicus et Orientalis 3; Göttingen: Vandenhoeck & Ruprecht, 1974), pp. 100–115.

3. The parable of the weeds and its interpretation (Mt 13:24–30, 36–43)

Bacq, P., 'Reading a Parable: The Good Wheat and the Tares (Mt 13)', *Lumen Vitae* 39 (1984), 181–194.

Bergmann, *Die Zehn Gleichnisse vom Reich der Himmel* (Lahr-Dinglingen: St. Johannis Druckerei, 1976), pp. 19–27.

Catchpole, D. R., 'John the Baptist, Jesus and the Parable of the Tares', *Scottish Journal of Theology* 31 (1978), 557–570.

Corell, J., 'La parábola de la cizaña y su explicación', *Escritos del Vedat* 2 (1972), 3–51.

Crossan, J. D., 'The Seed Parables of Jesus', *Journal of Biblical Literature* 92 (1973), 244–266, especially 259–261.

Doty, W. G., 'An Interpretation: Parable of the Weeds and Wheat', *Interpretation* 25 (1971), 185–193.

Ellena, D., 'Thematische Analyse der Wachstumsgleichnisse', *Linguistica Biblica* 23–24 (1973), 48–62.

Goedt, M. de, 'L'explication de la parabole de l'ivraie (Mt XIII, 36–43)', *Revue Biblique* 66 (1959), 32–54.

Jeremias, J., 'Die Deutung des Gleichnisses vom Unkraut unter dem Weizen (Mt XIII, 36–43)' in *Neotestamentica et Patristica. Festschrift für Oscar Cullmann* (Leiden: E. J. Brill, 1962), pp. 59–63.

Kevers, P., 'De gelijkenis van het onkruid tussen de tarwe (Mt. 13,24–30. 36–43)' in *Parabels Meerstemmig* (Antwerp: Patmos, 1980), pp. 116–121.

Kiehl, E. H., 'Jesus Taught in Parables', *Concordia Journal* 7 (1981), 221–228.

Kingsbury, J. D., *The Parables of Jesus in Matthew 13* (London: SPCK/Richmond, Va.: John Knox Press, 1969), pp. 63–76, 93–110.

Klauck, H.-J., *Allegorie und Allegorese in Synoptischen Gleichnistexten* (Münster: Aschendorff, 1978), pp. 207–208, 226–227.

Künzel, G., *Studien zum Gemeindeverständnis des Matthäus-Evangeliums* (Stuttgart: Calwer Verlag, 1978), pp. 125–134.

Lange, J., *Das Erscheinen des Auferstandenen im Evangelium nach Matthäus* (Forschung zur Bibel 11; Würzburg: Echter Verlag, 1973), pp. 181–187.

Marguerat, D., 'L'Eglise et le monde en Matthieu 13: 36–43', *Revue de Théologie et Philosophie* 28 (1978), 111–129.

Marguerat, D., 'Church and World in Mt 13:36–43', *Theology Digest* 27 (1979), 158–160.

Pregeant, R., 'The Explanation of the Parable of the Tares: Matt 13:36–43' in *Christology Beyond Dogma. Matthew's Christ in Process Hermeneutic* (Philadelphia: Fortress Press, 1978), pp. 107–113.

Weder, H., *Die Gleichnisse Jesu als Metaphern* (Göttingen: Vandenhoeck & Ruprecht, 1978), pp. 120–128.

Zumstein, J., *La Condition du Croyant dans l'Évangile selon Matthieu* (Orbis Biblicus et Orientalis 16; Göttingen: Vandenhoeck & Ruprecht, 1977), pp. 187–195.

4. The parable of the good Samaritan (Lk 10:25–37)

Bailey, K. E., *Poet and Peasant. A Literary-Cultural Approach to the Parables of Luke* (Grand Rapids: Eerdmans, 1976), pp. 72–74.

Bailey, K. E., *Through Peasant Eyes* (Grand Rapids: Eerdmans, 1980), pp. 33–54.

Bartsch, H. W., *Wachet aber zu jeder Zeit. Entwurf einer Auslegung des Lukasevangeliums* (Hamburg-Bergstedt: H. Reich, 1963), pp. 96–100.

Binder, H., 'Das Gleichnis vom barmherziger Samariter', *Theologische Zeitschrift* 15 (1959), 176–194.

Biser, E., 'Wer ist meiner Nächster?', *Geist und Leben* 48 (1975), 406–414.

Bishop, E. F., 'Down from Jerusalem to Jericho', *Evangelical Quarterly* 35 (1963), 97–102.

Bishop, E. F., 'People on the Road to Jericho: The Good Samaritan – and the Others', *Evangelical Quarterly* 42 (1970), 2–6.

Borsch, F. H., *Power in Weakness. New Hearing for Gospel Stories of Healing and Discipleship* (Philadelphia: Fortress Press, 1983).

Busse, U., *et al.*, *Jesus zwischen arm und reich. Lukas-evangelium* (Bibelauslegung für die Praxis 18; Stuttgart: Katholisches Bibelwerk, 1980), pp. 73–80.

Clucas, R. S., 'The Neighbor Questions', *Theologia Evangelica* 17 (2; 1984), 49–50.

Cranfield, C. E. B., 'The Good Samaritan', *Theology Today* 11 (1954), 368–372.

Crespy, G., 'The Parable of the Good Samaritan: An Essay in Structural Research', *Semeia* 2 (1974), 27–50.

Crossan, J. D., 'Parable and Example in the Teaching of Jesus', *New Testament Studies* 18 (1971–72), 285–307, especially 285–296.

Crossan, J. D., 'Structuralist Analysis and the Parables of Jesus', *Linguistica Biblica* 29–30 (1973), 41–51.

Crossan, J. D., 'The Good Samaritan: Towards a Generic Definition of Parable', *Semeia* 2 (1974), 82–112.

Daniel, C., 'Les Esséniens et l'arrière-fond historique de la parabole du Bon Samaritain', *Novum Testamentum* 11 (1969), 71–104.

Daniélou, J., 'Le Bon Samaritain' in *Mélanges bibliques rédigés en l'honneur de André Robert* (Paris: Bloud & Gay, 1967), pp. 457–465.

Derrett, J. D. M., 'Law in the New Testament: Fresh Light on the Parable of the Good Samaritan', *New Testament Studies* 11 (1964–65), 23–27.

Diezinger, W., 'Zum Liebesgebot Mk XII, 28–34 und Parr.', *Novum Testamentum* 20 (1978), 81–83.

Egelkraut, H. L., *Jesus' Mission to Jerusalem. A Redaction-Critical Study of the Travel Narrative in the Gospel of Luke, Lk 9:51 – 19:48* (Frankfurt am Main: P. Lang, 1976), pp. 83–90.

Eichholz, G., *Jesus Christus und der Nächste. Eine Auslegung des Gleichnisses vom Barmherziger Samariter* (Neukirchen: Buchhandlung des Erziehungsvereins, 1955).

Entrevernes Group, '"Go and Do Likewise". Narrative and Dialogue (Luke 10:25–34)' in *Signs and Parables. Semiotics and Gospel Texts* (Pittsburgh: Pickwick Press, 1978), pp. 13–64.

Ernst, J., 'Die Einheit von Gottes- und Nächsteliebe in der Verkündigung Jesu', *Theologie und Glaube* 1 (1970), 3–14.

Eulenstein, R., '"Und wer ist mein Nächster?" Lk 10, 25–37 in der Sicht eines klassischen Philologen', *Theologie und Glaube* 7 (1977), 127–145.

Feuillet, A., 'Le Bon Samaritain (Luc 10, 25–37). Sa signification christologique et l'universalisme de Jésus', *Esprit et Vie* 90 (1980), 337–351, 369–382.

Frankemölle, H., *In Gleichnissen Gott erfahren* (Stuttgart: Katholisches Bibelwerk, 1977), pp. 93–99.

Fuchs, E., 'Was heisst: "Du sollst deiner Nächsten lieben wie dich selbst?"' in *Zur Frage nach dem historischen Jesus* (Tübingen: J. C. B. Mohr, 1960), pp. 1–20.

Fuchs, E., 'Gott und Mensch im Text und als Text', *Zeitschrift für Theologie und Kirche* 67 (1970), 321–334.

Funk, R. W., 'How Do You Read? A Sermon on Luke 10:25–37', *Interpretation* 18 (1964), 25–37.

Funk, R. W., 'The Old Testament in Parable. A Study of Luke 10:25–37', *Encounter* 26 (1965), 251–267.

Funk, R. W., *Language, Hermeneutic, and the Word of God* (New York/London: Harper and Row, 1966), pp. 199–222.

Funk, R. W., 'The Good Samaritan as Metaphor', *Semeia* 2 (1974), 74–81.

Funk, R. W., 'Parable, Paradox, and Power: The Prodigal Samaritan' in *Parables and Presence* (Philadelphia: Fortress Press, 1982), pp. 55–65.

Furness, J. M., 'Fresh Light on Luke 10:25–37', *Expository Times* 80 (1969), 182.

Furnish, V. P., *The Love Command in the New Testament* (Nashville: Abingdon Press, 1972/London: SCM Press, 1974), pp. 34–45.

Gerhardsson, B., *The Good Samaritan—the Good Shepherd?* (Coniectanea Neotestamentica XVI; Lund: Gleerup, 1958).

Gewalt, D., 'Der "Barmherzige Samariter". Zu Lukas 10, 25–37', *Evangelische Theologie* 38 (1978), 403–417.

Glen, J. S., *The Parables of Conflict in Luke* (Philadelphia: The Westminster Press, 1962), pp. 40–53.

Gollwitzer, H., *Das Gleichnis vom barmherziger Samariter* (Neukirchen: Neukirchener Verlag, 1962).

Hermann, I., 'Wem ich der Nächste bin. Auslegung von Lk 10, 25–37', *Bibel und Leben* 2 (1961), 17–24.

Heuschen, J., 'De parabel van de barmhartige Samaritaan', *Revue Ecclésiastique de Liége* 46 (1959), 153–164.

Heyer, H., *Denket um. Überlegungen zu Worten und Gleichnissen Jesu* (Munich: Don Bosco Verlag, 1970), pp. 40–46.

Hultgren, A. J., 'The Double Commandment of Love in Mt 22:34–40. Its Sources and Composition', *Catholic Biblical Quarterly* 36 (1974), 373–378.

Hultgren, A. J., *Jesus and His Adversaries. The Form and Function of the Conflict Stories in the Synoptic Tradition* (Minneapolis: Augsburg Publishing House, 1979), pp. 47–50.

Jens, W. (ed.), *Der barmherzige Samariter* (Stuttgart: Kreuz, 1973).

Jones, P. R., 'The Love Command in Parable. Luke 10:25–37', *Perspectives in Religious Studies* 6 (1979), 224–242.

Kahlefeld, H., '"Wer ist mein Nächster?" Das Lehrstuck vom barmherziger Samariter und die heutige Situation', *Bibel und Kirche* 24 (1969), 74–77.

Kieffer, R., 'Analyse sémiotique et commentaire. Quelques réflexions à propos d'études de Luc 10.25–37', *New Testament Studies* 25 (1978–79), 454–468.

Klemm, H. G., 'Schillers ethisch-aesthetische Variationen zum Thema Lk 10, 30 ff.', *Kerygma und Dogma* 17 (1971), 127–140.

Klemm, H. G., *Das Gleichnis vom barmherzigen Samariter. Grundzüge der*

Auslegung im 16/17. Jahrhundert (BWANT 103; Stuttgart: Kohlhammer, 1973).

Lambrecht, J., 'De Barmhartige Samaritaan (Lk 10. 25–37)', *Ons Geestelijk Leven* 51 (1974), 91–105.

Lambrecht, J., 'The Message of the Good Samaritan (Lk 10:25–37)', *Louvain Studies* 5 (1974), 121–135.

Lambrecht, J., *The Parables of Jesus. Insight and Challenge* (Bangalore: Theological Publications in India, 1978), pp. 93–130.

Linskens, J., *The Great Commandment* (San Antonio, Texas: MACC, 1974), pp. 14–22.

Manek, J., . . . *Und brachte Frucht. Die Gleichnisse Jesu* (Stuttgart: Calwer-Verlag, 1977), pp. 82–90.

Mattill, A. J., 'The Good Samaritan and the Purpose of Luke-Acts: Halevy Reconsidered', *Encounter* 33 (1972), 359–376.

Mattill, A. J., 'The Anonymous Victim (Luke 10:25–37). A new look at the Story of the Good Samaritan', *Unitarian Universalist Christian* 34 (1979), 38–54.

Mayers, M. K., 'The Filipino Samaritan: a Parable of Responsible Cross-Cultural Behaviour', *Missiology* 6 (October 1978), 463–466.

Merklein, W., *Die Gottesherrschaft als Handlungsprinzip* (Forschung zur Bibel 34; Würzburg: Echter Verlag, 1978), pp. 250–253.

Monselewski, W., *Der barmherziger Samariter. Eine auslegungsgeschichtliche Untersuchung zu Lukas 10, 24–37* (Tübingen: J. C. B. Mohr, 1967).

Montefiore, H., 'Thou Shalt Love thy Neighbour as Thyself', *Novum Testamentum* 5 (1962), 157–170.

Mussner, F., 'Der Begriff des "Nächsten" in der Verkündigung Jesu. Dargelegt am Gleichnis vom barmherziger Samariter' in *Praesentia Salutis* (Düsseldorf: Patmos Verlag, 1967), pp. 125–132.

Naastepad, T. J. M., *Acht gelijkenissen uit Mattheus en Lukas* (Kampen: J. H. Kok, n.d.), pp. 68–87.

Patte, D., 'An Analysis of Narrative Structure and the Good Samaritan', *Semeia* 2 (1974), 1–26.

Patte, D., 'Structural Network in Narrative: The Good Samaritan', *Soundings* 58 (1975), 221–242.

Patte, D., *What is Structural Exegesis?* (Guides to Biblical Scholarship; Philadelphia: Fortress Press, 1976), pp. 76–83.

Perpich, S. W., *A Hermeneutic Critique of Structuralist Exegesis, with Specific Reference to Lk 10:29–37* (Lanham, Md.: University Press of America, 1984).

Perrin, N., *Jesus and the Language of the Kingdom* (Philadelphia: Fortress Press/London: SCM Press, 1976), *passim*.

Pilgrim, W. E., *Good News to the Poor. Wealth and Poverty in Luke-Acts* (Minneapolis: Augsburg Publishing House, 1981), pp. 141–143.

Piper, J., 'Is Self-Love Biblical?', *Christianity Today* 21 (1977), 1150–1153.

Ramaroson, L., 'Comme "Le Bon Samaritain" ne chercher qu'à aimer (Lc 10, 29–37)', *Biblica* 56 (1975), 533–536.

Reicke, B., 'Der barmherzige Samariter' in *Verborum Veritas. Festschrift für G. Stählin zum 70. Geburtstag* (ed. O. Böcher and H. Haacker; Wuppertal: Theologische Verlag R. Brockhaus, 1970), pp. 103–109.

Royse, J. R., 'A Philonic Use of *pandocheion* (Luke X. 34)', *Novum Testamentum* 23 (1981), 193–194.

Sellin, G., 'Lukas als Gleichniserzähler: Die Erzählung vom barmherziger Samariter (Lk 10: 25–37)', *Zeitschrift für die neutestamentliche Wissenschaft* 65 (1974), 166–198; 66 (1975), 19–60.

Sellin, G., 'Luke as Parable Narrator', *Theology Digest* 25 (1977), 53–60.

Seven, F., 'Hermeneutische Erwägungen zur poetischen Realisation eines neutestamentlichen Textes', *Linguistica Biblica* 29–30 (1973), 52–55.

Soares Prabhu, G. M., 'The Synoptic Love-Commandment: The Dimensions of Love in the Teaching of Jesus', *Jeevadhara* 13 (74; 1983), 85–103.

Spencer, F. S., '2 Chronicles 28:5–15 and the Parable of the Good Samaritan', *Westminster Theological Journal* 46 (1984), 317–349.

Spicq, C., 'The Charity of the Good Samaritan. Lk 10:25–37', *The Bible Today* no. 6 (April 1963), 361–366.

Stein, R. H., 'The Interpretation of the Parable of the Good Samaritan' in *Scripture, Tradition, and Interpretation. Essays presented to E. F. Harrison by his Students and Colleagues in Honor of his Seventy-fifth Birthday* (Grand Rapids: Eerdmans, 1977), pp. 278–295.

Stockum, T. C., 'Vijf variaties op een thema: Schiller en de gelijkenis van de barmhartige Samaritaan', *Nederlands Theologisch Tijdschrift* 17 (1963), 338–347.

Suzuki, S., 'Verantwortung für den andern: Lk 10,25–37 bei Bultmann, Barth, Bonhoeffer und K. Tagawa', *Die Zeichen der Zeit* 30 (1976), 331–338.

Sweetland, D. M., 'The Good Samaritan and Martha and Mary', *The Bible Today* 21 (5; September 1983), 325–330.

Ternant, P., 'Le bon Samaritain', *Assemblées du Seigneur* 46 (1974), 66–77.

Thomas, K. J., 'Liturgical Citations in the Synoptics', *New Testament Studies* 22 (1975–76), 205–214, especially 209–212.

Trudinger, L. P., 'Once Again, Now, "Who is my Neighbor?"', *Evangelical Quarterly* 48 (1976), 160–163.

Uleyn, A., 'Exegese en psychoanalyse. Een psychoanalytische lezing van de parabel van de barmhartige Samaritaan', *Collationes* 10 (1980), 405–423.

Via, D. O., Jr, 'Parable and Example Story. A Literary-Structuralist Approach', *Semeia* 1 (1974), 105–133.

Wink, W., 'The Parable of the Compassionate Samaritan: A Communal Exegesis Approach', *Review and Expositor* 76 (1979), 199–217.

Young, N. H., 'Once Again, Now, "Who is my Neighbor?" A Comment', *Evangelical Quarterly* 49 (1977), 178–179.

Young, N. H., 'The Commandment to Love Your Neighbor as Yourself and the Parable of the Good Samaritan (Luke 10:25–37)', *Andrews University Seminary Studies* 21 (1983), 265–272.

Zimmermann, H., 'Das Gleichnis vom barmherzigen Samariter: Lk 10, 25–37' in *Die Zeit Jesu. Festschrift für H. Schlier* (ed. G. Bornkamm and K. Rahner; Freiburg: Herder, 1970), pp. 58–59.

5. The parable of the rich fool (Lk 12:13–21)
Birdsall, J. N., 'Luke XII, 16ff. and the Gospel of Thomas', *Journal of Theological Studies* 13 (1962), 332–336.

Busse, U., *et al.*, *Jesus zwischen arm und reich. Lukas-evangelium* (Bibelauslegung für die Praxis 18; Stuttgart: Katholisches Bibelwerk, 1980), pp. 85–88.

Crossan, J. D., 'Parable and Example in the Teaching of Jesus', *New Testament Studies* 18 (1971–72), 285–307, especially 296–297.

Degenhardt, H.-J., *Lukas – Evangelist der Armen* (Stuttgart: Katholisches Bibelwerk, 1965), pp. 69–80.

Derrett, J. D. M., 'The Rich Fool: A Parable of Jesus Concerning Inheritance', *Heythrop Journal* 18 (1977), 131–151.

Dupont, J., *Les Béatitudes*, III: *Les Évangélistes* (Paris: J. Gabalda, 1973), pp. 113–118, 183–185.

Dupont, J., 'Die individuelle Eschatologie im Lukas-Evangelium und in der Apostelgeschichte' in *Orientierung an Jesus. Zur Theologie der Synoptiker. Für Josef Schmid* (ed. P. Hoffmann; Freiburg: Herder, 1973), pp. 37–47, especially 38–41.

Eibach, U., 'Jesus und die Güter dieser Erde! – Oder "Von der Pflicht eines biblischen Exegeten!" Einige Anfragen zu einer höchst bedenklichen Art, biblische Exegese zu "verwerten"', *Theologische Beiträge* 6 (1975), 27–30.

Elliott, W. M., Jr, 'The Man Was a Fool!', *Presbyterian Journal* 36 (23 November 1977), 7–8.

Gaide, G., 'Le riche insensé (Lc 12, 13–21)', *Assemblées du Seigneur* 49 (1971), 82–89.

Glen, J. S., *The Parables of Conflict in Luke* (Philadelphia: The Westminster Press, 1962), pp. 77–87.

Johnson, L. T., *The Literary Form of Possessions in Luke-Acts* (Missoula, Mont.: Scholars Press, 1977), pp. 153–154.

Lüthi, W., *Einer aus dem Volk: Predigt über Lukas 12, 13–21, gehalten im Berner Münster* (Basel: F. Reinhardt, 1976).

Magass, W., 'Zur Semiotik der Hausfrommigkeit (Lk 12, 16–21). Die Beispielerzählung vom reicher Kornbauer', *Linguistica Biblica* 4 (1971), 2–5.

Maier, G., 'Verteilt Jesus die Güter dieser Erde? Eine Untersuchung zu Luk. 12, 13–15', *Theologische Beiträge* 5 (1974), 149–158.

Mealand, D. L., *Poverty and Expectation in the Gospels* (London: SPCK, 1980), pp. 52–53.

Mees, M., 'Das Sprichwort Mt 6, 21/Lk 12, 21 und seine ausserkanonischen Parallelen', *Augustinianum* 14 (1974), 67–90.

O'Brien, I., 'Three Parables: The Rich Fool, the Barren Fig Tree, the Great Supper', *Friar* 21 (June 1964), 47–53.

Pilgrim, W. E., *Good News to the Poor. Wealth and Poverty in Luke-Acts* (Minneapolis: Augsburg Publishing House, 1981), pp. 109–113.

Schottroff, L., and Stegemann, W., *Jesus von Nazareth – Hoffnung der Armen* (Stuttgart: Kohlhammer, 1978), pp. 125–127.

Seccombe, D. P., *Possessions and the Poor in Luke-Acts* (Linz: SNTU, 1983), pp. 139–145.

Selms, A. van, '"Zeg tot mijn broeder, dat hij de erfenis met mij dele." Een Oudtestamentische exegese van Lc 12:13', *Kerk en Theologie* 27 (1976), 18–23.

Seng, E. W., 'Der reiche Tor: Eine Untersuchung von Lk XII. 16–21 unter besonderer Berücksichtigung form- und motivgeschichtlicher Aspekte', *Novum Testamentum* 20 (1978), 136–155.
Weisskopf, R., 'Lächeln reicht nicht', *Theologische Beiträge* 6 (1975), 23–27.

6. The parable of the great supper/wedding feast (Lk 14:15–24; Mt 22:1–14)

Adaszek, M., *'Ecce prandium meum paravi, venite ad nuptias' (Mt 22:1–14). I temi teologici spirituali e catechetici de Convito escatologico (Domenica 28ª 'per annum' Ciclo A)* (Collectio Urbaniana 3249; Rome: Pontificia Universitas Urbaniana, 1983).
Bailey, K. E., *Through Peasant Eyes* (Grand Rapids: Eerdmans, 1980), pp. 88–113.
Ballard, P. H., 'Reasons for Refusing the Great Supper', *Journal of Theological Studies* 23 (1972), 341–350.
Bergmann, W., *Die Zehn Gleichnisse vom Reich der Himmel* (Lahr-Dinglingen: St. Johannis Druckerei, 1976), pp. 77–87.
Bultmann, R., 'Lukas 14, 16–24' in *Marburger Predigten* (Tübingen: J. C. B. Mohr, 1956), pp. 126–136.
Crossan, J. D., *Four Other Gospels. Shadows on the Contours of Canon* (A Seabury Book; Minneapolis: Winston Press, 1985), pp. 39–52.
Derrett, J. D. M., 'The Parable of the Great Supper' in *Law in the New Testament* (London: Darton, Longman and Todd, 1970), pp. 126–155.
Dormeyer, D., 'Literarische und theologische Analyse der Parabel Lukas 14, 15–24', *Bibel und Leben* 15 (1974), 206–219.
Dupont, J., *Les Béatitudes*, II: *La Bonne Nouvelle* (Paris: J. Gabalda, 1969), pp. 259–276.
Dupont, J. (ed.), *La parabola degli invitati al banchetto. Dagli evangelisti a Gesù* (Teste e recerche di Scienze religiose 14; Brescia: Paideia, 1978).
Eichholz, G., 'Von grosses Abendmahl (Luk 14, 16–24) und von der königlichen Hochzeit (Matth 22, 1–14)' in *Gleichnisse der Evangelien. Form, Überlieferung, Auslegung* (Neukirchen: Neukirchener Verlag, 1971), pp. 126–147.
Ernst, J., 'Gastmahlgespräche: Lk 14:1–24' in *Die Kirche des Anfangs* (ed. R. Schnackenburg; Leipzig: St. Benno Verlag, 1977), pp. 57–78.
Fabris, R., 'La parabola degli invitati alle cena. Analisi redazionale di Lc 14,16–21' in *La parabola degli invitati al banchetto* (ed. J. Dupont; Brescia: Paideia, 1978), pp. 127–166.
Frankemölle, H., *In Gleichnissen Gott erfahren* (Stuttgart: Katholisches Bibelwerk, 1977), pp. 69–74, 130–133.
Fuchs, E., 'Trace de Dieu: la parabole', *Bulletin du Centre Protestant d'Études* 25 (1973), 19–39.
Funk, R. W., *Language, Hermeneutic, and the Word of God* (New York/London: Harper and Row, 1966), pp. 163–198.
Gaeta, G., 'Invitati e commensali al banchetto eschatologico. Analisi letteraria della parabola di Luca (14,16–24)' in *La parabola degli invitati al banchetto* (ed. J. Dupont; Brescia: Paideia, 1978), pp. 103–125.
Haacker, K., 'Das hochzeitliche Kleid von Mt 22, 11–13 und ein

palästinisches Märchen', *Zeitschrift des Deutschen Palästina-Vereins* 87 (1971), 95–97.

Haenchen, E., 'Das Gleichnis vom grosses Mahl' in *Die Bibel und Wir. Gesammelte Aufsätze* II (Tübingen: J. C. B. Mohr, 1968), pp. 135–155.

Hahn, F., 'Das Gleichnis von der Einladung zum Festmahl' in *Verborum Veritas. Festschrift für G. Stählin zum 70. Geburtstag* (ed. O. Böcher and K. Haacker; Wuppertal: R. Brockhaus, 1970), pp. 51–82.

Hasler, V., 'Die königliche Hochzeit, Matth 22, 1–14', *Theologische Zeitschrift* 18 (1962), 25–35.

Heyer, H., *Denket um. Überlegungen zu Worten und Gleichnissen Jesu* (Munich: Don Bosco Verlag, 1970), pp. 24–28.

Johnson, L. T., *The Literary Function of Possessions in Luke-Acts* (Missoula, Mont.: Scholars Press, 1977), pp. 146–147.

Linnemann, E., 'Überlegungen zur Parabel vom grosses Abendmahl (Lc. 14, 15–24; Mt 22, 1–14)', *Zeitschrift für die neutestamentliche Wissenschaft* 51 (1960), 246–255.

Matura, T., 'Les invités à la noce régale. Mt 22, 1–14', *Assemblées du Seigneur* 59 (1974), 16–27.

Meyer, P. D., 'The Gentile Mission in Q', *Journal of Biblical Literature* 89 (1970), 405–417, especially 412–415.

Musurillo, H. A., 'Many are called, but few are chosen', *Theological Studies* 7 (1946), 583–589.

Navone, J., 'The Parable of the Banquet', *The Bible Today* 1 (1964), 923–929.

Nirwood, F. A., 'Compel them to come in. The history of Lk 14,23', *Religion in Life* 23 (1954), 516–527.

Ogawa, A., 'Paraboles de l'Israël véritable? Réconsidération de Mt XXI, 28 – XXII, 14', *Novum Testamentum* 21 (1979), 121–149, especially 130–149.

Palmer, H., 'Just Married, Cannot Come', *Novum Testamentum* 18 (1976), 241–257.

Pilgrim, W. E., *Good News to the Poor. Wealth and Poverty in Luke-Acts* (Minneapolis: Augsburg Publishing House, 1981), pp. 73–74.

Pousset, E., 'Les invités du banquet (Luc 14,15–24)', *Christus* 32 (125; 1985), 81–89.

Radl, W., 'Zur Struktur der eschatologischen Gleichnisse Jesu', *Trierer Theologische Zeitschrift* 92 (1983), 122–133.

Rengstorf, K. H., 'Die Stadt der Mörder (Mt 22, 7)' in *Judentum—Urchristentum—Kirche. Festschrift für J. Jeremias* (ed. W. Eltester; BZNW; Berlin: Töpelmann, 1960), pp. 106–129.

Sanders, J. A., 'The Ethic of Election in Luke's Great Banquet Parable' in *Essays in Old Testament Ethics. J. P. Hyatt in Memoriam* (ed. J. L. Crenshaw and J. T. Willis; New York: Ktav, 1974), 245–271.

Schlier, H., 'Der Ruf Gottes. Eine biblische Besinnung zum Gleichnis von königlichen Hochzeitmahl', *Geist und Leben* 28 (1955), 241–247.

Schottroff, L., and Stegemann, W., *Jesus von Nazareth – Hoffnung der Armen* (Stuttgart: Kohlhammer, 1978), pp. 128–133.

Swaeles, R., 'L'orientation ecclésiastique de la parabole du Festin Nuptial en

Mt. XXII, 1–14', *Ephemerides Theologicae Lovanienses* 36 (1960), 655–684.

Swaeles, R., 'La parabole des invités qui se dérobent', *Assemblées du Seigneur* 55 (1962), 32–50.

Thevissen, G., 'Gereed voor het bruiloftsmaal. Bezinning op Mt 22, 1–13', *Getuigenis* 7 (1962–63), 273–279.

Tilborg, S. van, *The Jewish Leaders in Matthew* (Leiden: E. J. Brill, 1972), pp. 58–63.

Trilling, W., 'Zur Überlieferungsgeschichte des Gleichnisses von Hochzeits-mahl. Mt 22, 1–14', *Biblische Zeitschrift* N.F. 4 (1960), 251–265.

Via, D. O., Jr, 'The Relationship of Form to Content in the Parables: the Wedding Feast', *Interpretation* 25 (1971), 171–184.

Via, D. O., Jr, *The Parables. Their Literary and Existential Dimension* (Philadelphia: Fortress Press, 1974), pp. 128–132.

Vögtle, A., 'Die Einladung zum grossen Gastmahl und zum Königlichen Hochzeitsmahl. Ein Paradigma für den Wandel des geschichtlichen Verständnishorizonts' in *Das Evangelium und die Evangelien. Beiträge zur Evangelienforschung* (Düsseldorf: Patmos, 1971), pp. 171–218.

Weder, H., *Die Gleichnisse Jesu als Metaphern* (Göttingen: Vandenhoeck & Ruprecht, 1978), pp. 177–193.

Weiser, A., *Die Knechtgleichnisse der synoptischen Evangelien* (Munich: Kösel Verlag, 1971), pp. 58–71.

7. The three parables of Luke 15

Adell, A. V., 'Nietzsche and a Man with Two Sons', *Religion in Life* 45 (1976), 499–504.

Alonzo Diaz, J., 'Paralelos entre la narración del libro de Jonás y la parábola del hijo pródigo', *Biblica* 40 (1959), 632–640.

Arai, S., 'Das Gleichnis vom verlorenen Schaf – Eine traditionsgeschicht-liche Untersuchung', *Annual of the Japanese Biblical Institute* 2 (1976), 11–137.

Aus, R. D., 'Luke 15:11–32 and R. Eliezer ben Hyrcanus' Rise to Fame', *Journal of Biblical Literature* 104 (1985), 443–469.

Bailey, K. E., *The Cross and the Prodigal* (St Louis: Concordia Publishing House, 1973).

Bailey, K. E., *Poet and Peasant. A Literary-Cultural Approach to the Parables in Luke* (Grand Rapids: Eerdmans, 1976), pp. 142–216.

Bartolomé, J. J., 'Comer en común. Una costumbre típica de Jesús y su propio comentario (Lc 15)', *Salesianum* 44 (1982), 669–712.

Bartolomé, J. J., '*Synesthiein* en la obra lucana: Lc 15,2; Hch 10,41; 11,3. A propósito de una tesis sobre la esencia del Cristianísmo', *Salesianum* 46 (1984), 269–288.

Beirnaert, L., 'The Parable of the Prodigal Son (Lk 15:11–32) Read by an Analyst' in *Exegesis* . . . (ed. F. Bovon and G. Rouiller; Pittsburgh: Pickwick Press, 1978), pp. 197–210.

Bethge, E., 'Grenzüberschreitung: Eine Paraphrase zu Lukas 15, 11–32', *Reformatio* 25 (1976), 68–74.

Bishop, E. F., 'The Parable of the Lost or Wandering Sheep. Matthew 18, 10–14; Luke 15,3–7', *Anglican Theological Review* 44 (1962), 44–57.

Blinzler, J., 'Gottes Freude über die Umkehr des Sünder: Lk 15, 11–32', *Bibel und Liturgie* 37 (1963–64), 21–28.

Bonnard, P., 'Approche historico-critique de Luc 15', *Cahiers bibliques 'Foi et vie'* 12 (1973), 25–37.

Bonnard, P., 'La parabole du père et des deux fils. Lc 15,11–32. Écriture et prédication 26', *Études Théologiques et Religieuses* 53 (1980), 77–85.

Bovon, F., and Rouiller, G. (eds), *Exegesis. Problems of Method and Exercises in Reading (Genesis 22 and Lk 15)* (Pittsburgh: Pickwick Press, 1978).

Braumann, G., 'Tot—lebendig, verloren—gefunden' in *Wort in der Zeit. Neutestamentliche Studien. Festgabe für K. H. Rengstorf* (ed. W. Haubeck; Leiden: E. J. Brill, 1980), pp. 156–164.

Broer, I., 'Das Gleichnis vom verlorenen Sohn und die Theologie des Lukas', *New Testament Studies* 20 (1973–74), 453–462.

Bussby, F., 'Did a Shepherd Leave Sheep upon the Mountains or in the Desert? A Note on Matthew 18,12 and Luke 15,4', *Anglican Theological Review* 45 (1963), 93–94.

Busse, U., *et al.*, *Jesus zwischen arm und reich. Lukas-evangelium* (Bibelauslegung für die Praxis 18; Stuttgart: Katholisches Bibelwerk, 1980), pp. 105–124.

Carlston, C. E., 'Reminiscence and Redaction in Luke 15:11–32', *Journal of Biblical Literature* 94 (1975), 368–390.

Crawford, R. G., 'A Parable of Atonement', *Evangelical Quarterly* 50 (1978), 2–7.

Crespy, G., 'Psychoanalyse et foi' in *Essais sur la situation actuelle de la foi* (Paris: Éditions du Cerf, 1970), pp. 41–56.

Cromphout, F., 'Een man had twee zonen' in *God is een verhaal. Over de taal van het geloven* (Tielt: Lannoo, 1975), pp. 39–45.

Crossan, J. D., 'A Metamodel for Polyvalent Narration', *Semeia* 9 (1977), 105–147.

Derrett, J. D. M., 'Law in the New Testament: The Parable of the Prodigal Son', *New Testament Studies* 14 (1967–68), 56–74.

Derrett, J. D. M., 'The Parable of the Prodigal Son', *Studia Patristica* 10 (1970), 219–224.

Derrett, J. D. M., 'Fresh Light on the Lost Sheep and the Lost Coin', *New Testament Studies* 26 (1979–80), 36–60.

Drury, J., *Tradition and Design in Luke's Gospel* (Atlanta: John Knox Press/London: Darton, Longman and Todd, 1976), pp. 75–77.

Du, J. le, *Le fils prodigue ou les chances de la transgression* (Série Évangile 1; Paris: Centre Documentation Recherche, 1977).

Du, J. le, *et al.*, *Wie is eigenlijk de verloren zoon? Dieptepsychologische lezing en exegetische studie van Lucas 15, 11–32* (Antwerp: Patmos, 1977).

Dumais, M., 'Approche historico-critique d'un texte: la parabole du père et de ses deux fils (Luc 15,11–32)', *Science et Esprit* 33 (1981), 191–214.

Dupont, J., 'La parabole de la brebis perdue (Matthieu 18, 12–14; Luc 15, 4–7)', *Gregorianum* 49 (1968), 265–287.

282   *The Parables of Jesus*

Dupont, J., 'Le Fils prodigue: Lk 15, 1–3, 11–32', *Assemblées du Seigneur* 17 (1970), 64–72.

Dupont, J., 'Réjouissez-vous avec moi! Lc 15, 1–32', *Assemblées du Seigneur* 55 (1974), 70–79.

Dupont, J., 'Les implications christologiques de la parabole de la brebis perdue' in *Jésus aux origines de la Christologie* (ed. J. Dupont; Louvain: Leuven University Press, 1975), pp. 331–350.

Eldernbosch, P. A., 'Het verhaal van de vader en de twee zonen (Lucas 15)', *Rond de Tafel* 35 (1980), 163–167.

Entrevernes Group, '"We must make merry. . ." Controversy and Parallels (Luke 15)', in *Signs and Parables, Semiotics and Gospel Texts* (Pittsburgh: Pickwick Press, 1978), pp. 117–183.

Faley, R. J., 'There was once a man who had two sons', *The Bible Today* no. 18 (April 1965), 1181–1186.

Focant, E., 'La parabole de la brebis perdue. Lecture historico-critique et réflexions théologiques', *La Foi et le Temps* 13 (1983), 52–79.

Frankemölle, H., *In Gleichnissen Gott erfahren* (Stuttgart: Katholisches Bibelwerk, 1977), pp. 55–61, 65–69.

Fuchs, E., 'Das Fest der Verlorenen. Existentiale Interpretation des Gleichnisses vom verlorenen Sohn' in *Glaube und Erfahrung. Zum theologischen Problem im Neuen Testament* (Tübingen: J. C. B. Mohr, 1965), pp. 402–415.

George, A., 'Les paraboles', *Lumière et Vie* 23 (119; 1974), 35–48.

Giblet, J., 'La parabole de l'accueil messianique (Luc 15, 11–32)', *Bible et Vie Chrétienne* 47 (1962), 17–28.

Giblin, C. H., 'Structural and Theological Considerations on Luke 15', *Catholic Biblical Quarterly* 24 (1962), 15–31.

Giblin, C. H., 'Why Jesus Spoke in Parables (Lk 15)', *Chicago Studies* 7 (1968), 213–220.

Golenvaux, C., 'L'enfant prodigue', *Bible et Vie Chrétienne* 94 (1970), 88–93.

Grelot, P., 'Le père et ses deux fils: Luc XV, 11–32. Essai d'analyse structurale', *Revue Biblique* 84 (1977), 321–348, 538–565.

Harrington, W., 'The Prodigal Son', *The Furrow* 25 (1974), 432–437.

Hermant, D. K., 'A Conference on Luke 15', *Monastic Studies* 10 (1974), 155–163.

Hickling, C. J. A., 'A Tract on Jesus and the Pharisees? A Conjecture on the Redaction of Luke 15 and 16', *Heythrop Journal* 16 (1975), 253–265.

Hofius, O., 'Alttestamentliche Motive im Gleichnis vom Verlorenen Sohn', *New Testament Studies* 24 (1977–78), 240–248.

Hoogen, T. van den, 'Omgaan met een niet-vanzelfsprekend Evangelie. Een theologische bezinning op het traditie-begrip', *Tijdschrift voor Theologie* 17 (1977), 225–249.

Hoppe, R., 'Gleichnis und Situation. Zu den Gleichnissen vom guten Vater (Lk 15,11–32) und gütigen Hausherrn (Mt 20,1–15)', *Biblische Zeitschrift* 28 (1984), 1–21.

Jeremias, J., 'Tradition und Redaction in Lukas 15', *Zeitschrift für die neutestamentliche Wissenschaft* 62 (1971), 172–189.

Jones, P., 'La parabole du fils prodigue: Deux méthodes d'interprétation', *Revue Réformée* 34 (1983), 122–137.

Kossen, H. B., 'Quelques remarques sur l'ordre des paraboles dans Luc XV', *Novum Testamentum* 1 (1956), 75–80.

Kruse, H., 'The Return of the Prodigal. Fortunes of a Parable on its Way to the Far East', *Orientalia* 47 (1978), 163–214.

Lambrecht, J., 'Parabels over "het verlorene" (Lc. 15)', *Collationes* 22 (1975), 449–479.

Lohfink, G., '"Ich habe gesündigt gegen den Himmel und gegen dich." Eine Exegese von Lk 15, 18.21', *Theologische Quartalschrift* 15 (1975), 51–52.

Magass, W., 'Geben, Nehmen, Teilen als Tischsequenz in Lk 15, 11–32', *Linguistica Biblica* 37 (1976), 31–48.

Merklein, H., *Die Gottesherrschaft als Handlungsprinzip* (Würzburg: Echter Verlag, 1978), pp. 186–197.

Meynet, R., 'Deux paraboles parallèles. Analyse rhétorique de Luc 15,1–32', *Annales de Philosophie* 2 (1981), 89–105.

Mourlon-Beirnaert, P., 'Quatre lectures méthodiques de la "brebis perdue" (Luc 15, 1–7)', *La Foi et le Temps* 9 (1979), 387–418.

Mourlon-Beirnaert, P., 'The Lost Sheep: Four Approaches', *Theology Digest* 29 (1981), 143–148.

Naastepad, T. J. M., *Acht gelijkenissen uit Mattheus en Lukas* (Kampen: J. H. Kok, n.d.), pp. 88–107.

Nützel, J. M., *Jesus als Offenbarer Gottes nach den lukanischen Schriften* (Würzburg: Echter Verlag, 1980), pp. 234–255, 264–270.

O'Rourke, J. J., 'Some Notes on Luke XV, 11–32', *New Testament Studies* 18 (1971–72), 431–433.

Osborn, R. T., 'The Father and His Two Sons: A Parable of Liberation', *Dialog* 19 (1980), 204–209.

Patte, D., 'Structural Analysis of the Parable of the Prodigal Son: Towards a Method' in *Semiology and Parables* (ed. D. Patte; Pittsburgh: Pickwick Press, 1976), pp. 71–149.

Pesch, R., 'Zur Exegese Gottes durch Jesus von Nazaret. Eine Auslegung des Gleichnisses vom Vater und den beiden Sohnen (Lk 15. 11–32)' in *Jesus. Ort der Erfahrung Gottes. Festschrift B. Welte* (Freiburg: Herder, 1976), pp. 140–189.

Petersen, W. L., 'The Parable of the Lost Sheep in the Gospel of Thomas and the Synoptics', *Novum Testamentum* 23 (1981), 128–147.

Plotzke, U., *De Parabel van de barmhartige Vader* (Brussels: Jecta, 1971).

Pöhlmann, W., 'Die Abschichtung des Verlorenen Sohnes (Lk 15, 12f.) und die erzählte Welt der Parabel', *Zeitschrift für die neutestamentliche Wissenschaft* 70 (1979), 194–213.

Price, J. L., 'Luke 15: 11–32', *Interpretation* 31 (1977), 64–69.

Ramaroson, L., 'Le coeur du Troisième Évangile: Lc 15', *Biblica* 60 (1979), 348–360.

Rengstorf, K., *Die Re-Investitur des Verlorenen Sohnes in der Gleichnis-erzählung Jesu. Luk. 15,11–32* (Cologne: Westdeutscher Verlag, 1967).

Rasco, E., 'Les paraboles de Luc XV. Une invitation à la joie de Dieu dans le Christ' in *De Jésus aux Évangiles* (ed. I. de la Potterie; Gembloux: J. Duculot, 1967), pp. 165–183.

Rickards, R. R., 'Some points to consider in translating the parable of the prodigal son (Luke 15.11–32)', *The Bible Translator* 31 (1980), 243–245.

Robillard, J. A., 'La parabole du fils ainé. Jésus et l'amour miséricordieux', *Vie Spirituelle* 106 (1962), 531–544.

Rosenkranz, G., 'Das Gleichnis vom verlorenen Sohn im Lotos-Sutra und im Lukas-evangelium', *Theologische Literaturzeitung* 79 (1954), col. 281–282.

Sanders, J. T., 'Tradition and Redaction in Luke XV, 11–32', *New Testament Studies* 15 (1968–69), 433–438.

Schnider, F., 'Das Gleichnis von verlorenen Schaf und seine Redaktoren', *Kairos* 19 (1977), 146–154.

Schnider, F., *Die verlorene Söhne: Strukturanalytische und historisch-kritische Untersuchungen zu Lk 15* (Orbis Biblicus et Orientalis 17; Göttingen: Vandenhoeck & Ruprecht, 1977).

Schottroff, L., 'Das Gleichnis vom verlorenen Sohn', *Zeitschrift für Theologie und Kirche* 68 (1971), 27–52.

Scott, B. B., 'The Prodigal Son: A Structuralist Interpretation', *Semeia* 9 (1977), 45–73.

Smit, J., *Speelruimte. Een structurele lezing van het evangelie* (Hilversum: Gooi en Sticht, 1981), pp. 37–61.

Strunk, R., and Mausshardt, M., 'Leistung des Schöpferischen (Lk 15, 11–32)' in *Doppeldeutlich, Tiefendimensionen biblischer Texte* (Munich: Kaiser, 1978), pp. 59–78.

Suermann, M., 'Das Gleichnis vom verlorenen Sohn in Kunstwerken der Vergangenheit und Gegenwart', *Katechetische Blätter* 106 (1981), 322–332, especially 323–325.

Thorn, J. C., 'Gelijkenisse en Betekenis', *Scriptura* 9 (1983), 30–43.

Tolbert, M. A., 'The Prodigal Son: An Essay in Literary Criticism from a Psychoanalytic Perspective', *Semeia* 9 (1977), 1–20.

Trilling, W., 'Gottes Erbarmen (Lk 15, 1–10)' in *Christusverkündigung in den synoptischen Evangelien* (Munich: Kösel Verlag, 1969), pp. 108–122.

Via, D. O., Jr, *The Parables: Their Literary and Existential Dimension* (Philadelphia: Fortress Press, 1974), pp. 162–176.

Via, D. O., Jr, 'The Prodigal Son: A Jungian Reading', *Semeia* 9 (1977), 21–43.

Vogel, H.-J., 'Der verlorene Sohn. Lukas 15,11–32', *Texte und Kontexte* no. 18 (1983), 27–34.

Waelkens, R., 'L'analyse structurale des paraboles. Deux essais: Luc 15, 1–32 et Matthieu 13, 44–46', *Revue Théologique de Louvain* 8 (1977), 160–178.

Walls, A. F., 'In the Presence of the Angels (Luke XV, 10)', *Novum Testamentum* 3 (1959), 314–316.

Weder, H., *Die Gleichnisse Jesu als Metaphern* (Göttingen: Vandenhoeck & Ruprecht, 1978), pp. 168–177, 249–262.

Wittig, S., 'A Theory of Multiple Meanings', *Semeia* 9 (1977), 75–103.

8. The parable of the unjust steward (Lk 16:1–13)

Bailey, K. E., *Poet and Peasant. A Literary-Cultural Approach to the Parables in Luke* (Grand Rapids: Eerdmans, 1976), pp. 86–118.

Barth, M., 'The Dishonest Steward and His Lord. Reflections on Luke 16:1–13' in *From Faith to Faith. Essays in Honor of Donald G. Miller* (ed. D. Y. Hadidian; Pittsburgh Theological Monograph Series 31; Pittsburgh: Pickwick Press, 1979), pp. 65–73.

Bigo, P., 'La richesse comme intendance dans l'Évangile. A propos de Luc 16, 1–9', *Nouvelle Revue Théologique* 87 (1965), 267–271.

Bouwman, G., *De Derde Nachtwake* (Tielt: Lannoo, 1968), pp. 161–166.

Busse, U., *et al.*, *Jesus zwischen arm und reich. Lukas-evangelium* (Bibelauslegung für die Praxis 18; Stuttgart: Katholisches Bibelwerk, 1980), pp. 115–120.

Caemmerer, R. R., 'Investment for Eternity. A Study of Luke 16, 1–13', *Concordia Theological Monthly* 34 (1963), 69–76.

Colella, P., 'Zu Lk 16:9', *Zeitschrift für die neutestamentliche Wissenschaft* 64 (1973), 124–126.

Comiskey, J. P., 'The Unjust Steward', *The Bible Today* no. 52 (February 1971), 229–235.

Degenhardt, H. J., *Lukas – Evangelist der Armen* (Stuttgart: Katholisches Bibelwerk, 1965), pp. 114–131.

Derrett, J. D. M., 'Fresh Light on St Luke XVI: I. The Parable of the Unjust Steward', *New Testament Studies* 7 (1960–61), 198–219.

Derrett, J. D. M., '"Take Thy Bond. . . and Write Fifty" (Luke XVI,6). The Nature of the Bond', *Journal of Theological Studies* 23 (1972), 438–440.

Descamps, A., 'La composition de Luc XVI, 9–13', *Novum Testamentum* 1 (1965), 47–53.

Dominguez, B., 'Call for a New Responsibility (Luke 16:1–13)' in *The Human and the Holy: Asian Perspectives in Christian Theology* (ed. E. P. Nakpil and D. J. Elwood; Quezon City: New Day Publishers, 1978), pp. 81–88.

Drexler, H., 'Zu Lukas 16 – 17', *Zeitschrift für die neutestamentliche Wissenschaft* 58 (1967), 286–288.

Dupont, J., *Les Béatitudes*. III: *Les Évangélistes* (Paris: J. Gabalda, 1973), pp. 118–122, 168–172.

Dupont, J., 'L'exemple de l'intendant débrouillard. Lc 16, 1–13', *Assemblées du Seigneur* 56 (1974), 67–78.

Dupont, J., 'Dieu ou Mammon (Mt 6:24; Lc 16:13)', *Cristianesimo nella Storia* 5 (1984), 441–461.

Fassl, P., '"Und er lobte den ungerechten Verwalter" (Lk 16,8a). Komposition und Redaktion in Lk 16' in *Eschatologie. Bibeltheologische und philosophische Studien zum Verhältnis von Erlösungswelt und Wirklichkeitsbewaltigung. Festschrift für E. Neuhäusler* (ed. R. Kilian, K. Funk and P. Fassl; St. Ottilien: EOS Verlag, 1981), pp. 109–143.

Feuillet, A., 'Les Paraboles de Luc: Chap. 16. Recherches sur la conception chrétienne du droit de propriété et sur les fondements de la doctrine sociale de l'Église', *Esprit et Vie* 89 (1979), 241–250, 257–271.

Feuillet, A., 'La Parabole du mauvais riche et du pauvre Lazare (Lk 16, 19–31) antithèse de la parabole de l'intendant astucieux (Lc 16,1–9)', *Nouvelle Revue Théologique* 101 (1979), 212–223.

Fiedler, P., 'Lk 16:1–13: Entschlossene Reaktion auf das Gebot der Stunde', *Am Tisch des Wortes* 124 (1972), 82–88.

Fitzmyer, J. A., 'The Story of the Dishonest Manager (Lk 16, 1–13)', *Theological Studies* 25 (1972), 23–42.

Fletcher, D. R., 'The Riddle of the Unjust Steward: is Irony the Key?', *Journal of Biblical Literature* 82 (1963), 15–30.

Fossion, A., 'Tromper l'argent trompeur. Lecture structurale de la parabole du gérant habile, Luc 16,1–9', *La Foi et le Temps* 13 (1983), 342–360.

France, D., 'Serving God or Mammon?', *Third Way* 2 (10; 1978), 3–8.

Francis, F. J., 'The Parable of the Unjust Steward', *Anglican Theological Review* 47 (1965), 103–105.

Fuchs, E., 'L'Évangile et l'argent: la parabole de l'intendant intelligent', *Bulletin du Centre Protestant d'Études* 30 (1978), 3–14.

Gächter, P., 'Die Parabel vom ungerechter Verwalter. Lk 16,1–8', *Orientierung* 27 (1963), 149–150.

Gunneweg, A. H. J., and Smithals, W., *Achievement* (Biblical Encounter Series; Nashville: Abingdon Press, 1981), pp. 145–149.

Hendricks, W. L., 'Stewardship in the New Testament', *Southwestern Journal of Theology* 13 (1971), 25–33.

Herrmann, J., 'Rechtsgeschichtliche Überlegungen zum Gleichnis vom ungerechten Verwalter (Lk 16:1–8)', *Jahres- und Tagesbericht des Görresgesellschaft* (1969), 27–33.

Hiers, R. H., 'Friends By Unrighteous Mammon: The Eschatological Proletariat (Luke 16:9)', *Journal of the American Academy of Religion* 38 (1970), 30–36.

Kamlah, E., 'Die Parabel vom ungerechter Verwalter (Luk 16.1ff.) im Rahmen der Knechtsgleichnisse' in *Abraham unser Vater. Festschrift O. Michel* (Leiden: J. Brill, 1963), pp. 276–294.

Kannengiesser, C., 'L'intendant malhonnête (Lc 16, 1–8a)', *Christus* 18 (1970), 213–218.

Kosmala, H., 'The Parable of the Unjust Steward in the Light of Qumran', *Annual of the Swedish Theological Institute* 3 (1964), 114–121.

Krämer, M., *Das Rätsel der Parabel vom ungerechten Verwalter Lk 16, 1–13. Auslegungsgeschichte – Umfang – Sinn. Eine Diskussion der Probleme und Lösungsvorschläge der Verwalterparabel von den Väter bis heute* (Bibl. di Sci. Religiose 5; Zürich: Pas-Verlag, 1972).

Lunt, R. G., 'Expounding the Parables. III. The Parable of the Unjust Steward (Luke 16:1–15)', *Expository Times* 37 (1966), 132–136.

Maass, F., 'Das Gleichnis vom ungerechter Haushalter. Lc 16, 1–8', *Theologia Viatorum* 8 (1961–62), 173–184.

Maillot, A., 'Notules sur Luc 16.8b–9', *Études Théologiques et Religieuses* 44 (1969), 127–130.

Marshall, I. H., 'Lk 16,8 – Who Commended the Unjust Steward?', *Journal of Theological Studies* 9 (1968), 617–619.

Merkelbach, R., 'Über das Gleichnis vom ungerechter Haushalter (Lucas 16, 1–13)', *Vigiliae Christianae* 33 (1979), 180–181.

Miranda, J. P., *Communism in the Bible* (Maryknoll, N.Y.: Orbis Books, 1981/London: SCM Press, 1982), pp. 50–52.

Molina, J. P., 'Luc 16:1–13', *Études Théologiques et Religieuses* 53 (1978), 371–376.

Moore, F. J., 'The Parable of the Unjust Steward, Lk 16, 1–9', *Anglican Theological Review* 47 (1965), 103–105.

Naastepad, T. J. M., *Acht gelijkenissen uit Mattheus en Lukas* (Kampen: J. H. Kok, n.d.), pp. 108–124.

Noonan, J. T., Jr, 'The Devious Employees', *Commonweal* 104 (1977), 681–688.

Osborn, E., 'Parable and Exposition', *Australian Biblical Review* 22 (1974), 11–22.

Paliard, C., *Lire l'Écriture, écouter la Parole. La parabole de l'économe infidèle* (Lire la Bible 53; Paris: Éditions du Cerf, 1980).

Pilgrim, W. E., *Good News to the Poor. Wealth and Poverty in Luke-Acts* (Minneapolis: Augsburg Publishing House, 1981), pp. 125–129.

Reumann, J., *Jesus in the Church's Gospels* (Philadelphia: Fortress Press, 1968/London: SPCK, 1970), pp. 189–198.

Rüger, H. P., 'Mamonas', *Zeitschrift für die neutestamentliche Wissenschaft* 64 (1973), 127–131.

Safrai, S., and Flusser, D., 'The Slave of Two Masters', *Immanuel* 6 (1976), 30–33.

Schwarz, G., '". . . lobte den betrügerischen Verwalter"? (Lukas 16, 8a)', *Biblische Zeitschrift* 18 (1974), 94–95.

Scott, B. E., 'A Master's Praise: Luke 16,1–8a', *Biblica* 64 (1983), 173–188.

Seccombe, D. P., *Possessions and the Poor in Luke-Acts* (Linz: SNTU, 1983), pp. 160–172.

Topel, L. J., 'The Injustice of the Unjust Steward: Lk 16:1–8', *Catholic Biblical Quarterly* 37 (1975), 216–227.

Via, D. O., Jr, *The Parables. Their Literary and Existential Dimension* (Philadelphia: Fortress Press, 1974), pp. 155–162.

Weder, H., *Die Gleichnisse Jesu als Metaphern* (Göttingen: Vandenhoeck & Ruprecht, 1978), pp. 262–267.

Williams, F. E., 'Is Almsgiving the Point of the "Unjust Steward"?', *Journal of Biblical Literature* 83 (1964), 293–297.

9. The parable of the rich man and Lazarus (Lk 16:19–31)

Bigo, P., 'Richesse et Évangile', *Revue de l'Action Populaire* no. 96 (1956), 257–272.

Bishop, E. F., 'A Yawning Chasm', *Evangelical Quarterly* 45 (1973), 3–5.

Busse, U., *et al.*, *Jesus zwischen arm und reich. Lukas-evangelium* (Bibelauslegung für die Praxis 18; Stuttgart: Katholisches Bibelwerk, 1980), pp. 121–125.

Cadbury, H. J., 'A Proper Name for Dives', *Journal of Biblical Literature* 81 (1962), 399–402.

Cadbury, H. J., 'The Name of Dives', *Journal of Biblical Literature* 84 (1965), 73.

Cantinat, J., 'Le mauvais riche et Lazare (Luc 16, 19–31)', *Bible et Vie Chrétienne* 48 (1962), 19–26.

Cave, C. H., 'Lazarus and the Lukan Deuteronomy', *New Testament Studies* 15 (1968–69), 319–325.

Crossan, J. D., 'Parable and Example Story in the Teaching of Jesus', *New Testament Studies* 18 (1971–72), 285–307, especially 297–299.

Derrett, J. D. M., 'Fresh Light on St. Luke XVI: II. Dives and Lazarus and the Preceding Sayings', *New Testament Studies* 7 (1960–61), 364–380.

Dunkerley, R., 'Lazarus', *New Testament Studies* 5 (1958–59), 321–327.

Dupont, J., *Les Béatitudes*, III: *Les Évangélistes* (Paris: J. Gabalda, 1973), pp. 60–64, 162–182.

Evans, C. F., 'Uncomfortable Words. V: "If they do not hear Moses and the prophets" (Lk 16:31)', *Expository Times* 81 (1969–70), 228–231.

George, A., 'La parabole du riche et de Lazare (Lc 16, 19–31)', *Assemblées du Seigneur* 57 (1971), pp. 80–93.

Feuillet, A., 'La parabole du mauvais riche at du pauvre Lazare (Lc 16, 19–31), antithèse de la parabole de l'intendant astucieux (Lc 16, 1–9)', *Nouvelle Revue Théologique* 101 (1979), 212–223.

Glombitza, A., 'Der reiche Mann und der arme Lazarus. Luk XVI. 19–31. Zur Frage nach der Botschaft des Textes', *Novum Testamentum* 12 (1970), 166–180.

Grobel, K., '. . . Whose Name Was Neves', *New Testament Studies* 10 (1963–64), 373–382.

Huie, W. P., Jr, 'The Poverty of Abundance. From Text to Sermon on Lk 16,19–31', *Interpretation* 32 (1968), 403–420.

Jensen, H. J. L., 'Diesseits und Jenseits des Raumes eines Textes. Textsemiotische Bemerkungen zur Erzählung "Vom reichen Mann und armen Lazarus" (Lk 16, 19–31)', *Linguistica Biblica* 47 (1980), 39–60.

Johnson, L. T., *The Literary Function of Possessions in Luke-Acts* (Missoula, Mont.: Scholars Press, 1977), pp. 140–144.

Lorenzen, T., 'A Biblical Meditation on Luke 16:19–31. From the Text toward a Sermon', *Expository Times* 87 (1975), 39–43.

Manrique, A., 'La Parábola del rico epulón y de Lázaro y la justicia social en la época de Jesús (Lc 16, 19–31)', *Ciudad de Dios* 191 (1978), 207–215.

Mattill, A. J., Jr, *Luke and the Last Things* (Dillsboro, N.C.: Western North Carolina Press, 1979), pp. 26–40.

Mealand, D. L., *Poverty and Expectation in the Gospels* (London: SPCK, 1980), pp. 46–49.

Miranda, J. P., *Communism in the Bible* (Maryknoll, N.Y.: Orbis Books, 1981/London: SCM Press, 1982), pp. 22–25.

Naastepad, T. J. M., *Acht gelijkenissen uit Mattheus en Lukas* (Kampen: J. H. Kok, n.d.), pp. 125–138.

Obermüller, R., 'La miseria de un rico: un juicio neotestamentario. Lucas 16,19–31' in *Los Pobres. Encuentro y compromiso* (ed. L. Brummel *et al.*; Buenos Aires: La Aurora, 1978), pp. 45–66.

Pax, E., 'Der Reiche und der arme Lazarus. Eine Milieustudie', *Studii Biblici Franciscani Liber Annuus* 25 (1975), 254–268.

Pesch, W., 'Lk 16, 19–31' in *Die Epistlen und Evangelien der Sonn- und*

Festtage fasc. 12 (ed. H. Kahlefeld and O. Knoch; Frankfurt/Stuttgart, 1971), pp. 362–365.

Pilgrim, W. E., *Good News to the Poor. Wealth and Poverty in Luke-Acts* (Minneapolis: Augsburg Publishing House, 1981), pp. 59–60, 113–119.

Rohrbaugh, R., *The Biblical Interpreter. An Agrarian Bible in an Industrial Age* (Philadelphia: Fortress Press, 1978), pp. 69–85.

Schnider, F., and Stenger, W., 'Die offene Tür und die unüberschreitbare Kluft', *New Testament Studies* 25 (1978–79), 273–283.

Scholtz, G., 'Ästhetische Beobachtungen am Gleichnis vom Reichen Mann und Armen Lazarus und an drei anderen Gleichnissen (Lk 16, 19–25, 26–31; 10:34; 13:9; 15:11–32)', *Linguistica Biblica* 43 (1978), 67–74.

Seccombe, D. P., *Possessions and the Poor in Luke-Acts* (Linz: SNTU, 1983), pp. 173–181.

Stubhahn, M., 'Vom reichen Prasser und armen Lazarus', *Am Tisch des Wortes* 107 (1970), 84–93.

Tanghe, V., 'Abraham, son Fils et son Envoyé (Luc 16,19–31)', *Revue Biblique* 91 (1984), 557–577.

Trudinger, P., '"A Lazarus Motif" in Primitive Christian Preaching', *Andover Newton Quarterly* 7 (1966), 29–32.

Wehrli, E. S., 'Luke 16:19–31', *Interpretation* 31 (1977), 276–280.

10. The parable of the judge and the widow (Lk 18:1–8)

Bailey, K. E., *Through Peasant Eyes* (Grand Rapids: Eerdmans, 1980), pp. 127–141.

Bindemann, W., 'Die Parabel vom ungerechten Richter', *Theologische Versuche* 13 (1983), 91–97.

Catchpole, D. R., 'The Son of Man's Search for Faith (Luke XVIII, 8b)', *Novum Testamentum* 19 (1977), 81–104.

Clark, W., 'The Meaning of *ara*' in *Festschrift für F. W. Gingrich* (Leiden: J. Brill, 1972), pp. 70–84, especially 75.

Cranfield, C. E. B., 'The Parable of the Unjust Judge and the Eschatology of Luke-Acts', *Scottish Journal of Theology* 16 (1963), 297–301.

Delling, G., 'Das Gleichnis vom gottlosen Richter', *Zeitschrift für die neutestamentliche Wissenschaft* 53 (1962), 1–25.

Derrett, J. D. M., 'Law in the New Testament: The parable of the Unjust Judge', *New Testament Studies* 18 (1971–72), 178–191.

Deschrijver, R., 'La parabole du juge malveillant (Luc 18,1–18)', *Revue d'Histoire et de Philosophie Religieuses* 48 (1968), 355–366.

George, A., 'La parabole du juge qui fait attendre le jugement. Luc 18, 1–8', *Assemblées du Seigneur* 60 (1975), 68–79.

Ljungvik, H., 'Zur Erklärung einer Lukas-Stelle (Luk XVIII. 7)', *New Testament Studies* 10 (1963–64), 289–294.

Mattill, A. J., Jr, *Luke and the Last Things* (Dillsboro, N.C.: Western North Carolina Press, 1979), pp. 89–96.

Ott, W., *Gebet und Heil. Die Bedeutung der Gebetsparänese in der lukanische Theologie* (Munich: Kösel Verlag, 1965), pp. 19–72.

Paulsen, H., 'Die Witwe und der Richter (Lk 18,1–8)', *Theologie und Glaube* 74 (1984), 13–39.

Riesenfeld, H., 'Zu *makrothymein* (Lk 18,7)' in *Neutestamentliche Aufsätze. Festschrift J. Schmid* (Regensburg: Pustet Verlag, 1963), pp. 214–217.

Ru, G. de, 'De gelijkenis van de onrechtvaardige rechter (Lucas 18, 1–8)', *Nederlands Theologisch Tijdschrift* 25 (1971), 379–392.

Sabbe, M., 'Het eschatologisch gebed in Lukas 18, 1–8', *Collationes Brugenses et Gandavenses* 1 (1955), 361–369.

Schneider, G., *Parusiegleichnisse im Lukas-Evangelium* (SBS 74; Stuttgart: Katholisches Bibelwerk, 1975), pp. 71–78.

Spicq, C., 'La parabole de la veuve obstinée et du juge inerte, aux décisions impromptues (Lc XVIII, 1–8)', *Revue Biblique* 68 (1961), 68–90.

Stählin, G., 'Das Bild der Witwe. Ein Beitrag zur Bildersprache der Bibel und zum Phänomen der Personifikation in der Antike', *Jahrbuch für Antike und Christentum* 17 (1974), 5–20.

Stramare, T., 'Oportet semper orare et non deficere (Lc 18,1): espressione di comando o segreto di successo?', *Lateranum* 48 (1982), 155–166.

Via, D. O., Jr, 'The Parable of the Unjust Judge: A Metaphor of the Unrealized Self' in *Semiology and Parables* (ed. D. Patte; Pittsburgh: Pickwick Press, 1976), pp. 1–32.

Weder, H., *Die Gleichnisse Jesu als Metaphern* (Göttingen: Vandenhoeck & Ruprecht, 1978), pp. 267–273.

Wifstrand, A., 'Lukas XVIII. 7', *New Testament Studies* 11 (1964–65), 72–74.

Wilson, S. G., 'Lukan Eschatology', *New Testament Studies* 15 (1969–70), 330–347, especially 340–341.

Zimmermann, H., 'Die Gleichnis vom Richter und der Witwe (Lk 18, 1–8)' in *Die Kirche des Anfangs* (ed. R. Schnackenburg; Leipzig: St. Benno Verlag, 1977), pp. 79–95.

11. The parable of the Pharisee and the tax collector (Lk 18:9–14)

Bailey, K. E., *Through Peasant Eyes* (Grand Rapids: Eerdmans, 1980), pp. 142–154.

Biesinger, A., 'Vorbild und Nachahmung, Imitationspsychologische und bibeltheologische Anmerkungen zu Lk 18, 9–14', *Bibel und Kirche* 32 (1977), 42–45.

Busse, U., *et al.*, *Jesus zwischen arm und reich. Lukas-evangelium* (Bibelauslegung für die Praxis 18; Stuttgart: Katholisches Bibelwerk, 1980), pp. 129–132.

Charpentier, E., 'Le chrétien: un homme "juste" ou justifié? Lc 18, 9–14', *Assemblées du Seigneur* 61 (1972), 66–78.

Cortes, J. B., 'The Greek Text of Luke 18:14a. A Contribution to the Method of Reasoned Eclecticism', *Catholic Biblical Quarterly* 46 (1984), 255–273.

Crossan, J. D., 'Parable and Example in the Teaching of Jesus', *New Testament Studies* 18 (1971–72), 285–307, especially 299–300.

Feuillet, A., 'La signification christologique de Lc 18, 14 et les références des Évangiles au Serviteur souffrant', *Nova et Vetera* 55 (1980), 188–229.

Feuillet, A., 'Le Pharisien et le publicain (Luc 18,9–14). La manifestation de la miséricorde divine en Jésus Serviteur souffrant', *Esprit et Vie* 91 (48; 1981), 657–665.

Frankemölle, H., *In Gleichnissen Gott erfahren* (Stuttgart: Katholisches Bibelwerk, 1977), pp. 111–117.

Frickel, J., 'Die Zöllner, Vorbild der Demut und wahrer Gottesverehrung' in *Pietas. Festschrift für Bernhard Kötting* (ed. E. Dassmann; Münster: Aschendorff, 1980), pp. 369–380.

Green, L. C., 'Justification in Luther's Preaching on Luke 18:9–14', *Concordia Theological Monthly* 43 (1972), 732–747.

Gunneweg, A. H. J., and Schmithals, W., *Achievement* (Biblical Encounters Series; Nashville: Abingdon Press, 1981), pp. 114–118.

Heimbrock, H. G., and Heimler, A., 'Das Gleichnis vom Pharisäer und Zöllner (Lk 18, 9–14)' in *Doppeldeutlich, Tiefendimensionen biblischer Texte* (ed. Y. Spiegel; Munich: Kösel Verlag, 1978), pp. 171–188.

Hengel, M., 'Die ganz andere Gerechtigkeit. Bibelarbeit über Lk 18, 9–14', *Theologische Beiträge* 5 (1974), 1–13.

Hoerber, R. G., '"God Be Merciful on Me a Sinner". A Note on Lk. 18:13', *Concordia Theological Monthly* 33 (1962), 283–286.

Mahr, F., 'Der Antipharisäer. Ein Kapitel "Bibel verfremdet" zu Lk 18,10–14', *Bibel und Kirche* 32 (1977), 47.

Merklein, H., '"Dieser ging als Gerechter nach Hause. . ." Das Gottesbild Jesu und die Haltung des Menschen nach Lk 18,9–14', *Bibel und Kirche* 32 (1977), 34–42.

Moltmann, J., *The Power of the Powerless* (San Francisco: Harper and Row/London: SCM Press, 1983), pp. 88–97.

Mottu, H., 'The Pharisee and the Tax Collector: Sartrian Notes as Applied to the Reading of Scripture', *Union Seminary Quarterly Review* 29 (1974), 195–213.

Nützel, J. M., *Jesus als Offenbarer Gottes nach den lukanischen Schriften* (Forschung zur Bibel 39; Würzburg: Echter Verlag, 1980), pp. 255–263.

Rondet, H., 'La Parabole du Pharisien et du Publicain dans l'oeuvre de S. Augustin', *Sciences Ecclésiastiques* 15 (1963), 407–417.

Schmitz, S., 'Psychologische Hilfen zum Verstehen biblischer Texte? Zum Beispiel Lk 18,9–14', *Theologie der Gegenwart* 26 (1983), 99–109.

Schmitz, S., 'Psychologische Hilfen zum Verstehen biblischer Texte? Zum Beispiel Lk 18,9–14', *Bibel und Kirche* 38 (1983), 112–118.

Schnider, F., 'Ausschliessen und ausgeschlossen werden. Beobachtungen zur Struktur des Gleichnisses vom Pharisäer und Zöllner. Lk 18, 10–14a', *Biblische Zeitschrift* 24 (1980), 42–56.

Schottroff, L., 'Die Erzählung vom Pharisäer und Zöllner als Beispiel für die theologische Kunst des Überredens' in *Neues Testament und christliche Existenz. Festschrift für H. Braun* (ed. H. D. Betz and L. Schotroff; Tübingen: J. C. B. Mohr, 1973), pp. 439–461.

Smit, J., *Speelruimte. Een structurele lezing van het evangelie* (Hilversum: Gooi en Sticht, 1981), pp. 73–78.

Wachler, G., *Wenn zwei dasselbe tun* (Berlin: Evangelische Verlagsanstalt, 1967).